APA ETHICS CODE COMMENTARY AND CASE ILLUSTRATIONS

APA ETHICS CODE COMMENTARY AND CASE ILLUSTRATIONS

LINDA CAMPBELL

MELBA VASQUEZ

STEPHEN BEHNKE

ROBERT KINSCHERFF

American Psychological Association • Washington, DC

Published by
American Psychological Association
750 First Street, NE
Washington, DC 20002
www.apa.org

To order
APA Order Department
P.O. Box 92984
Washington, DC 20090-2984
Tel: (800) 374-2721; Direct: (202) 336-5510
Fax: (202) 336-5502; TDD/TTY: (202) 336-6123
Online: www.apa.org/books/
E-mail: order@apa.org

In the U.K., Europe, Africa, and the Middle East, copies may be ordered from
American Psychological Association
3 Henrietta Street
Covent Garden, London
WC2E 8LU England

Typeset in Goudy by Circle Graphics, Inc., Columbia, MD

Printer: United Book Press, Baltimore, MD
Cover Designer: Mercury Publishing Services, Rockville, MD

The opinions and statements published are the responsibility of the authors, and such opinions and statements do not necessarily represent the policies of the American Psychological Association.

Library of Congress Cataloging-in-Publication Data

APA ethics code commentary and case illustrations / by Linda Campbell . . . [et al.].
  p. cm.
Includes bibliographical references and index.
ISBN-13: 978-1-4338-0693-3
ISBN-10: 1-4338-0693-2
 1. Psychologists—Professional ethics. 2. Psychology—Standards. 3. Psychologists—Professional ethics—Case studies. I. Campbell, Linda Frye, 1947–

 BF76.4.A63 2010
 174'.915—dc22

                                                    2009019512

British Library Cataloguing-in-Publication Data

A CIP record is available from the British Library.

Printed in the United States of America
First Edition

CONTENTS

APA ETHICS CODE COMMENTARY AND CASE ILLUSTRATIONS

INTRODUCTION

APA Ethics Code Commentary and Case Illustrations makes what we hope will be a unique contribution to the literature on ethics and psychology. At the heart of our approach to writing *APA Ethics Code Commentary and Case Illustrations* are two premises: First, ethics is better described as a process than as a set of rules, and second, most ethical dilemmas are neither straightforward nor easily resolved, so psychologists must tolerate a measure of ethical ambiguity in their professional lives. This latter statement, that ambiguity is inherent to psychologists' lived experience, is far from a criticism of the field or those who are privileged to engage in our profession. Instead, ethical ambiguity is a sign that psychologists' work is rich, rewarding, worthwhile, and complex. Those who choose to devote their professional lives to the science and practice of psychology will encounter many rewards along the way, but many challenges as well. *APA Ethics Code Commentary and Case Illustrations* is meant to serve as a supportive resource for psychologists as they encounter and think through these challenges.

The American Psychological Association's "Ethical Principles of Psychologists and Code of Conduct" (2002), hereinafter referred to as the Ethics Code, is a text based on a set of principles taken largely from the biomedical ethics literature. The five principles in the Ethics Code—Beneficence and

Nonmaleficence; Fidelity and Responsibility; Integrity; Justice; and Respect for People's Rights and Dignity—form the foundation for the 89 ethical standards that comprise the code. The five principles are aspirational and may be thought of as the ethical ceiling toward which psychologists should aspire in their professional work. The standards are enforceable rules of conduct and may be thought of as the ethical floor below which psychologists may not fall. The standards set the minimum bar for engaging in the work of the profession. It is a worthwhile exercise for students and seasoned psychologists alike to ponder the relationship between the principles and the standards, both in a general way and in terms of the relationship of specific standards to specific principles. Broadly speaking, we view the standards as operationalizing the principles, as the mechanisms through which psychologists ensure that the values of the profession are present and guiding them in their day-to-day professional lives.

The structure and organization of this book are intended to mirror this relationship between the principles and the standards. The chapters reflect on the text of the Ethics Code, with a focus on how the standards apply to specific principles and how the standards guide psychologists when conflicts among principles arise. Such conflicts occur frequently, and examples are easy to find. Psychologists struggle with whether to break confidentiality when a client poses a threat of harm to another person. Clients may be intent on behaviors that, although not harmful, are unhealthy and strike treating psychologists as working against clients' best interests so that psychologists must struggle with whether and how to promote healthier behaviors, sometimes against clients' stated wishes. These tensions—between confidentiality and safety and between beneficence and client self-determination—represent ethical dilemmas insofar as they pit one ethical principle against another. Although each side of the dilemma represents a value that is important to the profession, psychologists confront scenarios in which one value must take precedence over the other. Put simply, these psychologists are presented with ethical dilemmas.

The case illustrations are intended to offer psychologists a process as they encounter and work through their ethical dilemmas. Although responding to an ethical dilemma is always a fluid process, we have organized the case illustrations into four parts to provide a structure for a decision-making process. The first part of these vignettes, the case illustration, gives the scenario—what has happened, the facts of the matter. Sound ethical decision making is usually dependent on the facts of the case, and it can be both important and helpful for psychologists to distinguish between facts that are *known* to be true and facts that are *believed* or *speculated* to be true.

The second part, the ethical dilemma, identifies the relevant ethical principles and standards. At this point in the decision-making process, psychologists look to the text of the Ethics Code to explore how the language of the code speaks to the specific situation. At this juncture, psychologists may use the Ethics Code as something of a toolbox, to see what resources it offers.

The third part, the decision-making factors, explores the different values and interests afoot that create the potential for an ethical dilemma. Now psychologists begin to delve explicitly into the decision-making process. This part of the case illustration moves beyond the *what* one must consider to explore *how* psychologists will actively weigh and balance competing values and interests.

The fourth and final part of the case illustration discussion brings the previous three parts together to offer concrete and explicit possibilities for psychologists to resolve the dilemma and move forward in their professional lives. Psychologists will explore the possibilities that have been identified and consider the benefits and risks of each course of action. Finally, psychologists will choose one of the identified options. The four-part organization is intended to emphasize that resolving an ethical dilemma entails a thoughtful process of considering and integrating multiple, competing points of view.

Our approach in *APA Ethics Code Commentary and Case Illustrations* may not resonate with readers who have come to think of ethics and ethics codes as primarily about obligations and prohibitions imposed on psychologists in a top-down fashion, as if from a higher authority that leaves little room for professional discretion or judgment. Such an approach is oriented largely toward constraining psychologists' behavior—telling psychologists what they may not do—in order to minimize the harm to the individuals and groups with whom psychologists work. With its focus on avoiding harm (nonmaleficence), a top-down approach, in our opinion, leaves correspondingly less room for doing good (beneficence), and so tells only half the story.

We view ethics as based on the profession's core values and thus permeating every aspect of psychologists' work. Rather than solely imposed from above, we see ethics as rising from the ground up as well, as operative every time psychologists interact with clients, walk into a laboratory, teach classes, conduct assessments, publish articles, or supervise trainees. Ethics, from our perspective, is every bit as much about *doing right* as it is about *avoiding wrong*.

We want to emphasize that we view rules as essential. Each of us has spent, and will continue to spend, a good deal of our careers examining and teaching psychology ethics codes, statutes, regulations, and important legal cases. Nonetheless, a virtually exclusive focus on constraints, on the parameters of acceptable and unacceptable behavior, risks losing sight of a larger reality captured in why psychologists enter the field: to seek truths about the human condition, to advance our knowledge and understanding of thoughts and emotions, to contribute to the common good, to ease pain.

In our experience, the vast majority of psychologists are hard working, ethically minded, competent professionals. Of course, these psychologists need to know the "ethical rules of the road," in a manner of speaking, but their energies are not mostly spent on staying (just barely) on the right side of ethics codes and regulations; instead, their energies are spent advancing their work and, on occasion, navigating a thorny ethical dilemma. Our belief and hope is that these psychologists will be those who find this book most useful.

Some readers may interpret our position as being that ethical decision making is primarily instinctual, based on intuition and a personal, idiosyncratic sense of what is right and wrong. This interpretation of our position is incorrect. From our point of view, ethical decision making is a process of reasoning, not a visceral reaction. Although we do not want to ignore the importance of having a strong, internal sense of ethics in psychologists' professional lives, it is our view that a thorough working knowledge of relevant rules, regulations, and professional codes of ethics, combined with a systematic method of approaching and resolving dilemmas, are essential for the ethical practice of psychology.

The defining feature of rules and regulations and of a methodology for resolving dilemmas is their public nature. The public aspect of psychologists' work is easily confused with the concepts of privacy and confidentiality and is thus often ignored or misunderstood. Psychologists engage in a profession that is licensed and regulated by a governing authority, for the purpose of ensuring competent and ethical practice. A license to practice psychology is a public document, and psychologists must engage in public acts, such as attending an accredited degree program and taking an examination, in order to obtain the license. All psychologists, whether licensed or not, are expected to abide by a standard of care in practice, research, teaching and training contexts. By virtue of the public nature of the profession, psychologists may be called on in a public venue to account for their actions. Thus, psychologists' decision-making processes may be subject to public scrutiny.

To say that psychologists may be called to account in a public venue is not the same as saying that all information related to the psychologists' behavior will be disclosed in public forums, such as a newspaper. It means instead that there are public entities that may call on psychologists to give reasons for a particular decision or course of action in the context of a jurisdiction's laws, regulations, standards of care, and professional ethics codes. For this reason, decisions that psychologists make are never confined solely to the psychologist and client; such decisions are always, at least potentially, a matter of public accountability.

The public nature of the profession moves decision making out of the purely private realm of a personal, idiosyncratic morality. This move—from the private into the professional and public domain—entails a psychologist explicitly adopting the texts of the profession as formal and official standards of behavior. It also entails adopting a method of resolving conflicts and dilemmas that can be subjected to public scrutiny. As a consequence, our approach should not be characterized as saying that ethical decision making is a matter solely of personal morality, intuition, or idiosyncratic judgment. We believe that a disciplined, methodological approach, in the context of a jurisdiction's rules and the Ethics Code, is a defining feature of solid ethical practice.

In this book we attempt to demonstrate our approach to ethics and ethical decision making through the use of case illustrations. The four-part decision-making process, as applied to the case illustrations, should provide a reasonably comprehensive understanding of how the Ethics Code may be applied across the broad range of work psychologists do. Given the breadth of psychologists' work, no single volume could adequately address the ethics of the entire profession.

The Ethics Code has 89 ethical standards, all of which have potential applications in a variety of complex and nuanced situations and settings. For this reason, we were not able to offer a case illustration for each possible application of every standard—to do so would require many volumes. Neither were we able to provide an illustration for every single standard. In choosing among the standards, we drew on our experience in teaching and consulting on the Ethics Code. The result is a set of case illustrations that best reflect the ethical dilemmas and challenges psychologists across the United States from various work settings have brought to us. We hope and believe that the case illustrations in this book are reasonably representative of what psychologists confront in their day-to-day work and are fairly well distributed across the spectrum of the Ethics Code. We also hope that psychologists are able to take the illustrations we provide and use them as examples of a process that can be applied to the myriad situations we do not address.

At this point in our introduction, it may be clear to readers that our approach to ethics is better characterized as *proactive* rather than *reactive*. In a manner of speaking, we encourage psychologists to look forward over the ethical landscape to see where they are heading and where the pitfalls may lie, rather than to look up and out of a hole into which they have fallen. Taking a proactive orientation entails having a firm grasp of relevant laws and regulations, standards of practice and guidelines, and the Ethics Code, to anticipate what benefits and problems may arise from different courses of action. A proactive orientation develops and strengthens over time; as psychologists mature and garner more professional experience, it becomes easier to anticipate what is likely to happen and so to avoid pitfalls.

Standard 3.05, Multiple Relationships, helps to illustrate the benefits of a proactive stance. The second paragraph provides a test for when psychologists should refrain from a multiple relationship:

> A psychologist refrains from entering into a multiple relationship if the multiple relationship could reasonably be expected to impair the psychologist's objectivity, competence, or effectiveness in performing his or her functions as a psychologist, or otherwise risks exploitation or harm to the person with whom the professional relationship exists.

The first prong of the test set forth in Standard 3.05 calls on psychologists to refrain from multiple relationships that "could reasonably be expected to impair the psychologists' objectivity, competence, or effectiveness in performing their functions as psychologists." More and varied professional experiences should provide psychologists with a better sense of when a reasonable likelihood of professional incompetence is present and a correspondingly better sense of which multiple relationships to avoid. In short, as psychologists grow in their professional lives, they mature ethically.

Inherent in this and many other standards of the Ethics Code is the concept of reasonableness. *Reasonable* and *appropriate* are words that allow a measure of professional judgment and discretion, and so they are compatible with and even enhance a proactive stance. The Introduction and Applicability section of the Ethics Code gives reasons for why these words are important to include in the ethical standards:

> The modifiers used in some of the standards of this Ethics Code (e.g., *reasonably, appropriate, potentially*) are included in the standards when they would (1) allow professional judgment on the part of psychologists, (2) eliminate injustice or inequality that would occur without the modifier, (3) ensure applicability across the broad range of activities conducted by psychologists, or (4) guard against a set of rigid rules that might be quickly outdated. As used in this Ethics Code, the term *reasonable* means the prevailing professional judgment of psychologists engaged in similar activities in similar circumstances, given the knowledge psychologists had or should have had at the time.

The concepts of "reasonableness" and "appropriate" are essential to understanding the proper application of the Ethics Code, which is a living document that speaks to psychologists in a broad range of activities. Words such as *reasonable* and *appropriate* offer flexibility so that the Ethics Code simultaneously sets forth clear expectations for behavior and allows psychologists the ability to exercise professional judgment in their own area of expertise.

We hope this book will serve as a helpful ethics resource for psychologists, alongside other commentaries on the Ethics Code. Psychologists should be mindful that although the Ethics Code is the central text for determining what constitutes the ethical practice of psychology, it is not the sole determinant. As the code itself says (in the Introduction and Applicability section):

> In the process of making decisions regarding their professional behavior, psychologists must consider this Ethics Code in addition to applicable laws and psychology board regulations. In applying the Ethics Code to their professional work, psychologists may consider other materials and guidelines that have been adopted or endorsed by scientific and professional psychological organizations and the dictates of their own conscience, as well as consult with others within the field.

In addition to these many and varied sources that guide psychologists in their professional behavior, the code's preamble emphasizes that the ethical lives of psychologists are not static but rather involve an active, affirmative embrace of ethics across the professional life span:

> The development of a dynamic set of ethical standards for psychologists' work-related conduct requires a personal commitment and lifelong effort to act ethically; to encourage ethical behavior by students, supervisees, employees, and colleagues; and to consult with others concerning ethical problems.

APA *Ethics Code Commentary and Case Illustrations* is intended for psychologists at all levels of professional experience, from beginning students to those whose entire professional lives have been devoted to the field of psychology. Our purpose and goal is to gently encourage psychologists to accept the invitation offered in the Ethics Code's preamble, namely, to embrace a lifelong commitment to the highest ethical standards in the profession of psychology.

1

RESOLVING ETHICAL ISSUES

The 2002 American Psychological Association's (APA's) "Ethical Principles of Psychologists and Code of Conduct" (hereinafter the *APA Ethics Code* or the *Ethics Code*; see http://www.apa.org/ethics/code2002.html)[1] provides direction for psychologists engaged in the primary domains of professional activities, including Education and Training (Section 7), Research and Publication (Section 8), Assessment (Section 9), and Therapy (Section 10). The APA Ethics Code further offers guidance and rules by which psychologists must abide in enacting ethical processes that support these professional activities; these include Privacy and Confidentiality (Section 4), Advertising and Other Public Statements (Section 5), and Record Keeping and Fees (Section 6). The 2002 APA Ethics Code comprehensively directs psychologists to standards that may be used in developing their own skill competence and interpersonal competence (Section 2, Competence) and that inform them in their interpersonal relationships within professional realms (Section 3, Human Relations).

---

[1]American Psychological Association. (2002). Ethical principles of psychologists and code of conduct. *American Psychologist, 57,* 1060–1073.

The introductory section of the Ethics Code defines application of the Ethics Code. Psychologists must be mindful of the application of the Ethics Code to activities that are part of their scientific, educational, or professional roles. Such activities include psychotherapy, research, teaching supervision of trainees, public service, developing and conducting assessments, organizational consulting, forensic activities, behavioral interventions, and other activities that are conducted in a professional role. These professional activities apply regardless of modality or the means by which psychologists engage with those they serve. These modalities may include in-person, postal, telephone, Internet, and other electronic transmissions. Psychologists are purposeful in discerning professional activities from those of private conduct that are not within the auspices of the Ethics Code.

These aforementioned nine sections of the APA Ethics Code were developed with the intention of promoting and enhancing ethically characterized professional experiences. Section 1 of the Ethics Code, Resolving Ethical Issues, provides a blueprint for psychologists when questions of ethical conduct are encountered. Resolving Ethical Issues reflects two prominent themes that suggest a perspective through which psychologists are encouraged to view ethical issues and that provide a frame of reference for thinking about how one would engage in the resolution of an ethical issue: (1) a proactive stance and (2) utilization of reasonable professional judgment both proactively and in reaction to events that have occurred before professional judgment can be enacted.

Support for a proactive stance by psychologists engaged in ethical issues is evidenced throughout the 2002 Ethics Code. This section, however, directly reflects this stance through the intent and wording of the standards. Each of the eight standards within this section cites passages that include these phrases: "make known one's commitment," "take steps to resolve conflict," "take appropriate action," "cooperate," "take further action appropriate to the situation," and "take reasonable steps to correct or minimize [the problem]." These terms promote proactive and initiating actions in conjunction with ethically appropriate reactive and responsive actions to the applicable ethical standards.

A second theme of Section 1 is respect for reasoned judgment and decision making of psychologists. The Ethics Code does not impose a step-by-step approach to decision making but instead offers latitude for psychologists to weigh the factors of an ethical issue and then process the circumstances of the case to arrive at their best professional judgment in complying with the relevant ethical standard. Phrases used in these standards that support the value of professional judgment include "taking reasonable steps to correct," "minimize misuse," "clarify the nature of the conflict," and "bring to the attention of the individual if appropriate." Adoption of a proactive stance and the practice of reasoned professional judgment provide a frame of reference that psychologists may use to guide their engagement with ethical issues, questions, and dilemmas across the spectrum of the Ethics Code's standards. In specific application to Section 1, being mindful of a proactive stance and the importance of reasoned judgment is helpful in understanding these standards.

Section 1 comprises eight standards that cluster around four aspects of engaging ethical issues:

1. Others' use of psychologists' work (Standard 1.01, Misuse of Psychologists' Work)
2. Conflicts between ethics and legal authority (Standard 1.02, Conflicts Between Ethics and Law, Regulations, or Other Governing Legal Authority, and Standard 1.03, Conflicts Between Ethics and Organizational Demands)
3. Taking action on potential ethical violations (Standard 1.04, Informal Resolution of Ethical Violations, and Standard 1.05, Reporting Ethical Violations)
4. Cooperation in and treatment of those involved with ethical complaints (Standard 1.06, Cooperating With Ethics Committees; Standard 1.07, Improper Complaints; and Standard 1.08, Unfair Discrimination Against Complainants and Respondents).

OTHERS' USE OF PSYCHOLOGISTS' WORK

Standard 1.01, Misuse of Psychologists' Work
If psychologists learn of misuse or misrepresentation of their work, they take reasonable steps to correct or minimize the misuse or misrepresentation.

A proactive stance does not mean that psychologists are not reacting to an event. When psychologists learn that their work is not accurately depicted, they use reasoned judgment to determine what corrective steps might be taken. Psychologists are not expected to have extraordinary access to information on use of their work. The appropriate steps to take for corrective action are determined through a process using reasoned judgment. Documentation of the action and the decision-making process is also valuable in demonstrating the commitment of psychologists to protecting professional material and in promoting proper treatment of one's psychological work.

The venues through which professional work can be compromised are primarily verbal (e.g., court testimony, professional presentations and workshops, phone consultations and media interviews) and written (e.g., psychological report writing, research, forensic interviews, written articles, e-mail communications). Although not required by this standard, psychologists who participate in these activities may consider specialized training, continuing education, and consultation in improving means of controlling one's own work and reducing the chances of its misuse. For example, presentations and workshops might include handouts that specifically cite the author, date, and name of the workshop. Also, media workshops are an effective means to learn how to influence the content of an interview to ensure accuracy. Furthermore, psychologists may negotiate for access to review (nonrefereed) articles before publication. Copies of e-mail communications and psychological reports may be kept for substantiation of content. Additional monitoring methods may be cumbersome or time consuming; however, these actions do demonstrate advanced steps in protecting one's own professional contributions. Principle A: Beneficence and Nonmaleficence also cites support for psychologists to be alert to potential misuse of their own influence.

Standard 1.01, Case 1

Case Illustration. Dr. F. specializes in the assessment of children experiencing academic difficulties in school. Her standard approach includes integrated assessment of cognitive capacities, learning style, developmental needs, and emotional functioning relevant to learning capacities. At the request of the parents, Dr. F. completed an assessment of a 10-year-old, boy, T.G., and determined that he had some mild learning problems but that his current academic problems largely arise from severe anxiety symptoms reflecting his distress about his parents' bitter divorce and custody fight. Dr. F. mailed her report to the parents as they had requested. Two months later, Dr. F. received a telephone call from one of the parents instructing her not to respond to any communications from T.G.'s school. A day later, Dr. F. received a letter from the school indicating that T.G.'s parents had filed an appeal of a denial of special educational services with a copy of her report attached. The letter asked for a copy of the report signed by Dr. F. for inclusion in the appeal hearing. Upon reviewing the report, Dr. F. found that the copy of the report had been purged of any references to emotional and family functioning and included only the academic and cognitive portions. The report was unsigned because the portions following those sections had been removed, including the final page, which had contained her signature.

Ethical Dilemma. Here, the work of the psychologist has been misused and misrepresented by a third party. One the one hand, Dr. F.'s evaluation report had been selectively edited by parents and submitted in special education eligibility proceedings without Dr. F.'s knowledge. On the other hand, Dr. F. also had to consider the specific instruction from a parent that she not communicate with the school in any way lest she violate the confidentiality of the child and parents. Dr. F. is aware of Standard 1.01 and her obligation to take reasonable steps to correct misuse of her work. Also at risk in this situation is the potential for misclassification of T. G. and a distorted representation of his needs. Dr. F. thought about Standard 3.04, Avoiding Harm, and realized that misrepresentation in this case not only impacted the credibility and veracity of her work but also had greater implications for harm to the child. Dr. F. had always upheld the Ethics Code and thought of herself as an ethical psychologist, but she realized that she was finding herself in a situation in which confidentiality pledged to a client was in conflict with other ethical values, including General Principle C: Integrity, which reminds psychologists of the importance of honesty and truthfulness in science, teaching, and practice. What reasonable steps might Dr. F. take to correct or minimize the misuse or misrepresentation of her professional work?

Decision-Making Factors. Dr. F. recognized that there was a conflict between her duty to maintain confidentiality after being instructed not to communicate with the school and her duty to take "reasonable steps to correct or minimize" the misrepresentation of her evaluation report. Dr. F. was aware that the parents, and not the school, had retained her and were her identified clients. She reasoned that it was unlikely that the portion of her report detailing the testing evidence for a mild learning problem had been unduly persuasive because the boy had not been found eligible for special educational services. She considered the possibility that the parents had eliminated the sections that focused more on the anxious reaction their son was having to their divorce more out of a need to protect family privacy than in an effort to mislead special education staff.

On the other hand, Dr. F. also knew that the reason she was receiving the request from the school was that the parents were appealing the school's denial of special education services. Dr. F. was concerned that if she did not communicate to the school about the misrepresentation of her report that the parents may continue trying to place T.G. into special education services. Dr. F. believed that if they were successful in achieving such placement an injustice could well be done to the child in the inappropriate application of her recommendations, misdiagnosis, and psychological harm. The school was in receipt of Dr. F.'s partial report. On reading what the parents had submitted to the school, Dr. F. determined that the redacted portion remained confidential, but her role as evaluator was now known to the school. Dr. F. noted that the school might have its own suspicions about the integrity of the report because it had requested a copy from her office with her signature on it.

Decision Options. Dr. F. decided that she would defer to the parental assertion of confidentiality and not respond to the letter. She carefully documented the facts of the situation and the reasoning underlying her decision regarding the child's file. Dr. F. was fortunate to have maintained a reliable method of retaining copies of her own reports. She was also fortunate that in her specific circumstances she could infer that the misrepresentation of her work had not resulted in inappropriate assignment of T.G. to special educational services. Had it appeared that the misrepresentation had resulted in a fraudulent eligibility determination—or, worse, had it appeared that the boy was involved in toxic family dynamics that presented him as having significant neurocognitive deficits when he did not—Dr. F. may have come to a different decision. Indeed, in circumstances where the child may be factitiously presented as having significant cognitive or social impairment, a mandated child protection report might be triggered. Dr. F. also was aware that the school officials had the option to have their own psychologist review Dr. F.'s report and perhaps conduct an independent evaluation of the child.

Dr. F. contacted the parents to discuss her concerns about the submission of the partial report, the potential inadvertent consequences to them and their child if they were found to be relying on a partial report in proceedings in a legal context, and the potential difficulties that could arise for their son if he were awarded a potentially inaccurate special education classification based (at least in part) on an incomplete report. Dr. F. further explained to the parents that if they continued to seek the placement she would need to directly communicate with the school and voice her opposition to the use of her report in a placement that was inappropriate and possibly harmful to the child. Dr. F. documented her communications with the parents in the case record in the event that the legal proceedings resulted in efforts to discover her records and/or the parents or others later complained about her role in the matter.

Standard 1.01, Case 2

Case Illustration. Dr. Z. is a psychologist who works in programs for adults with major mental illnesses and teaches part time at a local college. The college media relations department referred to her a newspaper reporter covering a local trial in which the insanity defense was raised by a defendant who had been diagnosed with schizophrenia. Dr. Z. reluctantly agreed to be interviewed after the reporter told her that she was interested in a "fair and balanced" article about the relationship between violence and mental illness and that she understood that Dr. Z. could make no comment about this particular defendant. During the interview, Dr. Z. carefully explained that, statistically speaking, persons with schizophrenia are actually less violent than community samples, although "all bets are off when the person with schizophrenia is acutely psychotic, especially if he or she is paranoid." She was shocked when persons with mental illness were portrayed in the article in a stigmatizing fashion and that she was quoted as commenting that "all bets are off regarding violence when people are mentally ill" and that "paranoid people like the defendant" are especially dangerous. When she called the reporter to express her concern she was told that a story about the complex relationship between major mental illness and violence was "not the story I wanted to write" and denied recalling that Dr. Z. had told her that nothing she said in the interview was about a defendant she had never seen. Dr. Z. was told "Papers don't write retractions for stuff like this."

Ethical Dilemma. Here the work of the psychologist has been misused and misrepresented by a third party (Standard 1.01). On the one hand, Dr. Z. has given an appropriately limited interview in an effort to provide public education and challenge the stigma and misinformation often associated with major mental illness. She has attempted to correct the misrepresentation of her interview material. On the other hand, she has not actually succeeded in her efforts to correct the misrepresentation of her work or to minimize the impact of that misrepresentation on her clients and others. What additional reasonable steps might Dr. Z. take to correct or minimize the misuse or misrepresentation of her professional work?

Decision-Making Factors. Dr. Z. was concerned about the stigmatizing portrayal of mentally ill persons in the article, how other mental health professionals would perceive her professionally, and how her own patients would react when they read the quotations attributed to her. She reasoned that she had made efforts consistent with her obligation to take steps to correct the misrepresentation to the best of her ability but that these efforts had not yet been effective. Dr. Z. considered that her failed efforts to that point may not be sufficient to constitute "reasonable steps," particularly where the misrepresentation of her work had been conveyed to so many persons through a mass media publication and when the misrepresentation may have a specific impact upon the high-visibility trial of a defendant with a mental illness.

Decision Options. When the reporter rebuffed her, Dr. Z. phoned the editor of the paper and insisted on an opportunity to respond in a letter to the editor. She submitted a letter to the editor setting the record straight. Two weeks went by without publication of the letter, and the editor did not respond to voicemails inquiring whether it would be published. Dr. Z. subsequently wrote a column correcting the misinformation and misquotes in the article, which was published in another local paper.

If Dr. Z. is to continue taking referrals from the college media relations department, she should consider consulting with the media professionals at the time of each referral; investigating the professional reputations of print, radio, and television reporters in her area; and taking a workshop on interacting with the media. Some psychologists seek additional protection by insisting on receiving complete and unedited copies or any audio- or videotaped interviews they grant, or they make their own recordings of interviews when no electronic copy is created by the interviewer.

CONFLICTS BETWEEN ETHICAL AND LEGAL AUTHORITY

The following two standards—Standard 1.02, Conflicts Between Ethics and Law, Regulations, or Other Governing Legal Authority, and Standard 1.03, Conflicts Between Ethics and Organizational Demands—describe conflicts between professional ethical and other rules conflicts. These two standards might be viewed as psychologists in conflict with policy entities (Standard 1.02) and psychologists in interrelational conflicts (Standard 1.03); that is, when psychologists experience a conflict with policy and regulatory entities procedural options are often known or knowable to psychologists and may depend on whether state or federal regulations are applicable or whether state laws or rules or state licensure or state ethical committee issues are in question. In contrast, when psychologists experience a conflict with an affiliated organization many variables of professional relationships, including delegation of work to others, informed consent, supervisory and consultative roles and other interrelational factors, affect the conflict in complex ways. Both of these conflict clusters call on psychologists to be proactive and to exercise reasoned judgment in identifying both the conflict and options for resolution.

Standard 1.02, Conflicts Between Ethics and Law, Regulations, or Other Governing Legal Authority[2]
If psychologists' ethical responsibilities conflict with law, regulations, or other governing legal authority, psychologists make known their commitment to the Ethics Code and take steps to resolve the conflict. If the conflict is irresolvable via such means, psychologists may adhere to the requirements of the law, regulations, or other governing legal authority.

Professional judgment and decision making are very important competencies in this standard in that psychologists are not mandated to choose between an ethical value and legal or regulatory bodies or to violate one set of standards or values in order to comply with another. Rather, Standard 1.02 indicates that a psychologist may adhere to the law in resolving an "irresolvable" conflict between ethical responsibilities and "law, regulations, or other governing legal authority," but it does not require the psychologist to adhere to the law. As a consequence, the Ethics Code relies on the professional judgment and decision making of psychologists to weigh the respective values and standards implicated in this dilemma. Standard 1.02 calls on psychologists to engage actively in a process of ethical decision making by identifying the con-

---

[2] As this book is going to print, the explicitness of the language in Sections 1.02 and 1.03 of the 2002 Ethical Principles of Psychologists and Code of Conduct (the APA Ethics Code) is being examined. Further clarification is likely to emerge in early 2010. Please check this web page, http://www.apa.org/pubs/books/4312011-footnote.aspx, at that time for updates by the authors of this volume.

flict, voicing professional commitment to the Ethics Code, and taking steps to resolve the conflict.

A conflict between ethics and law occurs when a psychologist has legal and ethical obligations that are mutually exclusive such that the psychologist cannot fulfill the requirements of both. In certain instances, the law imposes requirements that the Ethics Code does not; at other times, the Ethics Code may require more than law, regulation, or other governing legal authority requires. These instances do not necessarily entail a conflict between ethics and law because, although the requirements may differ, the professional may nonetheless meet the requirements of both. A conflict arises when fulfilling the requirements of one results in violation of the other; in other words, when following the law necessarily entails violating the Ethics Code and, conversely, following the Ethics Code necessarily violates the law.

True Standard 1.02 conflicts are very rare. When such an exceptional circumstance arises, Standard 1.02 calls on the psychologist to engage in a process of attempting to resolve the conflict. If the psychologist's attempts are unsuccessful, the Ethics Code places the locus of ethical decision making on the psychologist, insofar as the psychologist must then decide the most appropriate course of action. The psychologist will choose whether to follow the Ethics Code and violate the law or whether to follow the law and violate the Ethics Code. Adhering to the Ethics Code in this circumstance may therefore constitute an ethically permissible act of civil disobedience.

Before engaging in an act of civil disobedience, a psychologist would follow a process of confirming that a true Standard 1.02 conflict exists. In addition, the psychologist would actively explore, with the aid of consultation, whether there are possibilities for resolving the conflict that the psychologist had not yet considered as well as the intended and unintended consequences of various courses of action. If the psychologist ultimately determines that the conflict is irresolvable and chooses to follow the Ethics Code, thereby violating the law, the psychologist must then be willing to accept the consequences of this choice. Such is the nature of civil disobedience.

It is important to note that there has been some confusion about what constitutes a conflict under Standard 1.02. A scenario that is often offered as an ethical conflict is one in which the psychologist is court ordered to produce confidential records against the wishes of the client/patient. The psychologist may well encounter a moral dilemma in this case, but if he or she refers to Standard 4.05 he or she will realize the following:

> Psychologists disclose confidential information without the consent of the individual only as mandated by law, or where permitted by law for a valid purpose such as to (1) provide needed professional services; (2) obtain appropriate professional consultations; (3) protect the client/patient,

psychologist, or others from harm; or (4) obtain payment for services from a client/patient, in which instance disclosure is limited to the minimum that is necessary to achieve the purpose.[3]

Disclosure of confidential information when mandated or permitted by law is, therefore, not a violation of Standard 1.02 and is not an example of an ethical conflict.

Several other standards within the Ethics Code contain language regarding legal requirements and are helpful to psychologists who are assessing whether there is a conflict between the Ethics Code and legal or regulatory policies. Such standards may or may not present an example of a conflict between an Ethics Code standard and the law, depending on the facts of a given situation. The following numbered compendium of ethical standards makes reference to decisions to disclose information, forgo informed consent, or release data that are permitted by law or regulation.

Ethical decision making often involves one of these three professional actions, and psychologists are respectful and mindful of their importance and the consequences of misjudgment. Psychologists are called on to use reasonable judgment in deciding a course of action in these and other scenarios involving potential legal or regulatory actions. In fact, Standard 1.02 would not be applicable in the following cases because the standards include the exception of a mandate or permission by law or regulation.

1. Standard 3.05(c), Multiple Relationships, cites the circumstance in which psychologists are required by law to serve in more than one role in judicial proceedings with the expectation that psychologists would clarify their roles and the extent to which confidentiality would be protected.

2. Standard 3.10(a), Informed Consent, states that when services are mandated by the court, psychologists inform the client/patient of the nature of services, mandatory status, and any limits of confidentiality.

3. Standard 3.10(b), Informed Consent, notes that for persons who are legally incapable of giving informed consent, psychologists obtain permission from a legally authorized person if a substitute consent is permitted or required by law and, if not, psychologists still take reasonable steps to protect the individual's rights and welfare.

4. Standard 3.10(c), Informed Consent, states that when services are mandated psychologists still inform the individual of the

---

[3]See Standard 4.05(b), Disclosures.

nature of the services, indicate whether they are court ordered, and explain any limits of confidentiality.

5. Standard 9.03(a), Informed Consent in Assessments, cites the importance of psychologists obtaining informed consent for assessments and other diagnostic services, except when testing is mandated by law or governmental regulation.

6. Standard 9.03(b), Informed Consent in Assessments, notes that when working with individuals whose capacity to consent is limited or for whom testing is mandated, psychologists inform the persons of the nature and purpose of assessment services using reasonable language for the individuals being assessed.

7. In describing release of test data, Standard 9.04(a), Release of Test Data, states that with a client/patient release psychologists may still refrain from release in protection of the client/patient or (b) in the absence of a client/patient release, psychologists provide data only as required by law.

In summary, psychologists are assisted in dealing with ethical conflict through several sections of Standard 1, Resolving Ethical Issues, and several additional sections of the Ethics Code as cited in the Standard 1.02 commentary. Resolving ethical issues requires psychologists to practice, effectively and competently, a proactive stance and reasonable professional judgment. Conflicts between ethics and law inevitably present some of the most challenging dilemmas a psychologist could face, so consultation with knowledgeable colleagues will be an invaluable resource in choosing a course of action.

Standard 1.02, Case 1

Case Illustration. Dr. G. has been providing cognitive rehabilitation services to Mr. J. in a nursing home setting after Mr. J. sustained a head injury. Mr. J.'s parents have filed a petition for guardianship of him that would essentially give them authority to make all decisions for him. Dr. G. is subpoenaed to give testimony in the guardianship hearing. Following his testimony about the clinical presentation of Mr. J., the judge asked Dr. G. whether in his opinion Mr. J.'s parents should be made his guardians. Dr. G. explained that he had been providing rehabilitation services and had not conducted either a forensic assessment of Mr. J.'s legal competencies or an assessment of whether Mr. J.'s parents would adequately protect Mr. J.'s interests should they be appointed guardians. The judge listened to Dr. G. and then said, "Frankly, Dr. G., I am not interested in those kinds of details and am ordering you to render an opinion on whether or not Mr. J. should be placed under the guardianship of his parents." Dr. G. responded that rendering such an opinion could very well violate the Ethics Code and that he is committed to the

Ethics Code as a psychologist. The judge responds, "I will give you one more opportunity to respond to my order to render an opinion, or I may well hold you in contempt."

Dr. G. felt very pressured by the judge and so testified while still on the record. Dr. G. stated that, on the basis of Mr. J.'s clinical presentation, he would think it probable that a more specific assessment of his legal competencies might well demonstrate that he is significantly impaired. "Because I have not assessed his parents, I can offer you no opinion as a psychologist as to whether they should be his guardians. However, I did speak briefly with them before the hearing today for the first time. Speaking now as an individual and not professionally as a psychologist, they seemed reasonable and concerned about their son's well-being."

In responding to the judge's order and threat of citation of contempt for failure to render an opinion, Dr. G. emphasized the limits of his professional role when making a reasonable effort to respond to the order of the judge. He also expressed his very limited basis for any impression he had of the parents and tried to distinguish his individual impressions from a professional opinion as a psychologist.

Ethical Dilemma. This is only one of many potential situations in which the ethical responsibilities of a psychologist may conflict with law, regulations, or other governing authority. In this case, a "governing authority" in the form of a trial judge is ordering a psychologist to render an expert forensic opinion regarding guardianship that extends beyond the clinical data he has developed in providing services to Mr. J. and that is well beyond his scope of practice. Dr. G. realized that in question was not only Standard 1.02 but also Standard 2.01(a), Boundaries of Competence. Dr. G. thought that the judge was assuming that because Dr. G. is a rehabilitation psychologist he was competent to do forensic assessments. Dr. G. works with the recommendations made by neuropsychologists in his rehabilitative treatment of patients, but he does not conduct evaluations himself. Furthermore, Dr. G. is aware of Standard 9.01, according to which psychologists do not base their opinions on forensic testimony or information that is not sufficient to substantiate their findings. In addition, Standard 9.02(a), Use of Assessments, cautions psychologists to "use assessment techniques, interviews, tests, or instruments in a manner and for purposes that are appropriate." Dr. G. did not perform any assessment with instruments while working with Mr. J., but he did conduct an intake interview before starting treatment, and he pursued several lines of inquiry that could have been considered interviews. In the context of considering interviews as assessment, Dr. G. may also have violated this standard in that interviews conducted for the purpose of rehabilitation services would not be used to make a competency decision or a guardianship decision.

Decision-Making Factors. Dr. G. had a sinking feeling in realizing that, under the pressure of the judge, being the focus of those in the courtroom, and his desire to be cooperative, he went beyond his scope of practice and made statements that he should not have made. Standard 1.02 would permit but not require Dr. G. to render an opinion as the judge had ordered; however, this standard is meant to give psychologists the authority to exercise their professional judgment in "adhering to the requirements of the law, regulations, or other governing legal authority" when psychologists have the competence and expertise to render an opinion. In this case, Dr. G. not only had not conducted a competency evaluation for Mr. J. or an evaluation of the parents for guardianship, but also he did not have the necessary training to do either of these assessments. Dr. G. wondered whether the judge thought that he was reluctant because he was testifying not as an expert witness but as a treating therapist or if the judge realized that Dr. G. did not have the training to conduct forensic assessments. Any opinion Dr. G. rendered on assumptions about Mr. J.'s functioning and on the fitness of the parents is outside of his scope of practice even if he did conduct neuropsychological assessments and fitness evaluations, but professionally, he had in fact not conducted them and therefore would be relying on insufficient information to substantiate his opinion.

Dr. G. was quite distraught about his actions in the courtroom. He feared that he may have risked undermining Mr. J.'s legal or civil rights; also, he had no information about whether Mr. J.'s parents might have a conflict of interest or improper motive that might preclude them from acting properly if appointed legal guardians for their son. He has not conducted an evaluation of the parents to determine their fitness for guardianship, which he realized would be necessary to make an informed recommendation. Dr. G. knew that an appropriate evaluation of the parents to determine their fitness for this role has not been done. Mr. J. certainly has cognitive limitations resulting from his injury, but Dr. G. cannot attest to the necessity for Mr. J. to have a guardian.

Dr. G. further realized that, in an attempt to frame his answer in a context that would clearly indicate that he was not providing expert testimony, he had presented himself as an "individual" rather than a psychologist. Dr. G. knew that psychologists who are testifying because they are either treating professionals or expert witnesses cannot divorce their role from that of psychologists. They cannot be psychologists one minute and members of the community moments later. If he had been a typical person from the community, he would not be testifying in any capacity, except possibly as a character witness.

Decision Options. Dr. G. saw that his duty, at this point, was first to consult with the judge and second to talk with Mr. J. about the effect of his testimony on their relationship and the outcome of the testimony. Dr. G. would want to tell the judge of his error in giving an opinion, not because of Standard 2.01 but because he was not competent to render those opinions.

He would think about explaining to the judge that any decisions made on the basis of his opinion would be made erroneously and that refusal to consider Dr. G.'s explanation to the judge could result in an injustice to Mr. J. He would urge the judge to appoint a neuropsychologist to evaluate Mr. J.'s functional needs and abilities and to appoint a psychologist to evaluate Mr. J.'s parents for the potential need for guardianship.

Dr. G. would want to talk with Mr. J. and explain his actions. He would want Mr. J. to know that he had asked the judge to reconsider his testimony. Dr. G. may also express to Mr. J.'s parents that he wants the most appropriate treatment possible for Mr. J.

Standard 1.02, Case 2

Case Illustration. Dr. K. accepted an appointment to the state board that is responsible for the supervision of convicted sex offenders. This appointment was offered in large part because the statute specifically requires appointment to the board of at least one licensed mental health professional and because Dr. K. has developed expertise in the assessment and treatment of sex offenders. He learns, on taking his position on the board, that the staff who assign risk levels to the offenders are required to rely solely on factors listed in the statute. Although these factors reflected the state of sex offender risk assessment when the law was passed over a decade ago, Dr. K. realizes that they no longer reflect best practice in this area. In fact, the list is so outdated that relying on it alone would involve acting below the standard of care if Dr. K. were engaging in his professional practice as a psychologist. Dr. K. had been pleased to join the board because this was his particular area of expertise and he had been anticipating the contribution he might make and the progress that could be made through board procedures and policies. Now Dr. K. was dismayed because none of the other board members seemed concerned about this practice gap. When he expressed his concern to the chair of the board he was told that his votes as a board member in regard to reviewing the assigned risk levels must be based exclusively on the factors required by the law. The chair was concerned about following procedures and going by the book, not with making changes. Dr. K. knew that he was in a quandary on how to proceed. He was a new member, and he certainly felt like he did not have the influence that other, more tenured, members had, yet he felt obligated to try to deal with this significant problem. The other appointed board members represented various areas of specialty, but none were functioning in a career role in which they would understand the importance of the changes that had occurred in classification; thus, Dr. K. felt as though he were on his own and would need to make a reasoned decision about how to proceed.

Ethical Dilemma. Dr. K. is in the unenviable position of recognizing that the classification procedures relied on by his state board have gradually drifted below the standard of care that would be required if Dr. K. were to be producing recidivism risk assessments of sex offenders in his professional practice. Here, the basic problem is that Dr. K. is responsible for reviewing and voting on work that, in his view, has become scientifically incompetent because the risk determination and classification procedures relied on have not kept up with developments in the field. Hence, he would be forced to vote "no" or to abstain in all cases reviewed by the board for approval of the proposed classification, or to vote "yes" to approve classifications that he finds based on inadequate methods.

Dr. K. is aware of Standard 1.02 and that the Ethics Code may be in conflict with, in this case, a governing legal authority. For Dr. K., this predicament goes beyond the authorization to adhere to the governing legal authority that the Ethics Code grants and extends into the fair and just treatment of the individuals whose risk levels he is assessing (General Principle A: Beneficence and Nonmaleficence and General Principle D: Justice). In addition, Standard 9.02, Use of Assessments, typically applies to the "use of instruments in a manner and for purposes that are appropriate in light of the research on or evidence of the usefulness and proper application of the techniques." Dr. K., however, believed that assigning risk levels to individuals was a means of assessment and that use of an outdated categorization system could be applicable to the Standard 9.02. Dr. K. was further stymied because his board acted as an extension of state government with all of the implied legal authorization and that to question the procedures that other members had practiced for years would put him, politically and practically, in a very tenuous position. Dr. K. would need to think about any recourse and well as consequences to himself should he further act.

Decision-Making Factors. The chair of the board had suggested to Dr. K. that in his role as a board member he is acting in a "ministerial" administrative role instead of in his role as a psychologist, so arguably the Ethics Code might not apply. He also argued that Mr. K., as a board member in an administrative role, had a duty to vote on whether the state board has complied with the process and standards defined in the law, not whether those processes and standards are sufficiently within a professional standard of care for psychologists. These stances of not being in the role of a psychologist and being in the job only to verify compliance with processing did not seem tenable to Dr. K. because, in fact, he was a board member not as a private citizen or a public member but as a mental health professional.

Psychologists would hold that the Ethics Code would apply, pointing to the requirement that the board member holding Dr. K.'s position be a licensed mental health professional (albeit not necessarily a psychologist) and asserting that his function as a board member is akin to the function that clinical supervisors often provide when reviewing the work of supervisees: ensuring adherence to the relevant standard of practice. Dr. K. was cognizant of his short tenure on the board and the need to decide how he should approach other members as well as how he should present his proposed changes. Dr. K. is aware of his responsibility to those he serves (Standard 3.05, Avoiding Harm) and his obligation to make known his commitment to the Ethics Code.

Decision Options. Because there may be a lack of consensus about the application of the Ethics Code to his participation as a board member, Dr. K would be advised to seek one or more formal consultations from sources such as the APA Ethics Office, his state or provincial board of licensure for psychology, or recognized authorities in the field of ethics in psychological practice.

Dr. K. has expressed his concern to the chair of the sex offender classification board; however, Dr. K. would be in a stronger position if he had explicitly expressed his commitment to the Ethics Code and specifically identified the conflict between his role as a board member and what he believes is expected of him by the Ethics Code. Specifically, Dr. K. may articulate the discrepancy between the classification process reflected in the statute and current best practices in the field and attempt to enlist the support of the chair in bringing this discrepancy to the attention of the state legislature.

In either event, Dr. K. will need to make a reasoned judgment about how to proceed. Depending on additional circumstances, such as the likelihood of success in amending the statute to require procedures consistent with professional standards of care, or his ability to create a record that could be relied on by a further reviewing body, such as a court, Dr. K. might decide to resign his board position. Alternatively, he may choose to remain at least for a time if there is a reasonable belief that his continued participation may result in appropriate reform of the statute and/or the risk assessment and classification procedures. As can occur in a true dilemma, reasonable persons might reasonably disagree about which decision would be best and why. In any case, his efforts to secure a formal ethics consultation from an appropriate individual or organization, and an ability to clearly articulate the basis for the decision he makes, would reflect professional prudence in making his decision.

Standard 1.02, Case 3

Case Illustration. Dr. V. works in an incarceration setting for violent men. Among her duties are screening the mental status of men who have been placed in the disciplinary segregation unit where they are held in extreme isolation for periods of weeks to months. Legal challenges to this practice have consistently failed in the courts. Dr. V. observed that prolonged isolation often produces psychosis and significantly self-harming behavior on the part of the inmates. She discovered that this observation is consistent with the clinical experience of other psychologists in similar settings and is reflected in research on the impact of prolonged isolation on human beings. She informed the prison administration of her observations and her concerns that periodically screening the segregation unit inmates is insufficient to prevent or promptly detect severe clinical deterioration. She informed them further that she believed the mental health interventions provided once an inmate manifests a severely deteriorating mental status are commonly insufficient to stabilize the inmate or help maintain safety for the inmate and the unit. She was told to continue her screening or face employment disciplinary proceedings.

Ethical Dilemma. Dr. V. has identified one dimension of her role as a clinical duty to detect and respond to severe clinical deterioration with the goal of ameliorating the human suffering of the inmate, including self-harm and suicidality. Another dimension is to help identify and manage the symptoms and behaviors associated with severe clinical deterioration that could pose safety risks to other inmates and the correctional staff on the unit. A third dimension is to stabilize the inmate's mental status so that the inmate can understand and appreciate that assignment to the segregation unit is a punishment for misconduct elsewhere in the prison. Dr. V. appreciates that the practice of extreme isolation of inmates itself creates some of the outcomes she is asked to address (e.g., increased safety risks on the unit at times of severe clinical deterioration) and that the existing screening and mental health interventions available to her are inadequate to discharge her clinical and institutional responsibilities. She identified these ethical and professional practice conflicts to prison administrators, and thus far they have failed to respond.

Decision-Making Factors. Bringing the situation to the attention of prison administrators has failed to resolve the conflict. Where, as in this case, the risks to mentally ill inmates, other inmates on the unit, and correctional staff remain significant and unaddressed, the psychologist arguably has a duty to take further steps to resolve the conflicts.

Standard 1.02 does not require Dr. V. to stop participating in existing segregation unit policies and procedures, although it does require her to "take steps to resolve the conflict" that she has identified. The additional steps that would be required or prudent to take under Standard 1.02 might depend on other factors, such as the frequency with which inmates show significant clinical deterioration associated with prolonged isolation; the severity of the psychosis, self-harm, or other manifestation of the clinical deterioration; the likelihood that adequate reform can be initiated within the correctional system and the length of time it may take for those reforms to take place; or whether inmates would be exposed to further risk of harm if the psychologist quit or asked for a transfer to another facility or assigned different duties.

Decision Options. To be fully consistent with Standard 1.02 Dr. V. will also need to communicate her commitment to the Ethics Code and take steps to resolve the conflict. Depending on the information associated with these and other factors in Dr. V.'s specific situation, she might choose from among these or other options:

- continue in her role on the unit but also continue to advocate for reform of relevant institutional policies and practices regarding prolonged inmate isolation,
- seek a transfer to another assignment or facility where this specific conflict between organizational and professional organization demands does not exist,
- remain in her role on the segregation unit but work with external legal or advocacy organizations to minimize the use of prolonged isolation as an inmate behavior management or disciplinary strategy,
- advocate through her employment union and professional associations to reform policies and practices regarding segregation units, or
- find professional practice opportunities outside of the correctional system entirely.

Standard 1.03, Conflicts Between Ethics and Organizational Demands
If the demands of an organization with which psychologists are affiliated or for whom they are working conflict with this Ethics Code, psychologists clarify the nature of the conflict, make known their commitment to the Ethics Code, and to the extent feasible, resolve the conflict in a way that permits adherence to the Ethics Code.

Conflicts with organizational entities are often more complex and difficult to manage because, in contrast to having a conflict with a governmental policy or regulation, psychologists are working with other individuals with whom they have varying degrees of relationships. The scope of practice for psychology has expanded rapidly, resulting in many developing and changing venues for psychological activities. Some of the organizational agencies with which psychologists now typically work include hospitals, mental health agencies, insurance companies, schools, corporate/business entities, governmental agencies, managed care companies, correctional systems, and funding agencies (governmental, public, and private).

Psychologists may have very different, but specific, relationships with each of these entities, determined in part by the psychologist's status as employee, consultant, or affiliate (e.g., working privately or for another company in a collaborative model). The Ethics Code cites the importance of making known an ethically related conflict and of psychologists' citing their commitment to the standards of the Ethics Code; however, resolution of the conflict is viewed within the parameters of "the extent feasible." The extent feasible may be influenced by several variables pertaining to the role of psychologists in the organization in addition to employment status, including balance of decision-making authority within the organizational structure, the line of reporting authority, the status of established versus developing policies that affect the ethics context, budgetary implication for implementation of change, and interpersonal relationships. These factors may not affect psychologists' interpretation of compliance for the Ethics Code in context of organizational policies, but psychologists may consider these and other variables in deciding how to facilitate compliance with the Ethics Code effectively. Instead of thinking of themselves as mediators between organizations and the Ethics Code, psychologists may serve the role of facilitators and educators in enhancing the quality of practice, promoting sound and defensible policies, and assisting organizations in advancing professionalism.

Psychologists are encouraged to include in their frame of reference other standards within the Ethics Code that may facilitate the resolution of organizational conflicts. Standard 3.06, Conflict of Interest, cites restraint from professional activities that may affect psychologists' objectivity, competence, or effectiveness or expose others to harm or exploitation. Standard 3.11(a), Psychological Services Delivered to or Through Organizations, offers several points of information that clarify and define the role and function of the psychologists in service provision. Psychologists must obtain informed consent for assessment and evaluation with specific elements included (e.g., nature and purpose of assessment, limits of confidentiality, and involvement of third party; Standard 9.03a, Informed Consent in Assessments). Standard 10.01(a), Informed Consent to Therapy, additionally offers aspects of informed consent for therapy that assist psychologists in conveying their purpose. Standard 9.03, Informed Consent in Assessment; Standard 3.11, Psychological Services Delivered to or Through Organizations; and Standard 10.01(a), Informed Consent to Therapy all offer variables for consideration in defining the role and function of psychologists in working with populations who may not be informed of the role of psychological services in their work environments.

Standard 1.03, Case 1

Case Illustration. Dr. L. is a school psychologist in a district where his duties include evaluation of students for behavioral management plans and special educational services. The common practice in his school district is for guidance staff to refer students to him. After working there for some months, he discovers that he was wrong when he assumed that guidance staff routinely obtained informed consent from parents before referring the students to him for professional services. When he brought this to the attention of the district superintendent, he was told that parents receive a handbook of policies and procedures at the time they first enroll their child in school and that this handbook includes a statement that school authorities may refer their children for educational and psychological assessment services at their discretion and without prior notice. The superintendent insists that he has been told by the school district's attorney that this is adequate for informed consent and that it would be "too much of a hassle to ask parents first every time we wanted to do some psych assessments on a kid."

Dr. L. had been working for the district for a little over a year and therefore was quite shocked to learn of this practice and to realize that he had been there for this length of time and did not have a hint of the problem. Dr. L. liked working in the district very much and actually did like the individuals with whom he worked. He was quite surprised at the dismissal of the seriousness of the practice and realized that he would need to approach this problem with thoughtfulness. He wondered also whether other psychologists and related staff in the district knew of the practice or if they, as he, had simply assumed that informed consent was being acquired. He had to admit, also, that he had not paid close enough attention to the handbook of policies and procedures and had not made an inquiry when he was hired about how procedures were carried out and how the district practices would affect his work as a school psychologist. He had expected some variance, because he worked with all the schools in the district, but he was exasperated with himself that he would be in this situation.

Ethical Dilemma. This case illustrates conflicts between demands of an organization and the Ethics Code. Dr. L.'s conflict exists between ethical duties involving informed consent and practices of the school district that Dr. L. thought violated the autonomy, self-determination, and decision making of parents. On the one hand, Dr. L. is obligated to provide professional services to students only after he has obtained adequate informed consent from parents or guardians. On the other hand, the superintendent has informed him that, in the opinion of the school district, it is sufficient that the parents/guardians are provided a statement in a school handbook indicating that students may be referred for assessment services without prior or additional notice to the parents or guardians. Dr. L. thought about the fact that he had not had a complaint or question from parents during the time he had been there, and so he wondered if this particular community simply did not question or disagree with school policy. Dr. L. knew, however, that number of complaints is not the litmus test for ethical behavior. In fact, the position of the school in presuming authority to test conveyed a sense of potential exploitation because the parents were not being given a choice about their children's evaluation or the consequences of placement or behavioral regimen resulting from the evaluation.

Decision-Making Factors. Dr. L. clearly identified the nature of the ethical conflict and its implications for professional practice in his educational setting. The case illustration is silent as to whether Dr. L. specifically made known his commitment to the Ethics Code as required by Standard 1.03. Ideally, he would be able to cite the specific standards implicated in creating a conflict between organizational demands and the Ethics Code in his discussions with the superintendent or other school officials. Standard 1.03 also requires that psychologists, "to the extent feasible, resolve the conflict in a way that permits adherence to the Ethics Code." Dr. L. will have to consider whether he believes notification of parents through distribution of a school handbook is adequate to discharge his duties to obtain informed consent or whether in his circumstances his professional practices are permitted under Standard 9.03.

Standard 9.03(a) applies to informed consent in assessment and holds that informed consent is required for "assessments, evaluations, or diagnostic services" unless "testing is mandated by law or governmental regulations." One could argue that psychological services required for the determination of eligibility or provision of legally authorized or mandated special educational services are a form of testing mandated by governmental regulations. This standard also waives informed-consent obligations when it is "implied because testing is conducted as a routine educational, institutional, or organizational activity." Dr. L. will have to decide whether his psychological services are part of the provision of routine educational services, in particular in light of a formalized policy of notification of the provision of psychological services in the school handbook provided to parents.

If Dr. L. is not persuaded that Standard 9.03(a) resolves the potential conflict regarding informed-consent duties, then he will have to decide how he can resolve this conflict "to the extent feasible." What is feasible is a fact-sensitive judgment whereby the psychologist will have to weigh the range of potential outcomes, the risks and benefits associated with each of them, the vulnerability of various parties to the process, and other factors.

Decision Options. To aid his assessment of his obligations and options, Dr. L. should consider seeking formal consultation regarding professional practice standards in school psychology from the APA Ethics Office, APA Division 16 (School Psychology), or recognized authorities in ethics and professional practice in school psychology.

Dr. L. considered his situation and obtained a second appointment with the superintendent that was also attended by an attorney for the school district. During that discussion Dr. L. was able to persuade the superintendent to approve a process that included three provisos: (a) specific attention would be drawn to the provision for referral for psychological assessment in the handbook at school orientation and a mailing home to parents at the beginning of each school year, (b) parents were provided an "opt out" choice for referrals for assessment without prior notification, and (c) Dr. L. was permitted to call parents to discuss the assessment process with them when receiving a referral from school staff. They agreed that, should a parent object to the assessment, Dr. L. would notify school authorities to attempt to resolve the situation with parents before Dr. L. would proceed with assessment. Dr. L. agreed to proceed in this manner pending more detailed consultation from knowledgeable colleagues in school psychology and from the Ethics Code.

Standard 1.03, Case 2

Case Illustration. Dr. M. is a psychologist working for an organization that is contracted to provide assessments of recently sentenced inmates on a correctional classification unit. Inmates who show indications of significant distress or symptoms of mental illness are then provided treatment by Dr. M. and her colleagues during the weeks before they are transferred to other prison units. After a series of violent disruptions on the unit that resulted in injury to inmates and correctional officers, the prison administration sent senior correctional staff to inspect the assessment and treatment records maintained by the organization. Dr. M. and her colleagues understood from their contracting organization that treatment records were confidential, and they had been informing the inmates of such. The assessment records were provided to prison authorities to make assignments to facility units; however, treatment had been provided with a standard informed consent that included confidentiality of treatment. When Dr. M. declined to provide treatment records she was informed that all records generated on the classification unit are owned by the correctional agency and that she will be removed from the prison immediately and permanently if she does not provide access to them immediately.

Ethical Dilemma. On the one hand, Dr. M. is contracted to provide clinical services in a correctional setting where maintaining physical safety is a paramount concern. The inmates were informed that assessments generated were used for assignment to prison units, but they also were informed that any records regarding treatment provided after assessment were confidential. If, in fact, all the clinical records are the work product of the contracting corrections authority, then the corrections authority is the client, and Dr. M. may be obligated to provide the records for inspection even if the inmates had been informed otherwise. Dr. M. realizes that she should have determined the policies and the status of the records before beginning treatment with the inmates. She knows that the correctional agency is the client of her organization and, therefore, her client, but she had thought that the informed consent given to the inmates was an agreement to respect confidentiality by the correctional agency. Dr. M. believes that she has reason to defend against the release of records and to attempt to protect confidentiality of the inmates to the best of her ability. She does not have much time to decide how to proceed.

Dr. M. is well aware of Standard 1.03, Conflicts Between Ethics and Organizational Demands, and its relevance in her present situation. She is also cognizant of Standard 4.01, Maintaining Confidentiality, and Standard 4.02, Discussing the Limits of Confidentiality. Dr. M. was confident that inmates had been more disclosing than they would otherwise have been given her understanding about the confidentiality agreement. She knew that if confidentiality were not respected, her work with the inmates would, in some cases, be irreparably damaged and in other cases the inmates may not be able to trust her as they once had.

Decision-Making Factors. Dr. M. will have to determine what is "feasible" under Standard 1.03 in her difficult circumstances. She will have to consider what is feasible with the correctional authorities, the organization that employs her, as well as with the inmates who have received treatment services and whose treatment records are being demanded by prison staff. She is reminded that Standard 1.03 states that "psychologists clarify the nature of the [organizational] conflict, make known their commitment to the Ethics Code, and to the extent feasible, resolve the conflict in a way that permits adherence to the Ethics Code."

Dr. M. considered all levels of authorization to be involved in this process: her organization, the correctional staff at the facility, the correctional administration, and the inmates. She feels ethically obligated to engage each group that has a participatory role in this situation. Her organization has a contract with the correctional system, and she will want to learn more about the elements of that contract in regard to informed consent, confidentiality, and the authority of the correctional agency.

Dr. M. knows that she must make a decision about permitting access to the inmates' treatment records immediately or be removed permanently from the prison where she works.

Decision Options. This situation might have been avoided entirely had proactive consideration been given to the confidentiality status of records generated by Dr. M.'s contracting organization. For example, if prison authorities insisted on having on-demand access to treatment records, then the informed consent given to inmates at the time treatment began could have reflected that fact from the outset. Alternatively, protections for the confidentiality of inmate treatment records might have been negotiated with correctional administration prior to the initiation of treatment services to unit inmates.

Many situations that ultimately give rise to conflicts between ethical duties and organization demands could be addressed proactively. In thinking through her situation, Dr. M. decided that she would make significant changes to her consulting agreements, whether they be with a third party or through her organization. In hindsight, she recognizes that if she discusses and negotiates or agrees on all of the elements of Standard 3.07, Third-Party Requests for

Services, and Standard 3.11, Psychological Services Delivered To or Through Organizations, with the client that she would greatly reduce the likelihood of another situation such as the one she is now facing. Psychologists employed by or affiliated with organizations are advised to identify and resolve areas of potential conflict and areas in which ambiguities about professional duties and organizational demands could be resolved in advance.

In this situation, Dr. M. decided to take several steps. First, she informed the corrections staff that she would be in contact with the correctional authorities and that she would not release records until further discussions were held. She then called the chief operating officer of the clinical services organization that employed her under the contract with the corrections system. In turn, the chief operating officer phoned the warden of the prison to arrange for a discussion. During this time, Dr. M. took the opportunity to seek consultation from several colleagues regarding her options. She would consider communication with the inmates whose confidentiality was at risk depending on the outcome of the discussions. If Dr. M. and her company could maintain confidentiality, then she would not need to have the same conversation with the inmates, but she would surely understand the status of confidentiality for future services and would want to change the informed consent to reflect the actual status of the inmates on several ethical standards. If the discussions are unsuccessful, then Dr. M. will individually consider the inmates she saw for psychotherapy and decide how and what to say to them.

TAKING ACTION ON POTENTIAL ETHICAL VIOLATIONS

The following two standards—Standard 1.04, Informal Resolution of Ethical Violations, and Standard 1.05, Reporting Ethical Violations—cluster together on the theme of taking action on potential ethical violations. The Ethics Code requires psychologists to take several actions. The first is to decide whether an ethical violation may have been committed. The second is to decide the appropriateness of directly calling the issue to the attention of the relevant individual. An additional concern to address is whether the intervention would violate confidentiality rights. Psychologists then determine whether informal resolution is indicated as provided in the standard. There are similar aspects of professional judgment in each phase of decision making regarding potential ethical violations.

Standard 1.04, Informal Resolution of Ethical Violations

When psychologists believe that there may have been an ethical violation by another psychologist, they attempt to resolve the issue by bringing it to the attention of that individual, if an informal resolution appears appro-

priate and the intervention does not violate any confidentiality rights that may be involved. (See also Standards 1.02, Conflicts Between Ethics and Law, Regulations, or Other Governing Legal Authority, and 1.03, Conflicts Between Ethics and Organizational Demands.)

The factors that may be considered in applying this standard, and Standard 1.05, are complex. Some of the questions psychologists may ask themselves in this determination include the following:

- How credible is the alleged charge; is the source reliable; do I believe the alleged behaviors may have occurred?
- If the behaviors occurred, do I believe this would violate one or more standards in the Ethics Code?
- If the alleged behavior is true, has it caused harm, or is it likely to cause harm, to clients or others?
- If the alleged behavior is true, is the charge serious enough (e.g., having caused, or likely to cause, substantial harm to persons or organizations) to suggest that an informal resolution would not be appropriate?
- What is the relationship between the two psychologists, and how would a question regarding ethical behavior likely evolve?
- Does the charge suggest a skill deficit or a more complex judgment deficit?
- Is a compromised course of action a likely factor in the decision of the psychologist?
- Does the psychologist appear to have self-monitoring and self-regulatory ability?

These variables do not represent a comprehensive list, but they illustrate ways in which psychologists may consider information in making a determination as to their course of action.

Skill deficits may range from very minor instances, such as inaccurate information in a brochure, to attempts to practice in a domain in which one has no experience or training (e.g., performing a child custody evaluation when one has general assessment training only). Skill deficits can often be corrected informally when psychologists can self-monitor and exercise reasoned professional judgment and therefore can decide to cease and desist in the practice once they learn of the problem.

Relational violations (e.g., inappropriate behavior with clients/patients) also can range from minor situations, such as a psychologist sitting with a client/patient at their children's soccer game, to sexual misconduct. Relational violations may result when judgment is impaired or self-monitoring and self-regulation are not accessible. Often, misconduct characterized by inappropriate interpersonal behavior occurs when individuals are no longer able to process their actions objectively and are unable to discern the potential for exploitation. These situations are likely to signal a level of severity that may warrant action beyond informal resolution because the individual is unable or unwilling to cooperate effectively.

Standard 1.04, Case 1

Case Illustration. Dr. Z. had a long and amiable professional relationship with Dr. U. Both psychologists had focused on providing similar kinds of professional services but had never really been competitors because each lived in a different nearby city. Instead, they had developed a collegial relationship and often relied on one another for consultation, shared activities within their state professional association, and activities within the APA division that reflected their mutual professional interests. Over the years, Dr. Z. had become aware that Dr. U. was a very smart, affable, and competent psychologist but one who was somewhat disorganized and preoccupied by the daily demands of his professional work and who did not excel in long-range personal or professional planning. After a meeting of their professional association, Dr. U. shared over coffee that he had recently been diagnosed with what would likely be a manageable but chronic illness that typically required suspension of professional activities for short but unpredictable periods and that could result in a more rapid deterioration. When Dr. Z. sympathetically inquired what sort of plans Dr. U. had made for his family and his professional patients/clients in light of these circumstances, Dr. U. smiled and commented, "You have got to be kidding; I've never even had a will in my entire adult life and, to start planning now would feel like I am giving in to the illness—it's not going to happen. I'm sure I'll be fine, and I'll just manage things until I am back on my feet."

Ethical Dilemma. Dr. Z. recognizes that Dr. U. may be in violation of Standard 3.12, Interruption of Psychological Services, which calls, in part, for psychologists to "make reasonable efforts to plan for facilitating services in the event that psychological services are interrupted by factors such as the psychologist's illness, death, unavailability, relocation, or retirement." Because of the similarity of their professional practices, Dr. Z. appreciates that if the services provided by Dr. U. were interrupted, his referred and current clients/patients could be disadvantaged and potentially harmed. Because of the potential downside to Dr. U.'s clients/patients from an interruption, and the potential risk to Dr. U.'s professional reputation if he failed to adequately make preparations, Dr. Z. felt the need to point out to Dr. U. the potential seriousness of the situation. Dr. Z. does not have reason to think that Dr. U. has fallen into a questionable status of practice yet, but because the potential seems possible

Dr. Z. decides to attempt an informal resolution of the potential for untimely interruption of services.

On the other hand, Dr. Z. also appreciates that Dr. U. may have made that comment in jest (although he seemed to be serious), to deflect further conversation out of a sense of wanting to maintain his privacy or to avoid conversation about the potential course of his illness that may prompt his own anxiety or an unwanted sense of sympathy from others. Although Dr. Z. has always found Dr. U. to be very professionally competent, he does not really know in detail how Dr. U. arranges the staffing and supervision of his employees in his professional practice. He is concerned that if he presses the point about the potential interruption of professional services that Dr. U. may simply decline to discuss it with him and may even just choose to stop communicating with him as a long-time colleague about his health.

Decision-Making Factors. Dr. Z. may weigh several factors in deciding whether to proceed to press the point with Dr. U. at all, to attempt to discuss the issue informally, or to move in a more formal manner. These factors include the potential risks and harms to Dr. U.'s clients/patients from an interruption of service given the specific nature of his professional practice and the specific vulnerabilities or needs of those receiving services; how imminent those potential risks and harms might be should there be an interruption of services, and reasonable options available to those served by the particular kind of professional practice; the potential exposure of Dr. U. to damage to his professional reputation and practice (including license and ethics complaints), and that of the profession in general, should his services be substantively interrupted; and the likelihood that attempting to resolve the issue informally appears appropriate and would not violate any confidentiality rights.

Decision Options. Consistent with Standard 1.04, Dr. Z. decides that he should at least try to establish whether Dr. U. has in fact failed to take reasonable steps to minimize the impact of any interruption of services through Dr. U.'s illness or death. Sensing that Dr. U. did not seem amenable to having that discussion at that moment, he decides to wait until after the dinner of their professional association that evening. Although Dr. Z. appreciated that an interruption of services could have very unfortunate consequences for individuals receiving the kinds of professional services they both offer, he decided to rely on their years of collegial interaction to try to learn more about the situation and resolve any ethical issue informally. He believed Dr. U. to be a fundamentally competent psychologist who cared deeply about his clients/patients and likely to understand Dr. Z.'s concerns if he could articulate them well and without seeming threatening or self-righteous.

After the association dinner was over, Dr. Z. asked Dr. U. if he might sit with him for a moment and talk. He told Dr. U. that it was out of a sense of collegial respect (and gently reminded him of the years they had known each other), a sense of obligation to the work they did with similar clients/patients, and to ensure that Dr. U. himself was not personally or professionally compromised that he felt he must learn more about how the practice would be managed if Dr. U. were unavailable due to his illness. He offered to help Dr. U. consider how to best plan for any interruption and to minimize the impact of an interruption on those in Dr. U.'s practice. To his relief, Dr. U. told Dr. Z. that he had, in fact, been making some plans for his practice and for his family. Dr. U. explained that the high anxiety prompted by his recent diagnosis and unease about the potential course of illness "makes it very hard for me to have conversations about it and what it may mean for me and my family, even with old friends like you. You know, until this happened, I really didn't have a will for my own family, and never thought about planning for what would happen with my practice if something happened to me. I'm sorry I was so flip earlier today with my comment, but I appreciate that you wanted to make certain that I was doing what I needed to be doing, and were willing to help me out with planning if I needed it."

Standard 1.05, Reporting Ethical Violations

If an apparent ethical violation has substantially harmed or is likely to substantially harm a person or organization and is not appropriate for informal resolution under Standard 1.04, Informal Resolution of Ethical Violations, or is not resolved properly in that fashion, psychologists take further action appropriate to the situation. Such action might include referral to state or national committees on professional ethics, to state licensing boards, or to the appropriate institutional authorities. This standard does not apply when an intervention would violate confidentiality rights or when psychologist have been retained to review the work of another psychologist whose professional conduct is in question. (See also Standard 1.02, Conflicts Between Ethics and Law, Regulations, or Other Governing Legal Authority.)

Psychologists are required to take formal action in the case of an apparent ethical violation either when informal resolution was not effective or not appropriate and/or when substantial harm has occurred or is likely to occur. Substantial harm may result from actions based on deficits, such as a psychologist who conducts a custody evaluation without necessary competency, resulting in a harmful placement of a child, or from unethical acts of commission, such as sexual misconduct, insurance fraud, felony conviction, plagiarism, noncooperation in an ethics or legal inquiry, misrepresentation of the facts of a case, or other, similar behaviors.

Psychologists should be alert to the relationship between a persistent failure to meet the spirit of the APA Ethics Code and the subsequent engagement in violations of enforceable standards. A failure to value professional integrity may lead to behaviors such as insurance fraud, and a failure to exercise a sense of justice may lead to criminal behavior that could result in a felony conviction. Psychologists who determine that a formal reporting of an ethical violation is appropriate then would decide their course of action, which involves a reporting process. Psychologists use their judgment in reviewing factors involved with the violation to determine the most appropriate route for reporting. If the violation is not illegal and affects individuals in the person's workplace without substantial harm, psychologists may report the violation to persons in the organization or institution in which the violations are occurring. If the violation affects current or potential clients/patients, but not with substantial harm, psychologists may decide to make a report to an ethics committee. If the violation affects clients/patients in a harmful way and/or affects the profession, psychologists may determine that the APA Ethics Committee or state licensing board is the most appropriate entity for reporting. Psychologists are aware that regardless of whether an alleged violation affects the workplace, client/patients, and/or the profession some violations, such as sexual misconduct, violation of confidentiality, and failure of informed consent, by their very nature deserve very serious and consequent action.

The decision to treat a question of ethical violation informally or through formal processes is a judgment made by the observing psychologists on the basis of the factors that define the behavior and the actions in question. Psychologists recognize the range and degree of severity in the criteria of substantial or likely substantial harm and the importance of decision making and action that is appropriate and fair. After making this determination psychologists then also use their professional judgment in determining the specific engagement they will have in attempts to resolve the potential ethical problem. Psychologists are not required by the Ethics Code to make a report when confidentiality would be compromised or when the psychologist learns of the violation while being retained to review the work of another psychologist.

TREATMENT OF THOSE INVOLVED IN ETHICAL COMPLAINTS

The following three standards—Standard 1.06, Cooperating With Ethics Committees; Standard 1.07, Improper Complaints; and Standard 1.08, Unfair Discrimination Against Complainants and Respondents—cluster around the theme of treatment of persons involved in ethical complaints. According to the APA Rules and Procedures these three standards underscore the privilege and responsibility of a profession and its members to self-monitor, commit to consensual principles and standards, and to hold in high value the willingness to represent and promote the ethical tenets of the profession. Applicants for membership in APA agree to endorse and to uphold the APA "Ethical Principles for Psychologists and Code of Conduct." Members become stewards of the profession not only in practicing high standards but also in participating in the self-management of the profession, including due process and fair treatment of individuals involved in evaluating violations.

Standard 1.06, Cooperating With Ethics Committees
Psychologists cooperate in ethics investigations, proceedings, and resulting requirements of the APA or any affiliated state psychological association to which they belong. In doing so, they address any confidentiality issues. Failure to cooperate is itself an ethics violation. However, making a request for deferment of adjudication of an ethics complaint pending the outcome of litigation does not alone constitute noncooperation.

Whether psychologists file a complaint, are the respondent to a complaint, or are a third party to a complaint, cooperation with ethics committees promotes both due process for the person being questioned and the welfare of the public. Cooperation maximizes information access and thereby increases the likelihood of just and fair treatment for psychologists and the public.

When psychologists who have knowledge of a case and the psychologist in question have professional relationships, participating in any role or function in a complaint can be very difficult. The commitment to self-regulation by psychologists is a value held and is described through this group of standards (i.e., Standards 1.06, 1.07, and 1.08). Members of professional associations tend to support self-regulation over external regulation. When the enactment of this value, however, affects persons known to each other, cooperation can be challenging. Psychologists may be mindful that consultation with colleagues is a means of processing difficult decisions with additional expertise, knowledge, and collaboration.

Standards 1.05 and 1.06, Case 1

Case Illustration. Dr. C. was the chair of the state psychological association ethics committee, which received a complaint regarding Dr. A. The complaint was from Ms. J.,. who had been a client in Dr. A.'s group practice. Ms. J. had accused her own individual psychotherapist, Dr. B., of sexual misconduct and had registered her complaint with the state licensing board. The board adjudicated the case and after several months did find Dr. B. in violation of the sexual misconduct rule in the psychology law of the state. The board revoked Dr. B.'s license after a lengthy period of hearings and appeals. Ms. J. was now filing a complaint with the state ethics committee because she was certain that Dr. A., who was a practice partner of Dr. B., knew that Dr. B.

had been engaging in ethical and legal misconduct. Ms. J. specifically charged Dr. A. because she knew that Dr. A. and Dr. B. spent much time together and co-led groups; also, after the complaint became public, Ms. J.'s friend, who had been in therapy with Dr. A. when he was in another practice, told Ms. J. that she too had earlier been in therapy with Dr. B. and that he had engaged in sexual misconduct with her as well. She immediately terminated therapy with Dr. B. and went into therapy with Dr. A., to whom she told everything about her traumatic experience but also indicated that she did not want to pursue a complaint. Ms. J. also had additional, substantial information that Dr. A. knew of the sexual misconduct from sources other than clients for whom confidentiality must be respected.

When the ethics committee received permission from Ms. J. to share the complaint with Dr. A., they sent him the complaint material and asked for a response within 30 days. Members of the state psychological association sign a commitment to uphold the APA Ethics Code when they become members of the association. When the committee next met, no response had been received from Dr. A. The committee then sent a return-receipt letter requiring Dr. A. to respond. Thirty more days went by, and still no response was received. The committee now not only needed to pursue Ms. J.'s complaint but also would act on Dr. A.'s failure to respond.

Ethical Dilemma. As a result of Ms. J.'s complaint, Dr. A. was facing a potential violation of Standard 1.05, Reporting Ethical Violations, and now, because of his failure to respond, was also potentially facing a sua sponte complaint from the ethics committee itself for violation of Standard 1.06, Cooperating With Ethics Committees. The ethics committee was certain that Dr. A. had received the letter, because they received a return receipt of successful delivery. Standard 1.05 is applicable when a potential violation has "substantially harmed or is likely to substantially harm a person or organization and is not appropriate for informal resolution." Furthermore, Standard 1.06 requires psychologists to cooperate with state ethics committees in the investigation of a complaint, and in this case the complaint was against Dr. A for failure to have taken appropriate action. Regardless of whether the complaint filed by Ms. J. is substantive, Dr. A. is failing to cooperate with the ethics committee investigation and thereby may be risking the welfare and rights of Ms. J. (General Principle A: Beneficence and Nonmaleficence). The committee is also cognizant of the fact that when psychologists are friends or are in practice together, an informal resolution and a formal resolution are both very difficult because of the potential professional and personal cost to the relationship.

Decision-Making Factors. Dr. C. and the ethics committee were in receipt of the documentation provided by Ms. J. and had thoroughly reviewed the material. The case seemed substantive; however, the ethics committee considered due process an important part of their procedures and, except in rare circumstances, would not typically pursue a case unless the psychologist charged had an opportunity to be informed and to understand the case, had access to the documentation representing the charges, and had a reasonable opportunity to respond. The ethics committee realized that Dr. A. may have adopted a strategy of not responding in order to avoid questioning; however, there could also be other reasons for his lack of response. The committee members did not consider nonresponsiveness an acceptable final action, and they knew that they would need to decide a length of time to allow before taking further action.

In regard to an alleged violation of failure to take further action (Standard 1.05), the committee discussed the three elements of the standard that are important for application: (a) the apparent violation has substantially harmed or is likely to substantially harm a person, (b) the apparent violation is not appropriate for informal resolution, and (c) the psychologist has not resolved the violation in a proper fashion. The committee determined that because this ethical violation, if true, is such an egregious act of misconduct, it would not be appropriate for informal resolution. In addition, the experience has very likely already harmed Ms. J., and there is no indication that Dr. A. had taken steps to resolve the situation. The committee is mindful that Standard 1.05 does not compel psychologists to report a violation to any of various authorities but does compel them to take further action appropriate to the situation. Had Dr. A. reported to the ethics committee that he was engaged in corrective action, the committee could decide whether the action was appropriate and sufficient for the situation. In the case of failure to take further action on alleged knowledge of sexual misconduct, however, the ethics committee determined that compliance with Standard 1.05 would unequivocally be expected.

Decision Options. The ethics committee may decide to attempt contact several times before proceeding. The committee would want to hear from Dr. A., but if Dr. A. is not willing to communicate the ethics committee may proceed with the information they currently have. The committee, however, would likely think it most important that before acting on the information from Ms. J. they would make certain that the information was reliable and credible, and provided evidence beyond a reasonable doubt. The ethics committee could be quite certain that Dr. A. had in fact violated Standard 1.06 and that, considering all of the other circumstances, they would consider this a very severe violation. Unless the committee heard from Dr. A., or other evidence appeared to counter the complaint, the committee would have the authority to remove Dr. A. from membership in the association and forward the findings of their investigation based on failure to respond to the state licensing board and to the APA Ethics Committee. If Dr. A had come forward and engaged with the ethics committee, the committee may have considered enacting sanctions other than expulsion, such as supervision and continuing education, had Dr. A. been found in violation.

Standard 1.07, Improper Complaints
Psychologists do not file or encourage the filing of ethics complaints that are made with reckless disregard for or willful ignorance of facts that would disprove the allegation.

Evaluation of a complaint's merit is determined by criteria such as whether the behaviors at issue would be violations of the Ethics Code and whether the allegations can or cannot be proven or are only minor or technical violations. These and similar criteria may require information and documentation that are not knowable by a psychologist who is trying to decide whether to file a complaint or to encourage a client or other person to file a complaint. The previous Ethics Code handled this issue by focusing on whether potentially improper complaints "are frivolous and are intended to harm the respondent rather than to protect the public." The 2002 Ethics Code standard offers a different perspective on determining the impropriety of a complaint by valuing the treatment of knowable information. The measure of impropriety is that either psychologists willfully ignore information that would or should affect their judgment or they disregard available information that would or should affect their judgment. A consistent theme of the APA Ethics Code across standards is encouragement to use reasoned professional judgment. In deciding whether to file or to encourage the filing of a complaint, the judgment is to be based on knowable facts and information and specifically not to disregard or ignore facts that would disprove the allegations.

Standard 1.08, Unfair Discrimination Against Complainants and Respondents
Psychologists do not deny persons employment, advancement, admissions to academic or other programs, tenure, or promotion, based solely upon their having made or their being the subject of an ethics complaint. This does not preclude taking action based upon the outcome of such proceedings or considering other appropriate information.

Ethical complaints often occur within the context of organizations, institutions, and other entities in which professionals are affected or perceived to be affected by the complaint action. Complaints against psychologists that have been disclosed in their work settings, whether in business, government, or other institutional entities, often result in the release of these individuals from employment, and often with great personal hardship and professional damage to reputation and career. Standard 1.08, Unfair Discrimination Against

Complainants and Respondents, describes discrimination within a professional career frame of reference by noting actions that can do irreparable harm to psychologists' reputations, professional advancement, and livelihood. The Ethics Code encourages psychologists to use restraint and due process in making a sound determination regarding a complaint.

There are several significant conditions in which decisions may be made, or action taken, that stand apart from the status of an ethics complaint. If a faculty member has been proven to commit plagiarism, or a practicing psychologist has committed insurance fraud, action may certainly be taken based on these separate violations. Furthermore, after a complaint has been fully considered and acted on the individuals and organizations of interest may decide to take action based on full due process and the evidentiary findings of the case.

CONCLUSION

The APA Code of Ethics endorses cooperation in ways that demonstrate respect for psychologists' judgment and that value protection of the public. Specifically, the Ethics Code entrusts psychologists to be proactive through actions determined by psychologists themselves and to use their judgment in making decisions regarding responses to misuse of work and conflicts with legal and regulatory bodies and organizations. Psychologists are encouraged to use their judgment in determining the most appropriate venue in which to address an ethical violation and, subsequently, specifically how they choose to respond. Last, the Ethics Code emphasizes the importance of due process, fair and just treatment for all parties involved in a complaint, attendance to factual information in making judgments, and cooperative participation in self-regulation.

2

COMPETENCE

Professional competence is the cornerstone of the ethical practice of psychology. The perspective through which psychologists view practice, research, and training is based on the value of and professional commitment to competence. Competence is a consensually accepted value that psychologists endorse, and the standards in the 2002 American Psychological Association's (APA's) "Ethical Principles of Psychologists and Code of Conduct" (hereinafter the *APA Ethics Code* or the *Ethics Code*; see http://www.apa.org/ethics/code2002.html)[1] incorporate the assumption of competence in the enactment of each standard.

In the 1992 Ethics Code[2] several standards and General Principle A: Competence described the application of competent practice; however, the dynamic evolvement of practice, research, and training areas within the profession in recent years called for a comprehensive section in which various derivations of competence could be identified and defined. The general principle

---

[1]American Psychological Association. (2002). Ethical principles of psychologists and code of conduct. *American Psychologist, 57*, 1060–1073.
[2]American Psychological Association. (1992). Ethical principles of psychologists and code of conduct. *American Psychologist, 47*, 1597–1611.

with which competence is primarily aligned in the 2002 Ethics Code is Principle A: Beneficence and Nonmaleficence, according to which psychologists must strive to benefit those with whom they work and to do no harm through their professional actions. Without the foundational presence of professional competence, the ability to act with beneficence and nonmaleficence and the ability to ethically enact the additional standards are both significantly compromised.

The standards of competence in this chapter and throughout the 2002 Ethics Code may be conceptualized as skill-based competence and relational competence. *Skill-based competence* refers to abilities learned through formative education and training, maintenance of abilities through continuing education, and postdoctoral training in new areas of expertise. *Relational competence* refers to process abilities in self-assessment; self-monitoring; self-evaluation (intrapersonal abilities); and recognition of one's impact on others, power status in professional relationships, and intentional use of influence (interpersonal abilities).

Failure to exercise skill-based competence often manifests as scope-of-practice violations and failure to realize skill limitations. Standards 2.01, Boundaries of Competence, through 2.05, Delegation of Work to Others, directly define and illustrate these implications (e.g., population expertise; emergency services; services not available otherwise; emerging areas of practice; and new areas of expertise for psychologists, such as assuming forensic roles; see Exhibit 2.1). Failure of relational competence may be evidenced through activated vulnerabilities such as loss of judgment and inaccurate assessment of risk condition (e.g., Standard 2.06, Personal Problems and Conflicts; see Exhibit 2.1). The ability to make accurate observations and to negotiate interpersonal interactions contributes to appropriate and effective relationships with clients/patients. Correspondingly, the ability to gain accurate and useful insight into one's own values, attitudes, biases, and self-perception can contribute to effective self-monitoring.

Psychologists' decision-making capability depends on their ability to assess not only the situation at hand but also their own ability to make a sound judgment. This ability to make a sound judgment may be reflected in the skill-based competency area. For example, a well-meaning psychologist who is quite competent in executing general psychological reports or psychoeducational reports may try to assist a friend who is involved in a custody case by participating in a custody evaluation. The psychologist exercises competent assessment skills that are suitable for conducting a general psychological report but inadequate for a custody evaluation. The psychologist may not realize that a custody evaluation is being made, or that the psychologist does not realize how much specialized knowledge and experience are required to do a competent child custody evaluation. This is a case of skill-based incompetence in that the psychol-

EXHIBIT 2.1
Types of Competence and Evidence of Competence Failure

Types of competence	
Skill-based competence	Relational-based competence
a. Training	a. Interpersonal—Observation
b. Continuing education	b. Intrapersonal—Insight
c. Supervised experience	
d. Consultation	
e. Professional experience	

Failure of competence	
Limitations	Vulnerabilities
a. Overextension of expertise	a. Failure to identify vulnerabilities
b. Needed training with defined populations	b. Identification but loss of judgment
c. Monitoring evolving scope of practice	c. Inaccurate assessment of risk
d. Defining boundaries when services are not available	conditions
e. Overextension of existent skills in application to emerging areas	
f. Defining role in emergencies	

ogist does not have the skills to do the assessment. It is also a case of relational-based incompetence because the psychologist allowed an inappropriate blending of a personal and professional relationship. Competence is the foundation from which other standards are built. The ethical implementation of all standards of the 2002 Ethics Code is contingent on skill competence, and many standards throughout the code—including Multiple Relationships (Standard 3.05), Conflict of Interest (Standard 3.06), Assessing Student and Supervisee Performance (Standard 7.06), Bases for Assessments (Standard 9.01), and Sexual Intimacies With Current (Standard 10.05), and Former Therapy Clients/Patients (Standard 10.08)—are affected by relational competence.

Standard 2.01, Boundaries of Competence

Boundaries of competence is meant to be a very useful standard for psychologists in that the standard directly and specifically explains the thoughtful course of action for several variations on Standard 2.01(a) of working within one's boundaries of competence. The standard identifies the most typical circumstances in which ethical psychologists may need or want to consider provision of services or research in settings, with populations, or in emerging contexts that move psychologists outside of their defined areas of competence. Those circumstances include populations in which diverse factors must be recognized and respected (Standard 2.01b), circumstances that are new to the psychologist (Standard 2.01c) or in which the services are not available from other competent mental health professionals (Standard 2.01d), emerging areas for which training is not yet established (Standard 2.01e), and participation in forensic settings (Standard 2.01f). The guidance provided by these areas anticipates that as psychologists move away from formal training into lifelong learning, education and training will take different forms. Psychologists are expected to seek out these expanded training and learning opportunities and to be competent in understanding when the boundaries of their existing competencies are being approached or crossed.

Standard 2.01(a)

Psychologists provide services, teach, and conduct research with populations and in areas only within the boundaries of their competence, based on their education, training, supervised experience, consultation, study, or professional experience.

Psychologists must engage in professional activities only within their areas of competence. This standard has remained essentially unchanged from the 1992 Ethics Code and therefore is a well-established expectation for ethical practice, research, and training. This standard has not changed; however, scope of practice, research methodology, and training models during these years have. Failure to perform within one's areas of competence can correspond to psychologists' failure to recognize two things: (a) that an area of professional activity is different enough from their area of expertise to warrant additional training or, (b) that they have moved into a different area of expertise altogether but have not recognized that they are performing in a new area that requires additional skills and a knowledge base. These misperceptions can occur when psychologists' area of competence and areas of professional activity that require additional professional development share a common skill.

For example, in the practice area, psychologists who have expertise in assessment and have typically completed psychoeducational assessments, general psychological reports, and developmental evaluations may note that the performance of child custody evaluations includes assessment with some of the same instruments that are used in the psychologists' practices. The clinical intake may be similar, and the report may be similar in format. Psychologists who have a clinical practice with individuals and families may observe that their work involves interviewing skills, consultation with schools and agencies, and systems intervention with families and other entities. These activities imply some shared common skills with organizational psychology and may seem to be transferable. In both cases, psychologists may mistakenly rely on these common skills in their practice to begin expanding their professional activities into these areas of their own expertise or into new areas of practice.

Correspondingly, faculty members who have an area of expertise, such as psychotherapy training, may be asked to teach a research methodology class that includes psychotherapy research. Psychotherapy is a common element in the two teaching areas, but the faculty member may not have worked in statistical analysis or research methodology in the years since the development of new and sophisticated analytic methods. As another example, a researcher may be interested in a very lucrative grant that calls for a longitudinal study that is a methodological area of expertise for the researcher, but the subject of the investigation is a new field of study.

Psychologists who wish to transition into different areas of expertise can do so ethically through supervision, consultation, and additional training. The ability to recognize one's actual area of competence and to be cognizant of moving toward the boundary can be a difficult discernment of that competence. Failure to realize accurate boundaries can lead one down a slippery slope.

Standard 2.01(b)

Where scientific or professional knowledge in the discipline of psychology establishes that an understanding of factors associated with age, gender, gender identity, race, ethnicity, culture, national origin, religion, sexual orientation, disability, language, or socioeconomic status is essential for effective implementation of their services or research, psychologists have or obtain the training, experience, consultation, or supervision necessary to ensure the competence of their services, or they make appropriate referrals, except as provided in Standard 2.02, Providing Services in Emergencies.

General Principle E: Respect for People's Rights and Dignity is reflected in the intent of this part of Standard 2.01. Psychologists are instructed to be cognizant of three specific requirements in working with special populations: (a) be familiar with scientific or professional knowledge essential for effective implementation, and (b) if an identified knowledge base exists, then obtain the necessary competency or (c) make an appropriate referral. Acting in response to scientific or professional knowledge is an added element from the 1992 Standard 1.08, Human Differences. Reliance on scientific or professional knowledge is meant to assist psychologists in making decisions regarding their ability to self-assess competence with special populations.

An important factor in decision making with special populations is the balance between respect for group characteristics and individual differences. Psychologists are aware and respectful of values within identified populations and are respectful of the individuality of clients/patients. For example, knowing that a client/patient who is living in the United States was born in India of parents who still live in India may not in itself give a psychologist enough information with which to proceed. Generalization to group characteristics in developing a conceptualization of the client/patient would be unjustified. Exploration of the client/patient's cultural identity, degree of assimilation, family context, language, and individual goals is central to an understanding of the client/patient's frame of reference.

A caution for psychologists working with identified populations concerns the assumption that membership in the identified group renders special insight into and understanding of the client/patient. For example, a psychologist who grew up in a lower socioeconomic-status family and community, or a female psychologist who grew up in a single-parent family and who assumes a level of empathy, insight, and understanding of a client/patient with the same characteristics, can make significant errors in judgment. Shared characteristics cannot be assumed to be active factors in competent provision of psychological services. This assumption can lead to problematic countertransference, loss of objectivity, ineffective treatment planning, and unrealistic expectations of the clients/patients and their goals.

Scientific and professional knowledge are always in development, and there are no evidence-based findings available to guide psychologists in their decision making. This part of the standard requires psychologists to acquire skills that are, in fact, known to the profession or to make a referral. When scientific or professional knowledge has not been established, psychologists must be sensitive to the potential factors involved with regard to provision of services and must proceed with respect and commitment to understanding the individual client/patient.

Standard 2.01(c)

Psychologists planning to provide services, teach, or conduct research involving populations, areas, techniques, or technologies new to them undertake relevant education, training, supervised experience, consultation, or study.

Psychology is a dynamic and evolving profession that continues to present new dimensions of practice, research, and training to the field. With a few exceptions (e.g., the psychopharmacology training model), specific requirements for postdoctoral training in expanded or new areas of expertise have not been endorsed by the profession. Guidelines for practice have been adopted in several practice areas of expertise; however, the responsibility for developing an adequate level of competence in a new professional area rests with individual psychologists. Standard 2.01(c) identifies education, training, supervised experience, consultation, or study as routes to competence. Psychologists must monitor the quality and sufficiency of their additional efforts as evaluated by colleagues who are competent in the field in which they are seeking expertise.

Standard 2.01(d)

When psychologists are asked to provide services to individuals for whom appropriate mental health services are not available and for which psychologists have not obtained the competence necessary, psychologists with

closely related prior training or experience may provide such services in order to ensure that services are not denied if they make a reasonable effort to obtain the competence required by using relevant research, training, consultation, or study.

The intent of this standard balances the importance of General Principle A: Beneficence and Nonmaleficence with General Principle D: Justice and the right of all persons to benefit from services rendered by psychologists. Psychologists must make measured judgments regarding the relevance of their prior training as well as determine the means by which to achieve the necessary competency. If appropriate services are not available for clients/patients, then appropriate research, training, consultation, and study also may not be easily accessible. Psychologists should be able to demonstrate that they have made a reasonable effort to obtain the necessary competence for the needed services.

Standard 2.01(e)

In those emerging areas in which generally recognized standards for preparatory training do not yet exist, psychologists nevertheless take reasonable steps to ensure the competence of their work and to protect clients/patients, students, supervisees, research participants, organizational clients, and others from harm.

As the profession continues to develop, new areas of potential practice and scientific inquiry will emerge. The absence of established standards of practice, research design, or methods of inquiry does not relieve psychologists of their obligation to exercise competence; protect others from potential harm; or monitor the implementation of emerging areas through consultation, education, and research and training. When psychologists are involved in emerging areas of practice or scientific inquiry the informed consent of the individuals with whom they are working is an important factor in the protection of others and in respecting the choice of those who may be impacted by the activity. These include Standards 3.10 (Informed Consent), 8.02 (Informed Consent to Research), and 8.04 (Client/Patient, Student, and Subordinate Research Participants).

Standard 2.01(f)

When assuming forensic roles, psychologists are or become reasonably familiar with the judicial or administrative rules governing their roles.

Because of the evolving scope of psychology, coupled with the expanding role of legal activity in U.S. society, psychologists cannot declare nonparticipation in forensic settings. Practice, research, organizational, and training psychologists may be called on to be percipient witnesses (i.e., to present testimony of fact or perception), although this is rare. Psychologists are more or less likely to be called in court situations depending on their area of practice. Even psychologists who do not engage in forensic work as a specialty but who practice in areas that lend themselves to periodic forensic participation (e.g., marital and family therapy) should become reasonably familiar with rules of the court and legal principles that pertain to psychologists' roles. Psychologists practicing in fields that are more likely to be involved in court proceedings (e.g., trauma) would benefit from understanding court procedures and rules of protocol and from knowing their state laws pertaining to mental health when there is an occasion for court appearance or testimony. Psychologists who work in forensic psychology as expert witnesses or evaluators have a heightened responsibility to understand court procedures, judicial rules, and the laws of the state in matters in which they are involved.

Standard 2.01(b), Case 1

Case Illustration. Dr. M. has been asked to provide an evaluation of a child's parents after the parents were reported by hospital staff to child welfare authorities. The parents are relatively new immigrants to the country and are not able to communicate understandably with the hospital staff. The hospital staff reports that the parents are overly reliant on traditional healing methods practiced in their country of origin, to the detriment of caring for their child's fragile medical condition. In the hospital staff's view, this constitutes medical neglect, and the child welfare authorities are considering whether to take custody of the child. Unless Dr. M. is able to explain to the child welfare authorities why the parents' failure to provide medical care at home consistent with instructions from medical staff at the hospital does not constitute medical neglect, the child will ultimately be removed and placed in medical foster care pending the filing of a child abuse case in court. The child welfare authorities decide to give Dr. M. and the parents 3 weeks until they make that decision, and they place the child in the home of a relative until the decision is to be made. Dr. M. promptly recognizes that there may be several factors under these circumstances that could jeopardize his ability to provide a reliable evaluation of the parents. Dr. M. takes very seriously the ethical commitment to become culturally competent in professional work and to successfully accomplish training toward competence in multiple areas of diversity; as a result, Dr. M. does feel competent in several areas of practice. In this case, Dr. M. is not confident of competence, because Dr. M. is not versed in nontraditional healing practices, and realizes that the critical time factor determining the parameters of the evaluation required efficient and accurate decision making.

Ethical Dilemma. On the one hand, Dr. M. is required by Standard 2.01(b) to understand diversity factors "essential for effective implementation of services" or to "obtain the training, experience, consultation, or supervision necessary to ensure the competence of services, or make appropriate referrals" unless he is providing emergency services (Standard 2.02). On the other hand, although the 3-week time frame makes it more difficult to justify proceeding under these circumstances as an "emergency," Dr. M. is in a difficult situation given the absence of available supervision, consultation, or identification of a more knowledgeable professional to whom the parents can be referred. Failure to complete the assessment or the provision of an unreliable assessment that portrayed the parents as neglectful would result in the child's placement in medical foster care and initiation of legal action against the parents. Doing nothing, Dr. M. risks running out the 3-week clock, and failing to get adequate consultation/supervision support or to identify an appropriate professional to whom to make a referral Dr. M. risks unwarranted family disruption and legal action.

Dr. M. realizes that, in addition to a possible violation of Standard 2 .01, should be considered the importance of General Principle A: Beneficence and Nonmaleficence in psychologists' duty to "safeguard the welfare and rights of those with whom they interact professionally" and the application of General Principle E: Respect for People's Rights and Dignity in that Dr. M. has an obligation, in taking the case, to perform the evaluation objectively and at the same time to give rightful consideration to the clients' privacy, confidentiality, and self-determination.

Decision-Making Factors. In deciding on whether or how to proceed in these circumstances, Dr. M. can consider various factors, including the following:

- the likelihood that adequate supervision or consultation supports can be acquired in a timely enough fashion;
- the likelihood that Dr. M., the hospital staff, or the child welfare authorities can identify a professional to whom to make a referral in a timely enough fashion;
- the risks of providing an unreliable assessment (i.e., to the child, if the parents are depicted more favorably than is actually the case, and to the parents if they are portrayed as more neglectful than is the case) versus the certainty of family disruption and legal action against the parents if no assessment is done; and
- the likelihood that having a better understanding of the perspective of the parents would influence the decision to be made by the child welfare authorities.

Dr. M. considers the aspect of Standard 2.01(b) that "professional knowledge establishes that an understanding of factors . . . is essential for effective implementation." Dr. M. determines that very little is known or understood about what the family is actually doing in regard to traditional healing in the context of the child's medical needs. Greater interpretation and meaning in the parents' understanding of the child's medical care are needed. Dr. M. decides to take a broad and comprehensive view of the evaluation, hoping to gather the information needed to make an accurate determination.

Decision Options. Dr. M. agreed to begin providing services in the case but informed the child welfare authorities that if it appeared that the child was not at risk in placement with the relative, and if it appeared that progress was being made, then Dr. M. would ask for more flexibility in regard to the 3-week time frame. After reaching that agreement, Dr. M. arranged for the assistance of the hospital's interpreter service to find a suitable interpreter. One was found in a nearby community, and this interpreter began to work with Dr. M. on an expedited schedule to interview and assess the parents following an explanation of the child protection concerns and securing adequate informed consent from the parents. Dr. M. talked with the interpreter and did some research on the Internet, discovering that there was a medical anthropologist at a state university across the country who had written some articles on the traditional healing practices at issue and the "worldview about healing" characteristic of persons from the parents' culture and ethnic group. The anthropologist agreed to a telephone consultation with Dr. M., during which she explained that the parents' reliance on traditional healing practices when recently arrived in the United States did not itself necessarily reflect neglect of the child, in particular because it was not entirely clear that the parents knew precisely what the hospital expected by way of home care and probably did not share the same model of what was causing their child's illness.

The anthropologist suggested asking the parents to bring in the traditional healer on whom they were relying in the community. This could not be arranged until 2 weeks later, but the child welfare authorities agreed to extend the deadline for the assessment process. Utilizing the services of the interpreter, Dr. M. facilitated a joint conference among Dr. M., the traditional healer, the parents, and the physician who had been so concerned about the child. As the process unfolded it became very clear that there was no intent on the part of the parents to medically neglect the child; in fact, the situation was quite the contrary: Taking the child to the hospital was an additional step the parents had taken when there was no evidence of recovery after attention from the traditional healer. The traditional healer explained the perspective on illnesses and healing that informed his healing practice and explained the procedures that the parent had been instructed to perform. It became clear that the traditional healer had no hostility toward the use of prescribed medicines by the parents. After learning the specifics of the traditional healing rituals and herbs, the physician had no objection to the parents continuing to use them in conjunction with the Western medicine treatments. The physician explained the potentially serious consequences of failing to consistently take the medication as prescribed (which was also very valuable for Dr. M. in that it helped explain the heightened concern of the medical staff). The physician and Dr. M. also learned that, in the absence of adequate interpretation services, the parents simply did not understand the medication routine. Arrangements were made for the parents to bring the child to the hospital with a child welfare caseworker and for the interpreter to be available for the instruction session on medication management for the child.

Note that under Standard 2.01(b), the "training experience, consultation or supervision necessary to ensure the competence" of psychological services need not be services provided by psychologists. Here, the consultation that contributed to the positive result included the interpreter, the treating physician, a medical anthropologist, and a traditional healer. Without the contribution of each of these consultants it is unlikely that Dr. M. would have been able to adequately understand the perspectives and concerns of the parents, or to have achieved an outcome that so adequately supported the well-being of the child. Dr. M. realized that this case was not only unique but also exemplary of the breadth of assessment variables and the importance of psychologists adopting unconventional measures to achieve the most valid and accurate results.

Standard 2.01(f), Case 1

Case Illustration. Doctor N., an accomplished child psychologist, sends a letter to local family court judges noting that he is available for appointment as an evaluator in divorce child custody cases. Dr. N. soon receives his first appointment and begins a series of interviews with the separated parents and their child. Believing that the custody dispute could be resolved through mediation, Dr. N. suspends the evaluation process and initiates a process of mediation. Dr. N. uses common mediation practice and indicates to each parent that anything disclosed in the mediation process will be confidential unless a mandated reporting obligation were triggered. The mediation includes negotiation of financial issues and disclosure of complications about the visitation schedule arising from an ongoing affair about which the other parent is unaware. Unfortunately, the mediation effort fails. When Dr. N. resumes the custody evaluation he informs the judge and the attorneys that the information disclosed in the course of mediation is confidential, but the judge firmly instructs him to respond to the court and reminds Dr. N. of his obligation to be forthcoming with the court. Dr. N. realizes that he has acted without clearly identifying for himself four vital issues: (a) who his client was; (b) to whom, if anyone, he owed confidentiality; (c) the purpose of a custody evaluation versus mediation; and (d) what his own role would be and what his role would entail.

Ethical Dilemma. Standard 2.01(f) requires that psychologists be "reasonably familiar with the judicial or administrative rules governing their roles." Psychologists who are reasonably familiar with the rules governing their roles in legal or forensic contexts will be able to identify and distinguish clinical and forensic professional practices. They will also be sufficiently aware of relevant legal and administrative procedures to avoid inadvertently compromising the interests of participants in the legal process (including violations of confidentiality or privilege) or hampering the proceedings because of a lack of awareness. Although Dr. N. is described as an "accomplished child psychologist," his lack of familiarity with the judicial and administrative rules in his jurisdiction governing his appointment as a divorce child custody evaluator has resulted in misrepresentation, agreements that cannot be kept, and a jeopardizing of his ability to perform an objective custody evaluation. Dr. N. was appointed in the custody case to make a determination about custody. His decision to change the purpose of his service to mediation resulted in his taking a role as negotiator and, possibly, therapist, rather than evaluator. The parents, therefore, disclosed information in a negotiation setting that they may not have chosen to disclose had they been in an evaluative setting. Furthermore, Dr. N. offered confidentiality to the parents, who were not his clients; the court was his client. Actually, even though this standard alerts psychologists to understanding their forensic roles, this case would also be addressed by Standard 3.07, Third-Party Requests for Services. Regardless of whether the case was of a forensic nature, the parents would not have been Dr. N.'s clients and therefore would likely not have been included in a confidentiality agreement.

Dr. N. realizes that in addition to a violation of Standard 2.01(f), also in question as a result of his decisions are Standard 3.04, Avoiding Harm; Standard 3.05, Multiple Relationships; and Standard 2.01(a), Boundaries of Competence. Dr. N. had a very successful and effective career as a child psychologist and certainly had expertise in working with parents, conducting evaluations, and dealing with the effects of divorce and marital stress on children. The additional skill acquisition and competency involved in legal procedures took Dr. N. totally by surprise, and he now realizes the significance of these distinct roles.

Decision-Making Factors. First, in his jurisdiction Dr. N. is limited in his scope of practice by the terms of his appointment by the court; he is authorized by the court to conduct an evaluation in a divorce custody proceeding and has no authority to depart from that appointment by engaging in mediation without approval by the appointing court.

Second, in his jurisdiction it is considered to be the practice of law to engage in divorce mediation that includes financial agreements or other agreements of legal significance that are beyond the scope of psychological practice. Therefore, Dr. N. has potentially exposed himself to sanctions from the state bar authorities and others for the practice of law without a license.

Third, courts hearing divorce child custody cases often have extensive power to overcome privacy protections if doing so would be, in the court's opinion, in the best interests of the child. In this jurisdiction this includes the confidentiality of mediation efforts when cases are court involved, unless the court orders in advance of the mediation effort that they will be protected. Dr. N. did not know this and improperly offered confidentiality. Therefore, Dr. N. will have to disclose in response to questions from the attorneys what he has learned during the supposedly confidential mediation sessions. This would include (unless he is very lucky) disclosing the previously undisclosed marital affair. Perhaps Dr. N. was willing to hold the secret of the affair in his role as mediator, but in resuming his role as custody evaluator the affair may well be relevant information for the custody decision, at which point he could not fail to factor it in despite his confidentiality promise.

Finally, many jurisdictions extend *quasi-judicial immunity* to court-appointed experts and evaluators, which protects them against malpractice suits (although not licensure complaints). However, the immunity from being sued is limited only to those activities that are within the scope of the appointment from the court. Therefore, Dr. N. can be sued for malpractice for his mediation efforts, including his improper mediation of financial matters and improper assurances of confidentiality for mediation sessions.

Decision Options. Standard 2.01(f) and the unfortunate Dr. N. highlight the distinction between clinical roles and forensic roles. The standard requires that psychologists assuming forensic roles be, or become, "reasonably familiar" with the judicial or administrative rules governing their roles. What constitutes being "reasonably familiar" with the relevant rules requires a case-specific inquiry into factors such as:

- the complexity of the litigation;
- what is at stake in the litigation (e.g., money damages, loss of child custody, imprisonment, execution);
- the framework of rules of evidence governing the case and the psychologist's role within the case;
- and the likelihood that involvement in the case could precipitate a licensure complaint, ethics committee complaint, or malpractice lawsuit.

The administrative rules with which psychologists should be reasonably familiar include knowing how privilege works in the jurisdiction and should include rules or regulations promulgated by state licensing boards relevant to forensic roles.

Dr. N. should decide to forgo any additional forensic-related work until and if he gains considerably more knowledge and understanding of the prevailing judicial rules in his jurisdiction. In this case, Dr. N. should explain to the court the actions he has taken that have limited his ongoing role and created problems for the court in proceeding. He may suggest that the court appoint another psychologist with forensic expertise to perform the custody evaluation. He will need to tell the parents that he will not be able to ensure that their disclosures will be kept from the court record. Also, any agreements they reached on their divorce process will likely not be upheld in the court proceeding, because Dr. N. was not authorized to execute a mediation.

Standard 2.02, Providing Services in Emergencies

In emergencies, when psychologists provide services to individuals for whom other mental health services are not available and for which psychologists have not obtained the necessary training, psychologists may provide such services in order to ensure that services are not denied. The services are discontinued as soon as the emergency has ended or appropriate services are available.

This standard shares elements with Standard 2.01(d), Boundaries of Competence, in that both apply when mental health services are not otherwise available. Psychologists can provide services without an attempt to obtain competency and without prior training if an emergency prevails. An *emergency* is a time-limited and immediate need for assistance in natural disasters, large-scale catastrophes, and critical incidents of any scope.

Psychologists provide an important professional role in service to the public and are often needed for incident response even though they may not have emergency experience. Psychologists should be aware that they are providing psychological services that call for their expertise, albeit not in the specific area of need, as contrasted with a Good Samaritan act outside the scope of psychology (e.g., assisting in a medical emergency, such as a birth). Psychologists should be alert to the possibility that their particular mode of treatment could be harmful rather than helpful to the client/patient. A most natural human response is to go to the site at which assistance is needed. Response in emergency and disaster circumstances can be unintentionally harmful unless the service is delivered in a competent manner. Psychologists are mindful of the cultural, political, and social contexts of emergency or disaster situations in offering a competent response.

Standard 2.02, Case 1

Case Illustration. Dr. O. is a neuropsychologist whose practice is located in a small town in a very rural area. One afternoon, the town is suddenly struck by a tornado, resulting in devastation and multiple injuries to adults and children. Dr. O. is unhurt and is asked by a sheriff in a passing car to report to the elementary school gym, where injured persons are being brought for urgent attention. Dr. O. arrives to see adults and children in shock and is asked by the town physician to provide crisis intervention and psychological triage over the next few days until authorities can respond to the disaster with trained personnel. Dr. O. hesitates because she has not received any disaster response training and has never been in a situation in which her professional services were called on outside of her scope of practice. In fact, Dr. O. has a very specialized practice in which she does not conduct general psychotherapy or other broad psychological services. Her training is in a specific area of neuropsychology, and she has not worked with a general population since her graduate training days.

Even though Dr. O. is quite uncertain and anxious about how she might be able to contribute, she realizes the need from the community and decides to help in any way she can. She is still very aware of her limitations and wants to be conscientious about her participation.

Ethical Dilemma. Standard 2.02 applies directly to Dr. O.'s provision of services in these emergency circumstances. As Dr. O. thinks about her involvement in the triage, she begins to think about the ethical implications of her participation. She understands that she is being asked to provide services outside of her scope of practice but that the services would be rendered in an emergency situation applicable to Standard 2.02. Dr. O. begins to think that not only were boundaries of competence in question here but also, because this was a small rural community, that she likely will be administering to individuals with whom she has other, various relationships (Standard 3.05, Multiple Relationships). She is keenly aware of not wanting to act in any way that would bring harm to anyone (Standard 3.04, Avoiding Harm). Conversely, Dr. O. thinks about General Principle A: Beneficence and Nonmaleficence, according to which psychologists must seek "to safeguard the welfare and rights of those with whom they interact professionally and other affected persons." General Principle E: Respect for People's Rights and Dignity alerts psychologists that "special safeguards may be necessary to protect the rights and welfare of persons or communities whose vulnerabilities impair autonomous decision making."

Dr. O. feels confident that she is ethically on sound footing in participating in the triage; however, she now needs to think about the scope of her role, the duration, and the ways in which she could reasonably continue to participate. Dr. O. anticipates that during the course of her administering to individuals they could easily direct the interaction to personal problems, conflicts they may have, work-related problems, and other subjects that are not integral to the emergency situation but that are uppermost in their minds. She does not want to inadvertently drift into doing psychotherapy or engaging in decision making for which she is not prepared or that is not part of the emergency procedures.

Decision-Making Factors. The elements to consider are whether other mental health services are available (they are not) and whether there is an emergency (the tornado is gone, but individuals are in shelters and emergency personnel are still arriving). It should be noted that Dr. O. is not required by this standard to provide services, but she is allowed to even though she is not competent to provide the services. Even if not required by the Ethics Code, an important factor is the possibility that services will be denied to the victims of the tornado if Dr. O. does not assist. The final element in the standard requires a determination as to when appropriate services are available, because it appears that this will happen before the emergency ends. Emergency personnel will probably make that decision, but Dr. O should be aware of when trained personnel arrive and the adequacy of their numbers at the scene relative to the continued needs of the victims of the disaster. It is possible that Dr. O. can continue providing some services under supervision, if she has had "closely related experience or training" for the services to be provided under supervision (see Standard 2.01d) or if there are still not appropriate services available for the individuals with whom she is working.

Dr. O. realizes that she will need to monitor the experience as she provides services because she does not know what to expect. She may have myriad requests, demands, and circumstances that are unanticipated and unpredictable. Even though her participation is determined by the parameters of the Standard 2.02, her decisions on how she conducts her participation will be her responsibility.

Decision Options. Given the number of victims and the acuity of their psychological trauma following the devastation and loss of life, Dr. O. arguably would be permitted to continue to offer services until a sufficient number of trained personnel arrive to provide adequate services for the number of victims needing them. Dr. O. realizes that the disaster response coordinators would monitor and direct volunteers in accordance with expertise, experience, and training. It is likely that, as other volunteers arrive, some will have no more training than Dr. O.; others will be well trained and will have expertise. Depending on the number of individuals being served and the number of volunteers, the need for Dr. O.'s assistance may be there for an undetermined length of time. Dr. O. surmises that she will want to be of assistance as long as the disaster response team determines a need for her level of service and that she will be sensitive to the needs of the people she serves in relation to her ability.

Standard 2.03, Maintaining Competence
Psychologists undertake ongoing efforts to develop and maintain their competence.

In contrast to Standard 2.01, Boundaries of Competence, maintenance of competence requires psychologists to remain current in their present area of expertise. Failure to maintain competence can occur when psychologists are unaware that their standard of practice has changed, when new skills and knowledge bases have become part of the standard of competence, or when professional guidelines and criteria have been endorsed by the profession. Psychologists may develop reliance on and confidence and skill in using a particular test battery, format for clinical interviewing, and decision paradigm that once was the standard in the area but is no longer viewed as adequate.

Continuing education and peer consultation are viewed as means by which psychologists can remain current in their professional domain. Continuing education is often required for licensure; promotion is often a measure of development for teaching; grant acquisition is often a measure of success for researchers. All three areas of psychological activity, however, require initiation and self-monitoring by the psychologists themselves in order to maintain competence.

Standard 2.04, Bases for Scientific and Professional Judgments

Psychologists' work is based upon established scientific and professional knowledge of the discipline. (See also Standards 2.01e, Boundaries of Competence, and 10.01b, Informed Consent to Therapy.)

This standard specifically recognizes the dual importance of the scientific inquiry evidenced through empirical research and professional judgment evidenced through clinical expertise. This duality is often expressed as the *scientist–practitioner model* and conveys the shared significance of both aspects of the field in establishing effective methods by which clinical decisions are made. The scientific method of a controlled design, hypothesis testing, and interpretation of results is well established as scientific judgment based upon scientific knowledge. *Professional judgment* is the field application of the scientific inquiry based upon professional knowledge and expertise. Clinicians hypothesize across client/patient variables, diagnoses, treatment choices, and clinical decision making, and they exercise professional judgment in the interest of improved treatment outcome. Psychologists must be able to exercise competent judgment and decision making while adhering to the scientific principles established in the profession.

Standard 2.05, Delegation of Work to Others

Psychologists who delegate work to employees, supervisees, or research or teaching assistants or who use the services of others, such as interpreters, take reasonable steps to (1) avoid delegating such work to persons who have a multiple relationship with those being served that would likely lead to exploitation or loss of objectivity; (2) authorize only those responsibilities that such persons can be expected to perform competently on the basis of their education, training, or experience, either independently or with the level of supervision being provided; and (3) see that such persons perform

these services competently. (See also Standards 2.02, Providing Services in Emergencies; 3.05, Multiple Relationships; 4.01, Maintaining Confidentiality; 9.01, Bases for Assessments; 9.02, Use of Assessments; 9.03 Informed Consent in Assessments; and 9.07, Assessment by Unqualified Persons.)

Delegation of work inherently refers to responsibility for the actions of others in the work setting through supervision, consultation, or other reporting mechanisms. Psychologists specifically and clearly define the roles that they and those they delegate will hold. Several factors are important in determining these roles and responsibilities. Psychologists determine whether they are serving as supervisors or consultants. Supervision of others carries a level of professional responsibility that is quite different from the role of a consultant. Supervision most often occurs when the delegated person is not able to perform his or her assigned responsibilities independently because of skill deficits, an inability to qualify for the credential required by law, requirements of the organization within which the service is provided, or the delegated person cannot or is not meeting the criteria of a professional ethics code. Actions of supervisees are, by extension, actions of the supervisors themselves; consequently, psychologists are held as directly responsible for supervisees' actions as though they had committed the actions themselves. Accurate evaluation of the supervisees' level of competence and the ongoing monitoring that supervisees effectively perform their roles with competence is the full responsibility of the designated supervisors.

The profession of psychology is increasingly relying on the role of expert peer consultants when fully credentialed psychologists wish to expand their scope of professional work. Expert peer consultants may work with psychologists in developing a new area of expertise; fulfilling a professional role needed by the employing organization; responding to geographic regional needs; or in maintaining competence in a significantly changing area of practice, research, or training. Individuals involved in a collaborative, educative process should be certain to define and understand the roles and responsibilities of all parties. This standard specifically uses the term *delegation*, not *supervision*. Psychologist consultants should clearly establish their roles in both authority and responsibility for those to whom they are delegating professional work and should apply this standard accordingly.

Supervision primarily applies to two categories of oversight: (a) training supervision and (b) employment supervision. Training supervision includes training within a doctoral program, internship, postdoctoral or supervised work experience, and respecialization. Supervisees in training are working toward a level of competence represented by the acquisition of a credential such as a terminal degree or a state-issued license. Training supervisors typically hold full responsibility for the actions of the supervisees, and the supervisees are viewed by the public and the profession as performing under the credentials of the supervisors. The APA Ethics Code (Standard 10.01c, Informed Consent to Therapy) specifically notes that when a supervisor is legally responsible for the treatment provided by trainees the client/patients must be informed that the clinician is in training and is supervised, and the name of the supervisor must be provided. Many state licensing boards and other policy or regulatory entities similarly address this training relationship.

Employment supervision typically occurs when psychologists do one of three things: (a) hire individuals to assist them in their own work, (b) agree to supervise those who are not credentialed to work autonomously, or (c) are assigned supervision as part of their job responsibilities in an organizational entity. These three very different work relationships require psychologists to carefully determine their responsibilities and to understand the implications of their roles. Psychologists who employ individuals to assist them are fully responsible for ensuring the employees' competence and application of skills in their performance. In these situations, however, the psychologists also have direct authority over the work activities of the employees. When psychologists assist other professionals in performing activities that individuals are not able to perform autonomously psychologists may be vulnerable to signing off on work for which they are not actually responsible and that the individuals are not competent to perform. Psychologists should not participate in supervisory relationships in which they cannot ensure competence or monitor that competent activity is being performed.

This standard expressly cites that psychologists "take reasonable steps" in ensuring competence in delegation of work to others. The introduction to the APA Ethics Code explains that the term *reasonable* means "the prevailing professional judgment of psychologists engaged in similar activities in similar circumstances, given the knowledge the psychologist had or should have had at the time." This modifier conveys that psychologists cannot absolutely guarantee the competence of those they supervise and that they will be held accountable for what they actually did to ensure that competence and to limit delegation appropriately. Factors such as the following should be addressed and documented: what training has been obtained and provided; how often were supervision sessions held, and what was the content; and what were the competencies determined and what policies were used to enforce that only those areas were delegated. Appropriate delegation can be very difficult for psychologists working in organizational and institutional settings when they do not have the authority to decide on employment or work assignment of other employees. Psychologists can, however, make known their observations regarding the competence of others, encourage appropriate supervision and work assignment, and otherwise make every effort to correct the ethical vulnerability of the entity.

The importance of competence in serving diverse populations is addressed through several standards in the 2002 Ethics Code, including Standard 2.01(b), Boundaries of Competence; Standard 3.01, Unfair Discrimination; Standard 9.02(c), Use of Assessments; and Standard 9.06, Interpreting Assessment Results. This standard recognizes the increasing importance of interpreters in providing services and in conducting research with diverse populations. An interpreter who, for example, might be a family member or friend of the client could be vulnerable to exploitation or a lack of objectivity in providing interpretation. Furthermore, interpreters who do not have personal relationships with the patient/client but who are selected only because of language familiarity or competence with the means of communication needed may indeed have the skill of language but not the understanding of the importance of accuracy in conveying nuance, expression, and nonverbal communication in which psychologists are trained. Interpreters must also be trained in the importance of ethical standards, including confidentiality and informed consent.

Standard 2.05, Case 1

Case Illustration. Dr. P. has been hired by the local community hospital as a clinical supervisor for the field placement program for doctoral psychology trainees. The hospital has been asked to become a site for a doctoral practicum and has entered into discussions with the university and the community mental health center on possibly developing an internship site. Dr. P. completed her doctoral degree 5 years earlier and has worked in outpatient clinics and done adjunct supervision of trainees for the university doctoral program during that time. She was hired specifically to coordinate training for the new training role of the hospital. She is very pleased to have this position and hopes to do well in her role.

One of Dr. P.'s first supervisees at the hospital, Ms. A., reports that a young patient has been admitted to the medical unit for medical complications secondary to anorexia. It is determined that she needs a period of hospitalization to medically stabilize her, although she does not need to be on a tertiary medical care unit in a teaching hospital or other intensive medical setting. Psychological consultation is requested to help determine whether this patient should be admitted to a specialized eating disorders unit after medical stabilization. The doctoral student is in an advanced practicum; however, she had not worked with eating disorders in her earlier training. Dr. P. has had very limited experience with eating disorders, although she is familiar with the major concepts of eating disorders and she has experience in conducting general psychological evaluations. She also feels competent in cognitive and behavioral approaches to behavior change but has not applied these or other treatments to an eating disorder diagnosis. Dr. P. realizes that she does not have the experience that she would want to have in supervising this case, but hospital officials have informed her that they do not have anyone who can supervise the psychological aspects of this case and that they need her to be involved and to supervise the doctoral student on the case. Dr. P. does not want to jeopardize her new appointment at the hospital.

Ethical Dilemma. Dr. P. is aware that she could be in violation of Standard 2.05, Delegation of Work to Others. She also realizes that she does not have the competence to conduct this case on her own and so certainly is not able to supervise the case independently, either. Standard 2.05 requires that psychologists take reasonable steps to avoid delegating professional activities to persons who may have potentially compromising multiple relationships with those served or who may not be able to perform those professional activities competently given their education, training, experience, or need for particular levels of supervision. The standard also imposes a duty on psychologists to see that persons to whom they delegate professional responsibilities exercise those responsibilities competently. Dr. P. knows that there is not a multiple relationship problem in the case, but she is concerned that she is not able to provide the direction in supervision needed and that, if she could, the doctoral student's level of competence would be acceptable. However, because neither of them have a satisfactory level of competence, she is conflicted about how to proceed. In addition, Standard 2.05 requires not only that the person providing the psychological services be competent or be supervised by an individual who is competent but also that the supervisor ensure that the trainee follows through competently on services provided.

Dr. P. does not want to fall short of the hospital's expectations of her, but she also wants to conduct herself ethically and professionally. Dr. P. is well aware of Standard 3.04, Avoiding Harm, and she does not want to adversely affect the patient and does not want the doctoral student to have a negative experience in supervision. Standard 3.06, Conflict of Interest, directs psychologists to avoid a professional role, such as supervision of the patient with an eating disorder, and another interest, such as financial or employment-related reasons. Dr. P. realizes that there are competing interests for her in this case, and she wants to make professional and ethical decisions.

Decision-Making Factors. Dr. P. is concerned about her performance in her new position, but she does not want to risk an ethics breach by going forward on her own. Dr. P. realizes that she is at a tipping point in terms of her professional development, the training in progress in the hospital, and the training experiences that Ms. A. and other students will have in working with Dr. P. at the hospital site. Eating disorders will not be the only area in which Dr. P. will need to be skilled that may require an expansion of her training. Dr. P. notes that the hospital does not have staff who can supervise the case and that if the hospital is developing a training program, then eating disorders will be an area in which expertise will be needed. Cases being seen at the hospital will increasingly have primary care and integrated care implications, and Dr. P. now knows she needs to think about these areas of practice in her continuing education.

Dr. P. considers whether there is a means by which she can continue to work with the case and yet not be in an ethically untenable stance. She reflects on the conditions of Standard 2.01(d), Boundaries of Competence. If Dr. P. makes a commitment to gain the competency necessary to conduct assessments for eating disorders and to be able to supervise treatment, could she reasonably work with the case? Dr. P. feels confident about her general assessment skills, her therapeutic skills in evidence-based practice, and her supervision skills. None of these lends itself specifically to working with eating disorders, but Dr. P. wonders whether, if she gained the appropriate supervision, peer consultation, and focused training, she could proceed in working with this population. Dr. P. realizes that an organized and systematic approach to expansion of her scope of practice would be important for her continued supervision and training at the hospital and in her practice. She also thinks about Ms. A. and Dr. P.'s responsibility to bring her into the decision-making process and to explain the ethical implications to her so that this will be a learning experience for her also.

Decision Options. Dr. P. understands that there are several aspects of the decisions she must make and the actions she needs to consider:

- The patient's welfare must remain first in the consideration of Dr. P. and others in any decisions made about supervision and treatment. Dr. P. will commit to a course of action only if the patient's welfare is of primary consideration.
- Dr. P. will also consider Ms. A. and the importance of her training experience. Dr. P.'s decisions must be consistent with the training mission of the hospital.
- Dr. P. will likely decide to confer with the hospital administrator and discuss the options for treatment: the patient can be referred out of the hospital to a psychologist competent to work with eating disorders; a consultant with appropriate expertise may be brought in to supervise the doctoral student so that the case can remain a training case; Dr. P. could consider, with the hospital administrator, the option of supervising the student within Dr. P.'s own supervision and training experiences. Dr. P. has experience in behavioral interventions and in assessment and evaluation. She could consult an eating disorders expert to determine her skill level for training, and if the consulting expert agreed to work with her, she could begin her specialized training in this area, including ongoing supervision, consultation, and continuing education workshops.

An important consideration in thoughtful response and action regarding Standards 2.05 and 2.01 is that professional psychologists will continue to face a growing edge of practice in psychology and will need to assess advances in the field in concert with their own scope of practice. Psychology is a dynamic field, and the ability to ethically and professionally pursue new areas of interest and expertise is critical. Dr. P. inadvertently found herself in an untenable and unintended situation. The situation, however, gave her the opportunity to think about her obligation and her interest in finding ways to develop needed expertise and to remain competent in a changing practice environment.

Standard 2.05, Case 2

Case Illustration. Dr. G. is a supervising psychologist in a large outpatient clinic that is a training site for doctoral psychology students. Her ordinary practice for students assigned psychotherapy cases is to offer 1 hour twice weekly of individual supervision to each student. Mr. T. is one of her supervisees. She finds him smart and amiable in supervision. He seems well prepared. However, 3 months into the training year Dr. G. receives notice from the medical records department that Mr. T. is lagging far behind in writing his clinical notes from therapy sessions. She addresses that with him in supervision, and he agrees to complete the necessary documentation. One month later, she is informed that he is still missing half of the required documentation and that there is reason to believe that he has confused patients when writing notes in records. She also learns that he has not completed clinical notes that he had reported he had completed. She again addresses this with Mr. T., and he again agrees to complete the necessary documentation and to be more careful about writing the clinical notes in the correct records. He assures her that he had "just been confused" when he had reported to her that he had completed some notes that were actually not yet done.

Six months into the training year, Dr. G. receives a call from one of the patients assigned to Mr. T., who complains that "this therapy isn't anything like I expected"; that "this therapist says the meanest things to me"; and "my sessions are always about him, not about me." Dr. G. addresses this in supervision. Mr. T. points out that the complaining patient is diagnosed with depression, not otherwise specified; alcohol abuse; and borderline personality disorder. He states that he has merely been attempting to address her self-risking behavior and to set limits with her when she tries to stay beyond the scheduled appointment time or repeatedly call his office. He and Dr. G. agree on a strategy to address limit-setting in the treatment.

Two weeks later, Dr. G. is called and told that the patient has committed suicide. A review of the chart reveals that no clinical note had been entered on this patient for the month prior to the suicide. Careful reading revealed that at least two entries appeared to be those for other patients in Mr. T.'s caseload. It also revealed to Dr. G. that Mr. T. had apparently not been telling her in supervision some information that was reflected in the existing clinical notes, and this makes her wonder whether he had been adequately disclosing information in supervision that may not have made it into the notes.

Ethical Dilemma. Standard 2.05, Delegation of Work to Others, requires in 2.05(3) that psychologists who delegate professional activities to others take "reasonable steps" to "see that such persons perform these services competently." This places an affirmative duty on psychologists and requires a consideration of what those steps are. Dr. G. must consider not only a breach of Standard 2.05(3), performing services competently, but also 2.05(2), "authorize only those responsibilities that such persons can be expected to perform competently." Even though Mr. T. was a doctoral student and therefore had been evaluated for admission into the program, mounting evidence indicated that he may not have been competent to perform those assigned responsibilities in addition to not engaging in follow-through. Also possibly in question is Standard 7.06, Assessing Student and Supervisee Performance. This standard often serves to protect students from nonobjective evaluation and shifting program requirements. It also requires timeliness and specificity for the fair treatment and welfare of the students. In this case, Standard 7.06 brings into question whether Dr. G. had been evaluating Mr. T. on actual performance or on his professed performance.

Dr. G. engaged in a familiar model of supervision with a doctoral student, relying largely on the student's self-report in individual supervision sessions. At what point should Dr. G. have engaged more actively in ensuring that Mr. T.'s clinical notes were complete and that they reflected appropriate information about the therapy patients? At what point should Dr. G. have begun to wonder whether this student could be relied on to offer accurate information about his professional activities, including the content of psychotherapy sessions in supervision sessions?

Before receiving the telephone call from the complaining patient, Dr. G. was at least on notice that Mr. T. was not meticulous in his completion of clinical documentation and that he was sloppy enough to put patient notes in the wrong records. Given the discovery that he had not written notes that he said he had written, Dr. G. had reason to believe that Mr. T. was a particularly confused trainee or one who was actually willing to deceive her about professionally relevant responsibilities.

Decision-Making Factors. Dr. G. is distraught that a patient of Mr. T., the actual patient who called her to complain, has committed suicide. Dr. G. is faced with decisions that must be made now, and she will also face self-reflection on her role and her supervisee's role in the terrible outcome. Dr. G. must fact the possibility that she lost objectivity and reason early in the case. Five incidents presented her with conflicting information about Mr. T.'s performance versus his verbal testimony. Because Dr. G. did not verify or document any of the incongruences, she will need to reflect on the potential of negligence in supervision. She has always prided herself on being supportive to students, on working with those who have difficulties, and on accepting them at their own level of ability. She now faces the likelihood that her self-perception as an advocate of the student affected her objectivity and decision making. In reviewing her decision making, Dr. G. realizes the following failures:

- Had she reviewed the charts herself, she may have detected that Mr. T. was neglecting to offer in supervision important information that was contained in the charts.
- At the very least, it would have been reasonable for Dr. G. to have been more proactive in ensuring the production of clinical notes and the quality of their content.
- It would have been a reasonable step for Dr. G. to break from her ordinary supervision practice and communicate directly with the psychotherapy patients to determine whether the lack of diligence and care found in the medical records (absent notes, incorrect patient notes, information in notes not brought to supervision) was also present in the provision of psychotherapy. This would especially be the case when Mr. T. may have demonstrated a willingness to lie to her and when a patient had called to complain about psychotherapy sessions. Observing or recording sessions (with appropriate consent from clients) would have been another possibility.

Dr. G.'s distress is not only for the loss of the patient and the unanswerable question of whether the treatment the patient received was a factor in the devastating outcome but also for the unavoidable reality that she did not follow up on several signs that should have raised questions about Mr. T.'s competence and honesty.

Decision Options. Dr. G. has a difficult road ahead both in dealing with the reality of the event and in the steps she must take in the clinical follow-through and the training implications. Dr. G. will likely include the director of clinical training in her meeting with Mr. T. The faculty will want to fully examine the events leading up to the suicide and to hear an explanation from Mr. T. There will likely be an evaluation of Mr. T.'s clinical competence given the evidence of misrepresentation and failure to conduct himself professionally. Dr. G. would also need to meet with the clinic administrators to process the clinic aspects of the supervision.

This case of failure to delegate competently highlights the possibility that psychologists may have knowledge-based skills but not be competent in clinical judgment. There is evidence not that Dr. G. did not know how to supervise the actual clinical cases but that she missed all of the signs that the supervisee was not performing adequately and, furthermore, that he was exhibiting potential character problems. Dr. G. initially described Mr. T. as smart, amiable, and well prepared. The incongruence between her initial impression and the ongoing feedback about Mr. T. escaped her. She will need to understand and resolve this conflict before trusting her supervisory competency again.

Standard 2.06, Personal Problems and Conflicts

Personal problems may lead to the failure of skill-based competency or to the failure of relational-based competency, as outlined in Exhibit 2.1. Standard 2.06 alerts psychologists to the stage of professional interaction or provision of services at the time that personal problems become known. Standard 2.06 acknowledges that personal problems may precede professional service or that personal problems may develop or become known during the provision of professional service. Psychologists' response and understanding of responsibility should be timely and appropriate to each circumstance.

Standard 2.06(a)
Psychologists refrain from initiating an activity when they know or should know that there is a substantial likelihood that their personal problems will prevent them from performing their work-related activities in a competent manner.

Standard 2.06(b)
When psychologists become aware of personal problems that may interfere with their performing work-related duties adequately, they take appropriate measures, such as obtaining professional consultation or assistance, and determine whether they should limit, suspend, or terminate their work-related duties. (See also Standard 10.10, Terminating Therapy.)

Personal problems and conflicts are circumstances that result in vulnerability to relational competence, as described earlier in this chapter. Such problems may also include medical difficulties that have an effect on psychologists' work. The vulnerabilities can include a failure to identify that one has a developing personal problem, the ability to identify that one has a personal problem but failure to identify the effect the problem has on one's competence, or the ability to identify the personal problem and to acknowledge an effect on one's professional competence but a failure to accurately assess the risk condition resulting in an insufficient response to the problem or conflict. Other standards in this section address the importance of the development and assessment of skill-based competence. This standard addresses the case of skill-based competence being compromised because of interpersonal (e.g., divorce, illness of other, parental, family, or financial stress), intrapersonal (e.g., burnout, depression, phase of life concerns), or medical problems (e.g., chemotherapy, physical injury, fatigue due to illness).

These problems may manifest through compromised skill-based performance in practice, research, or training settings. Problems may also manifest in the blurring of boundaries in professional relationships that results in multiple role conflicts; sexual misconduct; and other inappropriate behaviors with clients, students, supervisees, employees, or teaching and research assistants.

Standard 2.06(a) calls on psychologists to be alert to compromised performance through self-monitoring when circumstances arise in their lives that would be expected to be problematic for any other professional. The standard applies the criterion of not simply knowing but that psychologists "should know" of the likelihood that problems will interfere with professional performance. This criterion introduces the importance of judgment and objectivity based on the standard of practice expected of others.

Standard 2.06(b) addresses the development of personal problems and conflicts after professional relationships have been established and psychologists are in a commitment to continue work with others. Consultation with other professionals regarding a course of actions or use of services often provided by professional associations and organizations are favorable options for problem resolution because compromised judgment would, by definition, impair a psychologist's ability to resolve these situations on his or her own. Consultation can not only inform the psychologist about how to proceed but also can assist in determining the degree of compromise that has already been committed.

Standard 2.06, Case 1

Case Illustration. Dr. V. maintained a successful private practice until she became addicted to prescription medication and started abusing alcohol following a series of painful surgeries. Eventually she recognized that her professional functioning was increasingly challenging and, after consultation with another psychologist, took the appropriate steps to suspend her practice until completing treatment for her addiction. This realization was most difficult for Dr. V., because she prided herself on her dedication and commitment to her practice and to her clients. She also was stunned that such an impactful problem could befall her without her awareness for weeks. The severity of her addiction required admission to a residential program. She twice relapsed within the first 6 months of discharge and was readmitted. After her relapses, Dr. V. became well aware that her recovery was a challenge of a lifetime and would require constant work. Dr. V. was confident that as soon as her realization of her addiction had occurred she took appropriate steps to suspend her practice and to seek treatment. She now believes that she is ready to resume her practice. She has maintained sobriety for 6 months and can avoid financial devastation and maintain her health insurance only if she resumes earning an income. Dr. V. is facing these two major circumstances that signal her need to work, but she also feels ready for work and thinks that she can handle it. Her relapses had occurred within 6 months. Dr. V. sees that she has maintained sobriety for 6 months and thinks that there is no evidence that she should wait any longer.

Ethical Dilemma. Dr. V. has acted consistently with Standard 2.06 by suspending her professional practice on recognizing that her functioning as a psychologist was increasingly impaired by her substance abuse. At this point she has been free of substances for 6 months and is under significant economic pressure to resume her livelihood. However, she has also twice previously relapsed within 6 months of discharge from a residential substance abuse treatment program to a degree that required a return to a residential treatment setting.

Dr. V. is well aware of the ethical expectations when personal problems affect psychologists' functioning. She notes to her colleagues that in Standard 2.06(a) "psychologists refrain from initiating an activity when . . . there is substantial likelihood that their problems will prevent their competent performance of professional activities." Dr. V. complied with the Standard 2.06(b) by suspending her practice when she became aware of her problems that could interfere with her work. Dr. V. says that the litmus test for resuming professional activity is whether there are identifiable or substantial reasons that her earlier problems would interfere with her performance now. She is very enthusiastic about getting back to her life as she liked it and about becoming a practicing psychologist again. Dr. V. thinks that even though she is at the brink of financial failure, this circumstance is minor in her motivation to resume.

Decision-Making Factors. How might Dr. V. proceed at this point? Standard 2.06 does not directly address the process of returning to professional practice after it has been limited, suspended, or terminated because of personal problems and conflicts; however, Standard 2.06(a) is applicable in that Dr. V. would be reinitiating her practice. Either part of the rule involves minimizing harm that arises when a psychologist cannot practice competently; therefore, Dr. V. might wish to consider the following kinds of factors when determining whether to resume her professional practice:

- Are there currently circumstances that make it more or less likely that she will be able to maintain her abstinence from substances should she return to practice; for example, is there evidence that she is further along in her recovery? Have there been changes in her network of interpersonal support, positively or negatively?
- Has she continued in appropriate substance abuse treatment?

- Has she continued to struggle with the physical pain that triggered her initial substance abuse, and/or does she face or anticipate stressors that may increase the risk of relapse?
- Does she have access to proper consultation or supervision as she resumes her practice?

Decision Options. Dr. V. came to rely on several colleagues and friends during her recovery, and she trusts their judgment about her progress. Dr. V. will weigh the feedback she receives as well as her own sense of being in control of her life. She may put measures into place of periodic contact with medical consults, therapists, and friends. Dr. V. may consider asking select clients to give her feedback and to be forthcoming in particular if they see any changes in her that she does not see herself. Dr. V. would want to be very careful enlisting clients for monitoring purposes, but she needs to know how she is relating to her clientele.

Dr. V. realizes that continued success will also continue to be hard work. She has talked openly about her need for continued therapy, consultation, and periodic coaching, which she began after the last hospitalization. Dr. V. will consider whether she should provide professional services to clients who are particularly vulnerable to the impact of impaired professional judgment and/or her sudden lack of availability should she need to return to residential substance abuse treatment. She should have in place a feasible plan that appropriately attends to the needs of her clients in the event of a relapse. She also would consider the circumstances of stress and other factors that were present when she first became sick. She intends to be alert to any events or experiences, either with clients or in her personal life, that might trigger her anxiety, stress level, or other mood factors that could send her back into a spiral. Dr. V. wants to conduct her professional behavior in a most ethical way and wants to have her professional life back. She understands that she could not rely on her insight for the first time around, but she hopes that she has some degree of self-awareness after successfully completing treatment that included self-regulation. In any case, she will have both support systems and health care monitors working with her.

CONCLUSION

Competence is the foundational standard on which professional services (Section 7, Education and Training; Section 8, Research and Publication; Section 9, Assessment; and Ethical Section 10, Therapy) and professional relationships (Section 3, Human Relations) rest. Section 1, Resolving Ethical Issues, is applicable on a failure of competence or a failure of professional decision making. The standards of the competence section provide psychologists with guidance in two realms of competency application: (a) expectations for maintenance of competency (i.e., Standard 2.01a, "providing services only within boundaries of . . . competence"; Standard 2.03, Maintaining Competence; Standard 2.04, Bases for Scientific and Professional Judgments; and Standard 2.05, Delegation of Work to Others). This section also provides and (b) guidance in decision making in circumstances that approach or exceed one's boundaries of competence (i.e., Standard 2.01b–f; Standard 2.02, Providing Services in Emergencies; and Standard 2.06, Personal Problems and Conflicts).

3

HUMAN RELATIONS

Section 3 of the American Psychological Association's (APA's) "Ethical Principles of Psychologists and Code of Conduct" (hereinafter the *APA Ethics Code* or the *Ethics Code*; see http://www.apa.org/ethics/code2002.html),[1] Human Relations, is a new category that was designed to more clearly encompass those standards relating to the responsibilities that psychologists have to consumers and the general public. Most of the standards in this section were previously in various forms in the General Standards section of the 1992 Principles of Psychologists and Code of Conduct,[2] which was deleted in the 2002 Ethics Code. As in the 1992 General Standards section, the standards in Section 3 are applicable to the professional and scientific activities of all psychologists. These standards deal with relationships that psychologists have with the individuals and groups with whom they work and the responsibilities that psychologists have to them. Section 3 frames the context of who psychologists are, what they do, and how they treat people.

---

[1]American Psychological Association. (2002). Ethical principles of psychologists and code of conduct. *American Psychologist, 57,* 1060–1073.
[2]American Psychological Association. (1992). Ethical principles of psychologists and code of conduct. *American Psychologist, 47,* 1597–1611.

All of the general principles (General Principle A: Beneficence and Nonmaleficence, General Principle B: Fidelity and Responsibility, General Principle C: Integrity, General Principle D: Justice, and General Principle E: Respect for People's Rights and Dignity) are applicable to this section and, in fact, are foundational to psychologists' interactions with the individuals with whom they work. In essence, General Principle A encourages psychologists to benefit those with whom they work, to take care to do no harm, and to safeguard the welfare and rights of those with whom they interact professionally. General Principle B underscores the importance of trust in the relationships psychologists have with others and their responsibility to society and to the communities in which they work. General Principle C informs psychologists of their obligation to bring honesty and truthfulness to the practice of psychology, to the teaching and training of others, and to scientific endeavors. General Principle D encourages psychologists to recognize that fairness and justice entitle all persons to access and benefit from the contributions of psychology and to equal quality in the processes, procedures, and services provided by psychologists. General Principle E encourages psychologists to respect the dignity and worth of all people. This includes people's rights to privacy; to confidentiality; to self-determination; and to the elimination of the effect of unfair, unjust, or inappropriate biases on psychologists' work.

As noted, all of the general principles are applicable to Section 3. It is evident that one of the challenges in application of this section is that it touches on so many facets of psychologists' work. Human relations are relevant to every interaction in which psychologists engage in their professional roles. The standards in this section are not technical in nature but instead permeate all of the dimensions of psychologists' activities that are defined and described in other sections of the Ethics Code.

The principles that underlie these standards attempt to ensure that psychologists' power is not abused intentionally or inadvertently and that psychologists' activities are carried out in fair and just ways and are communicated in a way that the individual clearly understands and desires. These standards are intended to position psychologists in such a way that their role, purpose, and goals are sufficiently transparent so that the individuals with whom they professionally interact can make reasonable decisions about the nature of the relationship and the level of the trust that should be invested into it. The concepts of *trust* and *transparency* are differentially referenced in this section . The standards in this section address circumstances and roles in which clients/patients should be able to expect *trustworthiness* from psychologists, as evidenced through the therapeutic relationship, advocacy, and other representational roles in which the client/patient views the psychologist as an ally. As well, the role and purpose of psychologists may call for *transparency* in the clarity and forthrightness with which psychologists explain their purpose, which may or may not be aligned with that of the client/patient. The level of the trust that a psychotherapy client/patient should be able to bring into the relationship will be different from the one he or she brings if the psychologist is acting in a forensic or research capacity, in which the primary interest of the endeavor is not necessarily the welfare of the individual. Clients/patients should have the information necessary to make their own decisions about level of trust by virtue of the transparency with which psychologists present themselves, their purpose, and role.

Regardless of the role or purpose of psychologists, they promote and engender trust in the relationships with those with whom they work in accordance with Standard 3.01, Unfair Discrimination; Standard 3.02, Sexual Harassment; Standard 3.03, Other Harassment; and Standard 3.04, Avoiding Harm.

Transparency is particularly relevant to Standard 3.05, Multiple Relationships; Standard 3.06, Conflict of Interest; Standard 3.07, Third-Party Requests for Services; Standard 3.08, Exploitative Relationships; Standard 3.09, Cooperation With Other Professionals; Standard 3.10, Informed Consent; Standard 3.11, Psychological Services Delivered To or Through Organizations; and Standard 3.12, Interruption of Psychological Services. These standards reference the nature and purpose of relationships that may not be in alliance with the goals of the individuals receiving psychological services. Psychologists do not behave in ways that would harm a person by distorting their role, and are mindful of the importance of clarifying and defining their roles to the recipients of their services so that those recipients do not have inaccurate expectations of confidentiality, trust, and an alliance with the psychologist.

Multiple relationships (Standard 3.05) are defined in this standard, and although the point is made that not all multiple relationships are unethical, guidance is provided to help psychologists refrain from entering into potentially harmful multiple relationships. Likewise, psychologists refrain from conflicts of interest that could be harmful, as noted in Standard 3.06, Conflict of Interest. Guidance is also provided in the case of Third-Party Requests for Services (Standard 3.07) to help psychologists clarify roles and limits to confidentiality. Acknowledgment of the potential for exploitation in authority roles is suggested in Standard 3.08, Exploitative Relationships, which emphasizes that psychologists are simply prohibited from engaging in exploitation. Psychologists are further encouraged to benefit people with whom they work, when appropriate, through Standard 3.09, Cooperation With Other Professionals.

Psychologists are encouraged to inform consumers or participants about aspects of the professional experience through informed consent (Standard 3.10). Those obligations are also required under Standard 3.11, Psychological

Services Delivered To or Through Organizations. Recommendations for facilitating services are made in the case of interruption of psychological services (Standard 3.12).

Standard 3.01, Unfair Discrimination

In their work-related activities, psychologists do not engage in unfair discrimination based on age, gender, gender identity, race, ethnicity, culture, national origin, religion, sexual orientation, disability, socioeconomic status, or any basis proscribed by law.

The title of this standard was *Nondiscrimination* in the 1992 Ethics Code. Because psychologists routinely use procedures in the course of their professional and scientific work that validly differentiate and discriminate among various categories of individuals, the standard was renamed to more accurately reflect the notion of *unfair* discrimination. Psychologists' work sometimes involves making valid discriminating judgments in the best interest of the consumers with whom they work. The intent of this standard is thus to clarify the prohibition of unlawful or invidious discrimination against people on the basis of such factors as age, gender, gender identity, race, ethnicity, culture, national origin, religion, sexual orientation, disability, or socioeconomic status. For example, unfair discrimination may take the form of the use of test or assessment procedures known to be culturally biased.

Just like all other people, psychologists may at times treat people unfairly, either intentionally or without an awareness of the impact that their behavior may have on the quality of care they provide. Psychologists may be uncomfortable or negatively influenced by treating clients who come from outside of their personal experience.

State and federal discrimination laws may also apply to psychologists' work. It is important for psychologists to be aware of state and federal laws that may govern discrimination in their professional activities. Because laws change, psychologists should take steps to be aware of relevant changes in laws in their jurisdictions.

Not all psychologists have the skills to work with all types of clients/patients, and this standard should not be interpreted to require that psychologists must offer services to all individuals regardless of training, experience, background, and competence. A tension may arise between General Principle D: Justice on the one hand, and General Principle A: Beneficence and Nonmaleficence on the other, such as when an individual may request or require services that the psychologist is not competent to provide. In chapter 2, we noted how Standard 2.01(d), Boundaries of Competence, addresses this tension by providing that psychologists "with closely related prior training or experience may provide such services in order to ensure that services are not denied" and "if they make a reasonable effort to obtain the competence required by using relevant research, training, consultation, or study."

Finding the line between what is unfairly discriminatory and what is not is sometimes a challenge, so psychologists are encouraged to closely attend to laws related to discrimination and to promote justice in such activities as ability testing and employment selection, in academia, and in research, as well as in the provision of mental health services.

The responsibilities to be knowledgeable and appropriately sensitive to the consumer's relevant demographic contexts are important, but psychologists must avoid acting on the basis of simplistic, unfounded stereotypes. The goals of benefiting clients; protecting them from harm; and promoting justice, dignity, and respect all underlie this standard.

Standard 3.01, Case 1

Case Illustration. Dr. D. is a psychologist in independent practice. He has approached the employee assistance program of a local factory to encourage the referral of clients to him. These clients will be predominantly from working-class and ethnic minority backgrounds. He sought these referrals because he needs to build his practice. At a meeting of the local psychological association, he reports that he has found this avenue to build his practice. Dr. D. does not seem to think about the importance of training and experience in working with a diverse group of clients/patients and talks as if his practice were driven by the market factors of availability of clients.

In a smaller group, Dr. E. hears Dr. D. belittle the cultures and customs of some of his clients. Dr. D. also states that he sees affirmative action as creating unfair advantages for people of color and that he privately opposes the scholarship program that the head of the factory had set up for children of the employees. Dr. E. is particularly surprised and concerned to hear Dr. D. communicate a sense of entitlement and to state that his work with this clientele is only temporary until he can build his practice with wealthier clients. Dr. E. is alarmed that Dr. D.'s discourse about the profession and his practice seem financially and expediency based only. He also hears Dr. D. brag about a strategy he used in order to "get out of" a required multicultural training course while in graduate school.

Ethical Dilemma. Dr. E. is familiar with the ethical responsibilities involved in Standard 3.01. General Principle A: Beneficence and Nonmaleficence guides psychologists in striving to benefit those with whom they work and to do no harm. General Principle D: Justice promotes the importance of recognizing that fairness and justice entitle all persons access to and benefit from the contributions of psychology and to equal quality in psychologists' processes, procedures, and services. General Principle E: Respect for People's Rights and Dignity cites the importance of psychologists trying to eliminate from their work biases that are based on diversity factors.

Dr. E. is amazed that Dr. D. has such negative stereotypes and biases and is engaging in provision of services with these populations only to promote his own economic agenda. Dr. E. had previously perceived Dr. D. to be highly confident but had not observed, until this meeting, the sense of entitlement and privilege that he communicates in discussing his attitudes toward the working-class clients with whom he plans to work. Dr. E. is also concerned that Dr. D. has not had the training to obtain competence in working with populations of which he apparently has little knowledge. He thus may likely be working outside the boundaries of his competence, in which case Standard 2.01(b), Boundaries of Competence, would be relevant. Dr. E. realizes that Standard 3.04, Avoiding Harm, directs psychologists to take reasonable steps to avoid harming their patients and others with whom they work. Dr. E. is fearful that Dr. D. could potentially cause harm through a lack of respect and understanding and a possible inability to establish a therapeutic alliance with many of his clients. Dr. E. is concerned that not only may training and skills incompetence be an issue but also that Dr. D. may be exhibiting interpersonal incompetence, insensitivity to others, and a failure of professional integrity.

Decision-Making Factors. Dr. E. considers Standard 1.04, Informal Resolution of Violations, which states that when psychologists believe that another psychologist may have made an ethical violation, they attempt to resolve the issue by bringing it to the attention of that individual if an informal resolution appears appropriate and the intervention does not violate any confidentiality rights that may be involved. In this case, it is not exactly clear that Dr. D. has committed a violation, but it seems likely that he will commit a violation given his apparent attitudes and biases. Consideration of Standard 1.04 suggests that a violation may have already occurred, because Dr. D. is already seeing some of these employees as clients, and the spirit of Standard 1.04 would support proactive involvement in a situation in which an ethical lapse is reasonably foreseeable.

It is possible that as Dr. D. begins seeing more clients, his basic humanity may be evoked, and he may treat his clients with respect and realize his responsibility to promote their welfare and well-being. However, the fact remains that Dr. D. has not had multicultural training, and because he bragged about it to colleagues it could be that he has not pursued continuing education in that area of content. Even if Dr. D. had not been so transparent about his biases, his statements about training lead Dr. E. to be concerned that he does not have the skill or competence to work with the client populations he is seeking. Dr. E. also finds the public comments Dr. D. made regarding his clients to demonstrate a lack of professional integrity. In considering whether to bring these concerns to Dr. D.'s attention, Dr. E. can imagine that it may indeed be an unwelcome and unexpected surprise for Dr. D. to hear that he is being perceived as holding prejudicial and biased perspectives. Dr. E., on the other hand, has been exposed to enough multicultural training to understand that harm can occur when people base their overt interactions with others on personal attributes about which they harbor negative thoughts and feelings; interpersonal prejudice and oppressive behaviors are often the result.

Decision Options. Dr. E. decides to approach Dr. D. with his perceptions and concerns in a manner that is as kind and compassionate as possible. He wishes to suggest that Dr. D. obtain training, experience, consultation, and/or supervision to ensure that his attitudes will be explored and sorted out, especially in regard to his socially constructed sense of entitlement. In addition, Dr. E. plans to suggest that working in a multiculturally competent context also means seeking skills training that would be not a single course but a commitment to a learning experience. Dr. E. will offer to attend a workshop on multicultural counseling with Dr. D. and to provide readings from which he has benefited.

If Dr. D. refuses to consider the need for such training, Dr. E. will suggest that he reconsider working with this clientele. Dr. D. may well be competent in specific content areas; however, Dr. E. realizes that in the community where both of them practice there is a substantial middle- and working-class population and that it is not reasonable or practical to think about factoring out segments of the populations for services. Even if Dr. D. does not accept clients toward whom he felt biases, his work with other clients will reflect his value judgments and his discriminatory perspectives. Dr. E. has reconciled himself to the possibility that if Dr. D. does not respond positively and demonstrably that Dr. E. will need to report his concerns to the licensing board or the national ethics committee, given that he is likely to substantially harm a person should he proceed to see working-class and ethnic minority clients without the benefit of proper training, supervision, and/or consultation.

Standard 3.02, Sexual Harassment

Psychologists do not engage in sexual harassment. Sexual harassment is sexual solicitation, physical advances, or verbal or nonverbal conduct that is sexual in nature, that occurs in connection with the psychologist's activities or roles as a psychologist, and that either (1) is unwelcome, is offensive, or creates a hostile workplace or educational environment, and the psychologist knows or is told this or (2) is sufficiently severe or intense to be abusive to a reasonable person in the context. Sexual harassment can consist of a single intense or severe act or of multiple persistent or pervasive acts.

(See also Standard 1.08, Unfair Discrimination Against Complainants and Respondents.)

This standard prohibits sexual harassment in as clear and specific a manner possible. When professional roles become sexualized in any way, conflicts of interest, role confusion, and the power differential become exacerbated. The goal of the standard is to educate psychologists as to what activities would be regarded as sexual harassment. This standard includes three defining elements: (a) an action that is sexual in nature; (b) a relationship that is professional in nature; and (c) the fact that the action is unwelcome, offensive, creates a hostile environment, or (d) is abusive to a reasonable person. Even when a sexual advancement is accepted or welcomed, the gesture may well violate other standards, such as Standard 3.08, Exploitative Relationships; Standard, 7.07 Sexual Relationships With Students and Supervisees; or Standard 10.05, Sexual Intimacies With Current Therapy Clients/Patients.

The standard is also designed to notify potential victims of sexual harassment of their rights to be free of such harassment and to clarify what conduct is prohibited as well as what conduct will not violate the standard. Sometimes psychologists exhibit poor judgment, but those instances may not rise to the level of harassment.

Verbal sexual harassment is defined by many as unwelcome or offensive remarks that create a hostile workplace environment. A psychologist may know or be told that the behavior constitutes sexual harassment. If a psychologist is notified by the subject of the harassment that the behavior is unwelcome and offensive, and the psychologist subsequently repeats the unwelcome behavior, then he or she risks being found in violation of this standard. Jokes or conduct with sexual overtones may or may not be offensive and unwelcome, but a pattern of such sexually offensive behavior after requests that it stop constitutes sexual harassment.

This rule is not meant to include minor insensitivities to which all people are subject, unless the individual has been notified that the behaviors are experienced as sexual harassment. The standard does not empower each person to define his or her own standard of sensitivity and require everyone else to meet it; however, especially where a power differential exists, such as teacher–student or supervisor–supervisee relationships, prohibitions may include flirtation in the workplace or other expressions of attraction.

There are certain verbal and other behaviors that are so offensive that no notice need be provided psychologists for them to be expected to know that the conduct is improper. For example, if even a single act of verbal behavior is of such severity that a reasonable person would agree that it is personally abusive, then it may be an ethical violation. Extremely offensive language, inappropriate touching or fondling, nonverbal communication that is overtly sexual, and offers of special attention or advancement in return for sexual favors are examples of behaviors that may constitute an ethical violation even without specific notice.

There may be questions about the changes between the 2002 Ethics Code and the 1992 Ethics Code, which provided protections for individuals who allege sexual harassments and those accused of it. However, those protections are modified in this standard and are addressed in Standard 1.08, Unfair Discrimination Against Complainants and Respondents.

Standard 3.02 thus describes the prohibition against sexual harassment and defines it. The standard provides general guidance for psychologists and recognizes that some psychologists will be guided by other, more specific definitions in various work settings.

Standard 3.03, Other Harassment

Psychologists do not knowingly engage in behavior that is harassing or demeaning to persons with whom they interact in their work based on factors such as those persons' age, gender, gender identity, race, ethnicity, culture, national origin, religion, sexual orientation, disability, language, or socioeconomic status.

This standard prohibits psychologists from knowingly harassing or demeaning others on the basis of the factors described. It is similar to Standard 1.12 of the 1992 Ethics Code and was modified only by the addition of "gender identity" and "culture" to the list of factors to which psychologists must be particularly sensitive. Sexual harassment is not the only type of harassment to be prohibited, because more subtle types of harassment and maltreatment are problematic. For example, telling offensive ethnic jokes and failing to manage one's dislike of students by treating them unfairly on the basis of religious preferences, disabilities, social status, sexual orientation, appearance, and other characteristics would be a violation of this standard.

The subjective state of mind of the psychologist is relevant in that, for this standard to be applied, the psychologist must be aware that his or her behavior is harassing or demeaning. This is designed to prevent a situation in which someone may perceive offense without psychologists being aware that it was perceived thus. Unless psychologists are made aware of the perception, they fail to have an opportunity to correct the behavior. Psychologists may not always know what behaviors may be considered harassing by an offended person. On the other hand, a psychologist who engages in behavior that would be considered improper to a reasonable person would not be able to defend such conduct on the basis of lack of awareness. If psychologists have been informed that certain behaviors are offensive, and they continue to engage in the behavior, they risk being in violation of this standard.

The fact that people from marginalized groups are often treated unfairly may indeed result in a discrepancy between the perceptions of the psychologist and the subject of the harassment. Thus, it is important for psychologists to remain current regarding the evolving societal sensitivities to language and behaviors considered demeaning to different groups in order to avoid acting and/or being perceived as acting in a pejorative manner.

Standard 3.04, Avoiding Harm

Psychologists take reasonable steps to avoid harming their clients/ patients, students, supervisees, research participants, organizational clients, and others with whom they work, and to minimize harm where it is foreseeable and unavoidable.

This standard is a more generic prohibition to take reasonable steps to avoid harm or to minimize it when it is possibly unavoidable. This standard is not intended to punish psychologists whenever a client/patient experiences discomfort.

It is important to distinguish between *harm* and outcomes that, from the perspective of the individual, may be painful, difficult, and unwelcome but nonetheless do not result in damage. An example of harm may be that a child custody evaluation incorrectly results in the loss of custody of a child. In general, harm arises because of incompetence, discrimination, unfairness, conflict of interest, or multiple relationships. Often, the psychologist has been charged with violation of this standard because the violation of another standard that speaks to specific harms has occurred and has been brought to bear on the individual. Several instances in psychologists' work may result in foreseeable distress, pain, or disappointment and unavoidable harm; for example, providing difficult feedback to a client/patient, student, organizational consultee, or colleague may be experienced as painful but may be necessary. The change process often results in periods of emotional pain and discomfort. Psychologists' various other responsibilities may result in the experience of foreseeable and unavoidable harm. For example, conducting child custody evaluations may result in a recommendation that may disappoint one of the parties. Other examples include evaluation of an individual's competency to stand trial, providing low grades or evaluations to students who have performed poorly, conducting personnel evaluations that lead to an individual's failure to attain employment, or disclosing confidential information to protect a child or elderly person from abuse. These are all important and legitimate responsibilities of psychologists that could result in foreseeable and unavoidable harm.

In such instances, psychologists can minimize harm by taking "reasonable steps" that demonstrate attempts to provide clarity about the psychological activity and avoid misunderstandings. Reasonable steps may include ensuring that informed-consent procedures adequately provide information about the risks and limits of confidentiality of the psychological activity in which the client/patient, student, supervisee, organizational consultee, or research participant may be involved. Following well-established research and treatment protocols, informing research participants of any possible negative aspects of the research project, and establishing a clear agreement with recipients of services to avoid misunderstandings in the future are all reasonable steps a psychologist may take to minimize harm. Also, selecting and using valid and reliable assessment techniques is important when one is engaging in any kind of evaluation, as is discussing the potential uses of test results with the persons to be evaluated. Evaluation and assessment techniques must be appropriate to the activity, nature of the problem, and characteristics of the individual. If an individual later claims harm due to an evaluation, referral, participation in a research project, or course of treatment, the reasonable steps, documented in the record, would help demonstrate ethical behavior.

Standard 3.04 provides educational value regarding the importance of avoiding harm and minimizing the foreseeable and unavoidable distress, pain, and disappointment that are sometimes the result of psychological work. Reasonable steps can help minimize those experiences. The standard is often cited in combination with other standards and is seldom charged in isolation.

Standard 3.05, Multiple Relationships

Multiple relationships have represented a significant portion of the ethical violations brought before the APA Ethics Committee, and attempts were made to clarify the risks of exploitation and harm as well as the fact that not all multiple relationships are necessarily harmful. This standard includes a definition of *multiple relationships*, one of the few definitions in the 2002 Ethics Code. This standard has three parts. Standard 3.05(a) defines a multiple relationship, describes when a psychologist should refrain from entering into a multiple relationship, and describes when multiple relationships are not unethical. Standard 3.05(b) speaks to the importance of taking reasonable steps to resolve a potentially harmful multiple relationship. Standard 3.05(c) emphasizes the importance of clarifying roles and confidentiality when psychologists are required by law, institutional policy, or extraordinary circumstances to serve in more than one role in judicial or administrative proceedings. General Principle A: Beneficence and Nonmaleficence is the primary basis for this standard.

Standard 3.05(a)
A multiple relationship occurs when a psychologist is in a professional role with a person and (1) at the same time is in another role with the same

person, (2) at the same time is in a relationship with a person closely associated with or related to the person with whom the psychologist has the professional relationship, or (3) promises to enter into another relationship in the future with the person or a person closely associated with or related to the person.

A psychologist refrains from entering into a multiple relationship if the multiple relationship could reasonably be expected to impair the psychologist's objectivity, competence, or effectiveness in performing his or her functions as a psychologist, or otherwise risks exploitation or harm to the person with whom the professional relationship exists.

Multiple relationships that would not reasonably be expected to cause impairment or risk exploitation or harm are not unethical.

For the first time, the Ethics Code defines a *multiple relationship* in the first paragraph of this standard. This standard provides guidance that psychologists should maintain only one role at a time with a client/patient, student, supervisee, research participant, consultee, or with someone close to or related to the person with whom the psychologist has the professional relationship, unless the psychologist is confident that a secondary role would not interfere with one's objectivity, impair competence, or result in harm or exploitation. In addition, the third point in the first paragraph of this prohibition indicates that psychologists should avoid promising, during the professional relationship, that a social or business relationship will occur after the professional relationship has ended. Implicit promises made through inferential comments may have an equally harmful effect on persons with whom psychologists are working.

The prohibition against harmful multiple relationships is one example in which conflicts of interest may be exploitative of the individuals with whom psychologists work. Thus, the second paragraph of Standard 3.05(a) sets out criteria to help assess whether the multiple relationship is problematic. Usually, the second role is social, financial, or professional if the multiple relationship is prohibited.

Also for the first time, the Ethics Code states clearly in the third paragraph of Standard 3.05(a) that not all multiple relationships are necessarily inappropriate, if they would not "reasonably be expected" to cause impairment or risk exploitation or harm. This is an attempt to acknowledge that not all multiple or dual relationships are problematic, or avoidable, such as in rural communities or small community populations. Psychologists should be mindful that even in large cities multiple relationships can have an uncanny manner of arising. There are situations in which it may not be feasible or reasonable to avoid social or other nonprofessional contacts with clients/patients, students, supervisees, research participants, or consultees, such as in small towns and in close-knit ethnic, religious, gay/lesbian/bisexual, or university communities. However, the emphasis on the term *reasonably* is critical in that a reasonable psychologist must be aware of transference, countertransference, or other clinical contraindicators that would make harm or exploitation foreseeable. What a reasonable psychologist would expect to occur is the test for determining the potential for exploitation or harm. For a violation to be considered, reasonable psychologists must have expected that the multiple relationship would lead somewhere problematic.

Psychologists' self-interests could blind them to the dangers of entering into an inappropriate multiple relationship. One of the most important cornerstones of ethical practice is that psychologists are required to set aside their own needs in the service of addressing their patients' professional needs. Boundaries are designed to minimize the opportunity for psychologists to use their consumers for their own gratification. Psychologists' responsibilities to, needs from, and expectations of a business partner are very different from those with a client/patient, student, supervisee, research participant, or consultee, to whom they have different sets of responsibilities. When one tries to maintain two different roles with a person, the potential for misunderstanding and harm increases because the incompatibility of the complex expectations and needs increase.

In decision making about these boundary issues it is important to be aware of how multiple relationships can be exploitative or cause harm to a person. A multiple relationship can erode and distort the professional nature of the therapeutic relationship. Multiple relationships can create conflicts of interest and compromise the objective basis that is necessary for sound professional judgment. Multiple relationships can also affect the cognitive processes that play a role in the beneficial effects of therapy and that help the patient maintain the benefits of therapy after termination. The power differential often interferes with the ability of clients/patients to enter into another relationship with the psychologist on an equal footing; they often remain vulnerable to exploitation even after termination of therapy. In addition, psychologists have several continuing professional responsibilities after termination, including the responsibility to maintain confidentiality and to realize that many clients/patients need to return to therapy. A good framework for the analysis of nonsexual relationships that would help decision making include the following factors: amount of time that has passed since therapy terminated, the nature and duration of therapy, circumstances of the termination, client's/patient's personal history, client's/patient's mental health status, likely impact of the relationship on the client/patient, and statements made by the therapist suggesting a future relationship. These factors are cited in Standard 10.08, Sexual Intimacies With Former Therapy Clients/Patients, and could lend guidance to decision making in nonsexual relationships also. Consulting with colleagues about the consideration to enter a multiple relationship can be helpful in the decision-making process.

The term *boundary crossings* refers to any activity that moves psychologists away from a strictly neutral position with their clients/patients. The notion of boundaries has evolved as an important strategy to "do no harm," because the needs of the psychologist could potentially obstruct therapy. Some boundary crossings may be subtle and/or helpful to clients/patients; others may reflect a mishandling of transference or countertransference issues. An example of a boundary crossing may include attending the wedding of a client/patient partly because the foci of therapy included clarification that marriage was indeed what the client/patient wished to do. Attending the same church as a person with whom the psychologist has the professional relationship, or shopping in the same grocery store (or other shops) that the person with whom the psychologist has the professional relationship does because they live in the same geographic area are other examples of boundary crossings that may or may not be problematic.

Activities considered to be gray areas in boundary maintenance by many psychologists include hugs with clients, gift giving or receiving, therapist self-disclosure, and extension of therapy beyond the scheduled time. It is often difficult to draw a clear line between subtle, harmless, or even helpful boundary crossings and those that may be problematic. Other issues involved in an analysis of decision making in such subtle areas include knowledge of the power dynamics in the situation and the psychologist's capacity to diagnose and conceptualize the client's needs and issues. Careful documentation of one's rationale and consideration of elements and potential for risk also are helpful strategies in minimizing potential harm. Clearly conceptualizing motivations of integrity, respectfulness, compassion, and trustworthiness can help one be clear about maintaining General Principle A: Beneficence and Nonmaleficence. Ultimately, psychologists' responsibility is to benefit the individuals with whom they work and to take care to do no harm, in this instance by minimizing the opportunity for psychologists to use those individuals for their own gratification and self-interest.

Standard 3.05(b)

If a psychologist finds that, due to unforeseen factors, a potentially harmful multiple relationship has arisen, the psychologist takes reasonable steps to resolve it with due regard for the best interests of the affected person and maximal compliance with the Ethics Code.

On occasion, psychologists may discover that they are involved in a potentially harmful multiple relationship. Multiple relationships arise in unexpected ways, and the APA Ethics Code recognizes that psychologists assume many roles in their work, family, community, and social roles. There are unlimited circumstances in which one may end up in overlapping roles, especially in small towns, rural areas, or small communities. You may discover that a client/patient is also joining community board that you just agreed to join, and that may result in contentious issues, or perhaps you discover that your child and your client's child are on the same baseball team, and your client is an aggressive coach! Perhaps you agreed to attend a special event meaningful to the client but realize that the client's transference issues were more of a problematic issue than you foresaw, and you end up in an uncomfortable position. In any case, Standard 3.05b requires that psychologists take "reasonable steps" to resolve the potential harm that might arise from such relationships. Such steps may include consultation with knowledgeable, objective colleagues. Communication with the person with whom one has the professional relationship about the pitfalls and risks may help prevent harm. Communication about the psychologist's avoidance of or refusal to enter or continue in a multiple relationship can help individuals accept the decision without feeling rejected, diminished, or devalued. Referral to another psychologist may be an option if the individual is unable to understand; however, it may be unwise to make a referral for the sole purpose of proceeding with a social, business, or other relationship.

Standard 3.05(c)

When psychologists are required by law, institutional policy, or extraordinary circumstances to serve in more than one role in judicial or administrative proceedings, at the outset they clarify role expectations and the extent of confidentiality and thereafter as changes occur. (See also Standards 3.04, Avoiding Harm, and 3.07, Third-Party Requests for Services.)

In general, psychologists are expected to avoid entering multiple professional relationships in forensically relevant situations or to resolve such relationships when they unexpectedly occur. In particular, psychologists should avoid mixing treatment and forensic relationships. However, that is not always possible. Standard 3.05(c), Multiple Relationships, recognizes that psychologists are sometimes required to serve in more than one role in judicial or administrative proceedings and so cannot always avoid or fully resolve a potentially harmful multiple relationship. Psychologists may work in small towns where no one else is available to provide treatment for a person the psychologist has evaluated for forensic purposes. A psychologist may provide treatment for someone who becomes involved in the court system and the records of the psychologist are relevant to the court proceeding. The latter situation is probably most common; however, the psychologist must inform the individuals affected about the change in expectations. In particular, the psychologist is expected to clarify that the confidentiality of the therapeutic content and process may be compromised if the client/patient chooses to enter mental health issues in the litigation and/or if the records are requested. In addition, the psychologist should clarify what his or her new role will be. For example, being available to be deposed or to testify in court may or may not serve the client's goals in the litigation, and the psychologist's role as a therapist may be negatively affected.

It is preferable for the treating psychologist to maintain only one role and to recommend that another psychologist be hired to conduct the forensic evaluation and provide the testimony. The Ethics Code envisions dual relationships in a forensic context as happening in extraordinary circumstances; for example, when there is only one psychologist on a hospital unit with the responsibility for conducting forensic assessments and providing treatment, the psychologist may be in the unenviable position of fulfilling both roles.

The general goal of Standard 3.05 is the welfare and protection of the individuals and groups with whom psychologists work. Psychologists' professional status with regard to privileges and power is unique, but in exchange for that status psychologists are expected do no harm and to engage in professional activities in a manner that is beneficial to clients/patients, students, supervisees, research participants, and consultants. Holding and protecting this trust is critical to the success of psychologists' professional work.

Standard 3.05(a)(3), Case 1

Case Illustration. Dr. P. is an amiable fellow who enjoys the occasional wagering game. He plays poker twice monthly with a group of like-minded friends. Dr. P. has a supervisory relationship with a doctoral intern, Mr. C. Over the course of several months, Dr. P. develops a close mentoring relationship with Mr. C, whom he perceives as a particularly promising psychologist in training. In the course of mentoring Mr. C., Dr. P. learns more about him, including the fact that Mr. C. also enjoys playing poker. Dr. P invites Mr. C. to join him at the poker games with his friends. Over time, Dr. P. makes statements suggesting that they have established a personal friendship that will extend beyond the training year. He makes comments suggesting that he has influence with a nearby teaching hospital that has a prestigious postdoctoral program and would be willing to use that influence to help Mr. C. secure a postdoctoral placement there in the future. Mr. C. shares with other interns that he has taken up playing cards with Dr. P., tells them about some of the comments Dr. P. has made about their friendship and his support for the postdoctoral application, and comments that this additional dimension to their relationship "sure can't hurt" his future career prospects. Other interns, who have not been included in the poker games, begin to believe that Dr. P. is unfairly favoring Mr. C. in making case assignments, being available for supervision time, and ultimately in providing feedback about progress to the faculty in their psychology program. Interns hoping to secure placements at the nearby postdoctoral program are particularly upset. The other interns become so upset at the perceived favoritism that they formally complain to both the field placement office in their psychology program and to the director of the clinical site where Dr. P. works.

Ethical Dilemma. Standard 3.05(a)(3) forbids "promises to enter into another relationship in the future with the person or a person closely associated with or related to the person" at the same time the psychologist is in a professional role with that person. Here, Dr. P. is clearly in a professional role with Mr. C. as a site clinical supervisor. He has engaged at the same time in a personal friendship with the intern. Dr. P. is described as making "comments suggesting" that he is willing to use influence to secure a future placement in a prestigious postdoctoral program. Whether those comments rise to the level of a "promise" forbidden by Standard 3.05(a)(3) will depend on what, specifically, was said, but it is notable that both Mr. C. and his fellow interns apparently took those comments as at least an implied promise by Dr. P. to use his purported influence over the postdoctoral application process. Standard 3.05 is not so definitive as to forbid any kind of additional relationship when a psychologist has a professional role with a person. It requires that a psychologist refrain from entering into a multiple relationship if that relationship could "reasonably be expected to impair the psychologist's objectivity, competence, or effectiveness in performing his or her functions as a psychologist, or otherwise risks exploitation or harm to the person with whom the professional relationship exists." How far a relationship with a trainee can evolve before the individual attention that is often part of an appropriate and effective mentoring relationship becomes a potentially problematic personal relationship is precisely what is at issue here.

Decision-Making Factors. This situation in which Dr. P. now finds himself is a reminder that it is often third parties who become upset when multiple relationships are established between a psychologist and a student or supervisee. Even if Dr. P. can establish that his objectivity and competence regarding the supervision of Mr. C. remain intact, clearly his effectiveness as a site supervisor for Mr. C. and the other interns has been compromised. This compromise of professional effectiveness is particularly likely to occur when, as in this situation, third parties come to perceive that the special relationship the psychologist has with an individual results in favoritism at a cost to themselves. Even when decisions made by the psychologist do not actually arise from favoritism, it is extremely difficult to combat the perception of favoritism once it has been established and in particular when there is a reasonable basis to believe that one person has been given special access or has a special relationship with the psychologist. It is also possible that Dr. P.'s indication that he would use special influence to favor Mr. C.'s application to the prestigious postdoctoral program might result in harm to Mr. C.

First, persons in the program may learn of this offer or be offended by Dr. P.'s efforts to secure a placement for Mr. C. and feel the need to review

Mr. C.'s application to the postdoctoral program more closely than they would have otherwise, to preserve the integrity and reputation of the admissions process. Second, interns who come to resent Mr. C. and to view him as willing to exploit personal friendships with a senior psychologist at their own expense may withdraw the peer support on which many students rely during doctoral training—or, worse, communicate with others in a way that damages Mr. C.'s emerging professional reputation. In addition, although all is currently going well in the personal friendship between Dr. P. and Mr. C., a situation might arise within the friendship that sours that relationship, and Mr. C. may come to perceive actions or decisions by Dr. P. as being driven by the circumstances in their friendship rather than strictly from their professional relationship. For example, should the friendship sour, Dr. P. may decline to support Mr. C.'s application to the postdoctoral program, raising the question of whether this decision is driven strictly on the basis of reasonable professional judgment of Mr. C.'s competence or whether Dr. P.'s objectivity and effectiveness have been impaired because of the friction within their personal friendship.

Decision Options. Dr. P. already finds himself facing resentment by students and complaints to the field placement office and the director of the clinical site where he is employed. His social relationship with Mr. C. has already compromised his capacity to function optimally as a supervisor with other students and may pose some risks to Mr. C.' s peer support network and emerging reputation as a professional among his peers. Consistent with Standard 3.04, Avoiding Harm, Dr. P. is obligated to takes steps to minimize any harm that may have already occurred and to forestall any that has not yet occurred. Dr. P. could do so by having a conversation with Mr. C. in which he acknowledges the difficult situation that his invitation to join a social activity at the exclusion of other students has caused both of them. He could clarify with Mr. C. the professional nature of their relationship, acknowledge that, as the more senior professional and supervisor, he "should have known better" and indicate that the poker game would not include Mr. C. from that point on. He might also advise Mr. C. that he would be offering to meet with the aggrieved students to acknowledge the difficult circumstances and his contribution to the situation. He will also arrange a meeting with the field placement office and his own clinical director to address the situation. Depending on the depth of the resentment that has emerged, he might also consider offering to transfer supervision of the students, including Mr. C., to another supervising psychologist. In addition to considering the degree of resentment that has been created, Dr. P. might discuss with the field placement office and his clinical director whether doing so would, on balance, be best for the students or inadvertently disadvantage them (e.g., the supervisor might not be able to write strong letters of recommendation if the period of supervision was not very long). If Dr. P. remains in a position in which he might be asked to write letters of recommendation for Mr. C. or any other of the supervisees, he might offer to have those letters independently reviewed by the clinical director as a safeguard for objectivity before they are mailed.

Standard 3.05(c), Case 1

Case Illustration. Dr. S. began treatment with Mr. A. after an industrial accident in which Mr. A. sustained a disfiguring injury. Dr. S. understood that the impetus for Mr. A. beginning therapy was the traumatic experience of his accident; however, as the therapy progressed, Mr. A. began to present personal concerns both contemporary and across life experiences. During the course of treatment, Dr S. learned of a history of sexual victimization suffered by Mr. A. during childhood. Dr. S. and Mr. A. began to talk about Mr. A.'s childhood experiences during the sessions. Dr. S. understood that Mr. A. did want to work on his ability to adjust to the effects of his injury, but they both agreed that these earlier experiences were also of importance.

Unknown to Dr. S., Mr. A. had started treatment at the suggestion of an attorney he had retained to represent him in a lawsuit against the manufacturer of the machinery he had been operating at the time. Dr. S. was under the impression that Mr. A. had begun therapy of his own accord, and nothing in the course of the therapy sessions led Dr. S. to think that there was a forensic component to the therapy. Furthermore, no contact was made by the attorney to Dr. S. requesting any evaluation, course of treatment, or other information that would be gathered in a workplace lawsuit of this nature. After 6 months of treatment with Mr. A., Dr. S. received a notice indicating that she would be deposed by Mr. A.'s attorney with the expectation that she would testify that Mr. A.'s anxiety and mood symptoms were caused by the industrial accident. Dr. S. was dumbfounded about the notice and the expectation for testimony. Even though Mr. A.'s emotional experiences had certainly been discussed, Dr. S. had not evaluated Mr. A.'s emotional state as a focus for therapy or as effects from the accident. Dr. S. felt manipulated and backed into a corner, because neither her client nor his representative had informed her of their expectation of court testimony. Even if Dr. S. would have considered taking the case as a forensic case, she had not conducted assessment and treatment planning in this case for that purpose.

Ethical Dilemma. Dr. S. has been in the role of a treating professional with Mr. A. for the duration of Mr. A.'s therapy. Dr. S. does do forensic work and provides testimony in custody, disability, fitness, and other cases in which she has conducted an evaluation and renders an opinion based on the evaluation. In this case, however, Dr. S. served in a treating role and therefore did not engage in the professional services that she would have had the case been one in which she would be an expert witness. Dr. S. also thinks that, as a treating therapist, she would not have had the objectivity to evaluate Mr. A. after working with him in a therapeutic role. Dr. S. not only is concerned about the conflict of interest created by a multiple role but also realizes that Mr. A.'s many symptoms that are being attributed to the accident are not documented as being of recent onset. This testimony seems to be the centerpiece for any subpoena, and she is well aware of the expectations for forensic testimony.

Even though Dr. S. could make a determination on whether the accident exacerbated Mr. A.'s mood state, without documentation of Mr. A.'s mood patterns and health history prior to the accident she cannot attribute the cause of his mood effects to the accident. A further complication is that the attorney presumably does not know of the abuse history, but opposing counsel may either know about the abuse or ask questions that would lead to Dr. S. either disclosing such knowledge or refusing the disclosure to the court.

Dr. S. realizes that several ethical standards may apply in this situation. Standard 3.05(c), Multiple Relationships, reflects the consensus that ordinarily a psychologist should not be in both a forensic and another professional role with an individual. However, when psychologists find themselves "required by law, institutional policy, or extraordinary circumstances" in a multiple role in "judicial or administrative proceedings, at the outset they clarify role expectations and the extent of confidentiality and thereafter as changes occur." Standard 3.06, Conflict of Interest, instructs psychologists to "refrain from taking on a professional role when . . . professional . . . or other interests or relationships could reasonably be expected to (1) impair their objectivity or . . . effectiveness or . . . (2) expose the person . . . with whom the professional relationship exists to harm or exploitation." Dr. S. may also apply Standard 3.04, Avoiding Harm, which states that "psychologists take reasonable steps to avoid harming their clients/patients" and General Principle A: Beneficence and Nonmaleficence supports psychologists in benefiting those with whom they work and doing no harm.

Decision-Making Factors. Note that Standard 3.05(c) may not yet apply in this case, because Dr. S has not been asked to serve in more than one role through a requirement of "law, institutional policy, or extraordinary circumstances." There is the possibility that Dr. S. will be ordered to do so by the court, but there appears to be no reason that an independent expert cannot be obtained to assess Mr. A. and testify as a forensic expert. For that same reason, this does not appear to be a situation that would constitute "extraordinary circumstances" for her serving in these two roles. However, there is no reason that Dr. S. may not testify as the treating psychologist as long as she is testifying to her services and appropriately limits her testimony to her treatment services. As soon as she is asked to testify to a forensic opinion that goes beyond the scope of treatment role (including an opinion that the industrial accident "caused" the symptoms with which Mr. A. presents), she should carefully consider her response to ensure that it does not extend beyond her role as a treating clinician. For example, it is highly unlikely that she can reliably assert that the industrial accident caused Mr. A.'s symptoms without extensive interviews of collaterals (e.g., family members, coworkers), a detailed review of documents, and independent verification of relevant history and self-report that is ordinarily beyond the activities of a treating clinician.

Should the attorney press Dr. S. to offer an opinion that the industrial accident caused Mr. A.'s distress, she may well find herself in the position of "expert by ambush," because she did not know that Mr. A. had been referred for treatment by his attorney or even that Mr. A. was considering filing a lawsuit. Once the attorney presses for a forensic opinion that pushes Dr. S. beyond her clinical role, Standard 3.05 may be implicated. There may also be other issues that arise should Dr. S. become involved in this legal case. For example, she has now been served with a notice for deposition from Mr. A.'s attorney. Ordinarily, testimonial privilege is waived when the attorney for a patient or client seeks to depose a psychologist on behalf of that patient or client. Also, once a plaintiff in a civil lawsuit puts his or her own mental functioning at issue, the latitude allowed opposing attorneys to inquire about history or functioning of the plaintiff is ordinarily extremely broad. For example, in this case it is highly likely that Mr. A.'s history of sexual abuse during adolescence would be reached through deposition of Dr. S. by opposing counsel.

Decision Options. How should Dr. S. proceed? First, she should make clear to Mr. A. and his attorney prior to the deposition that she has not conducted a forensic evaluation and will not be able to render an opinion that the industrial accident proximately caused Mr. A.'s psychological distress. She should explain to Mr. A. that, on the basis of the history she has obtained from him, she believes that at least some of his psychological distress arises from his history of sexual victimization and predates the industrial accident and that she would have to disclose this clinical opinion if asked for a clinical formulation.

Second, Dr. S. should work with Mr. A. and his attorney to clarify whether her participation in the legal proceedings will result in changes in what Mr. A. can expect regarding the confidentiality of his treatment. For example, deposition of Dr. S. by Mr. A.'s attorney may well constitute a waiver of Mr. A.'s psychotherapist privilege, resulting in the deposition of Dr. S. and Mr. A. by opposing counsel, turning over the treatment records to opposing counsel, or even compelled examination of Mr. A. by an expert retained by opposing counsel. Many persons who consider lawsuits are unaware of the extent to which their privacy can be compromised once the proceedings are begun, and Dr. S. should make sure that Mr. A. is making decisions with full and accurate information about involving his treatment relationship in the litigation.

Finally, consistent with her treatment relationship, or to the extent that Standard 3.05(c) becomes applicable with its requirement that psychologists "clarify role expectations," Dr. S. should have a clinical discussion with Mr. A. about the impact her involvement in the litigation would have on their treatment relationship. This is particularly important because it seems that Dr. S. will not be willing to blur her treatment role by offering forensic opinions on the proximate cause of his symptoms, and she cannot even offer a clinical opinion that his psychological distress arises solely from the industrial accident. Any resentment or disappointment on his part that she cannot play the role he had anticipated in the lawsuit should be directly addressed as part of clarifying her role going forward.

Standard 3.06, Conflict of Interest

Psychologists refrain from taking on a professional role when personal, scientific, professional, legal, financial, or other interests or relationships could reasonably be expected to (1) impair their objectivity, competence, or effectiveness in performing their functions as psychologists or (2) expose the person or organization with whom the professional relationship exists to harm or exploitation.

This standard requires that psychologists avoid taking on any number of professional situations or responsibilities for which other relationships could be harmful or exploitative. If there is a reasonable likelihood that other interests or relationships could detract from impartiality, proficiency, or competency, or if doing so would expose that person or organization to harm, mistreatment, or exploitation, then the professional relationship should be avoided. Trust is an important aspect of the professional relationship. Psychologists risk violation of that trust if they take on professional roles in circumstances under which competing professional, personal, financial, legal, or other interests or relationships could reasonably be expected to impair objectivity, competence, or ability to effectively perform this role.

Standard 3.06 also prohibits psychologists from taking on a role that would expose a person or organization with which a psychologist already works to harm or exploitation. Although this standard does not require that psychologists reject the added role in all circumstances, great caution is recommended. It is ultimately the psychologist's responsibility to make the often-complicated decisions that must be faced with due regard for the requirements of this standard and the Ethics Code.

This standard thus warns psychologists to avoid taking on responsibilities for which either previous, current, or future relationships could be harmful or exploitative. The same moral principles that underlie the cautions in Standard 3.05 apply here as well.

Standard 3.06, Case 1

Case Illustration. Dr. V. is a clinical psychologist who provides assessment and treatment services to children and adolescents within a department of psychiatry in an academic teaching hospital. Dr. V.'s work is largely done with youth with a specific diagnosis, and he works closely with psychiatrists on a team specializing in assessment and treatment of youth with that diagnosis. Dr. V. is aware that several of the psychiatrists have received large research grants from a pharmaceutical manufacturer over several years to conduct clinical trials with medications to treat this diagnosis, some of which have already been extensively marketed globally. Although Dr. V. receives no direct financial support from the pharmaceutical company, he is aware that his position as a psychologist is supported because of the large case flow of youth presenting with the diagnosis, which is due in part to the funded research program's reputation for excellence. He appreciates that his assessment and treatment approaches over the years have been shaped, at least in part, by the clinical presentations of clients/patients involved in the medication trials, and he generally believes that the medications used in the research trials are very helpful to his clients/patients.

Dr. V. is invited to a conference at a major medical school in another state to present a day-long workshop on assessment and treatment approaches for this diagnosis. Dr. V. will have his travel expenses covered and will be given a substantial honorarium for his workshop. He is provided a form on which to disclose whether he has a financial or other commercial interest in any medication or product that will be mentioned in his presentation. The form is clearly intended for physicians who may be receiving research support or other compensation by manufacturers of medications and medical devices and does not ask for disclosure of any indirect financial interests or support.

Ethical Dilemma. On the one hand, Dr V. has a great deal of experience in the assessment and treatment of children and adolescents with this diagnosis and presumably a great deal to offer participants in a lengthy workshop on this topic. He does not receive direct financial support in the form of fees or research grant support from commercial enterprises interested in the development of medications for the treatment of persons with this diagnosis.

On the other hand, Dr. V. provides professional services in an organizational environment whose involvement with medication research and development has shaped his approaches to assessment and treatment. Although he has no direct financial interest in the development of the medications, his position is supported indirectly by funds provided for medication research (as part of the department's general operating budget) and by the case flow of youth with this diagnosis who are referred because of the fine reputation for clinical care services provided youth with this diagnosis, at least in part because of the academic affiliation with a prestigious medical school and reputation for involvement in cutting-edge research.

Decision-Making Factors. Standard 3.06 obligates psychologists to "refrain from taking on a professional role when personal, scientific, professional, legal, financial, or other interests or relationships" might "impair their objectivity, competence, or effectiveness" when acting as psychologists or might "expose the person or organization with whom the professional relationship exists to harm or exploitation."

Dr. V. will have to determine whether his indirect financial interests arising from the funding of medication research within the Department of Psychiatry potentially constitute a conflict of interest that could impair his "objectivity, competence, or effectiveness" when teaching about the assessment and treatment of youth with this diagnosis, or "expose" either his department or the medical school offering him the invitation to present a lengthy workshop to "harm or exploitation." In addition, he may have to consider whether his long-standing professional and/or personal relationships with his colleagues in the Department of Psychiatry may have had an undue influence on his "objectivity, competence, or effectiveness" in presenting on the topic.

A strict reading of this ethical standard instructs the psychologist to refrain from taking on a professional role if there is a sufficient impact from a conflict of interest; note that it does not include a provision for a psychologist to proceed because the potential conflict of interest has been disclosed or even if the person or organization involved agrees to assume the risk of potential harm or exploitation.

Decision Options. Dr. V. is presented the challenge of judging whether he has interests or relationships that may impair his "objectivity, competence, or effectiveness" precisely at a time when his objectivity in doing so may be in question. For example, Dr. V.'s immersion in the activities of the Department of Psychiatry, including his personal and professional relationships with colleagues who do have more direct financial interests in funded medication trial research, may have substantially shaped his experiences in assessment and treatment of youth with this diagnosis. Dr. V. may not be in a good position to objectively determine how deeply he has been influenced by the organizational culture and activities that have evolved around the medication trials, much like physicians who receive gratuities, incentives, or perquisites from drug company representatives may not be entirely aware of how much these shape their prescription practices. In particular, because he has concluded that his clients/patients have generally benefited from medications that have been subjected to clinical trials through his department, Dr. V. may have been influenced in the weight that he assigns to the role of medication treatment for this diagnosis.

Dr. V. secures an ethics consultation that includes a detailed discussion of the evolution of his clinical perspectives on the assessment and treatment of youth with this diagnosis within the culture of his research-oriented department of psychiatry as well as his understanding of how his clinical perspectives may have been shaped by his years of clinical practice within that department.

After this ethics consultation, Dr. V. feels that he can present a fair and balanced workshop in an objective manner. However, to avoid potentially undermining his effectiveness as a workshop presenter on this specific topic, he decides to take steps to minimize the perception of lack of objectivity due to undisclosed real or perceived conflicts of interest; specifically, Dr. V. decides that he would disclose to the medical school officials who had invited him to present a workshop his indirect financial interests in the department's funded medication research and the potential impact of his personal and professional relationships with department colleagues who had made their professional reputations conducting medication trials. He decides that he would do this even though the disclosure form he was sent would have allowed him to avoid making these disclosures on the form itself.

Dr. V. also decides that if the medical school nonetheless offers him the invitation to present, he will begin his workshop with a disclosure to participants of his indirect financial interests and potential impact of his relationships with his colleagues on workshop content.

Standard 3.07, Third-Party Requests for Services

When psychologists agree to provide services to a person or entity at the request of a third party, psychologists attempt to clarify at the outset of the service the nature of the relationship with all individuals or organizations involved. This clarification includes the role of the psychologist (e.g., therapist, consultant, diagnostician, or expert witness), an identification of who is the client, the probable uses of the services provided or the information obtained, and the fact that there may be limits to confidentiality. (See also Standards 3.05, Multiple Relationships, and 4.02, Discussing the Limits of Confidentiality.)

At times, a third party—who may be a parent, teacher, court, employer, human resources office, training institution, referral source, or commanding officer—requests a psychological procedure. At those times it is vital that both the third-party requester, as well as the person receiving the services, receive clarification of the psychologist's roles ahead of time. In addition, the language in this version of the standards includes "an identification of who is the client." Clarifying the client's identity is essential. Problems can arise if one or more persons believe incorrectly that they are the psychologist's client (e.g., collateral contacts: employer, organization, family, school psychologist, family member). Not having identified the client, and perhaps not knowing exactly who the client is, can cause significant complications for all of the parties involved, including, and especially, the psychologist.

The term *client* sometimes refers to persons or organizations other than the person who is the direct subject of services. For example, when an attorney hires a psychologist to examine a defendant, the attorney is most often referred to as the "client," and the defendant is a recipient of services. The attorney is the one who presents the questions to be answered and who can authorize, direct, and terminate the professional relationship, including the handling of the work product or any confidentiality matters. Standards such as 3.04, Avoiding Harm, recognize this by using phrases such as "others with whom [psychologists] work" in addition to referring to "clients." In treatment of legal minors, the client is the child, in part because of insurance procedures, even though it is the parents who authorize treatment. Where one or more persons are to be identified as clients, that information must be clarified to all the parties; in addition, the psychologist's role in relation to all parties must be clarified.

Psychologists also must be clear about who controls the release of a report or who may receive other confidential information. Thus, Standard 3.07 requires that psychologists clarify at the outset of the service who their client is and the possible use of the information generated by the procedures, which requires careful thought. Who the client is drives the ethical and legal analysis. Communication of this information to the key parties involved can help minimize the likelihood that problems will arise later that interfere with the efficient and effective provision of psychological services.

Whether and how privacy and confidentiality will apply, including who will receive information, is important. Psychologists should also be aware that provisions of state and federal law may speak to these concerns, and they should be aware of how these legal provisions affect their practices. Although this standard does not require it, it is helpful to have a written release in order to clarify with clients the nature of the information to be released and the purpose of its release, and to document the authorization. It is often helpful to obtain written releases as circumstances warrant. A written authorization to release information can be helpful in clarifying the nature, extent, duration, and purpose of the information that is to be released or exchanged.

Standard 3.07 requires that psychologists explain to all parties involved, including the third party and the recipient of services, the nature of the relationship that the psychologist will have with all individuals and/or organizations involved. This explanation includes information about the role of the psychologist, who is receiving the services, who will receive information about the services, and how the use of information will be used.

Standard 3.07, Case 1

Case Illustration. Dr. B. is a licensed psychologist who performs contract testing and evaluation for the Department of Family and Child Services (DFACS). Dr. B. typically spends 1 day a week at DFACS, testing. She conducts evaluations for DFACS related to placement or decisions to be made, such as fitness to parent, foster placement, placement in rehabilitation groups (e.g., substance abuse), and back-to-work assessment. When Dr. B. is doing assessments at DFACS, she is evaluating people for different purposes.

During Ms. N.'s initial interview at DFACS, the caseworker tells her that DFACS conducted counseling groups, individual counseling, career exploration, and addiction counseling. Ms. N. knows that she has been negligent in taking care of her children, and she sees some of these services as being helpful for her to learn better parenting. Ms. N. is very interested in taking advantage of these opportunities, and when Dr. B. contacts her to set up an evaluation appointment Ms. N. thinks she is going to be assessed for counseling to learn how to interview for a job and to get help for her substance abuse, because these are the services she told the caseworker she would like to pursue. When Ms. N. comes in for the evaluation, Dr. B. gives her a uniform informed consent to sign and tells her that she works for DFACS and that anything Ms. N. tells her will not be confidential but could very well be referenced in the report. She tells every examinee the same thing. DFACS had asked Dr. B. to evaluate Ms. N. for fitness to parent and for her ability to function independently. In addition, Dr. B. was asked to evaluate Ms. N. for the purpose of determining whether her children should be placed in foster care as a result of her substance abuse, charges of neglect, and her inability to parent.

When Dr. B. completes the report and submits it to DFACS, she recommends foster care for the children at least for the current time, until Ms. N can receive rehabilitation. When Ms. N. finds out, she is furious and upset. She says that no one had told her that fitness for parenting was the purpose of the evaluation and that, had she known, she would not have cooperated. She blames Dr. B. for not being honest and forthcoming with her and threatens to make a complaint to the licensing board.

Ethical Dilemma. Dr. B. had very likely gotten into a pattern of consultation with DFACS in which she saw herself as conducting assessments and acquiring the requisite informed consent but had assumed that DFACS prepared the individuals for evaluations or other services they would receive with appropriate information. Dr. B. realizes that she may have violated Standard 3.07, Third-Party Requests for Services. Dr. B. understands that she is a contract psychologist for DFACS and thinks that she had explained her role adequately. Standard 3.07 instructs psychologists to clarify their roles to all individuals with whom they work. The clarification should include the role of the psychologist, which Dr. B. did in explaining that she would be conducting an evaluation. She had also informed Ms. N. that her client was DFACS and that confidentiality would be limited and that, in fact, several people on the staff would have access to her report. In thinking through Standard 3.07, Dr. B. realizes that she did not make explicit the fact that the probable use of the services and information provided would be for fitness to parent and could also have implications for custody of Ms. N.'s children, at least at this point. In compliance with Standard 3.07, psychologists "clarify at the outset of the service the nature of the relationship with all individuals or organizations involved." Dr. B. did explain the nature of her relation with DFACS and with Ms. N. in explaining that she would be evaluating her; however, in this case the probable use of the information was a key element not only in accurate explanation of the third-party request expectation but also in appropriate informed consent (Standard 3.10[c], Informed Consent, and Standard 9.03[a], Informed Consent for Assessment). Ms. N. very likely had been mandated for testing because the welfare of a child is involved; however, in a mandated-evaluation context psychologists still must inform the individual of the nature and purpose of the evaluation.

Decision-Making Factors. Dr. B. thinks back through the procedures she and DFACS had set up when she first became a consultant. Because of the volume of individuals to be tested, the decision had been made for Dr. B. to do the essentials of testing administration and the standard DFACS informed consent. Each client has a caseworker who conducts an interview, assesses the needs of the client, and determines the action to be taken in light of the responsibilities DFACS had to the state. Many of the clients at DFACS are mandated for services, including for evaluation. DFACS has an established protocol for informed consent and for communicating with mandated clients in legally required ways. Dr. B. begins to see that she had made assumptions about DFACS's preparation of clients and the level of informed consent, at least in regard to the clients she would be evaluating. Dr. B. considers that when other consulting professionals such as herself are working with DFACS clients, assumptions may have been made that she and other consultants were including the informed consent and third-party request information instead of it being acquired by the DFACS intake caseworker.

Dr. B. knows that she understands the intent of Standard 3.07 and that she had every intention of conducting her services ethically and professionally, but she had failed to ensure that all of the elements of the standard were properly enacted. Had this case occurred in her private practice, or in an agency setting in which the examinee was her client, she would have conducted all informed consent, an explanation of purpose, and an explanation of use of services herself. Because she was in a consulting role, she had not taken responsibility for communicating the essential elements of the services to the examinees and had deferred to DFACS. Dr. B. also realizes that DFACS had not attempted to influence her in any way regarding the degree of thoroughness or inclusiveness of her explanation of services to the clients; instead, she had made assumptions that proved to be a major contributor to the current dilemma.

Decision Options. Dr. B. thinks about her options as involving three areas of decision making: (a) how she would follow up with DFACS both regarding this case and future cases, (b) how she would engage with Ms. N. and her complaint, and (c) how she would change her consulting practice as a result of this experience. Dr. B. first contacts the administrator with whom she worked at DFACS and discusses the role of DFACS, her role, and the court's role, when applicable, in any evaluation case. She explains the ethical dilemma that has arisen because of the failure to communicate essential information between DFACS and herself. She makes clear that if she is to continue doing evaluations for DFACS there needs to be transparency and full informational disclosure between herself and DFACS in all future cases and that a protocol must be developed through which she would know what DFACS had told the clients, both voluntary and mandated, about the services they would receive. She also explains to DFACS that she will be giving a full informed consent and an explanation of the purpose and use of information gleaned from her evaluations even if DFACS includes that step in their informed consent.

Dr. B. develops her own procedural approach to future consulting work and includes specific steps that she follows when providing services for a third party. She realizes that it had been just a matter of time before she encountered this current dilemma, given that she had not worked through the important differential role responsibilities inherent in a third-party request for services.

Dr. B. thinks about whether and how to contact Ms. N. She discusses with the caseworker how to proceed and realizes that her decision for foster care of the children will likely be followed by the court regardless of whether the case had been mandated. She does not have doubts about her recommendation and therefore thinks it would be inadvisable to retract her clinical decision, because the welfare of the children is at stake. She remains very remorseful that her handling of the communication with Ms. N. would likely raise Ms. N.'s suspicion about working with child and family services and that she may well feel exploited. Dr. B. hopes that Ms. N. will remain in services at DFACS and make progress in her struggle with substance abuse and parenting skills so that a custody decision can be made in which the welfare of the children could be assured.

Standard 3.08, Exploitative Relationships

Psychologists do not exploit persons over whom they have supervisory, evaluative, or other authority such as clients/patients, students, supervisees, research participants, and employees. (See also Standards 3.05, Multiple Relationships; 6.04, Fees and Financial Arrangements; 6.05, Barter

with Clients/Patients; 7.07, Sexual Relationships With Students and Supervisees; 10.05, Sexual Intimacies With Current Therapy Clients/Patients; 10.06, Sexual Intimacies With Relatives or Significant Others of Current Therapy Clients/Patients; 10.07, Therapy With Former Sexual Partners; and 10.08, Sexual Intimacies With Former Therapy Clients/Patients.)

This standard is straightforward in prohibiting the exploitation of persons with whom psychologists work. There are various types of exploitative relationships. Exploitation may be sexual, financial, political, or of many other types. Some forms of exploitation, such as sexual relationships or extortion with clients/patients, students, supervisees, research participants, and employees, are clearly forbidden by this and other standards. Other actions that a psychologist may take are less clear. Exploitation may be seen as creating a differential in position such that the capacity of one individual to say no or to assert one's own needs and interests is compromised and the other individual then takes advantage of that compromise for his or her own purposes. Psychologists are to avoid taking unfair advantage of their ability to manipulate situations and people over whom they have authority for their own self-interests and needs.

Virtually all of the general principles underlie this standard. General Principle A: Beneficence and Nonmaleficence urges psychologists to strive to benefit those with whom they work and to take care to do no harm. General Principle B: Fidelity and Responsibility speaks of the importance of establishing trust with those with whom they work. General Principle C: Integrity encourages psychologists to seek to promote accuracy, honesty, and truthfulness and to avoid fraud, subterfuge, or intentional misrepresentation of fact and to strive to keep their promises. General Principle D: Justice encourages fairness, and General Principle E: Respect for People's Rights and Dignity encourages psychologists to safeguard the rights and welfare of persons. Maintaining awareness of the values of these principles can help inform one's actions.

More subtle forms of exploitation may occur in addition to obvious types of exploitation; these may include burdening persons with requests that they feel unable to keep and that go beyond their appropriate responsibilities. For example, asking a graduate student or employee to house-sit or run personal errands on a regular basis and without fair financial compensation may be exploiting him or her. Even though the people over whom psychologists may have power or authority (e.g., clients/patients, students, supervisees, research participants, consultees, and employees) may be very willing to provide more than a contract requires, psychologists are not entitled to that.

The perception of exploitation may be in the eye of the beholder. For example, a psychologist may hire a newly graduated psychologist at an hourly rate to provide services and to provide supervision for postdoctoral trainees. After a few months, the new psychologist may perceive and complain that the hourly rate is unfairly less than the profit that a supervising psychologist should receive for the services. If a complaint is made, it is the reviewing body that judges, on the basis of evidence, whether exploitation in an objective sense has occurred, regardless of whether it has been subjectively experienced by the complainant. The individual's subjective experience should not be taken as the sole determinant of exploitation; there is also an objective aspect.

Standard 3.09, Cooperation With Other Professionals
When indicated and professionally appropriate, psychologists cooperate with other professionals in order to serve their clients/patients effectively and appropriately. (See also Standard 4.05, Disclosures.)

Cooperating with other professionals speaks to a goal fundamental to psychology: to promote the welfare and protection of the individuals and groups with whom psychologists work, a value voiced in the Preamble of the APA Ethics Code. This standard focuses the concern on psychologists' clients/patients, not the concerns of the "other professionals." Psychologists typically collaborate with physicians, psychiatrists, and other health professionals with whom the client/patient works in order to enhance the benefit of services. Working effectively in schools, courtrooms, jails, hospitals, mental health settings, law enforcement, and the military often entails cooperating with other professionals. In addition, psychologists should cooperate and provide information to health care professionals, if a client/patient provides consent. Cooperation will often include conveying, disclosing, or receiving information. Psychologists should be aware of whether consent is required for a particular disclosure. When cooperating entails the sharing of information, psychologists should attend to the basis on which information is conveyed, which will often, but not always, be consent.

This ethical standard recognizes those situations in which other professionals may make requests that may not be appropriate or in the best interest of the client/patient. In addition, when information is provided, to be overly disclosing can reveal information that unnecessarily exposes the consumer of our services. Examples of inappropriate requests include someone asking for data that a research psychologist is not free to provide, trying to obtain agreement to a course of treatment that the referring psychologist views negatively, or a request by another professional who may just want to acquire privileged information from the psychologist. Standard 4.04, Minimizing Intrusions on

Privacy, reminds psychologists that, when cooperating with others, they are almost certainly sharing information but that they should be aware that only information pertinent to the particular circumstances in question should be shared.

Cooperating with other professionals may involve either obtaining or providing records of a person's previous treatment. In some instances, it may be helpful to the treatment for psychologists to do so. Cooperation with others does not just imply other mental health professionals, or even physical health professionals, but includes professionals in the broadening scope of psychologists' practice today.

Standard 3.10, Informed Consent

In the context of attention to human relations, the notion of informed consent provides a key to understanding the requirement of informed consent in other standards. *Informed consent* is an effort to ensure that the trust required from the individuals with whom psychologists work is truly justified, that the power of the therapist is not abused, and that the caring of the therapist is expressed in ways that are understood and to which are agreed. The right to informed consent reflects respect for individual freedom, autonomy, and dignity, and it is fundamental to relationships between psychologists and the individuals with whom they work. In essence, informed consent is the result of a process of reaching agreement to work collaboratively. It provides an opportunity to be sure that all parties involved adequately understand the shared venture, and it allows for communication and clarification. It is a recurrent process, and it must be repeated to clarify or renegotiate aspects of the process. This standard is written in four parts, and the obligations described in this standard apply to other consent-related standards (Standard 8.02, Informed Consent to Research; Standard 9.03, Informed Consent in Assessments; and Standard 10.01, Informed Consent to Therapy).

Standard 3.10(a)

When psychologists conduct research or provide assessment, therapy, counseling, or consulting services in person or via electronic transmission or other forms of communication, they obtain the informed consent of the individual or individuals using language that is reasonably understandable to that person or persons except when conducting such activities without consent is mandated by law or governmental regulation or as otherwise provided in this Ethics Code. (See also Standards 8.02, Informed Consent to Research; 9.03, Informed Consent in Assessments; and 10.01, Informed Consent to Therapy.)

The 2002 Ethics Code broadened the informed-consent requirement from research and therapy to research and most psychological services. Informed consent must be obtained for research participants, clients/patients, and organizational consultees, for example. As noted in the excerpt from the Ethics Code just given, specific elements of informed consent for specific areas of psychology are listed in other standards. This requirement may not apply to interventions mandated by law or governmental regulation or to other exceptions provided by the Ethics Code (e.g., when dealing with persons legally incapable of giving consent [Standard 3.10b], when to discuss confidentiality if not feasible or contraindicated at the onset [Standard 4.02b]). The requirement to obtain consent that is informed and understood by the client/patient, consultee, or research participant is a cornerstone of the trust inherent in the professional relationship. This standard is based primarily on the General Principle B: Fidelity and Responsibility and General Principle E: Respect for People's Rights and Dignity. Fidelity involves questions of faithfulness, loyalty, and promise keeping, all issues that are basic to trust. Fidelity is vital to all human relationships, and the professional relationships in which psychologists engage depend on honest communication and the assumption that the contract on which the relationship was initiated obliges both parties to fulfill certain functions. Psychologists also must respect the dignity and worth of all people and the rights of individuals to privacy, confidentiality, and self-determination to choose one's own course of action. The notion that consumers of services must consent to treatment and be informed of its implications stems in part from this value of respect for people's rights and dignity.

Although not specifically detailed in this standard, there are common expectations as to what constitutes appropriate informed consent, some of which are required in the standards that apply informed consent to research, assessment, and therapy. For example, the person who provides informed consent to the psychologist must *have the capacity to do so*, must have *received information relevant to the decision*, be *aware of the voluntary nature* of the participation, have *been given the opportunity to ask questions* about the processes and procedures, and *be able to exercise a voluntary choice*. The nature of the communication may vary according to the person's capacity, sophistication, and needs. The responsibilities include that psychologists convey to the individuals with whom they work, in clear language, what they can expect before beginning as well as throughout the work. In this way, respect for the rights and dignity of those people can be applied more broadly.

This standard also acknowledges that informed consent must be obtained whether the services are provided face to face or by means of the Internet, videoconference, or some other form of electronic communication. When using electronic forms of communication it is prudent for psychologists to take steps to ensure that the person who gave consent is in fact the one receiving the psychologist's services or participating in the research; this could be done, for example, through the use of a password. If services are provided through electronic communication, then possible limits of confidentiality must be included in the information to the individual or groups.

A basic premise of this standard is that psychologists should trust the ability of the persons from whom they are to obtain informed consent to decide what would be helpful to them, including their full and active participation in treatment decisions in a collaborative manner. Informed-consent forms, which often include basic information about billing policies, scheduling appointments, policy on cancellations, and common exceptions to confidentiality, may be helpful. Forms should supplement, not replace, the communication between psychologist and client/patient. In particular, clients/patients should have the opportunity to talk about their expectations, needs, and concerns about the procedures. They also should be allowed the opportunities to ask questions throughout the process. Standard 3.10(d), Informed Consent, is one of the standards within the Ethics Code that specifically requires appropriate documentation, either written or oral, for informed consent. Many state and federal laws require that informed consent be placed in writing. Psychologists would behoove themselves to be aware of these various laws. The process of informed consent is an ongoing method of communication and clarification.

Standard 3.10(b)

For persons who are legally incapable of giving informed consent, psychologists nevertheless (1) provide an appropriate explanation, (2) seek the individual's assent, (3) consider such persons' preferences and best interests, and (4) obtain appropriate permission from a legally authorized person, if such substitute consent is permitted or required by law. When consent by a legally authorized person is not permitted or required by law, psychologists take reasonable steps to protect the individual's rights and welfare.

Psychologists sometimes provide services to or conduct research with individuals who cannot legally give consent, such as children, adults who have been declared legally incompetent, or those who are not mentally or psychologically able to provide consent. In those cases psychologists must make attempts to communicate with the client/patient or research participant in a manner commensurate with his or her capacity. They must also take care to protect the best interest of such a person.

Seeking *assent*, an agreement to cooperate, is also the psychologist's responsibility. This attempt to gain agreement to cooperate should be sought even though the person may not be able to fully understand the research or intervention. For example, a child must be told about the nature of the testing, observation, or therapy and asked whether he or she will agree (i.e., assent) to the procedure. It should be noted that "seeking assent" does not mean that the child must agree. If a child says "no," then the psychologist should consider the child's preference not to be seen but might decide to see the child anyway, if doing so would still be in the child's best interest. Also, obtaining formal consent from a legally authorized person (e.g., parent, caretaker, legal guardian) is required if such substitute consent is permitted or required by law. The decision to proceed in the child's best interest is made only after obtaining the consent from a legally authorized person. When psychologists are uncertain about the ability of the client/patient to provide informed consent, they should proceed with caution. Documentation of this process is also important.

Standard 3.10(c)

When psychological services are court ordered or otherwise mandated, psychologists inform the individual of the nature of the anticipated services, including whether the services are court ordered or mandated and any limits of confidentiality, before proceeding.

This new standard was developed to more clearly provide guidance about forensic informed consent or other mandated contexts, such as in the military. In forensic evaluations the court may order individuals to submit to an evaluation against their will. Thus, the individual is not consenting to the evaluation. Even then, the psychologist still has the responsibility to give the individual relevant information about the service, the fact that it is mandated, the future use of information, and the limits of confidentiality. In addition, in a forensic situation an explanation as to how the role of the evaluator contrasts with the role of a psychotherapist may be relevant. Providing a client/patient with written explanations of these issues may be helpful. Documentation of this process in the psychological record is also recommended. When regulations permit, military psychologists should also inform active duty personnel of the psychologist's duty to report to appropriate military agency violations of the Military Justice Uniform Code if those violations were to be obtained during assessment or psychotherapy.

Standard 3.10(d)

Psychologists appropriately document written or oral consent, permission, and assent. (See also Standards 8.02, Informed Consent to Research; 9.03, Informed Consent in Assessments; and 10.01, Informed Consent to Therapy.)

Psychologists who provide services, including forensic services, or who conduct research, document that they have obtained consent or assent from the person and legal guardian, if relevant. A psychologist may do this either by including the signed consent, assent, or permission form in the record or through a progress note entry in the record if consent or assent was obtained orally. This standard does not specify the method of documentation and does not require a signed consent form. Legal requirements may be more specific regarding the methods of obtaining and documenting informed consent, and psychologists should know laws to which they are subject.

Standard 3.10 thus initiates the requirements of informed consent and is referenced throughout the rest of the Ethics Code. Standard 3.10 defines informed consent; 3.10(b) describes assent for persons legally unable to provide consent; Standard 3.10(c), which is new, provides guidance about forensic informed consent and other mandated contexts; and Standard 3.10(d) requires that psychologists note that appropriate informed consent procedures have been conducted and obtained.

Standard 3.10, Case 1

Case Illustration. Ms. B. contacts Dr. R., who is a child psychologist, regarding her concerns about her 12-year-old daughter, C.B., and her interest in Dr. R. providing psychotherapy for her. Dr. R. conducts an intake interview with Ms. B. and C.B. She acquires informed consent for services from Ms. B. and explains to C.B. the parameters of the services in appropriate terminology that she would understand, including limits of confidentiality. Ms. B. reports that her daughter is experiencing bullying at school and is now reluctant to go to school because of the experience. Her grades are slipping, and she is despondent much of the time at home. During the intake interview, Ms. B. reports that she had never married C.B.'s father and that they had permanently separated before the child's birth, adding that his whereabouts have been unknown since the separation. Dr. R. begins seeing the daughter and, as time goes on, thinks that she is benefiting from therapy. C.B. likes to come for sessions and reports to her mother that Dr. R. is helping her deal with her problems and seems to understand her.

Four months into treatment, Dr. R. receives a telephone call from a Mr. Q., who identifies himself as C.B.'s father and demands that Dr. R. immediately halt treatment until he has a chance to meet with Dr. R. He instructs Dr. R. to e-mail him a summary of C.B.'s intake information, diagnosis, and course of treatment. Dr. R. immediately contacts Ms. B and tells her of the call. She insists that Dr. R. continue to see C.B. without a break in the sessions and expresses that to halt the psychotherapy, even temporarily, would be harmful to her daughter. C.B. has never even seen her biological father, she explains, and to have a disruption in her life at such a difficult time by a virtual stranger would set her back significantly.

Ethical Dilemma. Dr. R. feels like she is in a quandary because she had conducted the initiation of psychotherapy appropriately and had engaged ethically in the informed consent procedures as well as in her explanation of confidentiality with the mother and with C.B. C.B.'s mother had agreed that she would receive only general information about how C.B. was progressing and would not ask for content information or other disclosures that C.B. wanted to be kept confidential. In fact, C.B. had been very concerned and attentive in the initial agreement regarding what would be told to her mother, and she has been very forthcoming with Dr. R., thinking that what she told Dr. R. would go no further.

Even though Dr. R. had acted ethically at the time, she is now unsure about the legal rights of the biological father in terms of consent for treatment. C.B.'s parents had not been married, but Ms. B. did acknowledge that Mr. Q. is C.B.'s father. Dr. R. likes to think that she was informed about state law regarding custody but realizes that she had not pursued with Ms. B. whether Ms. B. had gotten custodial rights, because it seemed that Mr. Q.'s departure had been impromptu and that he had not pursued any custody rights, visitation, or any contact with the daughter during these 12 years. Dr. R. believes that she had upheld Standard 3.10 in good faith at the time therapy was initiated. She also realizes that if C.B.'s father does in fact have a right to the records that she would, in essence, be breaking the confidentiality agreement (Standard 4.02, Discussing the Limits of Confidentiality) with her client and the mother if she complies with the father's demands. Dr. R. also is concerned about Standard 3.04, Avoiding Harm, for she believes C.B. is at a significant point in her therapy and that an interruption could be harmful. Dr. R. also thinks that she would not be respecting General Principle A: Beneficence and Nonmaleficence, or General Principle B: Fidelity and Responsibility, if she were to disclose the requested information because she believes that the client would be harmed by this intrusion into her privacy and that the trust Dr. R. has built with the client would be at risk.

Decision-Making Factors. Psychologists ordinarily do not have a duty to conduct an independent investigation of the legal custody of children unless there is some reason to suspect the representations by parents on whom the psychologist is relying to obtain informed consent or make professional decisions. Where legal custody may be an issue, such as after a parental marital separation or divorce, psychologists would be wise to ask to see a copy of a final divorce decree in which legal custody is described, if only to verify that the parent understands what is actually determined in the decree. However, in this situation the parent indicates there had never been a marriage, so no final divorce decree would even exist. It seems unreasonable, after Ms. B. has indicated that the whereabouts of C.B.'s father are unknown, to expect that

Dr. R. will insist on permission to contact C.B.'s father or would delay offering psychological services until he can be contacted. However, once Mr. Q. contacted Dr. R. there is reason to question the history provided by Ms. B. on which Dr. R. relied as an authorization of treatment for C.B.

Dr. R. knows that she would want to meet very soon with Ms. B. and to gain a full understanding of the legal status of the client and the custodial status of the parents. Dr. R. is certain that Ms. B. does have custodial rights but does not know what the rights of Mr. Q. would be in this circumstance. Dr. R. also needs to learn what the state statutes are regarding this circumstance. If Dr. R. learns that Mr. Q. does not have legal rights to C.B.'s psychotherapy record then, even though this development would be a major life event with which C.B. would need to cope, Dr. R. would feel confident that she had gained a sufficient amount of trust with C.B. that she could help C.B. deal with the sudden presence of her father. Dr. R. knows that if she finds that the father did have the right to the psychotherapy notes, then she would need to decide how to respond. She could refuse the records on the grounds of harm to the child but would then need to be prepared to go to court if a subpoena were issued. She would then possibly also be in violation of Standard 3.10 if she continued to see C.B. against the will of the father.

Decision Options. First, Dr. R. would promptly contact Ms. B. to report the contact by Mr. Q. and cite his demands. She should inquire about Mr. Q.: what Ms. B. can tell her about Mr. Q. and how he may have learned of the psychotherapy with C.B. and how Ms. B. wants Dr. R. to respond to his demands for suspension of treatment and an e-mailed summary of the treatment to date. Dr. R. would document the substance of this communication in the treatment record.

Second, Dr. R. would make certain that she understands how laws governing paternity and the rights of unmarried biological parents may apply in her jurisdiction. Jurisdictions vary in the extent to which uncontested acknowledgement of paternity without a formal determination of paternity by a court results in joint legal custody for purposes of making parental decisions about accessing professional services for a child. Dr. R. should be clear about what the rules in her jurisdiction are regarding parental rights of unmarried biological parents. If she accesses legal or other consultation to resolve any uncertainty about relevant law, this should also be documented in the treatment record.

If a relevant law requires that Mr. Q. be involved in obtaining an adequate informed consent for continuing treatment, then Dr. R. would invite Mr. Q. to meet regarding C.B.'s clinical needs and the course of treatment. Efforts to obtain Mr. Q.'s informed consent for the treatment of C.B. should be taken and documented in a manner consistent with Standard 3.10 and Standard 10.01 (Informed Consent to Therapy).

If Mr. Q. relents and authorizes psychotherapy to continue, then Dr. R. can continue to offer professional services to C.B. but will need to provide to Mr. Q. records and summaries if he continues to insist on the provision of information about the treatment. Furthermore, Dr. R. would need to explain to C.B. that, depending on the limits of confidentiality agreed to by Mr. Q., her disclosures may have a different level of confidentiality than they had earlier.

If a relevant law requires Mr. Q's informed consent for C.B.'s psychotherapy, but he declines to provide informed consent and authorization for continuing the treatment, then Dr. R. will be in a situation parallel to that when two divorced parents with legal custody disagree about authorizing treatment of a child. Unless C.B.'s clinical status is so fragile and the risk of harm from abruptly discontinuing treatment is so severe that her situation would rise to the ordinarily very narrow exceptions that authorize "emergency" care without informed consent under the law, Dr. R. should suspend treatment until the parental conflict can be resolved. This may require that Ms. B. go to court to seek sole legal custody or obtain a court order authorizing treatment of this minor child despite the absence of informed consent and authorization by Mr. Q. If Dr. R. does decide to continue treatment in the interim, she would be well advised to seek and document consultation regarding the urgent need for ongoing treatment and whether Mr. Q.'s failure to authorize urgent care triggers a mandated report to state child protection authorities.

If a relevant law does not require his involvement for informed consent, then the confidentiality of C.B.'s treatment should be maintained, unless Ms. B. authorizes further communication between Dr. R. and Mr. Q., or until Mr. Q. obtains a court order directing Dr. R. to act otherwise.

Standard 3.11, Psychological Services Delivered To or Through Organizations

This standard describes the general rule for organizational informed consent. It applies the informed consent principles to organizational settings, which are legal entities as opposed to individuals, and it supplements Standard 3.10.

Standard 3.11(a)
Psychologists delivering services to or through organizations provide information beforehand to clients and when appropriate those directly affected by the services about (1) the nature and objectives of the services, (2) the intended recipients, (3) which of the individuals are clients, (4) the relationship the psychologist will have with each person and the organization, (5) the probable uses of services provided and information obtained,

(6) who will have access to the information, and (7) limits of confidentiality. As soon as feasible, they provide information about the results and conclusions of such services to appropriate persons.

This standard is partly based on Standard 1.07a of the 1992 Ethics Code, Describing the Nature and Results of Psychological Services, and was significantly changed for the 2002 Ethics Code. This standard applies informed consent to the unique circumstances in organizational consulting. The informed consent procedures for clients/patients of psychotherapy or evaluation services or for research participation may not apply similarly to organizational contexts. The standard can be used as a tool to help psychologists think through the questions they will need to answer when working with or in organizations. The seven factors are new to the 2002 Ethics Code and can help structure psychologists' thinking about essential aspects of their services. Psychologists could possibly experience these factors as a burdensome imposition, but, considered from a decision-making perspective, the factors can be helpful in organizing psychologists' work. Often when psychologists have difficulties it is because they have not thought through one of these factors initially and a later situation arises in which they experience unintended consequences of their earlier decision.

This standard requires that the organizational client, employees, staff, or others involved in the psychologist's activities be provided information about the nature, objectives, and intended recipients of the services. Psychologists are to clarify which individuals are clients and the type of relationship the psychologist will have with those involved. In addition, psychologists provide the probable uses of the information gained, including who will have access to the information. They describe the limits to privacy and confidentiality that may apply, and they provide information to the proper parties about results and conclusions within a reasonable period of time.

Standard 3.11(b)

If psychologists will be precluded by law or by organizational roles from providing such information to particular individuals or groups, they so inform those individuals or groups at the outset of the service.

This standard is unchanged from Standard 1.07b in the 1992 Ethics Code, and it speaks to situations that restrict the parties affected by the services from receiving information and informed consent mandated by law or governmental regulations. When psychologists are not permitted to provide informed consent, or results of the procedures, they must discuss these restrictions with the persons with whom they work. In an organizational setting, this essentially suggests that the psychologist should have a clear understanding with the organization or agency of what his or her role is, including limitations that are imposed with regard to informing recipients of services of results or conclusions of the work. Situations that involve such preclusions are most likely to occur in organizational or forensic settings but may occur elsewhere as well. A corporation, for example, may have a policy not to share the results of personality assessments for security purposes when the assessments were completed at the request of the corporation.

When employed by or consulting with an organization, psychologists must be clear about their role within the organization and the limits placed on functioning. Because the clients are organizational entities, as opposed to individuals, there is more of a need to specify the intended recipient, identify which individuals are clients, and clarify the relationship of the consulting psychologist with each of those individuals. In a forensic setting, a psychologist may be prohibited from releasing the report to a client. If this is the case, the psychologist is required to inform the individual that the report will be written and that the individual may not have access to the report through the psychologist.

Standard 3.11 thus describes the need to specify the intended recipients of services; who the clients are; the relationship of the consulting psychologists to each of these entities; details about the nature and objectives of the services; how information obtained during the course of service delivery will be used, including the names of those individuals or organizations who will have access to the information; and limits to confidentiality and privacy.

Standard 3.11, Case 1

Case Illustration. Dr. H. is a consulting psychologist in training in an industrial and organizational psychology program. He primarily consults corporations in the evaluation of candidates for high-ranking management positions. Dr. H. is contacted by a computer company for which he had worked several times. The CEO tells Dr. H. that the company is looking for a vice president for research and development, someone who has expertise in the area of computer software innovations and who also has the management experience to step in and oversee the production in research and development. Dr. H. has developed an interview protocol over the years that he has determined was most effective in identifying individual traits, characteristics, and other variables important in high-level management. He has also developed several instruments that yield a wealth of information about the examinees, including measures of personality type, temperament in the workplace, decision-making skills, creativity, independence versus collaboration, coping under stress, and other important variables that assist Dr. H. in identifying individuals most likely to be successful in an executive position.

Four individuals are selected to be evaluated by Dr. H. He explains to the candidates that the CEO and other management officials would have access to the evaluation. He also explains that the candidates are not his clients—they would not have confidentiality with regard to their disclosures—and he describes how his evaluation will be used in making the selection for vice president. Dr. H. conducts his full battery with each of the four candidates and then gives the evaluations of each to the CEO, who then uses the evaluations to select one of the candidates for the position. Two of the other candidates are also hired, for other positions. Because this field of research and development in computer innovation is a small community, one of the candidates, Mr. S., learns that not only was he not hired for the vice presidency but he also was the only candidate not hired into a position.

Mr. S. contacts Dr. H. and says that he wants a copy of his evaluation. His reasoning is that, first, Dr. H. had possibly not been objective and that there must have been something negative conveyed about him because he was the only one not hired. Second, he thinks that the least Dr. H. can do would be to help him identify what was wrong with his performance so that he can improve for other job applications. His field is a niche area in software production, and he needs to know what happened in the testing so that he can correct the problems. Mr. S. comments that he is considering filing a complaint with the state licensing board.

Ethical Dilemma. Dr. H. is very much taken aback by this demand and in fact had not known that two of the candidates had been hired for other positions. Dr. H. is well aware of the ethical expectations when working with organizations as clients rather than individuals. He is accustomed to thinking about the factors important in organizational services. He realizes in this case that this examinee does know that management would have access to the information identified through the testing and that there was not confidentiality in the process, but apparently the examinee does not understand that he is not privy to the material. The results and conclusions of the services were provided to the appropriate persons, as required in Standard 3.11, but this did not include the examinees.

Dr. H. realizes that he cannot defend himself against the accusation that he had failed to be objective, because he does not want to review the information with Mr. S. The fact that the other two candidates were hired could further Mr. S.'s suspicion that something in the evaluation had been amiss. In regard to Mr. S.'s second demand, Dr. H. would never have intended that his battery be used in preparation for other interviews. Dr. H. worries that if Mr. S. pushes his complaint he would then have to reveal his test battery.

Decision-Making Factors. Dr. H. reflects on his handling of Standard 3.11 and reviews how he had approached each candidate regarding the conditions of the evaluation. Dr. H. thinks that he had explained the nature and purpose of the service: He told the candidates who would receive the evaluations, that the CEO was his client, how the information would be used in choosing the vice president, and that all senior executives may have access to the evaluations. Dr. H. thinks that he had been thorough in providing the information cited in Standard 3.11 but now realizes that he had not explicitly told the candidates that they would not have access to their own evaluations. Standard 3.11(a)(5) requires psychologists to provide information beforehand to clients and, when appropriate, those directly affected by the services about the "probable uses of services provided and information obtained." Dr. H. considers that he had not explained to the candidates that the evaluation could not be used for other purposes, such as feedback for corrective purposes. Dr. H. also is concerned that his evaluations may have been used to place two candidates in other positions. Some of his material could generalize to other career positions, but his evaluations were specifically tailored for the vice presidency of the company as described by the CEO. Dr. H. is not comfortable with the possibility that if the other candidates' performance in the other positions do not measure up, his evaluations would have been used inappropriately (see Standard 1.01, Misuse of Psychologists' Work).

Because he had worked with this software company for some time, Dr. H. had an agreement in place with them that they would consider his test materials proprietary. Dr. H. had spent years developing his evaluation model. He had to admit to himself that he was concerned not only about the unintended consequences of his evaluations but also the possibility that the proprietary status of his evaluation battery may be at risk.

Decision Options. Dr. H. decides to communicate with both the company and the disgruntled examinee, Mr. S. He will talk with the CEO about the use of his battery for purposes other than as prescribed and explain that the best fit for any specific position is not intuitive, that the evaluation needed to be tailored for the specific characteristics that would be a best match for the position. Dr. H. realizes he has no control over the use of his evaluations once they had been released, but he thinks it is important to clarify their specific use and to inquire about the use of his materials in selecting individuals for other positions.

Dr. H. also will contact Mr. S. and more thoroughly explain the use of his evaluations and why he could not share the information with Mr. S. Standard 3.11 is often a reference point in an organizational context when an employee provides information thinking it is confidential and that the employee is the client, when neither is the case. In this scenario the examinee understood the limitations of confidentiality and the access that others had to the material for decision-making purposes but did not understand the limitations of the examinee's own access. When individuals are assessed for specific performance purposes, such as fitness for duty or as a match for an executive management position, and are not selected for the position, the objectivity of the examiner and the accuracy of the examination material may be questioned. Dr. H. realizes that even though he had been doing this work successfully for some time, he had underestimated the importance of being thorough and deliberate about the factors cited in Standard 3.11, in particular in this case, regarding the use of information obtained and who will have access to the information.

Standard 3.11, Case 2

Case Illustration. Dr. M. is contacted by a vice president of a major national corporation and retained to provide an organizational consultation intended to improve communications between management and employees and mutual decision making among the middle-level managers at one of the regional offices managed by that vice president. In hiring Dr. M., the vice president is hoping to improve the organizational relationships within that office and bring those relationships on board with the other regions in terms of productivity, office climate, and a healthy workplace. Dr. M. meets with the director of the regional office, the head of the human resources division, and the vice president who had contacted him. The nature of the organizational problem is discussed and an agreement reached that Dr. M. will provide a written report of the consultation to the vice president. Dr. M. will not discuss the consultation process or results with any person other than the vice president, and she will complete the consultation within 30 days and for a specific fee. The vice president will then use the results as the upper level management group determined. Dr. M. describes to the group her consultation process, which includes individual interviews with the regional office employees and some key employees in the vice president's office. Over the next 30 days, Dr. M. meets with 14 regional office employees and 4 central office executives, formulates a series of recommended steps to improve internal communications and management decision making, and presents a final report to the vice president. The report included summaries of information provided by the individuals who had been interviewed during the consultation, with their remarks individually attributed in an effort to reflect the different perspective shared by employees serving in different roles within the regional and central offices.

Four days later, Dr. M. is contacted by one of the regional office employees, who furiously accuses Dr. M. of causing him to be fired by the regional vice president. The caller explains that after the consultation report had been submitted to the vice president he had been told that he was a "problem employee" who was "the cause of most of the problems" in that regional office "according to that psychologist." The caller indignantly states that his "observations and complaints should have stayed confidential since 'what you tell a psychologist is supposed to stay confidential—everybody knows that!'" Dr. M. is surprised and mortified to receive this call, in part because it had not occurred to her that her report might result in the termination of the employment of one or more regional office employers and in part because her intent in the written report had been to illustrate patterns of organization perspective and not to portray any individual as a "problem employee."

Ethical Dilemma. Standard 3.07 holds that in providing professional services from a third party, "psychologists attempt to clarify at the outset of the service the nature of the relationship with all individuals or organizations involved." This clarification includes

> the role of the psychologist (e.g., therapist, consultant, diagnostician, or expert witness), an identification of who is the client, the probable uses of the services provided or the information obtained, and the fact that there may be limits to confidentiality.

In this situation, Dr. M. is providing services at the request of one oversight office of the corporate organization to another office within the same organization. Dr. M. failed to meet the obligations of Standard 3.07 in not explaining her role and the nature of her work to all parties with whom she interacted. Furthermore, she did not explain that her client was the vice president, not the employees or the management staff of the office she was evaluating. She did not reveal that the vice president was intending to use the information to improve organizational structure and professional interaction among the employees and, most important, she did not explain that she did not consider her interviews with individuals confidential. Standard 3.11, Psychological Services Delivered To or Through Organizations, also clearly applies because Dr. M was providing services "to or through" an organization. Dr. M.'s situation demonstrates the potential overlap and interaction between Standard 3.07 and Standard 3.11. In addition to the elements of Standard 3.07, Standard 3.11 directs psychologists to inform others of the nature and objectives of the services, identify the intended recipients, and explain who will have access to the information.

Dr. M. is also mindful of Standard 3.04, Avoiding Harm, which holds that psychologists "take reasonable steps to avoid harming their clients/patients, students, supervisees, research participants, organizational clients, and others with whom they work, and to minimize harm where it is foreseeable and unavoidable." In these circumstances, a conversation with the CEO and other senior managers might have established the range of potential consequences to individual employees, and if she had done this Dr. M. would have been in a better position to foresee the likely harms and to avoid them or minimize their impact on individuals.

Decision-Making Factors. Dr. M. begins to realize that she had over-looked important ethical aspects of organizational consultation both in understanding the organizational structure into which she was going to work and in applying the ethical standards related to consultation. As Dr. M. begins to think through her actions and their implications for ethical conduct she becomes aware of several mistakes in her consultation process. Dr. M. knows she had not complied with Standard 3.07, because the nature of the complaint regarding confidentiality and the consequences of her omission had been made very clear to her from the employee. Dr. M. relates that interaction also to General Principle B: Fidelity and Responsibility, according to which individuals with whom she had worked had perceived themselves as having confidentiality in their disclosures, and she begins to feel that she had betrayed their trust in her as a professional.

In retrospect, Dr. M. realizes that she had implicitly seen the regional office as a part of the same corporate entity and had not considered her work a third-party request for professional services. She had not considered what steps she should have taken to either protect the confidentiality of statements made by individuals she interviewed or to inform participants of the limits of confidentiality. Dr. M. also begins to reflect on the purpose and function of including the names of individuals in such a report. She had thought that it would be helpful in understanding the organizational communication patterns and the task collaboration patterns.

Dr. M. thinks she has learned much from this experience and she will pursue continued education in organizational consultation. She is most saddened and concerned about the consequences to others of this occurrence. Whether or not her services were prompted by a third-party request, Dr. M. could also have taken guidance from Standard 3.11(a), Psychological Services Delivered To or Through Organizations, and Standard 4.02, Discussing the Limits of Confidentiality. As indicated earlier, Standard 3.11 provides statements of the ethical obligations for a psychologist providing services "to or through organizations," including disclosure of the identified client, the nature and objectives of the services, the probable uses of the services and information obtained, and any limits on confidentiality.

Decision Options. Dr. M. feels very humbled by this experience and reflects that she does not comprehensively understand the ethical parameters of her work in consultation. She decides that, in addition to continuing education, she will acquire consultation on her own to minimize the likelihood of having such an experience again. Several important elements of the Ethics Code became apparent to Dr. M. in this incident. Standard 3.07 and Standard 3.11 are most helpful in directing psychologists through decision making when one's client is not an individual or is not the psychologist's recipients of services. She also learned that the foundational concepts of informed consent and confidentiality have very distinct operationalized meanings that have diverse application. For example, knowing and acknowledging the limits of confidentiality are as important as understanding the obligation of confidentiality. Understanding the application of informed consent across different recipient groups and in specific legal, health, and institutional domains is necessary for competent practice.

In terms of the employee dismissal, Dr. M. writes a clarification letter to the regional vice president, specifying that she had not intended that any one individual be cast as a problem employee responsible in large measure for the problems in the regional office that had prompted the consultation. She emphasizes that her view was that, in this particular case, the problems were collective and would not be resolved simply by the termination of one individual and that she had included the remarks of that individual (just as with all of the others) to illustrate the many different ways employees in the regional office viewed the problems there. She points out the value of having an employee who is willing to share perspectives that were valuable to her consultation, even if the substance of them seemed annoying or provocative to senior administrators. She asks that the vice president reconsider the decision to fire the employee if the vice president had relied in any substantial way on her consultation report as the basis for the termination. She then calls the fired employee and explains that she had written the letter to the vice president and described its substance. She feels that she owes the fired employee information about what steps she had taken to try to minimize damage to him. She thinks that informing the employee of the letter still permits her to adhere to her agreement not to discuss the facts or the results of the consultation process with any person outside of the central office and regional office without prior authorization of the vice president. The circumstances in which Dr. M. found herself are a reminder to psychologists to be prudent and judicious when providing reports or other communication about their professional work.

Standard 3.12, Interruption of Psychological Services

Unless otherwise covered by contract, psychologists make reasonable efforts to plan for facilitating services in the event that psychological services are interrupted by factors such as the psychologist's illness, death, unavailability, relocation, or retirement or by the client's/patient's relocation or financial limitations. (See also Standard 6.02c, Maintenance, Dissemination, and Disposal of Confidential Records of Professional and Scientific Work.)

In essence, this standard requires that psychologists have a prior plan for addressing several potential interruptions to services, including their physical or mental illness, a disabling accident, death, retirement, or relocation, or if a client is unable to continue for financial or relocation reasons. This standard was new in the 1992 Ethics Code (Standard 4.08, Interruption of Services) and is slightly modified in the 2002 version to expand the requirement to all psychologists who are providing services, in addition to those providing therapy. The standard does not specify how those "reasonable efforts" are to be made; the list of potential interruptions is not exhaustive, and there is no requirement that the plan be written.

When interruption of services can be expected and planned for, a psychologist's "reasonable efforts" may include discussion of the expected interruption of services, including responses to a client's/patient's concerns. The psychologist might conduct pretermination counseling, refer the person to others, and if appropriate, communicate with the professional who will be responsible for the individual's case.

This standard requires that psychologists have a mechanism in place in case of an unplanned interruption of services, such as in the case of sudden illness or death. One option is for psychologists in independent practice to identify a trusted colleague who is prepared to contact clients and to have access to contact information; computer passwords; and documents such as contracts, including professional wills. Psychologists in group practices may have such an agreement jointly. Some states may have laws or licensure board rules that provide specific requirements. Organizational or agency contracts may provide rules about plans to facilitate services in the case of any of these potential interruptions of services.

CONCLUSION

Section 3 addresses areas that are relevant to every interaction of the professional role of psychologists. These standards are not technical in nature but instead permeate all of the dimensions of psychologists' activities that are defined and described in other sections. All the General Principles of the APA Ethics Code are the bases of these standards, and the standards in this section attempt to ensure that the power of psychologists is not abused intentionally or inadvertently. Psychologists' activities are expected to be carried out in fair and just ways and communicated in a way that relevant individuals clearly understand and desire.

4

PRIVACY AND CONFIDENTIALITY

The importance of maintaining privacy and confidentiality has long been recognized as a cornerstone to engendering the trust required in professional relationships in psychology. The General Principles in the "Ethical Principles of Psychologists and Code of Conduct" (hereinafter the *APA Ethics Code* or the *Ethics Code*; see http://www.apa.org/ethics/code2002.html)[1] that primarily underlie the standards in this section include General Principal A: Beneficence and Nonmaleficence, General Principle B: Fidelity and Responsibility, and General Principle E: Respect for People's Rights and Dignity. General Principle A encourages psychologists to maintain safety for clients by providing privacy and confidentiality; unwanted disclosures of client/patient information would be potentially harmful. General Principle B: Fidelity and Responsibility is applicable here, too, because privacy and confidentiality are essential in establishing relationships of trust with the individuals with whom psychologists work. *Faithfulness* partly means keeping information private and confidential. General Principle E: Respect for People's Rights and Dignity specifically articulates the rights of individuals to privacy, confidentiality, and

[1]American Psychological Association. (2002). Ethical principles of psychologists and code of conduct. *American Psychologist, 57,* 1060–1073.

self-determination. One of the values inherent in this principle is the right to *autonomy*, which involves the concept that a person has responsibility for his or her own behavior and freedom of choice and is at liberty to choose his or her own course of action. The right to privacy follows from the assumption that autonomous individuals have the right to make autonomous decisions about their own lives and the information relevant to these decisions. Psychologists respect the fact that individuals with whom they work have the power and skills to decide for themselves who knows what information about them.

The APA Ethics Code conveys the increasing complexity of the legal requirements for psychologists regarding privacy in reporting of information, including requirements of the Health Insurance Portability and Accountability Act and confidentiality issues generated by use of electronic transmissions and other technologies.

Privacy and confidentiality are perhaps more integrally involved with federal and state law and statutes than other sections of the Ethics Code. Statutes pertaining to a specific concept, such as limits of confidentiality, can be written in substantively different ways. To discharge their ethical obligations, psychologists must be familiar with the statutes of the jurisdiction in which they are practicing. For example, most states have statutes that define abuse and neglect, but not all track child abuse reporting requirements, reporting for disabled persons, or elderly persons in the same way, and some states are silent on some of these actions. Statutes can look different in significant ways from state to state and jurisdiction to jurisdiction depending on what the law says in that state.

The term *privacy* generally refers to individuals' right not to have information about them disclosed without their consent. Invasions, including those that occur through the inappropriate disclosure of any information related to the individual's physical, mental, or emotional processes, are to be avoided. Disclosures about clients/patients in reports or for other valid purposes are to be shared only for the appropriate purposes and include only information germane to the purpose for which the communication is made. In addition, psychologists discuss confidential information only with persons clearly concerned with the case or research.

Confidentiality means that nonpublic information about a person will not be disclosed without consent or special legal authorization. It is a promise of psychologists to keep information private about the persons with whom they work. The recipients of services retain the right to release confidential information about them, except in special circumstances, such as mandatory reporting laws.

The provisions in this section of the Ethics Code have potential broad applicability to psychologists' work in a wide variety of circumstances and situations, including various applied areas of practice (school, clinical, counseling, and industrial and organizational work) and in many different settings in teaching and in research.

Standard 4.01, Maintaining Confidentiality

Psychologists have a primary obligation and take reasonable precautions to protect confidential information obtained through or stored in any medium, recognizing that the extent and limits of confidentiality may be regulated by law or established institutional rules or professional or scientific relationship. (See also Standard 2.05, Delegation of Work to Others.)

This standard is slightly modified from the 1992 Ethics Code[2] to include the responsibility to protect confidentiality obtained or stored in any medium. It establishes that confidentiality is a primary professional obligation for all the work that psychologists do. At the same time, it recognizes that there are limits to what psychologists can do to protect such rights. The term *reasonable precautions* establishes not only that confidentiality is an important obligation but also that the ability to always maintain confidentiality may be limited despite a psychologist's best efforts and intentions. Therefore, psychologists carefully protect confidential information regardless of the method of storage. In addition, the standard recognizes that confidentiality is established by a variety of mechanisms in addition to the ethical imperative, including both legislative and case law and institutional rules.

The standard implies that it is the responsibility of psychologists to be familiar with the relevant state and federal laws, as well as organizational policies and regulations regarding confidentiality, and to be able to provide evidence that appropriate precautions were taken to protect confidentiality. The applicability of confidentiality requirements also varies according to the psychologist's role (as psychotherapist, teacher, supervisor, researcher, consultant), the psychological activity, and the status of the person with whom the psychologist is working.

Although addressed specifically in Standard 4.05, Disclosures, procedures used to protect confidential information include those used for releasing it. Neither that standard nor this one requires the person's written consent to reveal identifying information, whether the information is released orally or in writing, but obtaining the consent in writing is prudent and may be required by law. If the consent itself is provided orally, such as in an urgent request by phone, the psychologist should document the request but also obtain written consent as soon as possible.

---

[2]American Psychological Association. (1992). Ethical principles of psychologists and code of conduct. *American Psychologist, 47,* 1597–1611.

Standard 4.01, Case 1

Case Illustration. Dr. S. is employed part-time by University Health Services, located within the medical center of the university. In addition to the University Counseling Center, the university provides psychological services for students through the University Health Services. Additional services for students include physical health services, dental services, and psychiatric services. These services are partially provided as a benefit to the student population but also involve insurance payment when costs, type of services needed, and length of time of needed service extend beyond the parameters of the University Health Services' resources.

Dr. S. provides psychotherapy to individual students concerning personal and academic problems. Her caseload includes student clients who are dealing with eating disorders, relationship conflicts, and so on, and some have struggled with suicidal ideation. Dr. S. has worked at University Health Services almost 1 year and feels confident about her understanding of the policies and procedures as established by the medical center. She thinks that she is being professionally compliant with the University Health Services' expectations of her. The procedure for record keeping dictates that all clinicians enter their case notes electronically, and they are then stored in a specific drive maintained by the university computing service. Dr. S. is diligent in recording psychotherapy notes in a file separate from the client file that contains fee, attendance, demographic, and other pertinent information to the case file.

Dr. S. receives a call from one of her clients, who is in great distress. It seems that the client had received initial services for migraine headaches from a physician at the health services center. The physician had decided to refer the client on to a specialist in migraine headaches and had asked the client to sign a release so he could send her health records to the physician. The client signed the release. At the appointment with the migraine specialist, the specialist told the client that records of her psychotherapy had been a part of the materials received, and the specialist felt awkward that she had read some of the notes before realizing that they were for psychological services. The client is angry at Dr. S. and demands to know why and how she thought that she could violate the confidentiality of the relationship, especially when Dr. S. had made a point several times of reassuring her of the confidentiality of the sessions.

Dr. S. is very taken aback and confused about the predicament. She also is angry and feels betrayed by the administration of the health services center. When she meets with the administrator, she learns that the psychotherapy notes had not purposely been sent but that all health records regarding any service students receive are kept in the same file, and a request for the file would include information on all services. Dr. S. cannot believe what she is hearing and is at a loss about what to do next.

Ethical Dilemma. Dr. S. is caught in a circumstance in which the limits of confidentiality are limited by institutional rules by which University Health Services, in accordance with in the record-keeping procedure of the medical center, combined all material into one health file for an individual student. Dr. S. had been writing separate psychotherapy notes, thinking they were kept distinct from the other records in the electronic storage system, but she had no way of confirming this because she did not keep paper files and did not think to ask for access to clients' records in order to confirm or disconfirm her understanding of the record keeping. Dr. S. is very concerned that the client feels betrayed, and Dr. S. herself feels betrayed, although she realizes she had failed to thoroughly understand the procedures practiced at the University Health Services. Dr. S. is now uncertain whether she has violated confidentiality. She is unsure whether the university has met its obligation to explain the limits of confidentiality to her, whether she had failed to understand the record-keeping policies herself, and whether she is in ethical violation with the client. Even though university officials had the right to act as they did, Dr. S. wonders whether she acted unethically because she failed to underscore the policies with clients and therefore provided less than standard informed consent. She had explained the limits of confidentiality in terms of risk to self and others, but this was another ballgame altogether. She also realizes that she had included information in case notes of other clients that could be damaging to clients if read by others. What should she do?

Decision-Making Factors. Dr. S. decides that several areas of action are necessary in response to this circumstance.

- She would want to meet with the University Health Services administrator and discuss the record-keeping procedures, become aware of all policies and practices of the university, and decide whether she is in compliance with ethical standards and state statutes regarding confidentiality of her clients. She needs to reread all informed-consent and release forms that her clients signed in keeping with policies of the university.
- She reviews the informed-consent discussions that she herself has conducted with clients.
- She also reviews her state statutes in health service provision to ensure her own understanding of the state's expectations of confidentiality standards. After gathering all of the official policies and procedures that apply in her case, she consults colleagues who have similar positions at other universities. She also consults the state ethics committee as well as colleagues in her community who have also worked for the university. Dr. S. realizes that she should have become informed of all policies

and practices of University Health Services even before she began providing services there.

- Dr. S. knows that, aside from her ethical or legal circumstance, she must attend to the welfare of her client and attempt to preserve the therapeutic relationship so that she can continue assisting the client in the client's own distress.
- Dr. S. considers the possibility of meeting with the physician who received the information to limit the physician's access and to explain the dilemma.
- Dr. S. needs to consider the information that she has included in other clients' files and the unintended consequence of other health professionals reading her psychotherapy notes.
- Although this a very difficult situation, Dr. S. has to consider how to handle the fact that information on other clients might also be accessible and the limits of confidentiality of those materials.

Decision Options. Dr. S. sees her primary obligation as being to her client. She must also, however, work within the system regarding the practice of record keeping and the limits of confidentiality.

Dr. S. decides to meet with each current client and explain the limits of confidentiality and the implications of shared information. She sends letters to previous clients who had terminated therapy with a general statement about access to files and invites them to call her to discuss the matter, in particular if they had considered releasing, or had released, their university health files to a third party.

Dr. S. realizes that her own record keeping and format for maintaining client notes would need to change to still meet the expectations of useful records but to also provide greater protection for the clients.

Finally, Dr. S. decides to pursue a change of policy at University Health Services in health records maintenance and in consideration of limits of confidentiality. She realizes that the university is within its rights to maintain this policy; however, she considers the importance of students' access to confidential psychological services separate and apart from physical health information.

Regardless of how any modified policies would address the limits of confidentiality, Dr. S. develops her own informed-consent procedure for future clients and includes as part of her intake interviews a thorough discussion of the conditions of psychotherapy in University Health Services.

Standard 4.02, Discussing the Limits of Confidentiality

Confidentiality is the cornerstone of effective treatment; however, confidentiality is not absolute. This standard addresses the importance for psychologists of informing persons with whom they work of the limits of confidentiality. General Principle E: Respect for People's Rights and Dignity includes the right to autonomy, which, as discussed earlier, involves the concept that a person has responsibility for his or her own behavior and freedom of choice and is at liberty to choose his or her own course of action. Individuals have the right to determine the information they wish to share and to know and understand the limits to confidentiality. This information is to be provided as early as possible in the therapy relationship, and those explanations should extend to services, products, and information shared via electronic transmission.

Standard 4.02(a)

Psychologists discuss with persons (including, to the extent feasible, persons who are legally incapable of giving informed consent and their legal representatives) and organizations with whom they establish a scientific or professional relationship (1) the relevant limits of confidentiality and (2) the foreseeable uses of the information generated through their psychological activities (See also Standard 3.10, Informed Consent.)

This standard requires that psychologists discuss the multiple limits of confidentiality, to the extent that they are predictable, and how the information may be used in the future. Psychologists need to be mindful of the applicable law and regulatory statutes of the state in which psychological services are rendered. As mentioned earlier, not all states identify practices regarding reporting child abuse the same way or define neglect or abuse in the same way. In some states, the reporting of sexual misconduct by a psychologist is mandatory, whereas in other states statutes are silent on reporting. This is especially important, for example, when psychologists are providing services to individuals who may become involved in court cases such as marital separation, custody, visitation, relocation disputes, personal injury cases, or other legal matters.

It is also important to notify persons or organizations with whom psychologists work of state law *exclusions* to confidentiality, including child abuse reporting acts, situations involving the duty to warn or protect others from potentially dangerous clients/patients, responsibilities under commitment procedures, or the delivery of group therapy services. Psychologists who work or consult with organizations (e.g., military, corporations) may encounter unique conflicts around confidentiality issues, and in those cases they should be careful to define the limits of confidentiality with those with whom they work before the work starts and again when the work begins.

Psychologists are aware that once information leaves their offices their ability to exercise control over its use may be significantly compromised. Sometimes—for example, in the case of a referral from the court for an assessment—it is very clear how information is going to be used. In such cases, the psychologist knows the information will be used in a legal proceeding.

There are other times, however, when psychologists are less certain how information will be used (e.g., in organizational settings). They must then try to become aware of what they do know and what they do not know.

This requirement to discuss limits of confidentiality extends to minors or other individuals who are legally incapable of providing informed consent, such as adults with impaired cognitive capacity, and their legal representatives.

Standard 4.02(b)

Unless it is not feasible or is contraindicated, the discussion of confidentiality occurs at the outset of the relationship and thereafter as new circumstances may warrant.

The notification of confidentiality and the limits of confidentiality should be provided, as much as possible, before or at the beginning of services, whether one is conducting psychotherapy, teaching, supervision, doing organizational consultation, or conducting research. In addition, it is often necessary to continue to provide information or remind those with whom psychologists work of the limits of confidentiality throughout the process.

This standard recognizes that at times it may not be feasible, or may even be contraindicated, to provide the confidentiality information immediately, such as when the initial psychotherapy session is a crisis session and/or the client/patient is in an acute trauma state and may be upset or dysfunctional. In such cases, psychologists use their judgment to delay a discussion of limits of confidentiality until it is appropriate (e.g., when the crisis has subsided). The psychologist must share the relevant information as early as practical, as well as when new circumstances present themselves. For example, there are times when a client/patient may be on the verge of sharing information without awareness that such information could not be kept confidential. At those times, a psychologist may choose to remind the client of the confidentiality limit.

Standard 4.02(c)

Psychologists who offer services, products, or information via electronic transmission inform clients/patients of the risks to privacy and limits of confidentiality.

This is a new part of the standard that acknowledges the increased use of electronic transmission for either the provision of psychological services or the transmission of records over the Internet or via fax, phone, or other electronic media. Psychologists may think about compliance with and implementation of this standard through an examination of privacy and informed consent. Psychologists who use such technology should become knowledgeable about what might go wrong in using each technology in regard to limits of confidentiality or to obtain expert advice on such issues. To prevent compromising confidential information (in complying with Standard 4.01), special efforts may be taken to protect confidentiality, such as the use of passwords, encryption (encryption software is available through manufacturers of major operating systems), and firewalls (which can be in the form of software or hardware). For example, viruses or other Trojan horse computer programs can result in random transmission of electronically stored records, such as those stored by hospitals or large group practices. Psychologists can use anti-virus, anti-spyware, and other specialized programs to protect against such events. Psychologists use systems that protect privacy, and they may provide their clients/patients information on how to participate in electronic activity to protect their privacy and in actively monitoring their electronic interactions to promote safety and privacy.

Psychologists educate themselves and those with whom they work on the limitations of confidentiality and the types of risks that their particular electronic communication methods introduce into the provision of psychological services. They might cite as an example a situation in which a client is sitting in a coffee shop reading e-mail; in this instance, the e-mail is protected as long as no one passing by chooses to read it. If someone passing by takes an interest, however, then the e-mail is not protected. In other words, the protection is dependent on the interest and initiative of others. It is said that e-mail is not equivalent to a letter in terms of privacy but is more like a postcard. Likewise, if one is engaging in a cell phone call in the mall, the call is private only as long as no one chooses to listen. In addition to cautioning clients about such matters, psychologists should remind themselves that as required by Standard 4.01, they must be just as vigilant about privacy with cell phone calls, text messages, and e-mail as they are with face-to-face conversations in an office and with written records in an office.

In any case, clients/patients must be made aware of the potential limitations of confidentiality and of ways in which their privacy may be compromised when using electronic transmission.

Standard 4.02(a), Case 1

Case Illustration. Dr. C. is a psychologist who practices in marital and family psychotherapy. She has been seeing Mr. and Mrs. S. for several months and intermittently seeing the family, which includes two adolescent boys. The couple has several presenting problems: disagreements regarding parenting decisions and how they affect the boys; perceived resentment of Mrs. S. because she has taken a new job that requires her to spend more time away from home; disagreement about the veracity of reports from school that the older son is exhibiting behavioral problems; and incongruent priorities in their marriage regarding finances, extended families, and choice of friends.

Dr. C. has been working on these problems with the couple but realizes that the emotional discord and resentments run deep. The couple also is prone to raising questions regarding each other's parenting practices and to involving the sons in their marital disputes.

Mr. and Mrs. S. fail to attend sessions for several weeks. Dr. C. then receives separate phone calls from both of them requesting to come in for individual sessions. Dr. C. is reluctant but thinks that she should see them and hear them out. Both Mr. and Mrs. S. tell Dr. C. that they are divorcing and that alimony, child support, and custody are all on the table. Both of them want Dr. C. to give testimony on their respective behalf and to submit her client notes to their respective attorneys. They each think that they themselves would benefit by disclosure of their therapy sessions and that the spouse will be damaged in court for his or her disclosures in session.

Ethical Dilemma. Dr. C. is faced with several problems. She has engaged in marital therapy with this couple and does not see herself as having valid input into parental fitness, custody decisions, or any forensic aspects of the proceedings. Furthermore, she had not kept separate notes or included in her informed-consent procedures the conditions for differential disclosure or disclosure of information that could damage either party, both of whom are her clients. Each of the attorneys is pushing Dr. C. for disclosure of session material and both have in their possession the release consents from both parties. Dr. C. realizes that confidential information disclosed in the sessions could be damaging to each party for different reasons. First, information regarding the behavior of the older son in regard to vandalism and marijuana use could impact his application for scholarships in the coming year. Second, Mr. S. has discussed his alcohol use and his difficulties in controlling his drinking. He is being considered for promotion at his company, which takes particular pride in their employees being good family role models. Last, Mrs. S. had had several extramarital affairs in past years but considers these problems to be a thing of the past. These affairs occurred when the children were younger, and the local office of family services had been called in a couple of times.

Decision-Making Factors. The ethical implication of this situation for Dr. C. is not the waiver of confidentiality but psychologists' obligation to make limits of confidentiality known to persons with whom they establish a scientific or professional relationship. Once information is disclosed, neither the clients, the attorney, nor the judge could control additional access to that information because it would likely have been released to the public domain. Dr. C. should be certain who she considers her clients to be and that consent, in this case, means consent from the couple. Dr. C. will want to make clear that she did not conduct any evaluation. She should also be mindful of her role as the treating psychologist and not an evaluator. Clients do not always understand that they cannot have partial control or limited control of their information once a release is enacted. Further obligation for Dr. C. entails explaining to clients that once their information becomes public, the manner in which the information is used can take many different directions. Clients typically think of information released to the court as being used for judicial purposes only. Because the information is now public, employers, schools, organizations, and others do not need permission to draw on that information for making decisions and determining consequences that can affect the clients and their families.

Dr. C. can see no benefit to anyone of disclosing this information, yet the attorneys seem confident of their own ability to shape the information in the favor of their respective clients. Dr. C. realizes that she has three options. First, she can consent to testify and confine her testimony to the factual and observed information and perceptions that were evidenced in session and try to be as circumspect as possible. Second, she can continue to try to convince the attorneys of the risks involved in putting her on the stand. Third, she can meet with Mr. and Mrs. S. either together or separately and spell out the information that could come to light, the meaning of the information in the bigger picture, and the various potential consequences of the disclosures. Dr. C. is aware that once she reveals information in court she will not be able to control the use or the distribution of this information, and she knows that it is her obligation to explain this circumstance to her clients. The information not only could be used by each member of the couple to advance his or her own interests but also could be used by their elder son's school, by Mr. S.'s employer, and by other unidentified entities.

Decision Options. Dr. C. decides to meet with Mr. and Mrs. S. separately and explain these conditions and potential consequences to them as well as the likelihood of loss of control and use of information once it is released. If both members of the couple still want the release of records, she will comply, but she decides to have each of them sign an agreement that documents her concerns and cautions. Dr. C. further explains that, from her perspective, the client is the couple, and therefore if only one of them wants the release she will not be able to release information on one without revealing material regarding the other person. She realizes that if she receives a subpoena from the court she will decide to comply with the request, and if required to take the stand, she will explain her ethical obligation to respect the confidentiality of her clients. Dr. C. also is mindful that she needs to be consistent with the law and regulations regarding confidentiality in her jurisdiction.

Standard 4.02(a), Case 2

Case Illustration. Dr. B. is a rehabilitation psychologist who specializes in work-related problems and coping with chronic physical conditions. He practices in both psychotherapy and evaluation for these problems. Dr. B. has been seeing Ms. L. for several emotional and psychological problems as well as for coping with her chronic pain caused by rheumatoid arthritis. Ms. L. has a history of domestic violence in which she was battered by her former husband. They went through a very messy divorce that resulted in stress for Ms. L. and for her children. The children began having behavioral problems, including truancy from school, petty theft, and fighting.

Ms. L.'s job involves typing, sitting for long hours at a desk, and secretarial duties that aggravate her chronic pain. She cannot keep pace with the expectations of her supervisor and the rigors of the job. She has had several meetings with the supervisor and received a poor performance evaluation. She has become very stressed and emotionally debilitated, according to her account as told to Dr. B. Her supervisor eventually fired her, saying only that she was not able to do the job. Ms. L. wants to sue the company and her supervisor for emotional damages and wants Dr. B. to testify that her stress and emotional pain was caused by her job and her treatment on the job.

Ethical Dilemma. Dr. B. realizes that Ms. L.'s energy and motivation for "getting back at them," as she expresses it to Dr. B., are great. Dr. B. also thinks that the experience on the job did in fact contribute to Ms. L.'s stress and emotional state. Dr. B. also realizes, however, that he cannot attest to any causal reason for the increase in chronic pain, and he also is very aware that Ms. L. came into therapy with an impaired emotional condition that Ms. L. herself relates to the prior domestic abuse and to the challenge of dealing with her children's problems in school and with juvenile justice. Dr. B. has worked in psychotherapy with Ms. L. on her perception that others cannot be relied on to help her and that she is always totally on her own. He suspects that if he does not assist Ms. L. in her suit she will see him in the same light as others and that this will have a potentially detrimental effect on their therapeutic relationship.

Decision-Making Factors. Dr. B. considers the ethical implications that are influencing his obligation to explain to Ms. L. and about which he wants to reach an agreement before an action was taken. First, he realizes that Ms. L. thinks that her testimony regarding the damages she has suffered because of her job will be the focus of the case. She is unlikely to have realized that information on her prior life experiences, their effect on her life, and the events involving her children and their resulting problems will be accessible to the company's attorneys and the court. Second, she most likely has not thought about the risk of disclosing this information, that it would then be knowable in a public forum, and that neither she nor Dr. B. would have control over its use. Also, she has not factored in that because she came to this adversarial circumstance with prior physical and emotional health problems, she cannot truly demonstrate that her current problems were caused by job-related conditions and not by earlier problems.

Decision Options. Dr. B. decides that he has an ethical obligation to explain to Ms. L. the limits of confidentiality and the inability to control access to her information once it becomes public. Furthermore, he thinks that pursuing the lawsuit will be detrimental to her health and current functioning. He is concerned that Ms. L. will not understand that his opinion is offered in an attempt to support her and to promote her welfare but instead will discard his point of view and terminate the therapeutic relationship. He resolves to discuss these matters with her in the most supportive way possible but knows that ethically he must attempt to explain the implications of her intended actions.

Dr. B. also plans to discuss with Ms. L. the fact that if she continues with the case and he is called to testify, there are significant limitations to the testimony he would be able to give. He could attest to her emotional state during the time she was in therapy with him, but he could not speak to the effect of her prior abuse and parental stress on her current situation and therefore could also not say how much of her current functioning was caused by earlier trauma compared with her job-related stress now. Also, he has seen her for psychotherapy, not evaluation for fitness for work, worker's compensation, or for the emotional impact of her job on her condition. He would not be testifying out of his scope of competence, because he also performs evaluation in job-related cases, but in this case he had not been an evaluator. Also, if Ms. L.'s attorney asks for her records, Dr. B. might be conflicted about their release because of the possible detrimental effect of disclosure on his client. Dr. B. considers asking Ms. L. to authorize him to discuss with her attorney the record review and to collaboratively consider the level of risk for the material entering court, because once one's mental status has been put at issue all control of any related documents is lost.

Standard 4.02(c), Case 1

Case Illustration. Dr. T. and Dr. C. have practices in which they see clients face to face in their offices. Both are interested in developing an electronic means of providing services primarily through e-mail and Web-based communications. Dr. T. has expertise in technology based on her own professional interests. She has taken several courses in technology communication and has a good comfort level communicating through e-mail and developing listservs and Web-based programs. Dr. T. is considering providing electronic services because she has a natural interest in technology and because several of her clients who travel extensively for their work have inquired about the possibility of e-mail correspondence with her to maintain better continuity and greater availability to communicate when needed. Some of her clients' travel itineraries limit their sessions with Dr. T. to once a month, and neither Dr. T. nor the clients find this sufficient.

Dr. C., on the other hand, has not pursued technological interaction beyond word processing and basic e-mail communication. Dr. C. has clients who have inquired about e-mail communication because they, too, travel and some have difficulty, based on their geographical locations, obtaining the transportation means to meet in person consistently. Dr. C., unlike Dr. T., actually prefers to keep his practice as it is, but he thinks that he may lose those clients who travel as well as those who, for other reasons, experience logistical challenges in maintaining regular face-to-face sessions.

Ethical Dilemma. Both Dr. T. and Dr. C. realize that there are significant risks to privacy, confidentiality, and the potential to misunderstand the limits of confidentiality within any modality. Dr. T., however, is very motivated to develop an electronic component to her services and actually thinks that this could be a niche practice for her. She has considerable expertise in technological applications (e.g., facility with firewalls, passwords, and encryption) and believes that, for clients interested in this modality, she and they would benefit. On the other hand, Dr. T. knows that she is ethically obligated to explain the limitations and risks of this modality to clients, and she wonders whether this risk would affect the quality of the process and whether the clients really do understand the implications of their personal information being compromised. Dr. C., too, realizes the potential for compromise of confidential information and the possibility that even if clients agree to the change in modality and are attracted to the convenience of the services, if something went awry his working relationship with clients could be seriously damaged. Dr. C.'s clients predominantly present personal problems related to family, health habits, and personnel difficulties at work. Any of these subjects, if compromised, could be very damaging to them. Both psychologists worry that even though they would explain the risks to the clients, once something happened the clients would blame the psychologists.

Decision-Making Factors. Without specific protections installed in a computing system, e-mail and other electronic communication metaphorically are postcards that may retain confidential status as long as no one along the mail route is interested enough to read them. However, as with postcards, the contents are in public view, with no protection from disclosure should someone decide to read them. Psychologists should be aware also that electronic files may be hacked into or accessed by intentional means.

Psychological services delivered through electronic transmission bring to light the importance of thinking about privacy and informed consent and the respective implications in these scenarios. Psychologists who have sufficient expertise to protect privacy through firewalls, encryption, and other protective software mechanisms are better able to ensure a greater level of privacy and lower the risks to limits of confidentiality because they can both control their computing systems and assist clients in maximizing protection in their own systems through education and software.

Psychologists who do not have expertise in technological communication and who are unlikely to pursue additional abilities in these areas will rely more heavily on informed consent than in trying to control privacy; that is, psychologists are ethically expected to inform clients of the risks to privacy and limits of confidentiality. This expectation can be met through thorough and transparent informed consent. Clients who are clearly informed of the risks of electronic communication as distinct from in-person professional services may then make a choice for themselves. In these cases the clients are aware of the risks and, equally important, the potential consequences of loss of privacy and confidentiality.

In addition to their own ability to prepare competently to provide this service, psychologists must consider some of the following client factors that may affect the decision while realizing that there may also be many other influential factors:

- the geographical limitations or travel demands of the clients that affect the ability to meet in person,
- the personal nature of the content of the sessions in relation to risk of disclosure,
- the capability of the client to understand the risks and potential consequences of disclosure,
- the client's willingness to prepare educationally and technologically for the transition to electronic communication,
- assessment of the level of risk to the client's self or others and access to emergency backup services, and
- the licensing laws and rules relating to the geographical location of the client.

Decision Options. Dr. T. decides to develop electronic services to be offered to several of her clients. She pursues additional continuing education to learn systems of Internet protection using applications such as firewalls, encryption, and passwords. She realizes that this decision means ongoing education for herself in keeping up with technology and that she also has a responsibility to the clients with whom she will be working to ensure that they can enact the protections she identifies and instructs them to implement. Developing expertise in Internet communication does not relieve Dr. T. of the obligation to inform her clients of risks to privacy and limits of confidentiality; however, the level of protection she develops for her services may inform and affect the decisions of her clients.

Dr. C., in contrast, realizes that he does not want to undertake the additional educational activities necessary to become competent to practice electronically or to pay an expert to set up and monitor such systems for him. He does not feel comfortable with the implicit obligation to also educate his clientele and to assist in their continued updating of electronic security options. Given the nature of Dr. C.'s practice, he knows that confidentiality is of utmost importance to his clients and that disclosure could be very damaging to some. Dr. C. realizes that this decision could affect the developing nature of his practice and that electronic services may be a factor in the choice of some potential clients. He feels confident, however, in making a deliberate decision and building his practice around his areas of competence. Both Dr. T. and Dr. C. realize that maintaining privacy and confidentiality are responsibilities of all psychologists regardless of whether they are using technology or proceeding by conventional routes.

Standard 4.03, Recording

Before recording the voices or images of individuals to whom they provide services, psychologists obtain permission from all such persons or their legal representatives (See also Standards 8.03, Informed Consent for Recording Voices and Images in Research; 8.05, Dispensing With Informed Consent for Research; and 8.07, Deception in Research.)

In essence, this standard requires that psychologists obtain formal consent from clients/patients to use recording technology such as tape recording, videotaping, filming, or digital recording and explicitly specify that permission is obtained in advance. The legal representatives of minors or dependent adults are asked to provide the permission. Written permission may be prudent and may be required by law. No exceptions are allowed for service providers, despite the fact that exceptions are made for recordings for research purposes.

Standard 4.04, Minimizing Intrusions on Privacy

This standard recognizes that another aspect of respecting people's rights and dignity when providing information to others is the importance of releasing only information specifically relevant to the purpose in providing the communication. Release of other private information not particularly relevant to the purpose is a violation of several of the general principles, including General Principle B: Fidelity and Responsibility, because the trust in the relationship requires that psychologists use their good judgment in releasing only information that is necessary to release. Faithfulness in releasing information involves proactively minimizing intrusions to private information of the client/patient.

Standard 4.04(a)

Psychologists include in written and oral reports and consultations, only information germane to the purpose for which the communication is made.

Standard 4.04 essentially requires that psychologists limit the information they provide in reports, consultations, and other disclosures to that material that is relevant to the purpose of the release of information. Individuals with whom psychologists work, including clients/patients, students, supervisees, organizational consultees, and research participants, may share private information with psychologists that may not be relevant to the purpose of the report, release of information, or other disclosures. In essence, Standard 4.04(a) says that psychologists identify what information is necessary to fulfill the need for the disclosure and disclose only that information. Psychologists are prepared to provide a rationale of why particular information is necessary to disclose.

Third-party payors, for example, often require utilization reviews or outpatient treatment reports before they consider continuation of services. It is important to disclose only that essential information pertinent to the situation, not information that is beyond what is required or sufficient for the purposes of review. In forensic cases, reports and consultations may be subpoenaed or released by the client, and it is important to keep this possibility in mind when preparing reports and conducting consultations. When collaborating with other professionals, psychologists should provide only information relevant to the consultation. Psychologists do not release unnecessary, unjustified, gratuitous, or superfluous information in consultations or in reports.

Standard 4.04(b)

Psychologists discuss confidential information obtained in their work only for appropriate scientific or professional purposes and only with persons clearly concerned with such matters.

Standard 4.04(b) further defines the limits of release of information obtained in clinical, assessment, or consulting relationships, whether the persons with whom psychologists work be individual or organizational clients/patients, students, supervisees, research participants, or employees. The goal of this standard is to ensure that discussions with others necessary to conduct psychological activities is done without mention of superfluous or unnecessary confidential information and to avoid the use of confidential information as gossip or entertainment. Psychologists are aware that there is a distinction between consultation and gossip or the sharing of war stories. *Consultation* is the exchange of information toward a goal that serves the interest of the client/patient. Gossip and the telling of war stories is the exchange of information in service of the psychologists' own needs. The standard extends to relatives of a patient; it is inappropriate to discuss the treatment or assessment results with the spouse of a client/patient, for example, without the consent and without justification. Guidance about appropriate disclosures is provided in Standard 4.05, Disclosures, and Standard 4.07, Use of Confidential Information for Didactic or Other Purposes.

This standard recognizes the importance, when providing written and oral information, reports, and consultations, of releasing only that information that is specific to the purpose. Information that is irrelevant should not be disclosed. In addition, information should be shared only with persons concerned with the work.

Standard 4.04(a), Case 1

Case Illustration. Dr. B. has a broad-based practice that includes psychological services in long-term psychotherapy, psychoeducational assessment, career counseling, family therapy, and other direct services. Mr. J., whom Dr. B. has been seeing for interpersonal relationship and communication concerns, along with family-of-origin conflicts, had been diagnosed several months earlier with HIV. As a result, he and Dr. B. decide that the direction of the psychotherapy, for now, will be redirected to several specific aspects of the diagnosis because relationships and family are affected. Mr. J. has developed severe stress symptoms, both psychological and somatic in nature (i.e., sleep difficulties, anxiety attacks accompanied by headaches, depression, and short-temperedness). His parents are unaware of the diagnosis, and he feels certain that they would be not only upset but also judgmental and rejecting. His relationship with his parents is already on rocky ground, and before learning of the diagnosis he had been working toward trying to improve the relationship. Also, he has developed a new and promising relationship, which is not sexual at this point, but in psychotherapy he has expressed great interest in the growth of the relationship. The diagnosis has been very traumatic for Mr. J. and seems to throw all working issues in therapy up in the air. Dr. B. is planning to be out of the country for a month, and her clients, including Mr. J., will be seeing Dr. B.'s colleague for psychotherapy during that time. Dr. B. will be writing a summary of the therapeutic status of her clients for her colleague.

Ms. M., a second client of Dr. B.'s, has had an HIV diagnosis for several years. She had been referred by one of Dr. B.'s colleagues, who asked Dr. B. for a consultation regarding career assessment. Ms. M. had been working in what was considered a dead-end job, and she wants to take a different direction in regard to type of job and possibly even an entire career change. She has been doing the same work since college, which was 15 years ago, and has not given a lot of thought to emerging areas for career development. She wants to be thorough in this new career pursuit and go through a complete career exploration and decision-making process involving identification of skills, knowledge, interests, and values. Dr. B. has had training in career work and has all of the software and assessment materials necessary to accomplish this objective. Dr. B. will prepare a career assessment report to be given to Ms. M. and to the referring professional.

Dr. B. is fully trained to work in the content and process areas of interest to the clients, and she has considerable training and experience in working with HIV-positive individuals; therefore, she feels competent to treat the clients as well as their presenting concerns.

Ethical Dilemma. Dr. B. is experienced with regard to HIV diagnosis and the related working objectives in psychotherapy, and she has always been conscientious about how to respect and maintain privacy and confidentiality while also representing her clients and cases accurately. Dr. B. knows that in her reports she needs to acknowledge the role of the HIV diagnosis in the lives of Mr. J. and Ms. M. and that she needs to represent that diagnosis appropriately in order to build the most effective treatment plan for Mr. J. and to take into consideration for Ms. M. whatever personal and interpersonal characteristics, traits, conditions, or other variables that would affect the clients' abilities to achieve their respective goals.

Dr. B. needs to decide whether and how the clients' HIV status will be represented in the reports. Standard 4.04(a) requires that only information germane to the purpose of the communication is expected. Dr. B. does not want to disclose a client's diagnosis unnecessarily or in any way that could be detrimental to the client, but she also does not want to misrepresent the client's work in a way that would contribute to a misunderstanding of the client's treatment plan and needed psychological services.

Decision-Making Factors. Decisions regarding disclosure of information in reporting and consultation can be framed around four fundamental questions: (a) What has the psychologist been asked to answer? (b) How is the information at hand relevant to that question? (c) Does the information help in the understanding of the treatment plan? (d) Would a hypothetical psychologist providing psychological services in the future think that this information is important in order to effectively provide treatment?

In the case of Mr. J., Dr. B. realizes that the current treatment plan and conceptualization of the therapeutic work is integral to the client's reaction and adjustment to the diagnosis. The core treatment plan is now focused on dealing with significant others in relation to the diagnostic information. Even though, for example, a cognitive–behavior therapy–focused treatment for anxiety and depression and a psychodynamic-focused treatment for interpersonal and communication concerns could be typical choices, the context of the work and the application of the treatment would not be fully represented without the full diagnostic information.

In the case of Ms. M., Dr. B. thinks that the objective of determining a new career trajectory is not significantly affected by the client's HIV status. There are attributes that can affect the match between an individual and his or her career choice, such as personal values, attitudes, temperament, and interests. The diagnosis of HIV could in fact affect client changes in these areas. Dr. B., however, does not observe detrimental reactions with Ms. L. that could play a role in choices of career direction. Dr. B. reflects also that the purpose of the report is for the client to synthesize the information learned and to make decisions regarding the outcome of the career assessment.

Decision Options. In answering the preceding four questions for Mr. J., Dr. B. decides the following:

1. Dr. B. has been asked to provide relevant case notes in order for another psychologist to conduct psychological services for the short term. The HIV diagnosis is, therefore, important.
2. The information is relevant to the psychotherapy in that the diagnosis is central to the content and process of the sessions.
3. The information does assist in understanding the treatment plan.
4. The psychologist who is taking on the case would need to know the factors determining the working content of the case.

In answering these questions for Ms. M., Dr. B. decides the following:

1. Dr. B. has been asked to summarize career assessment information in order for a colleague to interpret the findings, and the HIV diagnosis would not inform the decisions emanating from the report.
2. The information is not relevant to the decision.
3. There is no treatment plan but rather recommendations that would not be impacted by the diagnosis.
4. Any subsequent professionals providing services related to the career assessment would not be advantaged by the diagnostic information.

Dr. B. determines that the HIV information should be included in the report for Mr. J. but not for Ms. M. Dr. B. also decides to discuss with both clients the implications of inclusion or omission of personal information in reports so that they will be fully informed about any other circumstance in which information may be disclosed. Dr. B. will explain to Mr. J. the purpose of including the information, the implications, and the possible outcomes. He will be given full informed consent as well as the opportunity to ask questions and discuss the treatment of the information in other possible circumstances.

Standard 4.04(b), Case 1

Case Illustration. Dr. H. will be attending her first conference since her move from her home state. She has focused her training in a specific area of forensics and is most hopeful of becoming acquainted with other psychologists in her same area of interest. She knows that several of the well-known psychologists in her field live in the state, and she is interested in becoming part of a peer consultation group, or at least in having an informal relationship with others in the field. She is invited to a meeting of those psychologists that would take place during the conference. She is quite excited to be included and is told that this would be an opportunity to discuss difficult aspects of cases and to receive peer consultation. She gladly accepts and is looking forward to the event. She prepares material from cases that represent difficulties she has had with some cases and thinks that this will be an opportunity to advance her conceptualization of cases and to learn from the experts.

On arriving at the appointed time for the meeting, she discovers that the gathering will take place at a restaurant rather than a private location. She thinks this might make the discussion a little more difficult in that the level and manner in which matters could be discussed will be more limited. She is still excited about the event and about meeting individuals whose reputations she knows are high in the field. She is prepared to ask questions about her cases and, she hopes, to make a contribution herself.

As the conversation progresses, Dr. H. begins to realize that the discussion of cases is quite casual and not directed particularly to input from others. The nature of the discussion is that some individuals tell stories about cases that have a sensational edge to them and, instead of giving feedback on the information that is being shared, subsequent speakers tell an unrelated story about another client that seemed to again be offered in the sensational or provocative realm. The stories are being told in a "can you believe that one" sense, and the resulting effect on the group is one of frivolity, laughter, and enjoyment. The psychologist who seems to be in charge of the group turns to Dr. H. and says "We haven't heard from you yet. Tell us about some of your cases."

Ethical Dilemma. Dr. H. is very disappointed, for several reasons, and she is quite anxious about the situation in which she now finds herself. All eyes have turned to her, and she knows that this is the first impression she will make on the individuals with whom she had hoped to affiliate. Dr. H. thinks about the ethical circumstances in which one would discuss cases. She still has confidence in the fact that her intentions certainly meet the ethical expectations in that consultation of her cases was meant to be done for professional purposes in order to better be informed and to serve her clientele effectively. She also still believes that the ethical expectation of discussing cases only with persons concerned with the matters would be met because these individuals are known to have expertise in her area. Dr. H. has ethical intentions but now questions whether her intentions can be conducted ethically in this context.

Decision-Making Factors. A delineation that can be helpful in thinking through these dilemmas is this question: Are cases discussed in the context of war stories or gossip, or are they discussed in light of the welfare of the client/patient? Two concepts can cloud psychologists' thinking on these matters. First, if the case is discussed with anonymity, does that release psychologists from further responsibility on how the case is discussed? Second, if psychologists talk about cases only with colleagues, is this a sufficient condition to meet ethical expectations? Anonymity and disclosure to colleagues who would have reason to have access to case material are certainly aspects of ethical expectations, and these factors must be considered in any decision regarding privacy. General Principle A: Beneficence and Nonmaleficence and General Principle E: Respect for People's Rights and Dignity are helpful in these decisions because they remind psychologists that discussion of confidential information is meant to be conveyed for the welfare of the client, not other interests or motives. The treatment of information is an important aspect of disclosure. One might imagine overhearing a discussion of one's sibling, child, or parent in a disparaging context even among rightfully appropriate professionals.

Dr. H. also has to admit to herself that she is in an awkward situation. These psychologists are experts in the field and could affect her participation in the local groups, her referrals, and her success in establishing herself in this community. Dr. H. is heartened by the fact that only a few of the psychologists are discussing their clients in the conversation and that others are not participating. She senses that, just as she is, several others are uncomfortable with the direction of the conversation.

Decision Options. Dr. H. decides that she will not discuss her cases in this group and that even though a few others had brought up cases and presented them in a very professional manner she cannot trust all of those present to respect the material even if she presents it ethically and professionally. She decides that her participation will be related to subjects of general professional information regarding the local psychological community. With deliberateness, she steers away from cases and makes comments related to contemporary matters in the field that would be of interest to the group.

Dr. H. also realizes that she does not want to participate in these meetings in the future. Even though she is conducting her discussion ethically, her very presence means that an observer overhearing this discussion would associate her with the quality and context of the conversation, and she does not want that affiliation. She also decides that the psychologists who also are uncomfortable with the discussion likely are individuals with whom she might want a continued professional association and that in the future she will contact them individually and control the setting and context herself. She still wants professional affiliation with ethically responsible colleagues but also realizes that she can seek consultation in a professional setting.

Dr. H. further decides that even though several of the psychologists who were telling stories are among the most recognized in the field, she will not seek consultation from them because, even though they have the expertise, they are not practicing within the ethical and values context that are important to her.

Standard 4.05, Disclosures

Standard 4.05, Disclosures, mirrors Standard 9.04, Release of Test Data, in that both describe release of information under two circumstances: (a) when psychologists have consent of the legally authorized person or persons and (b) when psychologists do not have authorization from the legally authorized person or persons.

Standard 4.05(a)
Psychologists may disclose confidential information with the appropriate consent of the organizational client, the individual client/patient, or another legally authorized person on behalf of the client/patient unless prohibited by law.

Standard 4.05(a) specifies when psychologists may and may not disclose confidential information. When provided appropriate consent by the psychotherapy client/patient or legally authorized person, or organizational client, psychologists may, but are not required to, disclose confidential information, unless prohibited by law. Even with consent, psychologists may decide that the confidential information is not appropriate for disclosure even though the standard allows for a presumption in favor of disclosure. The Ethics Code leaves open the possibility of an instance, even with consent, when, for ethical reasons, disclosure would not be appropriate.

If the consent is provided orally, the permission or request to disclose confidential information is documented in notes. A signed release authorization may be preferable, and under some circumstances may be required by relevant laws, such as the Health Insurance Portability and Accountability Act. The signed release or documentation may specifically identify the person, agency, or organization to whom confidential information may be released and be time limited (usually, 1 year is recommended). The choice not to release is not a violation of this standard, which does not require release, and such a choice may not violate other standards, if, even with consent, disclosure would be harmful to the client/patient.

Determination of "appropriate" consent requires additional attention when psychologists have to identify who the client is and confirm who has the legal authority to consent to the disclosure. For example, when working with minors or dependent adults who have a guardian, when a third party has requested the services, or when services are delivered through organizations, psychologists must take extra care to obtain appropriate assent and consent.

Standard 4.05(b)

Psychologists disclose confidential information without the consent of the individual only as mandated by law, or where permitted by law for a valid purpose such as to (1) provide needed professional services; (2) obtain appropriate professional consultations; (3) protect the client/patient, psychologist, or others from harm; or (4) obtain payment for services from a client/patient, in which instance disclosure is limited to the minimum that is necessary to achieve the purpose (See also Standard 6.04e, Fees and Financial Arrangements.)

Standard 4.05(b) provides a description of circumstances in which it is ethically permissible to disclose confidential information without the consent of the individual. Such disclosures can be made only if they are mandated or required by law, or are permitted by law and for a valid purpose. Before disclosing confidential information in the absence of client consent or a legal mandate, psychologists determine whether the law permits the release and whether there is a "valid purpose" for the disclosure. These provisions may vary significantly from state to state, either through legislative statute or case law, and psychologists become familiar with the laws that mandate reporting, such as child or elder abuse reporting acts and duty-to-protect statutes. All 50 states have mandatory reporting laws that require mental health professionals to report when child abuse or neglect is suspected. Some states have mandatory reporting laws for elder abuse, and some require or permit reporting for the intent to harm self or others; some states are silent on these last two issues. Child and elder abuse reporting laws are the result of legislative or court decisions that the need to protect children and older persons, who are often vulnerable and cannot protect themselves, outweighs the need for confidentiality.

Standard 4.05(b) provides several examples of valid purposes for disclosure where permitted by law. It is not necessarily an exhaustive list; neither does the list guarantee that state law allows the disclosure, nor that, if permitted, it applies in every specific instance. The standard is permissive rather than mandatory, and the psychologist's judgment determines when to disclose confidential information without consent. It is helpful to be familiar with research and clinical evidence with complicated obligations such as *duty to protect*. For example, assessing the degree of danger, developing an appropriate treatment plan, and implementing that treatment plan, including whether to "protect" or "warn," can be informed by the research and clinical evidence that guides psychologists through those steps. Remember also that Standard 4.02, Discussing the Limits of Confidentiality, requires that the individuals with whom psychologists work must be informed as early as feasible about the limits of confidentiality, including those listed in the Ethics Code. Engaging the client/patient of one's decision and plan to disclose information may also be a helpful strategy, increasing the probability that the client/patient will remain engaged in the treatment; however, this process is not required by this standard.

Psychologists should also note that, in general, as required by Standard 4.04, Minimizing Intrusions on Privacy, and specifically in regard to the fourth example listed in the standard—to obtain payment for services provided—the disclosure should be limited to the information necessary to achieve the stated purpose of the disclosure. Under no circumstances should psychologists intimidate a recipient of services by threats to disclose any confidential information in order to collect a debt. (Psychologists should refer to Standard 6.03, Withholding Records for Nonpayment, and 6.04e, Fees and Financial Arrangements, which set out the conditions under which psychologists may disclose information in order to obtain payment.)

This standard describes the conditions and situations under which confidential information may be disclosed. It is permissive rather than mandatory; Standard 4.05(a) permits psychologists to disclose confidential information if appropriate consent has been obtained, and Standard 4.05(b) identifies possible categories under which psychologists may decide to disclose confidential information without consent. However, clients/patients and others with whom a psychologist works must be informed as early as feasible in the relationship for those disclosures, and the standard prohibits disclosures of confidential information without consent for any purpose other than those listed.

Standard 4.05(a), Case 1

Case Illustration. Dr. C. is an organizational psychologist whose clients typically are businesses and corporations. He provides various consultative services, including testing candidates for management positions. Company A has hired Dr. C. to evaluate several candidates for a regional director's position. Dr. C. is conscientious in attending to ethical expectations, such as acquiring informed consent from the person who represented the client, which was the company. Dr. C. also acquires informed consent from individuals he evaluates, and he explains the nature of the testing, that his client is the company, the limits of confidentiality, and who is likely to have access to the information. The candidates all agree to comply. Dr. C.'s evaluation battery is quite extensive and identifies several domains of information regarding work style, personality traits, relationship patterns, coping mechanisms, and standard means of dealing with stress. Dr. C. believes his battery provides very descriptive and significant information on examinees, and he is confident that his early procedures regarding informed consent, explanation of limits of confidentiality, and transparency of relationships of all parties involved in the evaluation would meet all expectations of ethical conduct.

A few weeks after Dr. C. completes his work with Company A, he receives a call from the human resources director, who says that company officials have chosen one of the four individuals evaluated by Dr. C. for the regional director's job. The director goes on to say that one of the three candidates not chosen had subsequently applied for a similar job with another company (Company B) with which Company A has an affiliate relationship. Company B did not commission evaluations for their positions; however, because one of their five candidates had been evaluated by Dr. C., Company B wants access to the report, and Company A has agreed to give the company that information. Furthermore, Company B officials have told the candidate that they want to use the report in consideration of the candidate and that it would benefit the candidate to agree, especially considering that the other candidates were not receiving the evaluation and, therefore, that information would not be generated for them. The candidate then gave permission for Company B to use the report. Company A is giving a courtesy call to Dr. C. to keep him apprised of the use of his report.

Ethical Dilemma. Several ethical concerns run through Dr. C.'s mind when he receives this call, not the least of which are the perils of how one's generated materials are used once they have left one's control. Dr. C. is very conscientious in his contractual agreements with businesses and in his informed-consent procedures to explicitly require that the reports could be used only by the employing business for the purposes indicated at such time that his services were contracted; that is, Dr. C. suspects that Company A is calling because they, in fact, realized that Dr. C.'s permission may be necessary in order to pass along the report on a candidate who was not hired.

The dilemma for Dr. C. is that all parties have agreed to the sharing of the candidate's report, and to prevent the disclosure of the material Dr. C. will have to object to the transmission of the report and invoke the aspect of Standard 4.05(a) that states psychologists may (but by presumption are not required) disclose information. Dr. C. also surmises that even though the informed-consent document signed by the candidates for his testing was appropriate, he thinks that a new informed consent is in order for an individual applying for a different job and that appropriate consent has not been acquired.

Decision-Making Factors. Dr. C. understands that Company A is invested in fostering a good relationship with Company B, and he realizes that the candidate wants to be cooperative and not appear to be difficult to a prospective employer. Dr. C. would prefer that Company A decline to share the report and that the candidate decline to approve of the report being shared because he realizes that the ethical standard of disclosing confidential information with appropriate consent is meant to be presumptive in favor of disclosure and that relying on discretion to not disclose is meant to be an exception.

Dr. C. realizes that use of his report could have numerous negative consequences both to himself and to the other parties involved:

- The information could advantage the candidate but could also disadvantage the candidate because the others being considered for the job would not have been evaluated in an equivalent way. Regardless of how the information affects this particular candidate, the fact remains that Dr. C.'s report will be used differentially in a personnel decision.
- If the information is used and results in a negative outcome for Company B, both companies could misrepresent the role and the effect of Dr. C.'s testing even though it will have been used in an unintended context.
- If the information is used and the candidate does not get the job, Dr. C.'s evaluation could be seen by the candidate as not being fairly applied, resulting in the exploitation of the candidate.
- If Dr. C. objects, the consultation contracts he has been offered by Company A could be terminated. He knows that Company A is quite influential within the business community in which they both work.

Decision Options. Dr. C. decides that, regardless of the impact on his business, he must take steps to ensure the proper use of his evaluations and to attempt to prevent any exploitation or unfair treatment of the candidate. Dr. C., in considering his options, notes several relevant factors:

- He could object to the use of his report and reiterate the proprietary status of his testing materials. If Company A agrees, he simply need take no further action.
- He could ask to meet with his representative at Company A and discuss the implications for Company A in allowing disclosure of materials meant only for Company A and the potential negative consequences to Company A if the transaction goes badly. This action would be a type of informed consent for Company A.
- Dr. C.'s original informed consent, agreed to by Company A, allows him to talk at any point in the process to the candidates regarding their participation. On informing Company A of this

interest, Dr. C. could discuss with the candidate the implications of the use of materials that are not applicable to other candidates. This would also be considered an additional informed
consent for the candidate and the corporation.

- Dr. C. realizes that, on discharging his duties to fully inform
the company and the candidate of the potential negative
consequences of disclosure of his report, he could then make
a more equitable decision on whether to object to the use or
whether to allow the candidate to make the decision.

Standard 4.05(b), Case 1

Case Illustration. Dr. M. is a licensed psychologist who has been developing her practice for 4 years through working in several professional settings.
She has contracted with the local school system to perform psychoeducational assessments for educational placement; accommodation and remediation needs; and appropriate provision of psychological services, including
child and adolescent counseling and family services.

Dr. M. is conducting a psychological assessment for the local middle
school with a child client named Jimmy, a 10-year-old boy being tested for a
reading disability. During the intake interview, Jimmy begins to tell Dr. M.
how afraid he is of his father. Dr. M. knows through the intake interview she
had with the mother that she and Jimmy's father are divorced and that they
have joint custody. Jimmy visits his father every other weekend. When
Dr. M. interviews Jimmy by himself, he explains why he is afraid of his father.
He reports that his father is very punitive and gets mad at him for unexpected
reasons. He says his father "just seems to be mad all the time." When he is
angry at Jimmy, he withholds dinner and any subsequent food from Jimmy,
sometimes for a day at a time. For additional punishment, he makes Jimmy
stand in the corner for hours without being able to sit down. He calls it "time
out," but it goes on for hours, and sometimes when Jimmy cannot stand any
longer he adds not eating that night to the punishment. His father owns a factory, and on Saturdays when he is with his father Jimmy has to work in the
factory with the men who load trucks. Jimmy says it is very hard for him
because the freight is so heavy that he sometimes cannot carry the materials.

Dr. M. asks Jimmy if his mother is aware of the situation, and he says
yes, so she brings the mother in and asks her about Jimmy's report. Jimmy's
mother says it is all true and is upset that Jimmy has told. She says the testing
is supposed to be about Jimmy's reading problem, not their personal lives. She
begs Dr. M. not to tell, because the father is quite prominent, has financial
resources far beyond hers, and often reminds her that if she tries to interfere
with his means of disciplining his own son, he has enough money to buy total

custody of Jimmy and threatens to take him away from her. She knows that Jimmy's father is influential in town and could very possibly do just that. She also says that she had not been told that questions would be asked about their personal lives and that Dr. M. has no right to tell anyone what she has learned. She reminds Dr. M. that they had talked about confidentiality and that without the mother's permission, she expects Dr. M. to respect confidentiality.

Ethical Dilemma. Dr. M. thinks that the events she has heard from Jimmy are well within reportable circumstances. Dr. M. knows that she was contracted with the school system to conduct evaluations and that the school system has existing policies and procedures for responding to various categories of problems. Dr. M. knows also that she is ethically and legally bound to respond to what she has heard. Dr. M. is concerned also that Jimmy's mother does not seem to have a clear understanding of the informed-consent conditions, and she suspects that permission for testing might not have been treated as permission for counseling might. Dr. M. also worries that if what had been said is true, the father is disciplining Jimmy a way that leaves no physical marks or any way of detection, so if he contradicts Jimmy's story there will be no evidence to prove Jimmy is telling the truth. She knows that the mother could be right about the father's influence, and Dr. M. does not want to do anything to make Jimmy's situation any worse. Dr. M. takes very seriously the ethical standard of maintaining confidentiality, but she realizes that she has to choose between respect for confidentiality of the client and welfare of a child. She also now suspects that some or all of Jimmy's reading problems have to do with his anxiety about this situation, and she worries about how to address this in her report and whether doing so would be an ethical breach of confidentiality.

Decision-Making Factors. Dr. M. needs to determine what the policies and procedures of the school system—and, specifically, this school—are in regard to potential child neglect or abuse circumstances. She thinks that the school takes responsibility for notification, but she is concerned that the school defines mandatory reporting conditions differently than she understands them to be. Also, Dr. M. is aware that every state can differ in the mandatory reporting statutes and that she needs to ensure that she understand the specifics of the state statutes. Dr. M. also wants to reread the informed-consent paper signed by parents for specific services as well as the standing agreement that schools transact with custodial figures in order to conduct standard activities with children in the schools. Some activities require individual approval, and others are subsumed under the standing agreements.

Dr. M. is concerned about the implications of her actions in affecting both Jimmy and his mother. She realizes that if this information is true, the father could punish Jimmy for telling and the mother for asking for testing and creating a situation in which this information could be told to a third party.

Dr. M. is embarrassed to admit to herself that she also is thinking about her relationship with the school and the school system if she takes action that is counter to the policies and recommended action of the school. Half of her income comes from the services she provides to this school system, and her actions could have devastating consequences for her financial well-being.

Decision Options. Dr. M. decides that she must follow through with the pursuit of the behaviors in question and that the welfare of this child is more important than the commitment to confidentiality. Several factors come into play for Dr. M. that will determine her actual course of action. She considers the statutes of the state to be very instrumental in her decided actions, and if the statutes are in conflict with the policies of the school she will act in accordance with the statutes. Dr. M. also decides that if the school policy is one that would not include this situation in the mandatory reporting category she will pursue reconsideration with the school administrators. She wants to maintain a positive relationship with the school personnel and thinks that she can be persuasive in bringing them around to her point of view. If she is not able to achieve their cooperation then, regrettably but with resolution, she will pursue the school system at the administrative level in the hope of acquiring the administrators' cooperation. If the school and school system fail to categorize this circumstance as reportable, she will make the report herself.

Dr. M. also decides that because she is the examiner and the case is officially hers, she will take the initiative to talk with Jimmy's mother and explain the implications of not reporting this situation. She wants the mother to understand the ramifications for continuing to place Jimmy in these circumstances and gives her suggestions for resources the mother might pursue for her own support and decision making. Finally, Dr. M. also decides to meet with the mother and Jimmy together to talk through their next step and to make initial recommendations for resources for Jimmy in coping with his circumstances.

Standard 4.06, Consultations

When consulting with colleagues, (1) psychologists do not disclose confidential information that reasonably could lead to the identification of a client/patient, research participant, or other person or organization with whom they have a confidential relationship unless they have obtained the prior consent of the person or organization or the disclosure cannot be avoided, and (2) they disclose information only to the extent necessary to achieve the purposes of the consultation. (See also Standard 4.01, Maintaining Confidentiality.)

This standard recognizes that consultation with colleagues is an important way to ensure and maintain competence in one's work and to resolve ethical dilemmas. In the process of consulting, however, the privacy of the client/patient should be respected as much as possible. The standard thus allows for consultation without obtaining consent as long as identifying information is not revealed or if the disclosure cannot be avoided. Psychologists may be faced with circumstances in which a disclosure is necessary in order for the consultation to be successful. For example, when working with individuals who are struggling with a personality disorder, inability to understand the value or importance of consent to allow consultation may arise. Allowing disclosure when it cannot be avoided signals clear priority within this standard of the importance of General Principle A: Beneficience and Nonmaleficence over the autonomy aspect of General Principle E: Respect for People's Rights and Dignity.

Psychologists are required to limit the information disclosed to that necessary for the purposes of the consultation. The standard does recognize that at times the unique information about the client/patient that has to be disclosed to make the consultation worthwhile may cause the consultant to infer the name or identity of the client/patient. These circumstances may be unavoidable. One can obtain a signed consent to reveal identity and other information, in which case the client/patient is notified of the consultation and the information to be revealed.

Standard 4.06, Case 1

Case Illustration. Dr. B. has a hospital practice in which he works on the psychiatric unit primarily with patients who have Axis II diagnoses. Dr. B. seems to work successfully with this clientele and begins seeing similar outpatient clients in his private practice. Dr. B. has taken on several cases of individuals who had been diagnosed with borderline personality disorder (BPD), and he feels confident that he can work with this population because of his effectiveness working with the hospital clientele. However, Joan, one of Dr. B.'s clients, is becoming particularly challenging. She has begun calling him several times a week in an anxious state. She comes to his office at times when she does not have an appointment and waits for him outside his office when he goes to lunch. Dr. B. is not unfamiliar with these behaviors because he has several clients who have demonstrated variations of these symptoms, and he has been able to work effectively with those behaviors.

Dr. B. knows that an underlying condition with which Joan has had to deal in the past is an ongoing eating disorder. Joan has struggled with this problem for some time and had been successfully treated by Dr. J. Joan and Dr. J. had mutually agreed to terminate her psychotherapy 1 year ago, and she has not evidenced increased difficulty with this disorder since termination. Dr. B. is concerned that Joan's eating disorder symptoms were remanifesting during this time, when he has been seeing her for other presenting problems, including the BPD symptoms.

Dr. B. does not have expertise in the treatment of eating disorders and has not treated clients for this diagnosis in the past. Furthermore, he is concerned about the interaction of Joan's existing conditions and the recurrence of an eating disorder. Joan has told Dr. B. that she feels positive about her treatment with Dr. J. and that she thinks Dr. J. was effective and helpful with her.

Dr. B. decides that it would be important for him to consult with Dr. J. regarding Joan's treatment and the implications of emerging eating disorder behaviors. Dr. B. approaches Joan in session about giving him a release to talk with Dr. J. Joan becomes very upset, saying that she knows he is trying to "hand her off" to Dr. J. and get out of their relationship. She says that the need to consult with Dr. J. is an excuse to bring in someone else so that he Dr. B. does not have to work with her. She refuses to grant the release.

Ethical Dilemma. Dr. B. is very conscientious about ethical practice and has always attempted to conduct his professional practice with attendance to the standards of his profession and within the legal parameters of his jurisdiction of practice. Dr. B. knows that ethical practice would typically call for a release from the client in order to consult in a case in which the client's identity is known. Dr. B. thinks that if he does not consult with Dr. J. he might be missing critical information about Joan that would be necessary for continued treatment of her BPD symptoms and that an emerging eating disorder could become a manifested problem in itself, with the result being that, in terms of standard of care, Dr. B. could appear to be neglecting to treat the eating disorder and therefore applying targeted treatment to only a single component of the client's presenting problems.

If Dr. B. does consult with Dr. J. without a release from Joan, the therapeutic relationship could be damaged, and she could feasibly accuse him of violating confidentiality. He thinks, knowing Joan's coping options, that she will see this action as a betrayal and feel disrespected. He feels caught between what he thinks would be an ethical response and the need for a consultation with Dr. J. He knows that the consult could be seen as a violation of ethical conduct, especially considering the intense reaction that he expects from Joan. Psychologists must make treatment decisions that are in the clients/ patients' best interests. When psychologists make decisions for reasons other than clinical ones, such as avoidance of conflict with the client or anticipation of negative reaction by others, management of risk concerns can become heightened.

Decision-Making Factors. Dr. B. thinks about several different aspects of the case that he would take into consideration:

- His ethical standard of treatment for the problems Joan had presented to him are still of paramount importance. He wants to continue treatment for the symptoms of BPD and other concerns Joan has raised, and he still thinks he can effectively treat those problems.

- He also realizes, however, that an aspect of Joan's prior work and continued problem with eating disorders had to be treated and that he cannot ethically treat the eating disorder because doing so is beyond the boundaries of his competence (see Standard 2.01, Boundaries of Competence).
- If he proceeds with the treatment plan he has developed, he will be ignoring Joan's remaining problems, and this too would be ethically unsound.
- He also is committed to the proposition that confidential information should be released only with the consent of the client unless mandated by law or allowed under Standard 4.01, in which confidentiality is regulated by established conditions.
- He considers consulting an eating disorders expert other than Dr. J. This would enable him to discuss the case without revealing Joan's identity; however, he feels strongly that understanding Joan's prior history with eating disorders would be important to the treatment plan. He has determined that simply applying principles of treatment of eating disorders would not be sufficient in his work with Joan.

Decision Options. Standard 4.06 includes the proviso that consent for release is required unless "the disclosure cannot be avoided." This phrase allows for the condition that to be successful, consultation without consent may be necessary. The success of the consultation and the ability of the consulting psychologists to ensure that the client/patient's welfare is valued. In this case, Dr. B. has made a judgment that this decision is in the client's best interest, clinically and ethically. There are occasions on which ethical values are in conflict; in this case, these values are the autonomy of the client (General Principle E: Respect for People's Rights and Dignity) and beneficence toward the client (General Principle A: Beneficence and Nonmaleficence). Psychologists who work with clients who have diagnoses of personality disorders may often find themselves in the conundrum of competing ethical values with this particular client population.

Dr. B. does think that his need to consult with Dr. J. is justified and that revealing Joan's identity would be necessary for Dr. J to provide an informed perspective. The "disclosure cannot be avoided" provision in Standard 4.06 for release without consent seems applicable to him. He decides to consult select colleagues who have expertise in ethical and legal interpretation of standards of practice regarding his decision to consult with Dr. J. In this case, Dr. B. does not need to reveal the identity of Joan, or, for that matter, of Dr. J.

After consulting these colleagues, whose opinions are consistent with his own thinking, Dr. B. consults Dr. J. He realizes that Dr. J. would also need to agree on the exception cited in Standard 4.06 in order for Dr. J. to discuss the case with Dr. B. Dr. B. tells Dr. J. that he has consulted with other colleagues whom Dr. J. also knows have expertise in this area. He knows that if Dr. J. does not agree, he can go no further.

If Dr. J. agrees to consult, then Dr. B. would proceed with the consultation and incorporate Dr. J.'s views into his treatment plan. It is possible that Dr. B. would decide to present to Joan the inclusion of Dr. J. in the treatment plan. He also realizes that if Dr. J. does not agree to participate in the consultation then he will need to decide whether to continue in a limited way with Joan's treatment or to refer her to someone who could treat both disorders.

Standard 4.07, Use of Confidential Information for Didactic or Other Purposes

Psychologists do not disclose in their writings, lectures, or other public media, confidential, personally identifiable information concerning their clients/patients, students, research participants, organizational clients, or other recipients of their services that they obtained during the course of their work, unless (1) they take reasonable steps to disguise the person or organization, (2) the person or organization has consented in writing, or (3) there is legal authorization for doing so.

In their writings and professional presentations about work with clients/patients, students, supervisees, research participants, or organizational clients, psychologists are required to either obtain clear written consent for the information to be disclosed or change information that could lead to the personal identification of clients/patients. Gender, age, race/ethnicity, religion, physical disability, and geographic location are examples of characteristics that may be disguised to protect the identity of the client/patient. Legal authorization may be afforded if the information is already in the public domain by virtue of litigation or by authorized media presentations.

Psychologists may be mindful that it is easy to be lulled into a sense that because they are at a professional conference they can be less vigilant about confidentiality than they would be otherwise. The reality, however, is that often one cannot be entirely sure who is in the audience. On more than one occasion, material that should have been treated as confidential information was disclosed at a professional conference and, even though this might have been done in a professional manner, has found its way into the public domain and to the client who was being discussed, resulting in significant consequences.

Standard 4.07, Case 1

Case Illustration. Dr. M. is a professor in a doctoral training program in psychology at the local university. She primarily teaches practice and other applied courses and performs ongoing supervision of psychotherapy and other clinical services. Dr. M. enjoys teaching very much; she also enjoys giving presentations at professional meetings on education and training content areas. She is an effective and dynamic speaker, and therefore the state psychological association often asks her to present at their annual meeting.

At this particular conference, Dr. M. decides to present a case study of one of her supervisory experiences. She finds the case to be particularly interesting for several reasons. The client had presented with generalized anxiety, disconnection with friends, inability to maintain relationships, and preoccupation in her work setting. As the case progressed, the client disclosed that she had been sexually abused as a child. The student clinician had been particularly effective in working with the client and was able to effectively integrate the information about the childhood abuse into the client's existing treatment plan. The student clinician had disclosed to Dr. M. during supervision that she, too, had experienced childhood sexual abuse. She wanted to keep the case, and, in fact, it was important to her to be able to work with this client in self observation and evaluation of her own efficacy and ability to monitor her own parallel process and countertransference. These factors became the focus of the clinician's supervision.

In Dr. M.'s estimation, the case was a good one for demonstrating the importance of case conceptualization, prioritizing working issues, and sensitivity to client experience of trauma. Also, the case demonstrated successful processing of countertransference and other working alliance issues.

Dr. M. presents the case to a large audience at the state psychological association's annual meeting. She knows that some of the graduates of her program are still living and practicing in the community and could be in the audience, but she makes sure that the clinician cannot be identified by the descriptive information she provides. Dr. M. does not think about the fact that even though the identities of the two individuals are well masked the content of the client's presenting problem is rather unique. Furthermore, she has forgotten that this case was presented several times in group supervision. Two of the former graduate students who had participated in that group supervision are in the audience. They do not know, nor had they ever known, the identity of the client. They do, however, recognize the case because of the content and the outcome. Because they recognize the case they also know who the attending clinician had been. They do not, however, know that the clinician, who is now a friend and colleague of theirs, had experienced childhood sexual abuse. The psychologists (former graduate students) are now faced with how to ethically handle their receipt of this information.

Ethical Dilemma. Psychologists can be lulled into a sense of confidence, and sometimes carelessness, because they are attending a professional conference. They can be more lax about their engagement with others at professional conferences than they would be otherwise, but the reality is that one cannot be entirely sure who is in the audience and that, on occasion, material that should have been treated as confidential was disclosed within the professional context.

The psychologists are distressed about this disclosure, about their knowing the information, and about how to respond. They know that Dr. M. would never intentionally reveal this information, and they think that she had become focused on the teaching aspect of the case and had not been as careful of the use of didactic information in public as she should have been. Furthermore, they imagine that she is thinking that there is greater confidentiality assurance within the collegial context because clinicians understand the importance of confidentiality and know that the presentational context of this conference is different from a public presentation delivered to nonprofessionals. In this case, all of that is true, but a confidence was still violated, as they see it, and they are not sure how to proceed.

Decision-Making Factors. The psychologists are unsure whether they have an ethical obligation to tell Dr. M. about the disclosure. If Dr. M. made a strong effort to disguise the individuals, had she actually made an ethical error? It was clear that she did mask the individuals' identities, and the psychologists feel confident that no one else could have deduced the identity of either one, with the exception of the students who had participated in the group class.

They also consider whether they should tell the former clinician, their friend. On the one hand, they wonder what good could come of telling her, but on the other hand, perhaps it is her right to know that this information had been revealed. Could telling her cause a breach of sorts in their friendship because they now had information about her that she had not chosen to tell her peers? Would she have negative feelings toward them?

If the psychologists tell Dr. M., then Dr. M. has a decision to make also. Should she tell the former student about her disclosure? Dr. M. and the student had had a particularly good relationship, and the student had disclosed information to Dr. M., such as this current information, that she had not shared with others. Dr. M. has been proud of her mentoring of and relationship with graduate students and would need to deal with her own feelings about the disclosure as well as consider whether and how she would discuss this with the clinician.

Decision Options. The psychologists decide that they feel obligated, on the basis of Standard 1.04, to tell Dr. M. of the disclosure. Standard 1.04 allows psychologists to bring to the attention of an individual an apparent ethical violation—in this case, of confidentiality. In addition, they are aware that Principle A: Beneficence and Nonmaleficence's requirement that "psychologists seek to safeguard the welfare and rights of those with whom they interact professionally and other affected persons" could be applicable in this circumstance. The psychologists decide that depending on how Dr. M. proceeds, they may or may not approach the former student clinician with the information. If Dr. M. does discuss the breach with the former student clinician, then there will be no reason to raise the concern themselves. They realize, however, that even if Dr. M. tells the former student clinician, and the clinician knows that her colleagues are aware of this information, it could result in the same awkwardness in their relationships that they anticipated if they were to tell her themselves. They decide that it is important to talk with Dr. M. for several reasons. They hope she will learn from this mistake in future presentations. They also hope that she will make a reasoned decision on how to handle the breach, and they know they have several options as the situation unfolds. Above all, they are confident about the importance of telling Dr. M. of the situation, and they believe that, the friend eventually should be told, whether by Dr. M. or themselves.

Standard 4.07, Case 2

Case Illustration. Dr. K., a management psychologist, is presenting a seminar at a meeting of industrial and organizational psychologists and management psychologists. The attendees perform personnel selection and evaluation, efficiency evaluation, reorganization, and financial consultation. There are, however, other corporate domains represented at the conference, including legal professionals, accountants, and actuaries. Dr. K. wants to include several components to his presentation to make it relevant to the most attendees.

Dr. K. has consulted with a corporation during the past year and was contracted to do personnel evaluation and selection that involved testing, interviewing, and strategic planning. The consultation had been particularly difficult and complex because he had been hired to assist in personnel decisions, but information became known during his interview phase that affected the direction of the consult. Several executive management individuals whom he interviewed disclosed that a significant part of the internal problems of the company stemmed from the fact that some management-level employees think there were accounting irregularities and that there is speculation around the company about who might be involved. The executives told Dr. K. that they knew that if this rumor were investigated and were true, stock values would plummet and the entire company would be catapulted into a financial crisis. This would have a widespread effect on all employees and the welfare of the company. Dr. K. takes this information into consideration as he proceeds with his job, but he does not consider pursuing or investigating this possibility to be his responsibility.

Dr. K. thinks that this case would be interesting to present because of the twist in the consultation that affected his role and how he proceeded. In describing the corporation, he makes a great effort to disguise the identity of the corporation and any employees to whom he made reference. He does, however, make a brief comment about a product that the company manufactures. He does not realize that this company is the only one that makes that particular product. When he mentions the product, some individuals in the audience recognize the company and then know that the corporation is under a cloud regarding auditing and bookkeeping. Some of the psychologists in the audience, as well as other professionals, have been consulting with other companies that are in direct competition with the company cited in the case illustration Dr. K. provides. The psychologists are quite taken aback and are not sure how to respond to the information.

Ethical Dilemma. The psychologists are unsure whether there is actually an ethical dilemma to be considered. They are aware of Standard 1.03, which pertains to conflicts between ethics and organizational demands, and Standard 1.04, in which a violation by another psychologist could be handled by bringing the potential violation to the attention of the psychologist who, in this case, disclosed confidential information. The psychologists do not believe they have an obligation to the corporation to inform officials of the disclosure because any action taken on their part would be for the education and corrective response of Dr. K. They also question whether they are ethically bound not to repeat the information to other professionals, in particular, their current client, who is a competitor of the corporation discussed in the presentation.

Decision-Making Factors. The psychologists question whether they have an ethical obligation to Dr. K. to inform him that his description of the corporation contained identifying information. He had, after all, taken reasonable steps to disguise the client. It was just a fluke that the psychologists knew about this little-known product that the company manufactures. They wonder also whether they have an obligation to respect the confidentiality of the information, given that it was disclosed unintentionally and that to repeat the information to their client could be unprofessional, if not unethical.

The psychologists think about Standard 1.03, which pertains to conflict between ethics and organizational demands, but they do not see any conflict between their position in the circumstance and the corporation involved. The psychologists understand that if Dr. K. had not taken reasonable steps to disguise the client, then they may be obligated to attempt an informal resolution by telling Dr. K. about the disclosure. They are not sure that Dr. K. had not taken reasonable steps.

Decision Options. The psychologists decide that they will inform Dr. K. of the unintended disclosure. They realize that the ethical obligation described in Standard 4.07 is just as applicable to organizational clients as to individual clients. They also determine that even though repeating the information to their current corporate client might be advantageous to them in future contracts, they will not repeat the information because they came by it through unintended means. They realize how easily well-meaning and ethical psychologists can be lulled into careless disclosures, in particular in a professional setting with peers and colleagues. They know that it is easy to be lax in discussing professional issues, including presentational material, without thinking about the unintended consequences of a disclosure or unprofessional treatment of information.

CONCLUSION

Trust is a major theme in the relationship between psychologists and persons with whom they work. To maintain trust, psychologists must respect the rights to privacy and confidentiality as well as the limits to those rights. The importance of respecting people's right to privacy and of maintaining the confidentiality obtained in the course of their work with psychologists has been reflected in prior APA Ethics Codes. With the increased complexity of legal requirements, psychologists will also be mindful of issues generated by electronic and other technologies and the corresponding need for guidance in dealing with issues of privacy and confidentiality.

5

ADVERTISING AND OTHER
PUBLIC STATEMENTS

Psychologists are permitted a wide range of communications about their services and activities as long as the advertisements or public statements are not false, deceptive, or fraudulent. Three General Principles of the "Ethical Principles of Psychologists and Code of Conduct" (hereinafter the APA *Ethics Code* or the *Ethics Code*; see http://www.apa.org/ethics/code2002.html)[1] are foundational concepts in the framing of ethical conduct by psychologists in regard to advertising and other public statements: General Principle A: Beneficence and Nonmaleficence, General Principle C: Integrity, and General Principle E: Respect for People's Rights and Dignity. These General Principles remind psychologists that professional activities that are not in direct service, such as advertising and media engagement, hold potential for unintended exploitation or manipulation of others. General Principle A: Beneficence and Nonmalificence is an integral concept in this section of the Ethics Code because there is a nonexploitation component woven throughout these standards. General Principle C: Integrity is a primary principle that articulates the importance of promoting accuracy, honesty, and truthfulness in the science,

---

[1]American Psychological Association. (2002). Ethical principles of psychologists and code of conduct. *American Psychologist, 57*, 1060–1073.

teaching, and practice of psychology. Honesty and accuracy in all the public representations of psychologists help to ensure public trust and confidence in the profession as well as in individual psychologists. General Principle E: Respect for People's Rights and Dignity has an important application for this section of the Ethics Code in regard to the value and respect of self determination. The concept of informed consent ensures that the public has the information to make a fully informed choice. Public statements, defined in the first standard in this section of the Ethics Code, include everything that psychologists write, publish, broadcast, articulate, or communicate in any way. The standards in this section also require that psychologists take responsibility for statements made by others by correcting any erroneous statements.

There are often others standards that call for a negotiation of ethical dilemmas and in which there are competing principles. Standards in Advertising and Other Public Statements are not necessarily competing standards, but rather, these standards are important because psychologists know that if they are not careful about these activities, people can make uninformed choices. Psychologists will make reasonable attempts to ensure that people are informed and, because of their positions of greater power, they will be cautious that they do not knowingly or unknowingly act in ways that result in the disadvantage of others.

Several sections of the Ethics Code are structured in a way that offers definitions of the standards and frames the context in which the standards of the section are presented. Section 5, Advertising and Other Public Statements, is one such section. Standard 5.01, Avoidance of False or Deceptive Statements, introduces advertising with a definition of public statements that provides psychologists examples of the many means by which psychologists communicate publicly. Other standards that accomplish this same purpose are the following: Standard 3.05, Multiple Relationships, in which multiple relationships are first defined prior to describing ethical conduct in multiple relationships; Standard 4.05, Disclosures, in which disclosures are not defined per se but are bifurcated into treatment of confidential information with consent and without consent; and Standard 9.04, Release of Test Data, in which the term *test data* is defined prior to the explanation of ethical conduct in regard to the release of test data with and without consent.

Standard 5.01 has been modified in the 2002 Ethics Code for clarity, and Standard 5.01a includes definitions of public statements about work activities. Standard 5.01b includes expectations of public statements about credentials, and Standard 5.01c describes how psychologists represent their academic degrees. Standard 5.02, Statements by Others, is not significantly changed from the 1992 Ethics Code[2] and deals with responsibility for public statements,

---

[2]American Psychological Association. (1992). Ethical principles of psychologists and code of conduct. *American Psychologist, 47*, 1597–1611.

prohibitions of compensation to media employees, and requirements that psychologists identify their advertising as such when they do advertise. Standard 5.03, Descriptions of Workshops and Non-Degree-Granting Educational Programs, is also not significantly changed and requires that psychologists maintain responsibility for the accuracy of their advertisements for workshops, seminars, or other non-degree-granting educational programs. Standard 5.04, Media Presentations, was modified for clarity and describes the responsibilities psychologists have when providing public advice or comment in the media. Standard 5.05, Testimonials, is similar to the one in the 1992 Ethics Code and describes when psychologists can and cannot use testimonials. Standard 5.06, In-Person Solicitation, was expanded to more clearly define in-person solicitation and to identify activities that are not precluded by this standard. All of the standards in these sections apply to all psychologists.

The Federal Trade Commission (FTC) has had important historical influence on some of these standards, beginning in 1986. The Ethics Code has liberalized advertising over time, including the recognition, as a result of the FTC's Bureau of Competition, that some of the Ethics Code standards imposed impermissible restrictions on methods of competition. The FTC also has pursued changes in the ethics codes of the American Medical Association, the American Dental Association, and other groups, and the U.S. Supreme Court upheld action by the FTC against the American Medical Association in 1982. The American Psychological Association (APA) and the FTC entered into a consent agreement regarding various provisions (some were rescinded, some were modified) to make the advertising standards acceptable to the FTC. The agreement defines some terms for purposes of that agreement, and the definitions in this section (*psychotherapy* and *current psychotherapy patient*) are relevant only when applying those portions of the Ethics Code covered by the FTC agreement. The FTC consent order was published in its entirety in the March 1993 APA *Monitor on Psychology*.[3] The period of the active order by the FTC was complete as of 2002.

Standard 5.01, Avoidance of False or Deceptive Statements

This standard requires that psychologists be accurate and honest in their public statements, to ensure public confidence in the individual and the profession. Standard 5.01(a) defines public statements about work activities and prohibits "knowingly" making false statements, and Standard 5.01(b) describes expectations about public statements about credentials. Expectations

---

[3]American Psychological Association (1993). FTC consent order text is published in its entirety. *Monitor on Psychology, 24(3),* 8.

about how psychologists represent their academic and professional degrees as evidence of their competence to provide health services are described in Standard 5.01(c).

Standard 5.01 provides a specific definition of the moral principle expressed in Principle C: Integrity; that is, that psychologists should aspire to promote accuracy, honesty, and truthfulness in the science, teaching, and practice of psychology. They must not engage in subterfuge or intentional misrepresentation of fact. This standard articulates the expectations of this principle in the public representation of their work activities, description of credentials, and representation of degrees as evidence of competence. These are basic expectations to ensure public confidence in the individual psychologist as well as the profession.

Standard 5.01(a)

Public statements include but are not limited to paid or unpaid advertising, product endorsements, grant applications, licensing applications, other credentialing applications, brochures, printed matter, directory listings, personal resumes or curricula vitae, or comments for use in media such as print or electronic transmission, statements in legal proceedings, lectures and public oral presentations, and published materials. Psychologists do not knowingly make public statements that are false, deceptive, or fraudulent concerning their research, practice, or other work activities or those of persons or organizations with which they are affiliated.

This standard provides broad and inclusive exemplars of public statements, defines *public statements*, and then describes the prohibition to "knowingly" make public statements that are false, deceptive, or fraudulent concerning one's research, practice, or other work activities. It combines Standard 3.01 from the 1992 Ethics Code, which simply provided the definition of public statements, with Standard 3.03(a) from that same code, which described the requirement to avoid false or deceptive statements.

Public statements of all kinds make an impression, and these impressions should be designed to inform and help others in their decision making about involvement in psychological services; public statements must not deceive and mislead. The scope of public statements and advertising is broadly defined, and the list provided in the standard is not exhaustive. It applies to other public statements not listed, such as yellow pages listings, Web sites, newspaper articles, and radio and television interviews.

This standard covers problems of commission (what statements state, convey, or suggest) as well as omission (what they omit). Problems largely depend on context. For example, listing one's membership in APA or other organizations in a brochure for a workshop might be appropriate; however, listing such information after one's signature on a report might be considered misleading in that it suggests that APA membership is a credential, which it is not, or that it implies expertise.

Although this standard does not apply to private statements made in personal conversations, psychologists must also be cognizant of avoiding false, deceptive, or fraudulent statements in gray areas regarding psychological matters made at association gatherings, in community roles, or in other situations in which one's status as a psychologist is known. If a psychologist makes statements that are reasonably believed to be true, even if he or she at some later point discovers that they are false, this would not necessarily represent inconsistency with this standard because the term *knowingly* is used to qualify the intent of the speaker. Informed and good faith representations that later are learned to be controversial or problematic may themselves not be a violation of the Ethics Code.

Psychologists are permitted to advertise through any medium, including radio, television, Web sites, business cards, brochures, and newsletters. Only public representations that are known to be false, misleading, fraudulent, or deceptive are prohibited. Although some methods may not be considered by many people to be preferable, such as billboards or electronic pop-up advertisements, those are not inherently unethical.

Standard 5.01(b)

Psychologists do not make false, deceptive, or fraudulent statements concerning (1) their training, experience, or competence; (2) their academic degrees; (3) their credentials; (4) their institutional or association affiliations; (5) their services; (6) the scientific or clinical basis for, or results or degree of success of, their services; (7) their fees; or (8) their publications or research findings.

Standard 5.01(b) does not use the term *knowingly* as Standard 5.01(a) does because the subjective standard of "knowing" does not apply to statements that psychologists make concerning their training, experience, competence, academic degrees, credentials, institutional or association affiliations, services, basis for success of their services, fees, or publications or research findings. It is assumed that psychologists have accurate knowledge about these facts; therefore, psychologists must not misinform, mislead, or deceive others, either through commission or omission, regarding any of the descriptors listed in the standard.

Standard 5.01(c)

Psychologists claim degrees as credentials for their health services only if those degrees (1) were earned from a regionally accredited educational

institution or (2) were the basis for psychology licensure by the state in which they practice.

This standard specifically allows psychologists to claim for psychological work only two types of credentials: (a) those earned from regionally accredited schools or other similar regional accrediting body approved by the U.S. Secretary of Education and (b) a degree that may not be from an accredited university but whose curriculum and training experiences were approved as the basis for the granting of licensure in a state in which the individual is practicing. Thus, this standard applies only to psychologists who are claiming degrees or credentials as evidence of their competence to provide health services, such as a PhD, EdD, or PsyD.

A person who presents him- or herself as doing psychological work and who lists a degree that was not received in psychology (e.g., a PhD in English or economics) would be misleading potential clients and could be considered in violation of this standard. Psychologists may claim degrees as credentials for health services only if those degrees were earned from a regionally accredited institution and are relevant to the provision of health services or if those credentials were the basis for psychology licensure by the licensing board in the state in which they practice.

Standard 5.02, Statements by Others

This standard provides the expectation that psychologists retain professional responsibility for public statements made by others whom they have hired, including individuals who review the materials of psychologists. Psychologists avoid actions that might encourage others to make false or fraudulent statements about their work Standard 5.02 provides direction and conveys psychologists' responsibilities when they engage others to promote their work and advertisements. Psychologists are ultimately responsible for the accuracy, appropriateness, and actual wording of advertising. In addition, psychologists do not pay media employees for publicity, and they clearly identify paid advertisements.

Standard 5.02(a)
Psychologists who engage others to create or place public statements that promote their professional practice, products, or activities retain professional responsibility for such statements.

Standard 5.02(a) applies to situations in which the psychologist can control a public statement, such as in hiring a practice management firm or advertising agency to promote his or her practice or hiring a consultant to write a resume. The psychologist maintains responsibility in prior review of materials and requiring the delegated person to consult with the psychologist on professionally significant decisions about the statements, such as how to designate the psychologist's credentials. When errors are made in such statements, the psychologist is responsible for ensuring that corrections are made once the errors have been discovered and for discontinuing the use of erroneous materials. The important action for compliance with this standard is to determine appropriate professional responsibility in each advertising activity and to ensure that the required actions are taken where necessary. Failure to prevent or to correct false, deceptive, or fraudulent public statements may constitute a violation of this standard depending on specific facts or incidences.

Standard 5.02(b)

Psychologists do not compensate employees of press, radio, television, or other communication media in return for publicity in a news item. (See also Standard 1.01, Misuse of Psychologists' Work.)

The intent of this standard is to avoid the payment of a journalist or related professional in exchange for including a quote or related information from a psychologist. This standard does not restrict advertising, but it does not allow the practice of misleading the public by providing "bought" publicity in the form of a news story.

Standard 5.02(c)

A paid advertisement relating to psychologists' activities must be identified or clearly recognizable as such.

The issue addressed by this standard is whether the material is a paid advertisement versus a news item or educational piece for which no compensation is paid. A regular newspaper or magazine column or presentation for the media is clearly not creating an advertisement; however, a "canned column," whereby the psychologist buys a column and runs it in a newspaper or newsletter, may be a paid advertisement, and the psychologist should state that it is such. Camouflaging promotional messages as news stories or educational messages is not allowed. Advertising is allowed so long as it is labeled as such.

Standard 5.02(a), Case 1

Case Illustration. For several years, Dr. W. has been offering continuing education workshops through his state psychological association and through other mental health groups in his home region. Dr. W. finds that he really enjoys presenting workshops, and according to his evaluations his workshops are both popular and receive positive feedback from attendees. Dr. W. has begun to develop a series of workshops on several different topics and has become interested in generating advanced workshops for individuals who have attended his more basic content workshops. Dr. W. is accustomed to preparing his own materials and producing his own marketing brochures. The associations that sponsor him typically assist in the reproduction of his materials, but he always writes and edits his own information.

As Dr. W.'s workshops expand, he begins to offer workshops in different locations and to travel for his presentations. Dr. W. continues to produce his own presentational content, but within a few months he finds that tailoring his marketing materials for each different location is too difficult, and he has begun to redirect his energies. He finds that to offer continuing education credit in different states, considerable time will need to be spent acquiring sponsorship from the professional associations of which his attendees are members. He realizes that attendance at his workshops is greatly influenced by the continuing education certificates the attendees can acquire and that the process for acquiring each of these is time consuming and arduous.

Dr. W. learns that there are marketing companies that do most of the aspects of his work that he does not want to do and, in fact, does not have the expertise to do. Dr. W. hires a marketing firm to produce his brochures and all marketing materials that describe his workshops, objectives and goals of the presentations, location, continuing education credits to be offered, and his credentials and biographical information.

Ethical Dilemma. Dr. W. provides the information to the marketing company for his brochures and public information regarding his workshops. The timing is good because Dr. W. has the opportunity to conduct a series of workshops back to back within a limited number of months, and he needs to get the marketing materials out as soon as possible to the state associations that have offered to distribute the materials. His marketing company will do direct mailing, and the professional associations have offered to include marketing material on their state association Web sites and continuing education listservs, and to include the information in the regular mailings of continuing education opportunities to their members if his marketing company can deliver the material within the next 2 weeks.

Dr. W. is very fastidious in writing and editing his materials before delivering them to the marketing company. He realizes that the marketing company has a very short turnaround window, but his contact person says they can manage it. When Dr. W. receives the copies of the materials the marketing company has developed and sent out, he is very dismayed and upset. The marketing company had included information that was not true of Dr. W.: He was designated as having an American Board of Professional Psychology certification, his years of licensure and practice experience were listed as 10 years less than his actual practice, his area of special interest and competency was incorrect, and his geographical area of practice was incorrect. Furthermore, testimonials had been added that he had not provided.

When Dr. W. calls the manager of the marketing firm, the problems are investigated, and he learns that two errors have occurred. The company has also done work with another psychologist of the same first and last name, and the editor had pulled the wrong file. In addition, the written materials Dr. W. had given the company had included some course evaluations, and the editor had decided to include some of the statements made in the evaluation. One statement written by an attendee stated that "Dr. W. offers a one-of-a-kind presentation and gives solutions to many problems." This statement, when reproduced, included the statement only; it did not include the fact that the statement was a quote from a participant; instead, it appeared as though Dr. W. were offering this evaluation himself.

Decision-Making Factors. Many psychologists face situations in which they have done everything properly and still find themselves at ethical risk because of others' actions or inaction. The two defining criteria within Standard 5.02(a) are that psychologists have hired individuals and that these individuals were hired for promotion of the psychologist. Psychologists who engage others for reasons other than to promote their own practice, products, or activities are not addressed in this standard, and psychologists who promote themselves in ways other than through engagement of others are addressed in Standard 5.01. Dr. W. realizes that his actions meet both of these conditions. Furthermore, the statements are clearly public statements as defined in Standard 5.01.

The marketing firm is most apologetic and returns the payment Dr. W. had made for the materials, but they had already sent out the mass mailings to the Midwestern states mailing list and had forwarded the information to the state associations and other local sponsors of the workshops. Dr. W. knows he has an ethical obligation to be responsible for his public materials and must take corrective action but is now unsure what he could do.

- Dr. W. considers what he could ask the marketing firm to do in addition to refunding his money. He could ask for an additional mailing that would highlight the corrected information. Even if the firm agreed to this, the information would not arrive before the workshop, and people would have made their decision to attend on the basis of the original material. This action, however, would still be a proactive gesture in the effort ethically to correct the information.

- He also considers asking the state associations and other sponsors to hold the material if they have not sent them out already; however, again the edits would not arrive in time for the participants to be informed. Furthermore, the state associations are counting on income from the attendance and may want to negotiate how to proceed because they also have a financial interest in the workshops.

- Dr. W. considers making the correction himself and then sending a direct mailing to all of the potential attendees whose names he can obtain. He does have the names of many of the prospective attendees, but the marketing firm will not give him their list of former attendees of their promoted events.
- Dr. W. also knows that he can correct the information at the beginning of the workshops and apologize at that time for the misrepresentation.
- Dr. W. realizes, too late, that he had overlooked the critical role of reviewing the final copy because of the time pressure of action and in spite of this being a new company and a new activity for him. He also realizes that he knows colleagues who would have been good consultants regarding issues to consider when using a professional firm for promotion. Consultation is appropriate and desirable not only in expansion of scope of expertise but also in delivery, communication, and enactment of an already-established expertise.

Decision Options. The determining factors for engaging with others and promoting his services mean that Dr. W. will want to make all reasonable efforts to correct the misinformation so that others will not be misled or exploited. Dr. W. therefore decides to do all of the preceding actions considered in his decision-making factors. He knows that he will correct all misinformation at the beginning of his presentation, so no one would have paid fees under false pretenses, and he will make every effort to persuade the marketing firm and the sponsors take corrective actions. He does not have control over the responsiveness of any of these groups, but he can document a good faith effort.

Also, Dr. W. realizes that the materials he gave the marketing firm were correct and that the errors occurred in production. In the future, he will review and edit all materials after they have been typeset, not just received by the editor.

Standard 5.03, Descriptions of Workshops and Non-Degree-Granting Educational Programs
 To the degree to which they exercise control, psychologists responsible for announcements, catalogs, brochures, or advertisements describing workshops, seminars, or other non-degree-granting educational programs ensure that they accurately describe the audience for which the program is intended, the educational objectives, the presenters, and the fees involved.

In the 1992 Ethics Code (APA, 1992) this standard appeared in the Teaching section and was placed in the Public Statements section of the 2002 Ethics Code because it is more relevant to the broad activities of psychologists, such as workshops and other training activities not related to degree-granting educational programs. In essence, this standard prohibits deception or misrepresentations when describing educational programs such as workshops, seminars, continuing education, and Internet presentations. The standard does recognize that psychologists should not be held accountable for decisions that are out of their control, for example, when others determine what should be included in publications such as announcements, catalogs, brochures, or other advertisements. Errors or misrepresentations by others may occur during the production of materials. Psychologists should take reasonable steps to correct errors or misrepresentations when they are made and be able to demonstrate their efforts to inform those who commit errors or misrepresentations about the accuracy of the descriptions, including target audience, goals of the program, the presenters, and fees.

Standard 5.04, Media Presentations

When psychologists provide public advice or comment via print, Internet, or other electronic transmission, they take precautions to ensure that statements (1) are based on their professional knowledge, training, or experience in accord with appropriate psychological literature and practice; (2) are otherwise consistent with this Ethics Code; and (3) do not indicate that a professional relationship has been established with the recipient. (See also Standard 2.04, Bases for Scientific and Professional Judgments.)

The standard that appeared in the 1992 Ethics Code was modified primarily for clarity; however, the types of media presentations are presented in a different manner, and direct presentations (in the 1992 code, "public lectures" and "demonstrations") are no longer covered by this standard; the list is limited to those listed (print and Internet) and "other electronic transmission." In the 1992 Ethics Code, the list was extended to include "other media." Also, whereas the 1992 Ethics Code required that "recipients of the information are not encouraged to infer that a relationship has been established with them personally," the 2002 Ethics Code requires that psychologists "do not indicate that a professional relationship has been established with the recipient." This latter provision is more focused on the behavior of the psychologist but is also probably less restrictive than the previous provision.

The standard sets forth three criteria against which to judge advice or comment and against which psychologists weigh their own statements. It essentially applies to psychologists who provide public advice or comment via print and any electronic media; the list has been expanded to include public comment via electronic transmission, but public lectures and demonstrations have been removed. The standard is designed to ensure that statements are not sensationalized or exaggerated or do not create a misleading impression; they must be based on psychologists' professional knowledge, training, or experience in accord with appropriate psychological literature and practice. Also, other standards must be considered along with this one, including Standard 2.04, Bases for Scientific and Professional Judgments. Psychologists must comply with other standards in giving advice in the media. Serving as a media psychologist does not exclude psychologists from compliance with all other ethical standards.

Psychologists must not indicate that a professional relationship has been established with the recipient. In general, psychologists should restrict their comments to generic information, because very little or nothing is known about the individual, the scope of his or her problems, or history, as is required in appropriate assessment and treatment. Disseminating general psychoeducational information is permissible, but attempting to provide direct treatment through specific advice or guidance in a public setting will raise many ethical questions under numerous standards. Therefore, indicating to recipients of the public information that there is a professional relationship will be misleading. Psychologists can further avoid misunderstanding by using a statement to emphasize the difference in role of media advice-giver and educator by suggesting that the person might talk with a psychotherapist.

It should also be noted that Internet communication that is not public advice or comment is not subject to this standard, which does not address delivery of psychological services via the Internet.

Standard 5.04, Case 1

Case Illustration. Dr. B. is a practicing psychologist who, as media psychology has grown in the public sector, has become interested in a public media component for his professional work. He has been on his state association's referral list for media interviews and for consultation when local events happen that also involved psychological aspects. Dr. B. finds that he likes being interviewed and giving his opinion on public matters. He has begun to be called for a variety of events. As a result, his practice changes in two ways. First, he begins to publish his positions and viewpoints on psychological matters on his Web site and welcomes comments through a chat feature. He also begins to give interviews on the radio and soon is able to acquire a regular time frame on the local radio station. Dr. B. is very pleased with this added dimension to his practice because it gives him additional visibility, benefiting his practice, and because he really enjoys the media work.

Ethical Dilemma. Dr. B. readily answers questions on his radio show and offers his advice and professional opinions through his chat feature of his Web site. He also provides articles that he has written for his Web site on a variety of psychological subjects. Dr. B has an avid listener named Jane who never misses his radio show and thinks that he gives the best advice she has ever received from any professional. She sees him as having much common sense and believes that he actually understands people like her. Jane has made several suicide attempts in the past years and is struggling with both an abusive domestic situation and an eating disorder. She has been to several professionals, but no one like Dr. B.

One day, on the air, Dr. B. mentions his Web site and the service he provides there of giving advice to those who log in and ask questions. Jane is delighted and begins reading his articles and submitting questions, which he answers. Jane also begins to call in periodically to the show and asks questions that Dr. B. always answers; his input seems to help her a lot. Jane can hardly believe that after going to several mental health professionals she has finally found someone who understands her circumstances and who can tell her what to do.

Dr. B. knows that Jane has called in several times, because she always identifies herself. He does not think this is unusual, because several people have made repeat calls. He does not realize, however, that she is also writing in to his chat room, and he does not realize how often she is following through on his advice.

Jane and her partner begin having more frequent arguments, resulting in fights. Jane has been trying to implement some of the actions Dr. B. had said were important for people who were dealing with her situation. One evening, Jane and her partner have a very hostile, violent argument in which Jane is assaulted. She is distraught and dismayed that the new approaches she has been using were not only not working but also having worse results than before she began trying to change. She is in such despair that she takes an overdose of sleeping pills. She is found by her sister, who takes her to the emergency room. When the intake interviewer asks Jane whether she is in the care of any professional, she answers, "Yes, Dr. B."

Decision-Making Factors. Three criteria apply for psychologists making decisions about media activity. These are stated specifically in Standard 5.04, and Dr. B. realizes that he needs to consider each of those criteria in his future decision making and in how he responds to the current dilemma.

Dr. B. is shocked to receive the call from the emergency room. He remembers a person named Jane calling in as well as the general problem she presented, but he had had no idea that she had embellished his role in her life the way she had, and he had not realized that she was getting advice from him through both media and had pieced his radio show, his articles, and his chat feature together into what in her mind was a professional service specifically for her.

Dr. B. realizes that although his intentions were to be ethical in his increased scope of practice, he had indeed not considered the three criteria for media presentations as closely as he should have.

1. He had not been as careful as he could have been in consistently telling his listening public that his advice and opinions were not meant to be direct services and that he was not providing services for individuals. He had not implied in his show that he was doing this, but he also had not specifically warned listeners against interpreting his show as providing direct services to the public.

2. Dr. B. also realizes that even though he had general and accurate information about domestic abuse and eating disorders, he does not have expertise in either area. He has been repeating what he knows through professional contacts and continuing education, but he does not have a practice that includes either of these areas of service. This action falls short of the first criterion for media presentations of basing his statements on professional knowledge, training, or experience in accordance with the literature and practices. In the future, Dr. B. will seek consultation when engaging in a new area or an activity in which he does not have established expertise.

3. Dr. B. has not paid sufficiently close attention to the parameters of electronic services. His intention had been to have an electronic version of his radio show, similar to a newspaper advice column. However, Dr. B. underestimated the extent to which Jane was perceiving his radio advice as individualized and the way in which chat communication could have the appearance of even more individualized advice. Not only would a needy potential client such as Jane see Dr. B.'s media communications as psychological services, but also his media presence would begin to resemble an ongoing relationship between a psychologist and client. Although this standard does not prohibit conducting psychological services in public, it reminds psychologists that they must meet all other standards in the Ethics Code if doing so. Ongoing work of this nature would likely fail in regard to informed consent, competence, proper assessment and diagnosis and treatment planning, and ultimately would harm Jane by depriving her of needed services.

Decision Options. Dr. B. knows that he will need to revamp his radio show primarily by being very specific and intentional in stating the limitations of the information he is giving. He will need to be alert to and monitor repeat callers to the best of his ability. He also realizes that he needs to limit his statements in the future to areas of his practice in which he claimed expertise; that is, even though he is not providing a psychological service on his radio show, he now knows that he should not make general statements about clinical diagnoses, treatment plans, or etiology of conditions that are not within his area of expertise.

Dr. B. is disappointed but resolute in closing out his chat feature. He thinks it has increased his practice and referral sources, but he realizes that the risk of misinterpretation is great, and he decides that he will not continue to provide that service. He decides to continue uploading his articles and other material on his Web site, but he plans to limit all activity to one-directional information rather than interactive material.

Dr. B. knows that other colleagues are providing Internet services and, in fact, have clients who are receiving therapy over the Internet. Such an expansion had not been Dr. B's thought at any time. His intention had been to support media psychology and not to expand his Internet practice.

Dr. B. decides not to accept Jane as an Internet client or a conventional client and refers her to another professional with the necessary expertise to serve her. Dr. B. could decide with consultation from appropriate colleagues, to meet with Jane, at no charge, in order to correct the misinterpretations and misunderstandings about his services and his role as a media psychologist and to correct her perception of his role in her treatment; not to meet in person and instead write a letter; or to have no communication at all. The important factor is for Dr. B. to make a clinically sound judgment about how to communicate with Jane. He will need to be prudent and responsible in whatever choice he makes and to balance risk management with Jane's best interests.

Standard 5.05, Testimonials

Psychologists do not solicit testimonials from current therapy clients/patients or other persons who because of their particular circumstances are vulnerable to undue influence.

This standard prohibits solicitation of testimonials from all current therapy clients/patients on the assumption that a current client/patient might be susceptible to undue influence in the therapeutic relationship. The standard also prohibits solicitation of testimonials from former therapy clients/patients if their particular life circumstances result in their being vulnerable to undue influence. The prohibition against solicitation of testimonials from all current therapy clients/patients recognizes that the nature of the relationship between therapist and client/patient is such that the power differential, the dependence on the psychologist for treatment, the potential transference, as well as other factors, could result in undue influence. Because the needs of the psychologist could obstruct treatment, this boundary is essential to prevent potential exploitation. These dynamics sometimes continue for a period of time after treatment ends, depending on the length and intensity of treatment, and the client/patient's mental status. Thus, psychologists must approach former clients/patients for testimonials with caution, determining whether they are vulnerable to undue influence.

This standard does not prohibit the use of testimonials, although proof of exploitation would violate the Ethics Code; for example, other standards, such as Standard 4.01, Maintaining Confidentiality; Standard 3.05, Multiple Relationships; and Standard 3.08, Exploitative Relationships, might apply.

This standard does not cover testimonials from participants in activities other than psychotherapy. Thus, testimonials regarding a psychologist's workshops, seminars, or organizational/industrial work are not prohibited by this standard.

Standard 5.06, In-Person Solicitation

Psychologists do not engage, directly or through agents, in uninvited in-person solicitation of business from actual or potential therapy clients/patients or other persons who because of their particular circumstances are vulnerable to undue influence. However, this prohibition does not preclude (1) attempting to implement appropriate collateral contacts for the purpose of benefiting an already engaged therapy client/patient or (2) providing disaster or community outreach services.

This standard is designed to prohibit "ambulance chasing." It treats as vulnerable all actual or potential therapy clients, as well as any other person whose particular circumstances make him or her susceptible to undue influence. It does not prohibit solicitation so long as the vulnerability problem is not present. For example, soliciting mourners at a funeral home, or going by the residences of survivors located through names listed in obituaries, would be prohibited. However, the FTC has sought to ensure that this standard does not prohibit leaving professional cards or flyers on tables at a shopping mall, for example. The FTC is concerned that the standard allowed for activities that are in congruence with the First Amendment and the importance of permitting free competition.

An inherent conflict of interest exists in the act of solicitation of services when profit or personal gain is a factor. This prohibition does not preclude responding to others in circumstances of urgent distress or when a risk to self or others is posed.

The prohibition applies only to contacts that are uninvited and occur in person (including telephone contacts, according to case law), whether by the psychologist or through an agent of the psychologist. Contacts invited by the potential client/patient or conducted through general mailings or other methods are allowable.

The standard explicitly allows the invitation of a collateral contact (i.e., family member or significant other) of a current client/patient to participate in treatment to benefit the client/patient. Psychologists do not solicit collaterals such as family members or significant others of individual clients/patients for treatment, but there are times when psychologists working with clients/patients need to include these collateral contacts in the therapy process.

The standard was also modified to explicitly allow for participation in community outreach or disaster services. Psychologists may offer services through a community program for homeless persons, older adults, or others who may not ordinarily self-refer for mental health services, or emergency services to individuals who are vulnerable as a result of natural disasters such as hurricanes or earthquakes, or other disasters, such as terrorist activities.

Standard 5.06, Case 1

Case Illustration. Dr. S. is a community psychologist who has worked in the public sector for many years. He also has a small private practice and has been seeing an individual client named David in his general practice. David is working on several interpersonal and work-related goals in his psychotherapy, but his most pressing and important problem at present is the care of his aging father. His father had been very active in his community and continued living in his own home after David's mother had died. His father has begun to develop dementia during the past several years and now has been diagnosed with Alzheimer's disease. His father can no longer live in his home alone. David is distressed and concerned because he has two brothers whom he thinks need to be involved in the decisions regarding his father. David has been the primary caregiver through these past years, but he does not want to make decisions alone. He knows that Dr. S. cannot be involved in actual decisions about his father, but he thinks that Dr. S. might facilitate a conversation among the three brothers.

Dr. S. and David discuss this possibility, and Dr. S. agrees that he could try to be helpful in bridging the gap that has grown between David and his brothers. Dr. S. is mindful of the distinctive role delineations between providing services to multiple individuals as clients, such as families and couples, and providing service to an individual client for whom multiple individuals (i.e., collaterals) participate in the sessions for the benefit of the client. His intention is that the two brothers participate in David's sessions as collaterals, and he is careful to frame the invitation to sessions in that way as well as to restate the roles of everyone once the sessions are held. David speaks with his brothers about engaging with him in session and explains their roles and Dr. S.'s intentions and role.

Ethical Dilemma. Dr. S. begins a series of three sessions with all three brothers and quickly realizes that several dynamics are afoot that complicate the goal of bridging the gap among the brothers and that create some difficult decision making for him. David's brother Jim is married and has been in intense and ongoing marital conflict for some time. Jim has been so immersed in his own family difficulties that he feels unable to also attend to their father. Jim is having a struggle with his wife and her parents in regard to child-rearing practices and how to deal with some behavioral problems that have cropped up with their teenage son. This problem is exacerbating the difficulties Jim and his wife are having, and Jim seems to want to spend the sessions talking about his own marital problems and to use the sessions for his own edification and understanding of his own family difficulties.

David's second brother, Tim, had been diagnosed with schizophrenia 10 years earlier and has been able to live independently with the assistance of his parents and because he has been in a group home where his medications and his activities are somewhat monitored. However, various circumstances have resulted in Tim being taken out of the group home, and his living situation is now in question. He is currently homeless. Since their mother died and their father became ill, Tim's resources, both human and financial, have been dwindling. He is very scared about his future and what will happen to him. David cares about his brother but is unable to provide financial help. He also does not know where to turn for any public assistance or other mental health assistance for Tim.

Dr. S., through his public sector experience, has worked with couples in the very conditions that Jim is experiencing; he also has worked in outpatient community-based health centers and knows the possibilities for Tim in that community. But Dr. S. is also conscientious about the fact that he has invited the two brothers in as collateral participants, not as clients, and he wants to make an ethical decision about how to proceed with services.

Decision-Making Factors. Dr. S. thinks about the ethical standard that warns against uninvited solicitation of business from potential clients and other persons who are vulnerable to undue influence. The exceptions to this prohibition include collateral contact for current client benefit and disaster or community outreach services. Dr. S. thinks that both Jim and Tim need professional assistance with their respective personal circumstances. Dr. S. knows that had David told him about his brothers' circumstances that even though he had the expertise to provide professional assistance to both of them he would not have initiated such service because of the ethical implications of soliciting business from potential clients who were vulnerable. Both of these individuals, in

Dr. S.'s view, are vulnerable and may not be able to make an informed decision but instead might accept his services because of their circumstances.

Dr. S. also thinks about the two exceptions to this standard: (a) collateral inclusion for the welfare of the current client and (b) community service. He thinks through the fact that he is seeing Jim, who is financially and cognitively able to decide on and pursue his own psychological services, under the collateral conditions. Tim, on the other hand, is also being seen as collateral but is in dire need of help and is, in Dr. S.'s view, a person for whom services may be seen as providing community outreach service. Dr. S. will explore whether Tim is already in treatment and if so, with whom, so that care can be coordinated (see Standard 3.09, Cooperation With Other Professionals).

Decision Options. Dr. S. realizes that he must think about each of these individuals in light of Standard 5.06 and make a determination about each accordingly.

- The client, David, is being seen for individual therapy, and Dr. S. feels confident about the continued work with David in light of the ethical aspects of informed consent, human relations, and areas of his expertise.
- David's brother Jim needs psychological services just as David does, but Dr. S. determines that he is in fact vulnerable because he is beginning to feel desperate about his situation, and Dr. S. knows that agreeing to provide services for Jim would be done within the context of Jim's vulnerability. He is, in fact, seeing Jim but within the acceptable exception of collateral participation. He decides that his contact with Jim should remain so.
- Dr. S. is concerned about Tim and knows that if he continues without assistance and direction, or at least information that could assist him, Tim's circumstances are likely to further deteriorate. Dr. S. thinks that it would also be a multiple role conflict to work with Tim on his problems in the guise of collateral contribution within David's sessions.
- As a result, Dr. S. may decide to offer pro bono services to Tim in order both to give him information about the public sector that could be helpful to him and to give him direct services that might help stabilize him for the next set of decisions to be made regarding his living circumstances.

Overall, these sessions prove helpful for the original reason of David understanding the nature of the challenges in relation to his brothers, and he realizes their current and long-term limitations in caring for their father. Dr. D.

realizes the importance of having set goals for his inclusion of collateral family members toward David's objectives.

CONCLUSION

The Advertising and Other Public Statements standard provides guidance for psychologists about their communications about their services and activities. The principles of helping and not harming (General Principle A: Beneficence and Nonmaleficence); promoting trust for the individual psychologist and the profession by promoting accuracy, honesty, and truthfulness (General Principle C: Integrity); and protecting the rights and welfare of persons or communities who may be vulnerable (General Principle E: Respect for People's Rights and Dignity) are applied in this standard.

6

RECORD KEEPING AND FEES

Record keeping is not an end in itself but rather a process psychologists use to reflect their purpose, values, and roles in conducting themselves professionally. Psychologists should view the documentation of their professional activities through a frame of reference that weighs relevant factors such as work setting; population served; the nature of the activity; expected use of their records; jurisdiction; and, at times, client wishes, all of which result in considerable variance in record-keeping formats. Section 6 of the American Psychological Association's (APA's) "Ethical Principles of Psychologists and Code of Conduct" (hereinafter the *APA Ethics Code* or the *Ethics Code*; see http://www.apa.org/ethics/code2002.html),[1] Record Keeping and Fees, provides a context in which psychologists are encouraged to exercise their professional judgments in deciding how to document their work in order to respect the rights of the clients/patients whom they serve, to enact their professional roles responsibly, and to fulfill their specific documentation needs and obligations.

---

[1]American Psychological Association. (2002). Ethical principles of psychologists and code of conduct. *American Psychologist, 57*, 1060–1073.

The 2002 Ethics Code is written so that the enforceable standards incorporate key elements from the five general principles. General Principle B: Fidelity and Responsibility identifies the importance of trust and the corresponding responsibility in creating records regarding individuals' personal and private information, General Principle C: Integrity promotes honesty and truthfulness in the accuracy of record keeping and the transparency of fee arrangements, and General Principle D: Justice recognizes the importance of fairness and equal quality in how psychologists treat the documentation of information and in determination of fees. In making record-keeping decisions, psychologists think about objectives on multiple levels, asking themselves "What is the purpose of creating this record? How are record-keeping standards informing decisions, and what are the values being served through these standards?" The professional record-keeping activities cited in the Ethics Code of creating, maintaining, disseminating, storing, retaining, and disposing of records and data are reliable ways in which psychologists reflect their values through ethical and clinical decision-making processes in the exercise of prudent professional judgment.

The professional context and objectives of record keeping described in Standard 6.01 (Documentation of Professional and Scientific Work and Maintenance of Records) provide an overview of how psychologists may think about the application of documentation to their work. The remaining six standards identify two primary areas in which record keeping and documentation apply across aspects of professional activity: (a) confidentiality in the care of client/patient documents (Standard 6.02) and (b) financial transactions (Standards 6.03–6.07).

Standard 6.01, Documentation of Professional and Scientific Work and Maintenance of Records

Psychologists create, and to the extent the records are under their control, maintain, disseminate, store, retain, and dispose of records and data relating to their professional and scientific work in order to (1) facilitate provision of services later by them or by other professionals, (2) allow for replication of research design and analyses, (3) meet institutional requirements, (4) ensure accuracy of billing and payments, and (5) ensure compliance with law. (See also Standard 4.01, Maintaining Confidentiality.)

This standard invites psychologists to develop effective ways of documenting their work that are compatible with their purpose and approach and is one of the few instances in the Ethics Code in which the reason for the standard is offered. Psychologists reflect on what decisions will be made given the functional purpose for which the record is being kept. Considerations include the following four examples: (a) the likelihood that the record will be relied on by third parties for decision-making purposes; (b) continuity of care and urgent care needs with specific populations, such as older people and persons with developmental disabilities; (c) expectation of litigation with high-risk clients/patients; or (d) service to individuals who are geographically moving and need continuity of treatment. The five reasons for effective and purposeful documentation cited in this standard offer psychologists a framework in which to differentially identify the context of the work activity and the inherent record-keeping purpose. This knowledge enables psychologists to make choices about their documentation that are compatible with their professional values and ethical obligations.

Standard 6.01(1), Facilitate Provision of Services Later by [Psychologists] or by Other Professionals

A record that is written primarily from a clinical frame of reference is intended to clearly and accurately portray the salient features of a case so that the case can be understood across time and multiple professionals. Some of the decision factors that may go into a record could include questions such as the following:

- What do psychologists want the reader to know regarding the purpose, course, and outcome of treatment?
- How would psychologists want to differentially represent clinical information, for example, that describes recommendations that would result from an evaluation/assessment; describes psychotherapy treatment information directed at interpersonal or intrapersonal patterns; or lends itself to requests from educational, forensic, or unanticipated service entities (e.g., custody, educational placement)?
- How might records differ in a private practice versus a training setting? Records being written by private practice psychologists who expect to have control and responsibility over client/patient material are likely to take a different form than records being created by a trainee and supervised by a licensed psychologist who expects others in training and in later rotation of training services to view the records.
- How might psychologists incorporate developmental factors in a case such that descriptions made contemporarily about an adolescent or child could be interpreted differently or have differential treatment implications at a later time?

The obligation of psychologists in clinical record keeping is to ensure that the welfare of the client/patient has been protected and that the record is comprehensible for treatment, referral, and disposition purposes.

Standard 6.01(2), Allow for Replication of Research Design and Analyses

Four of the reasons to keep records enumerated in Standard 6.01 pertain to professional work; Standard 6.01(2) pertains to scientific work. Record keeping from the frame of reference of scientific inquiry may focus on the quality of data treatment for purposes of peer review, replication, content accountability, and financial accountability. Record keeping and documentation for research purposes may be subject to much greater prescription by authorizing entities than record keeping in other professional venues. Because of exploitation and abuse by some individuals in the past, research universities, funding agencies, publishers, and governmental entities have instituted requirements for conducting research that detail treatment of informed consent, manipulation of experimental variables, analysis of data, reported findings, and other factors. Furthermore, these entities often have specific requirements for data collection procedures; data retention time frames; conditions of data storage; and transmission of information among collaborators, multiple research sites, and data reporting systems (see also Standard 8.02, Informed Consent to Research).

The constituencies that researchers often consider in decisions of documenting scientific findings and judgments include peer reviewers; other scientists pursuing similar research; members of the public who may make decisions based on scientific findings; readers of scientific journals who may base research questions on existing findings; and funding agencies that have several vested interests, including ethical and legal treatment of subjects and others involved in the study, financial responsibility, accurate documentation of all phases of the study, and the validity of the eventual findings. Institutional review board approval is often required; when it is not required, it may be prudent (see also Standard 8.01, Institutional Approval).

Psychologists who are engaged in psychological research will want to consider several factors in record keeping and documentation, such as criteria of the authorizing entities, including institutional review board requirements; treatment of subjects; adequate description of the aspects of the study; and compatibility in documentation across governmental, university, and institutional entities. Record keeping for scientific purposes takes a course of development that is very distinct from other documentation efforts. Standard 3.10(d) states that when informed consent is required, it must be documented. In addition, Standard 8.02(a) identifies specific informational components of the research that are required when Standard 3.10 is applicable (see Standard 3.10, Informed Consent, and Standard 8.02, Informed Consent to Research).

Standard 6.01(3), Meet Institutional Requirements

Psychologists performing professional activities from an organizational frame of reference will be cognizant of informed-consent conditions; answering the questions of who the client is and who is receiving the services; identifying the control of the records, both during service provision and in later transfer or access to records; limitations of confidentiality; administrative roles; and other key procedural concepts that apply particularly to management and corporate systems. Furthermore, institutional requirements may apply to hospitals, Veterans Affairs institutions, and academic and educational settings in which the role of psychologists is one other than clinician, such as consultant, mediator, human resource specialist, or administrator of services. Individual institutions or organizations may have their own record-keeping policies of which psychologists would want to be aware.

Role diffusion may occur in these settings if the professional tasks and functions are not specified through documentation because some of the activities in organizational roles are similar to those in clinical roles. Questioning conducted during intake, administering assessments and evaluations, fostering a positive interaction during face-to-face transactions, and responding to personal expression are associated with clinical services. Documentation of the manner in which the professional role is distinctly conducted in organizational settings can assist psychologists in accurately representing themselves (see also Standard 3.11, Psychological Services Delivered To or Through Organizations).

Standard 6.01(4), Ensure Accuracy of Billing and Payments

Record keeping and documentation from a billing and payment frame of reference may include the reflection of transactions with private insurance companies; managed care companies; government entities, including Medicare and Medicaid; individual client billing; organizational billing; and forms that document services rendered, date of service, treatment, diagnosis, and other information requested. Accurate and understandable records that can explain the essential elements of services rendered are an excellent protection against misinterpretations of services and resulting difficulties in billing questions and payment. A psychologist may be asked for information for billing purposes that would not otherwise be included in the record and that the psychologist may think is detrimental to the welfare of the client; thus, the information included in a record may vary significantly depending on the purpose of the record and sometimes be at cross-purposes when the client's clinical well-being, for example, may not suggest the same course of action as record keeping for billing and payment.

Standard 6.01(5), Ensure Compliance With [the] Law

Statutes, regulations, and court cases at both the federal and state levels may address record keeping. We note from a legal frame of reference, however, that there are other federal and state laws with which psychologists become familiar. Federal regulations in provision of health care, including Medicaid and Medicare; federal regulations applied to education through the Family Educational Rights and Privacy Act and the Health Insurance Portability and Accountability Act (HIPAA); and many state regulations remind psychologists to be cognizant at all levels of legal jurisdiction of the rules and regulations governing them.

In addition, psychologists who work primarily in forensic settings become well aware of the jurisdictional implications, court proceedings, and regulations that affect their practice. This is an area of practice in which psychologists remain keenly aware that their records may serve many purposes and that their clinical records, evaluations, consultations, and all actions lend themselves to additional review by other professionals as well as the fact that others may have a specific investment in the psychologists' findings. Forensic records are expected to have a degree of specificity, focus, and treatment of content that may be quite different from clinical records, and psychologists are expected to be familiar with the protocols and procedures within court jurisdictions (see Standard 2.01[f], Boundaries of Competence).

Standard 6.01, Case 1

Case Illustration. Dr. D. is a psychologist in a large interdisciplinary organization. Because of the comprehensive services and scope of the practice, many referrals are received for the practice in addition to those received for individual professionals. Dr. D. has a practice within the organization but also has the administrative role of assigning the generic referrals to individual psychologists. The organization has developed a complex but fair and systematic way to carry out this function. Dr. D. receives two referrals from other psychologists in the community, both of which, coincidentally, reflect significant record-keeping problems, and he is concerned that these inadequate records could seriously impede the facilitation of services by psychologists in Dr. D.'s organization. The treating psychologists are transferring these clients for necessary and reasonable purposes, but the records of each challenge continuity of care.

Case 1 is a referral of an 87-year-old man whose record reflects extensive mental status testing, individual therapy, and family therapy. The client has been hospitalized several times related to his diabetes, and there is a brief mention of a psychiatric evaluation while he was in the hospital. The client's family members have already called Dr. D. to ask which psychologist the father will be seeing. They want to speak to that psychologist as soon as possible to learn more about why their father is being seen and what his treatment will be. Dr. D. realizes that the records do not identify any diagnosis; course of treatment plan; outcome of the hospital visit; or any informed consent, power of attorney, or guardianship documents. The fees for service collected have been well documented, and apparently the client had written personal checks for all services.

Case 2 involves a 26-year-old man who has applied with the local police department to become a police officer. The psychologist who evaluates applicants for the police department had asked the man for any health records pertaining to his physical or psychological status. When the applicant was beginning high school, his parents had been concerned about behavioral problems, including being oppositional, loitering after school, and two incidents of knocking over mailboxes with his buddies. He was evaluated by a psychologist, who described these problems and gave the opinion that this behavior would escalate as he grew older. On receiving a copy of this report, the psychologist working for the police department rejected the applicant on the basis of instability evidenced in this previous psychological report. The applicant is seeking a new evaluation from Dr. D.'s organization to clear his record.

Ethical Dilemma. Standard 6.01(1) requires psychologists to include in the psychological record information that is necessary to transfer that case to another professional with ease of continuity and that would typically apply, given the context of the case. Some information, in particular data regarding identification, purpose and course of treatment or service, and fees and disposition, would be provided in most cases. This specificity is important because an organizational case, a custody case, and an assessment case would all call for some differentiation of content, specificity, duration, jurisdictional authority, and other factors.

Dr. D. realizes that in Case 1 critical information is missing that would be needed for the appropriate disposition and subsequent transfer of the case and that in Case 2 the record contains information that likely misrepresents the client's status. Dr. D. begins to think about the application of Standard 6.01(1) in both cases, and even though neither he nor his colleagues have participated in the inadequate record keeping, he now wonders what his and his practice's roles are in working with these clients.

In Case 1 there is no coherent record of the reason for testing, individual therapy, family therapy, or hospitalization. There are indirect references to the client's memory problems but no diagnosis. Additional problems include inadequacy or absence of informed consent for the family access to records of the client and for authorization of mental status testing (Standard 3.10a; see also Standard 4.01a, which addresses breaches of the client's confidentiality with family members' access to information, and Standard 4.02a, which addresses the failure to explain the limits of confidentiality to the client and to the family).

In Case 2, Dr. D. continues to be primarily concerned about Standard 6.01(1) but also notes that he would have considered not releasing the report given that it could be used in misrepresentation of the client (Standard 9.04a). The test data are most likely outdated and should not be used in decision making (Standard 9.08a), and instead of just releasing the report, he would have explained the results and the limitations of their use (Standard 9.10).

Decision-Making Factors. Regarding both cases, Dr. D. should consider the purpose of the record, the content and detail needed for continuity of care, and how the information should be used and in what context. Dr. D. would need to consider contacting both psychologists regarding the problems inherent in each record.

In Case 1, Dr. D. is troubled by the failure of the record to reflect continuity of care, potential violations of confidentiality, and absence of informed consent. Dr. D. suspects that the client may have memory and other related problems and has been treated as though he had legal caretakers even though no legal transaction had transpired. Dr. D. is concerned that this client is vulnerable to exploitation given that he has been writing checks to pay for his care and that the client's best interest may not have been served given that the psychologist was meticulous with fee records but not treatment records.

In Case 2, Dr. D. might determine that a very different set of problems is presented. The original report could well have been appropriate for the purpose of testing at the time. The report, however, seemed to allude to treatment and the potential consequences of no treatment but did not make specific recommendations or qualify the evaluator's opinion that "behaviors could escalate." Dr. D. is inclined to think that even if the psychologist's report is accurate, the report does not facilitate provision of services these years later. Dr. D. would focus on the failure of this report to lend itself to future use and, more important, to continuity of care, in particular because the context of this case was one in which developmental changes and age-related behaviors should have been contextualized.

Decision Options. Dr. D. hesitates to accept Case 1 as a referral at that time before learning about the critical factors of purpose of treatment and current diagnosis so that he can understand the course of treatment. He is frustrated by how little helpful information the previous treatment professional has provided. He knows that an important reason for keeping accurate and thorough records is to facilitate transfer of services. He also realizes that, even though his organization includes several psychologists who work with older adults, a thorough consultation with the client would be needed in order to explain his rights to confidentiality, the limits of confidentiality, informed consent, and to hear from the client what services he wants. Dr. D. would want a release of information from the client in order to talk with the psychologists and to request testing data. Furthermore, if the client wants his family to have access to information, Dr. D. will need to execute an informed-consent authorization. He also will need to explain these limits and the necessary course of action to the family.

In Case 2, Dr. D. will consider the purpose of any further testing and whether this would be the best method to approach the case. Dr. D. realizes that outdated information had been used to make a decision and that the correction of this breach could take several forms. Dr. D. might envision a consultative role with both the police psychologist and the evaluating psychologist. A corrective recommendation to the evaluating psychologist might suggest a qualifying letter or statement that would explain the ethical and clinical problems in the use of outdated material. Furthermore, a consultation with the police psychologist could clarify developmental aspects of adolescent behaviors, in particular because the behavioral, academic, and interpersonal history of the client contraindicate the earlier concern. Dr. D. or the psychologist who would fulfill the consultative role would also inform the client of the needed transactions, obtain informed consent and a release for records, and ensure that the client understands every aspect of the case as it continues to evolve.

Psychologists are mindful in all of these professional transactions that the welfare of the client and the best interest of the client (General Principle E: Respect for People's Rights and Dignity) are paramount. Dr. D. might well surmise that these psychologists may have lost sight of this foundational concept in the execution of their judgment in these cases.

Standard 6.02, Maintenance, Dissemination, and Disposal of Confidential Records of Professional and Scientific Work

How might psychologists think about the purpose of documentation in the context of confidentiality? Confidentiality is one of the organizing concepts that define professionalism in psychology, so much so that Section 4 of the APA Ethics Code is devoted to the role of confidentiality and privacy in professional conduct. Psychologists convey information that is relevant to professional activities in a manner that is accurate and respectful, in particular when the information is relied on in making a professional judgment.

The purpose of a record varies within clinical, research, organizational, legal, and payment contexts. Confidentiality is a unified concept, yet it must often be implemented differently in these contexts. For example, psychologists' compliance with confidentiality might take a different form in a forensic child custody record or a management consultation record than in a fee-for-service psychotherapy record. Informed consent is a valued process for clarification in how confidentiality will apply in a given number of circumstances, the exceptions to confidentiality, the limits of confidentiality, and the purpose for which records are kept. Several standards incorporate a reference to application of confidentiality within informed-consent passages. These include reference to the limits of confidentiality as an aspect of informed consent in organizational settings with clients and those affected by the service (Standard 3.11a[7]); with persons with whom psychologists have a scientific or professional relationship (Standard 4.02a[1]); in the use of research data (Standard 8.02a[6]); in conducting assessments, evaluations, or diagnostic services (Standard 9.03a[3]); and in conducting psychotherapy (Standard 10.01a). In decision making regarding documentation and confidentiality, psychologists balance the dual values of (a) creating an effective record that serves the professional purpose within the specific setting and (b) respecting the welfare and rights of individuals with whom they work.

Decision-making questions that psychologists may consider in developing confidential records include the following:

- What is the context (e.g., clinical, research, organizational, legal, billing) in which the record is being created?
- What is the purpose of the record?
- Whose confidentiality is protected through the record?
- What entities and individuals may want access to the record, and what are the confidentiality implications of access to this material?
- Must the information be included in the record to demonstrate the basis of prudent and professional judgment? If so, how does this inclusion affect the understanding of confidentiality with the service recipients?
- How can the purpose of the record most effectively be achieved while also protecting the confidentiality of the clients/patients?
- If confidentiality cannot be ensured, what actions may be most effective in responding to the potential compromise?

Psychologists are aware that there are several sources of record-keeping information, some of which are recommended and some of which carry required compliance. These include the APA record-keeping guidelines as outlined in the Ethics Code, federal laws and regulations such as HIPAA (including the exemption for psychotherapy notes), state laws and regulations, university requirements for institutional review and grant oversight, and federal requirements for educational records (i.e., the Family Educational Rights and Privacy Act). The specific requirements for retention and for compliance may change over time. Psychologists stay informed of the current and changing status of the multiple entities within which they develop, retain, and dispose of records.

Standard 6.02(a)

Psychologists maintain confidentiality in creating, storing, accessing, transferring, and disposing of records under their control, whether these

are written, automated, or in any other medium. (See also Standards 4.01, Maintaining Confidentiality, and 6.01, Documentation of Professional and Scientific Work and Maintenance of Records.)

As the scope of professional and scientific activities has expanded, professional practices such as record keeping that support those activities have evolved in order for them to be effective and useful. Technological advances, including computerized record keeping, advancing access to information via electronic transmission, the ease of electronic transfer of information requested and received, limited means of monitoring transactions, and ease of altering information, are all relatively new electronic influences on psychologists' professional functioning. These advances present new challenges to the practice of confidentiality at every stage of record treatment. Furthermore, health services, organizational consultation, research collaboration, training, and the business of conducting psychological activity in these arenas require access and transfer by multiple entities and individuals through multiple professional settings, resulting in significant implications for dissemination of records. Psychologists maintain confidentiality in their own record treatment; however, these emerging expectations of multiple purpose and need for records may place limits on psychologists' control of records and potentially compromise confidentiality.

Psychologists are aware of the requirement to maintain confidentiality in the retention, dissemination, and disposal of records across varying settings and jurisdictions. Circumstances may vary regarding the need to retain, disseminate, or dispose of documents, and thus the appropriate means of enacting confidentiality may vary. For example, the need to keep records for organizational consultation services may differ from the need to keep records to facilitate the safety of a suicidal client/patient. In the latter case, the conditions of limits and disclosure on confidentiality may come into question. The context in which the psychological services are being rendered has implications for confidentiality in the maintenance and dissemination of records. Some examples of contexts include: (a) electronic transmission of records that comply with federal and state regulations, (b) retention of research records and data that are compliant with policies set by grantors (i.e., federal, state, private, or other) as well as the funding component within those grants that monitor the specific costs and compensation, (c) forensic records that comply with the requirements of the jurisdiction in which the case is being considered (the level of detail and timing of events can be significant in providing information for legal decision making, in particular in regard to provision of expert testimony), (d) clinical and other records that are psychological in nature and that are appropriate to consider within the professional, state, and federal guidelines. Psychologists adhere to ethical standards of confidentiality in these and other contexts. Confidentiality in application to Family Educational Rights and Privacy Act documents, HIPAA-compliant documents, and forensic records applicable to a state jurisdiction may require psychologists to practice confidentiality in consideration of various factors.

Psychologists are mindful of retention and disposal policies within the profession (e.g., record-keeping guidelines, forensic guidelines), the jurisdiction in which the records are kept, and through organizational agreements (e.g., companies, state agencies, community mental health centers, university counseling centers). Even though, for example, professional guidelines may establish a 7-year retention of records, a state statute may require a 10-year record retention. Confidentiality in retention of records, including storage and access of records over time, is an important determination. Records that may be archived but retained are kept in a location whose security is equal to that in which active records are kept. The disposal of records may occur through several different processes but must be treated with continued confidentiality.

Psychologists must also be mindful of the preservation of confidentiality in recorded transactions and may consider the following decision-making questions in regard to the purpose of the record:

- What entities are most likely to receive this information, and for what purpose? How will these factors affect confidentiality standards?
- Is the recorded information most likely to be needed in a clinical, research, organizational, legal, or billing settings, and how will these factors affect confidentiality in record maintenance and dissemination?
- What is the level of detail called for given the purpose of the record (e.g., basic data; background and history; legal engagement; hospitalization; prior diagnoses; relational information; focus on work, personal, academic, health data), and does this level of detail have implications for successful maintenance of confidentiality?
- What are the vehicles by which information will travel (e.g., electronic, paper, audio, video), and are there special considerations regarding confidentiality for these means of information access? What are the implications for information dissemination?
- What are the limitations of confidentiality in the record-keeping process in any specific case, and how should affected individuals be informed?
- What are the organizational procedures, federal or state policies, and professional guidelines for disposal of records in terms of length of time of retention? In the process of disposal, are these processes congruent with confidentiality standards for records?

Standard 6.02(b)

If confidential information concerning recipients of psychological services is entered into databases or systems of records available to persons whose access has not been consented to by the recipient, psychologists use coding or other techniques to avoid the inclusion of personal identifiers.

The business of practice as shaped by legal requirements, organizational regulations, and technology advancement has transformed record keeping from a paper file convention to include electronic record keeping. Psychologists will want to become aware of the means by which their records are available to others within organizational systems and to do two things: either (a) implement methods to restrict the access through protected passwords, the masking of clients/patients' identities, or other means of preserving confidentiality; or (b) take steps to inform affected individuals of the limitations on confidentiality of their records and the implications of the limitations.

Standard 6.02(c)

Psychologists make plans in advance to facilitate the appropriate transfer and to protect the confidentiality of records and data in the event of psychologists' withdrawal from positions or practice. (See also Standards 3.12, Interruption of Psychological Services, and 10.09, Interruption of Therapy.)

This standard may be interpreted in light of two additional standards that also address interruption of services. These standards consider unexpected interruption of services due to conditions unanticipated in the life of the psychologist or events in the lives of clients for which the psychologist could not have planned (Standard 3.12) and changes in the contractual status or employment of the psychologist (Standard 10.09) or in protection of the safety of the psychologist (Standard 10.10b). Standard 6.02(c) highlights the importance of advance planning for reasonably anticipated changes across time in the provision of psychological services. Written documents such as professional wills can be very helpful in fulfilling psychologists' obligations under Standard 6.02(c).

The specific focus of this standard is the transfer of information for continued services. The two important factors here are the (a) appropriate conditions for logistical transport (i.e., the HIPAA transaction and security rules, federal and state policies) and (b) orientation of individuals involved in the transfer to the importance and treatment of confidentiality.

Standard 6.02(a), Case 1

Case Illustration. Dr. B. is a psychologist who works in the local community mental health agency. The agency is part of the public sector, and most of the patients are seriously mentally ill, have multiple diagnoses, or are on complex medication regimens. The agency serves the lower socioeconomic status segments of the population, individuals without insurance, and Medicaid patients. One of Dr. B.'s patients has to be hospitalized for a diabetes condition. While in the hospital, the medical staff note a depressive state, refusal to eat, and other potentially psychological symptoms. The psychologist working in the hospital asks Dr. B. for the records of the patient so that the staff can provide continuity of care. The patient has given informed consent for the medical staff to receive this information. Two days later, Dr. B. receives a call from the patient's sister, who is very upset on learning that her brother had been diagnosed by Dr. B. with posttraumatic stress disorder subsequent to a sexual assault that occurred when he was a young adult. He is taking several medications and is participating in ongoing intensive treatment at the agency with Dr. B. Dr. B. explains that she cannot talk with the sister because of confidentiality. The sister retorts that all of this information is displayed on a chart hanging on her brother's bedside and that the whole family has read it. Furthermore, she adds, the hospital staff, including the hospital psychologist, has talked freely with her about her brother's conditions, so she doesn't know why Dr. B. is being so particular about it.

Ethical Dilemma. Dr. B. is stunned at hearing this news and knows that this patient has always been very private, in regard to his family, about his mental health treatment. Because Dr. B. had released the records to the psychologist specifically, and because the release named the attending medical staff as the only recipients of the records, Dr. B. had thought that confidentiality would be honored, and the explanation of the release form to the patient was consistent with that understanding. Dr. B. believes that the hospital psychologist had, perhaps willfully, violated Standard 6.02(a) by not protecting confidentiality in the maintenance and dissemination of records.

Decision-Making Factors. Dr. B. has not violated any of the standards in question, even though the subsequent events would bring her behavior under scrutiny and any technical problems in the language of the release could result in her being in violation. In any event, Dr. B. feels responsible for intervening at this point and doing what she can to correct any violations that have already occurred, to prevent continued breach of confidentiality and to minimize any harm to her client. Dr. B. would want to think through the pertinent aspects of Standard 6.02 and be able to discuss these cogently and clearly with others. Dr. B. might think about the context of a hospital setting and the vehicles for information dissemination that are different from those of her agency, including electronic transmission of records and possible hospital procedures for records, of which she is unaware. Dr. B. had appropriately cooperated with the hospital psychologist in the best interest of the care for the patient but had not included any consultation on the handling of the records or possible differences in procedures. The purpose of the records had been to assist hospital personnel in the treatment of the patient while he was still in the hospital. Dr. B. had no reason to think the records were being used for any inappropriate purpose. The focus of Dr. B.'s concern could be questions of who has access, who needs access, and who wants access to confidential information. Would Dr. B. have withheld some or all of the information had she known it would be easily accessible? Dr. B. might question the explanation of limits of confidentiality and whether, given a hospital environment, she might need to think about limits as being much broader or at least to explain the various potential policy interpretations of confidentiality between settings. Dr. B. would think about how psychologists can respond when the system in which they work does not respect or protect confidentiality of patients.

Decision Options. Dr B. might typically talk with her patient first, given the possible concerns and reactions he might be having. Dr. B. also realizes that she has not yet learned the conditions or policies pertaining to how information is handled within the hospital, she does not yet know what the continued practices will be after her consultation with the staff, and she does not know how the hospital psychologist is reconciling these apparent practices with his or her own ethical practice. Dr. B. would likely want to learn what will happen henceforth before giving the patient any more information that could be inaccurate.

Dr. B. would want to talk with the hospital psychologist about the maintenance and dissemination of psychological records within the hospital system. She also should express her concern about how the patient's information has been accessible to family and others and her concern regarding the responsibility to determine the use of records by the requesting professional. After learning the record-maintenance procedures from the psychologist, Dr. B. may also want to talk with the hospital administrator or the individual who coordinates the handling of records for the hospital in case there is a discrepancy between medical and psychological records or there is additional policy to understand. After Dr. B. thinks that she has a thorough understanding of all the elements of record maintenance and dissemination and confidentiality policy, she may have several courses of action. Dr. B. will want to talk with her patient about what has happened, how it seemed to happen, and what Dr. B.'s intended and unintended roles were in the dissemination. Dr. B. would attend as best she could to the reactions of the patient in the hospital and would want to make a priority of resolving this incident with the patient in therapy. Dr. B. would also discuss with the patient how he would want to proceed with his family members given what they now know. Dr. B. has learned that record maintenance and dissemination can be complicated, especially when more than one entity is involved in caring for the patient.

Standard 6.02(c), Case 1

Case Illustration. Mr. S. is the brother of Dr. G., who very unexpectedly passed away of a heart attack. Dr. G. had not had health problems and seemed to be physically fit. The last thing Dr. G. would have worried about was his health. As a result, Dr. G. had not thought about how his very full practice would be administratively handled or how his clients would be informed in the case of such an event and how their psychological needs would be looked after. Dr. G. had been in a solo practice and did not have close friends who are psychologists. Mr. S. is the sole heir to Dr. G.'s estate and is the executor of the will. He is a stockbroker and knows very little about psychological services. He is well aware that his brother had not left instructions regarding his practice. Because his brother had made him executor of the will and therefore in charge of all financial transactions regarding Dr. G.'s personal and professional lives, Mr. S. surmises that his brother would have wanted him to handle everything personally. Mr. S. does not think he can contact all of these clients personally, so he enlists the office staff in his practice to divide up the files and call the clients. Mr. S. knows nothing about transferring clients to another professional or about referring clients to other professionals. He therefore tells his staff to call the clients; inform them of his brother's death; and state that he, Mr. S., wishes the best for them. The community in which Mr. S. and his brother lived is a moderate size town. As his staff begins to call clients, several of them realize that they knew some of the people they are calling and are very surprised to read of the kinds of difficulties that these individuals have been having. One of the clients who is called by a staff member is shocked about the news—very saddened but also angry and in disbelief that she is being informed this way, that her confidentiality is being violated and that no effort to transfer or refer is being made. This client is also a psychologist and knows that this critical situation should be handled differently. She asks to meet with Mr. S. so she can explain to him the impact and consequences of what he is doing.

Ethical Dilemma. The psychologist/client thinks through the several ethical implications for the situation at hand. She may realize that Standard 6.02(c) had not been honored by Dr. G. because no plans had been made for transfer of records or for the protection of confidentiality. In addition, Standard 3.12 calls on psychologists to make reasonable efforts to plan for the interruption of psychological services caused either by factors affecting the psychologist's or clients' relocation or financial limitations. Standard 10.09 (Interruption of Therapy) may apply in similar cases; however, in these circumstances Dr. G.'s employment or contractual relationships were not factors in the interruption of services. The psychologist is aware that Dr. G. had not prepared for the possibility of circumstances that had, in fact, occurred. She has very mixed feelings given the loss of her own therapist. She does, however, feel the responsibility to meet with Mr. S. and explain the important ethical and professional factors of which he should be aware.

Decision-Making Factors. The psychologist realizes that she has no authority or direct decision capability in this case. She is involved as a client and has an investment in seeing that her own record, as well as those of others, is properly and ethically treated. She also thinks that she is the only professional link she knows between Dr. G. and his brother regarding Dr. G.'s professional responsibility. The psychologist could talk with Mr. S. in a consultative manner in order to explain the ethical obligations that she hopes he will honor. Important concepts to be considered in any action would include respect for the right of confidentiality held by the clients/patients and that, as a matter of administrative procedure, their records are not compromised. Mr. S. could not anticipate the emotional or psychological impact on the clients in the loss of their therapist, but being respectful of the grief from loss would be important. Mr. S. has no knowledge about psychological resources in the community but would want to understand the importance of appropriate transfer and referral of clients.

In addition to his brother's failure to meet ethical expectations, Mr. S. had further neglected the standard of care in disposition of the records by enlisting individuals who were not trained in the treatment of confidential records or in delivering such difficult news. As a client of Dr. G., the psychologist is aware that she would not want to assume any role in the disposition of the records, but in meeting with Mr. S. would hope to facilitate his more ethically appropriate treatment of the records. The primary objectives of Mr. S. at this point, she thinks, should include proper notification, protection of confidential information in the records, identification of whether the state licensure board rules lend any guidance, determination of whether a psychologist consultant should be contacted, and facilitation of referrals.

Decision Options. The psychologist explains to Mr. S. that notification of clients will need to be timely but that he should halt the involvement of his office staff in the review of records and disclosures to clients. Mr. S. has several options for conducting notification and for facilitation of referrals. He could contact the state psychological association, APA, or a practice group in town with a similar practice to Dr. G.'s. His contact should include inquiries about individual psychologists or a group to whom he could refer Dr. G.'s clients. Furthermore, he would want to ensure that any individuals who would have access to the records have been trained in how to handle confidential files. Mr. S. could conceivably hire a psychologist to train Mr. S.'s own staff for notification. They were not, at this point, professionally competent to make decisions about confidentiality. Mr. S. can also consider identifying, through psychological associations, psychologists who have practices similar to his brother's and offer this list of psychologists to the clients, encouraging them to use the list in making their own decisions about continued care. The primary purpose of Mr. S.'s response in considering all options is the welfare of Dr. G.'s clients and consideration of their best interest. This objective would include both the professionalism and sensitivity in which the death of Dr. G. is transmitted and the useful and appropriate provision of information regarding continuity of services, in particular the kind of care each patient would need after Dr. G.'s passing. This situation is a reminder of how important it is that psychologists identify another professional to maintain client/patient records for the required period of time after the death of a colleague.

Standard 6.03, Withholding Records for Nonpayment

Psychologists may not withhold records under their control that are requested and needed for a client's/patient's emergency treatment solely because payment has not been received.

The intent of this standard is to define a particular condition of release of records. The APA Ethics Code recognizes the value of psychologists' services and gives acknowledgement in this standard of that regard. Three key terms that facilitate interpretation of this standard are (a) *control*, (b) *emergency treatment*, and (c) *solely*.

Depending on contractual agreements, records that psychologists develop or use may not be in their own control if there are organizational entities responsible for services, prevailing law, or third-party payors with whom either psychologists, the clients/patients, or both have agreed to be custodian of the records. Not only must the psychological activity be described as emergency in nature, but it must also be a treatment component of the activity; that is, the record would contribute to decisions regarding a treatment needed by the client, such as hospitalization, medication, or emergency placement. Last, the term *solely* suggests that psychologists may withhold records for reasons other than nonpayment, such as the welfare of the client, potential exploitation of the client, or misinterpretation of the records.

Decision-making questions regarding withholding of records may include the following:

- What authority controls access to the records?
- Do the circumstances of the request qualify as an emergency treatment need?
- Are there reasons to withhold the record that could protect the client from exploitation or misrepresentation through the record?

Standard 6.04, Fees and Financial Arrangements

Standard 6.04 is among several standards in the Ethics Code that do not make use of the term *informed consent* yet rely on the fundamental meaning of informed consent within the Ethics Code. Informed consent is at the heart of Standard 6.04 because the standard ensures that individuals should have information relevant to the decisions they make. Standard 6.04 is also the embodiment of Principle E: Respect for People's Rights and Dignity and brings life to the meaning of Principle E in that psychologists respect the rights of individuals to self-determination. An important factor in self-determination is the ability to access information that will help one make decisions. An equally important value for Standard 6.04 is *transparency*. Transparency is the quality of clarity, full disclosure, and access to knowing the elements of information or action that may affect individuals. Without transparency, informed consent is compromised because neither the psychologists nor the clients can make informed decisions. The common threads running through the five areas of Standard 6.04 are the fundamental importance of informed consent and transparency. Standards 6.04(a) (agreement on compensation and billing arrangements), 6.04(d) (early discussion of anticipated limitations in service recipient's financing), and 6.04(e) (informing service recipients of the use of collection agencies) evidence the important function of informed consent in ensuring that clients understand the financial conditions of their participation. Standards 6.04(b) (fee practices being consistent within the law) and 6.04(c) (psychologists not misrepresenting their fees) both expect and reflect transparency in financial representation. These two areas rely on psychologists' transparency in representing themselves and their services to clients. Unlike the three other standards addressed in Standard 6.04, these two involve not negotiations or transactions with clients but rather the financial clarity and honesty with which psychologists choose to represent themselves.

Standard 6.04(a)

As early as is feasible in a professional or scientific relationship, psychologists and recipients of psychological services reach an agreement specifying compensation and billing arrangements.

Several key terms in Standard 6.04(a) highlight the important concepts in thinking about financial arrangements. *Agreement* between psychologists and recipients of services suggests recognition by both parties that the conditions of services are acceptable. Because recipients may not be familiar with the specific aspects of psychological services, psychologists attempt to affirm the recipients' understanding of compensation and billing. Also to be determined are the various charges to be made in addition to the identified fee for the service, such as costs for consultation, correspondence, copying, travel, and other collateral activities that incur costs to the psychologist. Although the term *informed consent* is not used in this standard, there is an implication of accurate informing in order to achieve consent in this aspect of psychological service.

Feasibility in timeliness of reaching an agreement allows latitude for psychologists to use their professional judgment to determine the client's/patient's immediate needs. It is advisable to consider the discussion of the fee agreement before actual psychological services are delivered because the perspective of the psychologist and the clients/patients could be affected once services have ensued. Professional judgment is used in determining the earliest appropriate discussion of fees. For example, if the first encounter is in an emergency situation, a discussion of fees may not be appropriate.

Professional and scientific relationships are both applicable in this standard, and the context in which services are being provided may affect the agreement. Clinical services through third-party payors, contrasted with fee-for-service activities; organizational services through corporate or institutional consultation fees; legal services through the court or adjudicating parties; and research activity in which federal, state, or other grant entities are financially responsible imply variation in how compensation and billing would be determined.

Last, the standard does not require specific record keeping for financial arrangements; however, psychologists may consider the means by which a record can serve as documentation of financial transactions and decisions.

Standard 6.04(b)
Psychologists' fee practices are consistent with law.

The term *fee practices* refers both to compliance with the law and to knowledge about the standard of practice and fee structure within one's state. Federal regulations (e.g., HIPAA, Medicare, other government services), state regulations (e.g., Medicaid and state programs), and insurance agreements require an understanding of the relationship among services, fees, and compensation. Psychologists should be in compliance with the law and regulations of their legal jurisdiction. This standard may be challenging because sometimes contractual arrangements, laws, or insurance policy provisions seem to prevent psychologists from giving clients/patients the ideal services and are perceived as standing in the way of providing appropriate services. Nonetheless, psychologists may not violate the law in their billing practices and have an ethical obligation to conform their billing practices to the law.

Standard 6.04(c)
Psychologists do not misrepresent their fees.

This standard makes clear that psychologists neither intentionally nor unintentionally misrepresent their fees to clients, payors of services, or any organizations with which psychologists transact services (e.g., Medicare, Medicaid, insurance companies, service recipients). Unintentional misrepresentation may arise by virtue of the complexity of billing given the various regulatory entities and the growth and scope of psychological activities. Such misrepresentation is corrected as soon as it is discovered.

The complexity of billing because of various regulatory entities and the growth in scope of psychological activities in clinical services, research, organizational services, and forensics can result in unintentional misrepresentation of fees. Psychologists are mindful that fee structure and subsequent billing can be both complicated and unfamiliar to clients/patients and that they therefore should attempt to clarify that the recipients have an accurate understanding of fees.

Ethical Standard 6.04(d)

If limitations to services can be anticipated because of limitations in financing, this is discussed with the recipient of services as early as is feasible. (See also Standards 10.09, Interruption of Therapy, and 10.10, Terminating Therapy.)

Psychologists are aware that limitations to services without notification and explanation to the recipient have significant ethical implications for premature or inappropriate termination. Clients/patients may develop a psychological investment in services, an expectation for treatment, and a commitment to a psychotherapeutic relationship and treatment plan. When services are interrupted, the effect on the clients/patients can be damaging. General Principle A: Beneficence and Nonmaleficence provides a foundational concept within this standard in the importance of striving to benefit those with whom psychologists work and to do no harm. Psychologists seek to safeguard the welfare and rights of those with whom they interact professionally. They also apprise themselves of the limitations of services and do three things: (a) enlist the clients/patients in problem-solving the choices of referral, altered sessions, reduced fees, and other options; (b) negotiate with payors for the needed service structure; and (c) alter treatment or services in order to work within the parameters of the limitations ethically and within professional boundaries.

Standard 6.04(e)

If the recipient of services does not pay for services as agreed, and if psychologists intend to use collection agencies or legal measures to collect the fees, psychologists first inform the person that such measures will be taken and provide that person an opportunity to make prompt payment. (See also Standards 4.05, Disclosures; 6.03, Withholding Records for Nonpayment; and 10.01, Informed Consent to Therapy.)

This circumstance is a difficult one for both psychologists and for service recipients. Psychologists are called on to be respectful of their clients/patients in pursuing collection of fees, yet the Ethics Code does recognize and respect the fact that psychologists have the right to receive payment for their services. Several concepts facilitate understanding of this standard:

- Psychologists may consider including, in initial written informed consent and privacy notices, the procedures used for nonpayment of fees, the confidentiality implications, and the probable course of action if necessary.
- Before taking action in a nonpayment situation, psychologists discuss the payment status with the clients/patients and attempt to resolve the issue. If the situation is not resolved, psychologists explain the implications of confidentiality and the probable course of action.
- Psychologists are mindful of the state law governing confidentiality parameters and use of collection agencies.
- If collection becomes the necessary course of action, psychologists provide only the minimum information necessary to process the transaction, such as name, address, dates of service, and amount owed.

Questions that promote sound decision making regarding Standard 6.04 include the following:

- What factors could affect the timeliness of the discussion with the recipients of fee and billing services?
- How has the agreement been determined or altered on the basis of the clinical, legal, organizational, or research context of the service?
- Are professional practices and state law reflected in the financial agreement?
- Have fees been explained in such a way that a layperson could understand the conditions?

Standard 6.04(a), Case 1

Case Illustration 1. Dr. A. is an organizational psychologist who consults with corporations regarding personnel selection, promotion, and employer–employee relations. Dr. A. receives a phone call from the vice president of a major company in town who has received a recommendation for Dr. A. from a colleague in another company who had contracted for Dr. A.'s consultation services several times. The vice president explains that the company is in an unexpected difficult situation and needs Dr. A.'s expertise. It seems that the vice president for finance suddenly left for a position with another firm, and the company needs to replace this person rather quickly. Company officials want Dr. A. to interview the four internal candidates for the position and tell the vice president whether one of them would be suited for the job or whether they should do an external search. Dr. A. accepts the job, tells the company of the fees charged for doing a personnel evaluation, and obtains consent to interview employees and others and to have access to company information. After completing the project, Dr. A. sends the vice president a bill of fees for service that was double the amount he cited for the personnel evaluation. When questioned, Dr. A. explains that the personnel evaluation included only interviews with candidates, the instruments administered, and the evaluation report. Dr. A. cites the additional costs as comprising travel costs to interview the applicants and billable hours for interviewing others in the company and the related travel expenses. Dr. A. explains that these additional costs are pro forma conventional costs and would be incurred with any similar job. Dr. A. adds that the usual fee is being charged, not inflated or unrealistic charges, and that company officials should have already assumed these fees and factored them in themselves.

Case Illustration 2. Dr. B. receives a call from a colleague whose adult client's adolescent daughter has made a suicide attempt. Dr. B. specializes in working with adolescents, which prompted the colleague's request that she agree to see the adolescent for therapy. The referring psychologist and the mother consider the timing critical and believe that the daughter is in a personal crisis. Dr. B. agrees to see the adolescent immediately.

Dr. B. talks with the mother and then conducts a clinical intake evaluation with the daughter with a special focus on suicidal ideation. During her interview, the mother reports that she has insurance that includes mental health services and a few days of inpatient care per year. Dr. B. determines that the adolescent is in fact at risk of harming herself. The adolescent is hospitalized for 3 days, during which time Dr. B. treats her. Dr. B.'s office staff set up additional sessions with the adolescent so that she can have an effective transition when released from the hospital. Six weeks later, the mother receives Dr. B.'s invoice and immediately contacts Dr. B. to express her dismay, saying that she had no idea the fees would be so high and that because insurance will pay for the inpatient treatment but no outpatient sessions that she cannot pay Dr. B.'s hourly rates. In the meantime, the daughter had seen Dr. B. during her hospital stay and for 6 subsequent weeks. She has developed a good relationship with Dr. B. and, for the first time in a long time, has begun to feel understood by and trusting of another person.

Ethical Dilemma. In both cases, the psychologists failed to explain the specifics of compensation and the billing arrangements before services were rendered. Standard 6.04(a) requires that the psychologist and client reach an agreement regarding both fees and billing arrangements, and it requires this to happen as early as is feasible. In the case of Dr. A., Standard 6.04(c), which states that psychologists do not misrepresent their fees, might also be in question. In assuming that certain costs were known and inherent in billing, Dr. A. did not provide a complete list of the charges that would be rendered; thus, the fee could be seen as misrepresented. In the case of Dr. B., the initial failure to thoroughly discuss fees was understandable given the emergency nature of the service. However, the patient's mother was also a psychologist, and it was not out of the question to discuss fees with the mother even during the emergency phase and certainly no later than discussion of discharge planning. It was determined that the hospital costs and initial out-patient costs would be paid by the insurance company; however, the continuing fees charged by Dr. B. were not discussed (Standard 6.04a). Three additional standards could be applicable in this case: (a) Standard 6.04(d), which explains the importance of discussing fees if there is any anticipation that the client may have limited financing, as well as (b) Standard 10.09 and (c) Standard 10.10, which direct psychologists to be sensitive to the effect that interruption of therapy or termination of therapy, respectively, may have on the therapeutic relationship, the continuity of services, and the patient's/client's psychological well-being. Both Dr. A. and Dr. B. made omissions in their presentation of fees. Dr. A. thought that there were conventions in billing costs that the client neither anticipated nor agreed were standard inclusions. Dr. B. did not discuss the specifics of fees during the emergency event but failed later, before additional services were offered, to inform the client of costs. Neither psychologist intentionally misrepresented fees but, through questionable judgments, omissions were made that affected compliance with Standards 6.04(a), 6.04(c), and 6.04(d).

Decision-Making Factors. The components of Standard 6 regarding fees and billing do not specifically reference informed consent and yet informed consent is an underlying premise in psychologists' responsibility to reach an agreement with clients/patients regarding fees in a timely, comprehensive, and clear manner. Informed consent serves the function of disclosing to clients/patients the effects; processes; and potential consequences, both positive and negative, of psychologists' services on them. General Principle E: Respect for People's Rights and Dignity alerts psychologists to the importance of the proper inclusion of informed consent into fee and billing information. The decisions clients/patients make about services may be based on several factors. Billing and fees are factors for which clients/patients have the right to full disclosure of all relevant information prior to making their decisions. Before they can optimally exercise self-determination and autonomy, clients must be equipped with information with which to make their decisions.

In the first case, Dr. A. did not provide all billing and fees information, because assumptions were made about billing practices. The client may have chosen another psychologist had the client known the fees up front. Because the service was time limited and involved a closed-ended service (e.g., testing, interviewing, and recommendations), the ongoing relationship between the psychologist and the recipient of service (e.g., the applicants), was not likely to be substantially damaged.

In the case of Dr. B., additional factors complicated the decision-making process. In contrast to Dr. A.'s case, ongoing services that built on a therapeutic relationship as well as on the importance of continuity were primary factors. Dr. B. took the case in an emergency situation and, reasonably, did not discuss the specifics of fees during the crisis. During the ensuing weeks, however, Dr. B., who realized that insurance paid for the hospital costs and the initial outpatient costs, did not inquire about any limitations of the insurance or, more directly, of any limitations of the mother to continue therapy for the daughter if insurance terminated payment. This case reflects more egregious violations of Standard 6.04(a) and 6.04(d) because the psychological well-being and health of a client (or service recipient), as well as access to needed services, may have been compromised.

Decision Options. Dr. A. may realize that even though services had been provided that were thought to be commonly understood in regard to billing, full discussion and clarification prior to services are desirable. In this case, the service was needed in a timely way, and this circumstance may well have affected Dr. A.'s priorities. Dr. A. could have declined the job if the standard protocol were questioned prior to delivery of services. In this case, the service has already been completed, and Dr. A. will need to decide whether to adjust the total billing and fees charged given the confusion about the financial arrangement.

Dr. B. will need to think about continuing to provide services to the adolescent at negotiated fees or to initiate preparation for pretermination counseling and referral to another professional. Dr. B. will want to weigh an assessment of the level of risk for harm and the general well-being of the client in making this decision and should remember that the best interests of the client must be a factor in any decision.

Both Dr. A. and Dr. B. will want to consider a means by which an agreement specifying compensation and billing may be determined before engaging in services in the future. This could involve a contract or memorandum of agreement that meets the spirit of informed consent.

Standard 6.05, Barter With Clients/Patients

Barter is the acceptance of goods, services, or other nonmonetary remuneration from clients/patients in return for psychological services. Psychologists may barter only if (1) it is not clinically contraindicated, and (2) the resulting arrangement is not exploitative. (See also Standards 3.05, Multiple Relationships, and 6.04, Fees and Financial Arrangements.)

In the 1992 Ethics Code the first sentence of this standard stated that psychologists should ordinarily refrain from bartering. Because of the response from psychologists practicing in rural and small communities, however, the policy was modified so that no ordinary condition was stated. However, both standards use the same two conditions for determining when bartering is allowable. The responsibility to ensure that the bartering is fair and equitable remains with the psychologist. Bartering is a means of payment for psychological services that may be considered by psychologists primarily for one of two reasons: (a) financial limitations of the clients/patients or (b) values of the community or the culture in which psychologists work. Financial limitations are sometimes dealt with through pro bono status; however, psychologists may not themselves be able to support a substantial pro bono service, and clients/patients may also have reluctance to accept a pro bono arrangement. The therapeutic impact of altered financial agreements within any working alliance may affect the quality of the relationship and the effectiveness of the outcome. Bartering for goods can be complex, but bartering for services is inevitably complex. Contracting with clients for services such as landscaping or housecleaning creates an ongoing relationship, not just a single transaction.

Bartering may be contraindicated for several clinical reasons. Bartering for services must be carefully considered because it often constitutes a dual relationship. Factors that psychologists may consider in determining potential counterproductive clinical impact are those also identified in other standards that address relational variations of psychologists and the recipients of their professional services (see Standard 10.08b). Factors that could be considered in the bartering decision making process include the following:

- Could the nature, duration, or intensity of the psychological services affect the likelihood of a sound bartering agreement (e.g., intense psychotherapy vs. career counseling, organizational consultation vs. court testimony in a custody case, a time management workshop vs. 3 years of intensive psychotherapy)?
- If a diagnostic impression has been made, might the nature of the characteristics be contraindicating for bartering (e.g., borderline personality disorder, schizophrenia, oppositional defiant disorder)?
- Does the nature of the problem suggest that fee arrangements could become working issues in therapy (e.g., boundary issues, generalized and protracted financial distress, dependency needs, countertransferential issues with finances)?
- Does the nature of the considered bartering arrangement suggest problems associated with pre-existing client/patient issues (e.g., bartering for artwork when the client/artist is unable to sell any works independently)?

Bartering may also be contraindicated for reasons of exploitation. The value of services or products may change over time, resulting in the bartering arrangement being inequitable in exchange value. The verifiable value of goods or services is an important aspect of equitable and successful bartering. When the value of the bartered conditions change, or the perception of the arrangement changes, the clients/patients may feel exploited, and psychologists may also feel exploited. For example, when artworks are bartered, the value of the work may increase, causing the client/patient to think that the arrangement now underestimates the worth of the work; however, if the work decreases to little commercial value, the psychologist may feel underpaid for his or her services.

If psychologists do enter into bartering agreements, they would do well to document the facts and conditions of the agreement. Record keeping and fees are subsumed with bartering under Section 6 of the Ethics Code because these two activities represent the means by which psychological services are defined and verified. Elements of this record could contain: (a) the rationale for bartering; (b) a discussion of the pros and cons with the client/patient; (c) consultation with other psychologists; and (d) specific bartering conditions agreed to by the client/patient, the psychologist, and any invested third parties.

Further decision-making questions could include the following:

- What is the reason for considering bartering?
- What is the likely consequence of not bartering?
- What are the potential unintended consequences for the client/patient and for the psychologist?
- Does the relationship created by bartering potentially rise to the level of a dual relationship?

Standard 6.05, Case 1

Case Illustration. Dr. K. has practiced in the same small farming community for several years. Quite a few of the residents have spoken to him about various psychological services, but many cannot afford to pay. Dr. K. is one of the few psychologists in the region, and the others, he understands, do barter for services with select clients. Dr. K. decides to begin consideration of bartering and has several current requests, including from two clients who are having difficulty paying.

Potential Client 1 is a farmer who wants Dr. K. to do some testing with his son, who is having learning problems in school. The farmer proposes that he provide Dr. K. fruits and vegetables produced in his fields.

Client 2 is already seeing Dr. K. but is having difficulty paying. She also proposes offering goods: her artwork. Dr. K. already knows, from his history of working with this client, that she has been unable to sell her artwork; this is one of the reasons she is in therapy. Furthermore, Dr. K. has been suspecting that this client has borderline personality disorder.

Potential Client 3 is a painter and requests to pay by painting Dr. K.'s house exterior or interior, or both, over time. This request involves a service, not goods, but it is not an easily quantifiable service. There would certainly be a comparative market price that Dr. K. could use as a reference point, but his satisfaction with this service would be based on the quality of the performance.

Client 4 is already seeing Dr. K. for services and is requesting to provide landscaping services. The client has presented in therapy with relationship problems. Dr. K. has begun to realize that the thematic nature of the relationship problems was a level of dependence and boundary problems that would sabotage this client's relationships. The client does not recognize this dynamic yet, however.

Ethical Dilemma. In all four cases, Dr. K. is considering implementation of a select bartering arrangement with some clients. Several of the requests for bartering arrangement could be problematic and pose ethical concerns. Dr. K. is aware that there are two prohibitions against bartering: (a) clinical contraindication and (b) the potential for exploitation. As Dr. K. thinks about these two criteria, he also thinks about General Principle D: Justice in that access to services and equal quality is an important value for psychologists. He realizes that Potential Client 1's proposal does not seem to be problematic. Dr. K. does not know the farmer yet, and so he cannot make a judgment about clinical conflicts. Client 2's suggestion for bartering could be conflictual for Dr. K. for at least one reason that may not meet the standard's criterion that, given the possibility of a personality disorder, bartering could be contraindicated. If he rejects this suggestion, then he may need to resolve the problem that the client cannot afford services otherwise. Potential Client 3 is proposing to do house painting for Dr. K. Dr. K. knows nothing about Potential Client 3's working problems at this point but does realize that house painting is valued on the basis of the performance, competence, and quality of the job done. Dr. K. is already thinking about what he would do if he does not like the job quality, the paint color, or some other aspect of the work. In addition, the risk of introduction of a dual relationship should be discussed. Last, Client 4 is suggesting that he provide a landscaping service for Dr. K. Dr. K. knows the client has boundary problems and dependency needs in relationships. He wonders whether this scenario would also be clinically contraindicated and, further, whether the client could perceive exploitation inasmuch as the value of the service would be difficult to determine. Also, the service would present an ongoing relationship with the client that could foster a dual relationship (see Standard 3.05, Multiple Relationships).

Decision-Making Factors. All four bartering arrangements present different vehicles of bartering and therefore different concerns. Psychologists must be mindful that unfair discrimination may develop when consequences of decisions result in conflict of interest, exploitation, or clinically contraindicated actions. Dr. K. is aware that all discrimination is not unfair and that discerning and discriminating decisions are regularly made in a professional context but that discrimination based on age, gender, gender identity, race, ethnicity, culture, national origin, religion, sexual orientation, disability, socioeconomic status, or any basis proscribed by law is unfair discrimination (see Standard 3.01, Unfair Discrimination). Two clients or potential clients have suggested bartered goods: (a) the produce, which has a fixed or market value, and (b) the artwork, the value of which may vary. The third and fourth proposals involve services rather than goods. Bartered services are more complex in nature than goods because services are evaluated by performance and competence of the provider and the quality of the job, and an agreement for services introduces the possibility of role conflict in that the psychologist is in one role as a therapist and another as a receiver of services. House painting lends itself to the variability of performance and competence, although in terms of value a market price could in fact be determined. Landscaping as a service is not time limited; neither is it a single action, such as painting a house. It would be an ongoing business relationship that introduces the potential for a longer term dual relationship.

The bartering arrangement with Potential Client 1 seems straightforward to Dr. K. because the goods can be assigned a market value, and the quantity purchased also can be varied. Dr. K. has no reason to think that the exchange would be clinically contraindicated or that exploitation could be a factor.

In regard to Client 2, Dr. K. fears that this type of arrangement would complicate the already-intense nature of the client's therapy and could set the stage for boundary violations given the likely diagnosis of a personality disorder. It occurs to Dr. K. that he, rather than the client, could be vulnerable to exploitation by purchasing art that has no known market value or that would potentially lose market value over time.

The house painting suggested by Client 3 seems reasonable initially, because the work would be a single service. As Dr. K. thinks it through, services are more difficult to measure qualitatively than are goods. If Dr. K. does not like the paint color, the paint job itself, or some other aspect of the painting, then the therapeutic relationship could be threatened.

Client 4 is very enthusiastic about landscaping and assures Dr. K. that he will do a good job; however, Dr. K. has an uncomfortable feeling just thinking about the arrangement. He is already working with this client on boundary problems and dependency needs. He thinks that this client could be at risk of perceived exploitation and rejection by Dr. K. when limits on access to the property are set or if Dr. K. does not want to pursue landscaping suggestions made by the client. Dr. K. realizes also that if he does not like the landscaping work the ensuing business discussion would most likely contaminate the therapeutic context. If he does like the landscaping, then the client's interest in pleasing Dr. B. and gaining approval could also contaminate the working relationship.

Decision Options. Dr. K. realizes the complex implications of bartering with these clients and potential clients, and he understands that there are several important variables to consider: a pre-existing therapeutic relationship; the fixed versus fluid value of goods; services that have a fixed value in terms of the existence of comparable pricing yet a fluctuating value when skill, reliability, and motivation are factored in; the potential for perception of exploitation even in the absence of exploitation; and the confounding effective of personality characteristics, disorders, and interpersonal dynamics that could affect the therapeutic relationship and the effect the therapeutic relationship could have on the quality of the services and goods rendered.

In consideration of these factors, Dr. K. decides to accept the bartering agreement of Potential Client 1, the farmer, and to reach a determination in collaboration with him on the market value of the produce that he would provide.

Dr. K. decides that the bartering of artwork would be fraught with problems based both on the variable value of the artwork and the current devaluation of the artwork as well as the possible borderline personality disorder characteristics of the client. Dr. K. thinks that the therapeutic relationship with the client is intermittently fragile as is and that additional factors the client could interpret as being influential in the relationship would be problematic and clinically counterproductive. Furthermore, it occurs to Dr. K. that if the client's artwork becomes popular and successful in the future questions may arise as to the relative value of the psychological fees charged and the value of highly priced artwork. Dr. K. is committed to working with the client to find a means for her to continue receiving services given that she is a current client.

Dr. K. is tempted to agree to Potential Client 3's barter offer of house painting. On second thought, however, the possibility of dissatisfaction with the service persuades Dr. K. to graciously decline the offer and to consider other means by which the client can receive services. Because Dr. K. is not already seeing this person as a client, the possibility of a referral could be considered in collaboration with the individual.

Dr. K. knows that Client 4 is not having difficulty in paying the fees for services and begins to think that the client might be proposing the landscaping service as an extension of the existing boundary difficulties. It would be consistent with the client's personality to want to offer services to Dr. K. in order to gain further approval as well as to find ways to be in contact with Dr. K. outside of the psychotherapy context. Dr. K. then determines to decline the bartering request and will be aware of these possible factors when discussing the matter with the client.

Standard 6.06, Accuracy in Reports to Payors and Funding Sources

In their reports to payors for services or sources of research funding, psychologists take reasonable steps to ensure the accurate reporting of the nature of the service provided or research conducted, the fees, charges, or payments, and where applicable, the identity of the provider, the findings, and the diagnosis. (See also Standards 4.01, Maintaining Confidentiality; 4.04, Minimizing Intrusions on Privacy; and 4.05, Disclosures.)

The two key elements of this standard are (a) taking reasonable steps and (b) accurate reporting. As has been described in other standards of Section 6, the context in which psychological services are delivered is a significant determiner of the content and procedures that psychologists use in conducting their responsibilities ethically. The nature of service delivered in a clinical context can mean that diagnosis, treatment plan, fees charged, dates of service, and coding classification are all accurate. Equivalent information in an organizational setting might include fees per hour, specific activities conducted in the fee-charged time frame, and materials charges (e.g., supplies, telecommunication, travel expenses). Research reporting might include personnel costs, materials and supplies, data analysis costs, and other time-on-task charges.

The responsibility for taking reasonable steps to ensure reporting accuracy reflects the complexity and breadth of psychological activity. An unintentional error made despite a psychologist's reasonable efforts may be contrasted with an error made by willful negligence such as an intent to collect fees not actually earned. Such a violation could be made by commission or by unreasonable omission, such as a failure to provide services (e.g., train and supervise employees) for which one has charged a client. Psychologists often work in reporting systems with multiple other individuals, agencies, and large entities. They oversee the appropriate and accurate treatment of their information to the extent possible but are not expected to have inordinate monitoring capability of information after it leaves the purview of psychologists.

Standard 6.07, Referrals and Fees

When psychologists pay, receive payment from, or divide fees with another professional, other than in an employer–employee relationship, the payment to each is based on the services provided (clinical, consultative, administrative, or other) and is not based on the referral itself. (See also Standard 3.09, Cooperation With Other Professionals.)

This standard reflects the professional value embodied in Principle A: Beneficence and Nonmaleficence and Principle C: Integrity in that referrals are made on the basis of the clinical, organizational, or forensic need of the client/patient and in the best interest of the client/patient, not for remunerative benefit. Clients/patients should be able to expect that when psychologists give recommendations for psychological services, the referral is to professionals who have the greatest expertise and likelihood of providing the most effective services. Employer–employee relationships are excepted in this standard because it would be evident to clients/patients that there would be shared financial advantages to services between employer and employees. Standard 6.07 does not prohibit psychologists from participating in service referral networks, professional associations, or institutions because all participating members of the referral systems would be equally eligible for referrals. Psychologists note that the identification of the client is an essential element of discharging the duty under this standard and that when an entity or organization other than the service recipient may be the identified client, they may need to take steps to clarify the relationship and purpose of the referral.

CONCLUSION

In summary of Section 6, Recordkeeping and Fees, the ethical standards primarily convey three important professional responsibilities for psychologists: (a) making decisions regarding the purpose of the record for any given client and the treatment of the records from creation to disposition, (b) maintenance of confidentiality of records and decision making regarding consent and disclosures, and (c) making determinations about the many aspects of fee and financial arrangements with appropriate informed consent and transparency. The recordkeeping standards promote the concept of records as a reflection of the type and purpose of psychological services provided and financial arrangements as an opportunity to convey transparency and appropriate informed consent.

7

EDUCATION AND TRAINING

The organizing principle of Section 7 of the 2002 American Psychological Association's (APA's) "Ethical Principles of Psychologists and Code of Conduct" (hereinafter the *APA Ethics Code* or the *Ethics Code*; see http://www.apa.org/ethics/code2002.html)[1] is the identification of expectations for programs, faculty, and students in the academic matriculation process. The underlying condition of a power differential between faculty and students creates an inherent vulnerability of students in training. This vulnerability can lead to unjust treatment or exploitation. The identification of expectations for programs, faculty, and students is a means by which the Ethics Code can provide tools with which faculty and students can manage the relational imbalance. Perhaps as much as any of the sections in the Ethics Code, Section 7 incorporates Ethical Principle B: Fidelity and Responsibility and Ethical Principle D: Justice. Training psychologists are expected to create an educational environment of fairness and equity in which students matriculate and to be trustworthy and responsible to students who are depending on them for guidance and knowledge.

---

[1]American Psychological Association. (2002). Ethical principles of psychologists and code of conduct. *American Psychologist, 57,* 1060–1073.

Informed consent has a bidirectional quality in that protection is also provided for the programs and the training psychologists. As a result of the information provided by programs, students can exercise autonomy and self-determination (Principle E: Respect for People's Rights and Dignity) in making their choices regarding selection of a training program. Students are then responsible for their decisions, and programs can require that students be responsible to the program for the cited expectations and requirements. Students may decide to matriculate in a particular program; if they do, then the program can hold them accountable for meeting requirements, and programs can make decisions that are based on the degree to which students fulfill those expectations.

The Education and Training Section comprehensively defines expectations from the initial stage of student interest in considering training programs through program matriculation to summary evaluation of students. These expectations are clustered into the following three areas.

1. *Informed consent for training* (Standard 7.01, Design of Education and Training Programs; Standard 7.02, Description of Education and Training Programs; and Standard 7.04[1], Student Disclosure of Personal Information).

   These standards reflect the opportunity and the right of informed consent for students and establish the profession's expectations of programs to fulfill their training commitments. Potential students may be assured that when they choose a training program they will have access to the program resources, faculty expertise, and particular curricula experiences that were stated as being offered when they applied for admissions. Standard 7.01, Design of Education and Training Programs and 7.04(1), Student Disclosure of Personal Information, describe the requirements of the program and faculty to meet expectations, and Standard 7.02 describes the requirements of students to meet expectations.

2. *Conditions for evaluation* (Standard 7.03, Accuracy in Teaching; Standard 7.04, Student Disclosure of Personal Information; Standard 7.05, Mandatory Individual or Group Therapy; Standard 7.06, Assessing Student and Supervisee Performance).

   After students have accepted an offer into a training program, they no longer have the leverage of comparative decision making across programs. Even though it is possible for students to change programs, the investment students make for advanced training is considerable. The financial, time, location, professional, and relational costs of changing programs can be staggering. When students accept a training program, much of their experience becomes predetermined, and students may not have choices. These standards offer parameters for faculty in establishing requirements and give students a frame of reference for students' reasonable expectations.

3. *Relational boundaries* (Standard 7.07, Sexual Relationships With Students and Supervisees).

The APA Ethics Code is alert to the condition that psychological activities are often conducted with individuals for whom there are inherent power differentials. The Ethics Code directs psychologists through several standards regarding professional boundaries that guard against loss of objectivity or risk of exploitation. Evaluation is an activity conducted by psychologists in clinical, organizational, forensic, and research settings in addition to training. Conducting evaluations is a fundamental role for psychologists, and therefore they are mindful of their actual and perceived influence over students.

Standard 7.01, Design of Education and Training Programs
Psychologists responsible for education and training programs take reasonable steps to ensure that the programs are designed to provide the appropriate knowledge and proper experiences, and to meet the requirements for licensure, certification, or other goals for which claims are made by the program. (See also Standard 5.03, Descriptions of Workshops and Non-Degree-Granting Educational Programs.)

Accountability has become a central feature of program and organizational evaluation across professions in recent years, including in psychology training programs. Accreditation, certification, or licensure requirements may well include standard criteria that all program applicants are expected to meet; however, given the breadth of practice in psychology and the continued expansion of the scope of psychology, training programs are also expected to define and describe the individual elements of the program. When programs decide to adopt these criteria, they must then show evidence that the educational experiences claimed to be provided were, in fact, offered. Within this standard, the phrase "for which claims are made by the program" is significant in that programs are expected to fulfill only those claims that are made by the program. This specificity calls on students and others to exercise a caveat emptor perspective in understanding the claims made as well as those requirements for a training goal that the program does not claim to meet.

The accountability for the design of the program in providing appropriate knowledge and proper experience also speaks to the expertise of faculty instructors, resources of department and field sites, competent supervision, library resources, and access to an adequate learning environment. Training directors and faculty may review information provided to the public by means of written materials, Web sites, and other public venues to ensure the accuracy and congruence of the materials with the actual program.

Standard 7.01, Case 1

Case Illustration. Dr. D. has accepted an adjunct position in a doctoral training program that has been developing for several years. The program is known in the community as a quality one, and so Dr. D. thinks this will be a good opportunity to gain academic teaching experience and to advance her interests in an academic career. The program is not APA accredited, but it is understood by faculty, students, and the community that it is committed to working toward that status. Dr. D. thinks that it would be rewarding to participate in this endeavor.

After teaching for a semester, Dr. D. begins to realize several things that make her very uneasy. The program advertises, through marketing materials and recruitment of students, that APA accreditation is imminent. The program materials imply that students entering the program now will be graduating from an accredited program by the time they finish their internships. The faculty seem to also talk in these terms to students and to individuals in the community who have developed interest in the program.

Dr. D. becomes uneasy about this process during several faculty meetings in which the training director talks about the curriculum, hiring of faculty, resources, assistantships, practicum availability, and other factors that would be variables in the preparation for an accreditation visit. Dr. D. realizes that the program is much earlier in development than has been portrayed and that in fact very little progress has been made toward preparation for accreditation. Dr. D. knows that students are coming into this program with the expectation of it being accredited. Dr. D. does not know if the training director and faculty realize the discrepancy, but she realizes that several classes of students had already graduated that had expected accreditation. She also has heard that some students who had graduated were able to take the licensure examination in their state on the basis of equivalency standards, but some were not.

Ethical Dilemma. Dr. D. is concerned that the program in which she is teaching is inadvertently violating Standard 7.01. She is confident that the program provides the "appropriate knowledge" for which claims of qualifying for APA accreditation are made, but because of practicum limitations the "proper experiences" necessary to meet accreditation standards are not in place. Other Ethics Code standards regarding misrepresentation might also be violated (e.g., Standard 5.01a), and Dr. D. is very concerned about misrepresentation to the students and the community. The implication that accreditation is imminent, in Dr. D.'s opinion, may be a violation of meeting the requirements for the goal of graduating with a degree from an APA-accredited program. If students are accepting admission to the program with the expectation that they will enjoy the status of an APA-accredited program, they may be misled. The duty under Standard 7.01 is for the program to provide the knowledge and experiences that will fulfill the students' expectations based on the program claims.

Dr. D. is not a tenured faculty member and, in fact, is adjunct faculty. She realizes that if she questions program administrators on this matter it could affect her teaching status and her access to academic experience that she needs for her professional advancement. Dr. D. has met and talked briefly with other faculty but does not know any of them well enough to privately pursue this concern. She feels quite alone in this dilemma but also thinks that students may be unfairly treated here, and she feels an obligation to pursue the question.

Decision-Making Factors. A key factor in interpreting Standard 7.01 is the phrase "for which claims are made." Dr. D. realizes that the program does not actually state that accreditation will be achieved within a certain time frame, but phrases such as "Students who are admitted now will not need to be concerned about APA accreditation" or "Students matriculating in our program now will be graduating from an APA-accredited program" are being used. The materials do not refer to how long the student could be in the program or what the average length of expected matriculation is. Dr. D. is confident that the spirit of Standard 7.01 is not being met but is unsure about any discretionary status and more generalized program descriptions that might mitigate the interpretation. On the basis of the discussions at faculty meetings, she is convinced that the program is not designed to provide the experiences required for APA accreditation to be achieved in the foreseeable future.

Dr. D. does not think there is intentional distortion or misrepresentation, and therefore she wonders about how and to whom she should speak if she decides to pursue this question. She does not want to alarm students or cause them unnecessary concern; therefore, she wants to be cautious.

Dr. D. realizes that if she does speak to the department head or the training director, her inquiry could be met with concern because they too may not have thought about the time frame involved and therefore would also be concerned about misrepresentation. If the director or department head are aware of the balancing act they are doing regarding the program's status, however, there is the possibility of defensiveness or rejection of Dr. D.'s concern. If this occurs, Dr. D. will think about other means of reporting the potential standard violation and a more effective way to try helping students who may be caught in the middle. Dr. D. will also need to consider the impact on her teaching agreement and the possible negative consequences.

Decision Options. Dr. D. realizes there are several difficult factors in this case, so she decides to consult with colleagues who are teaching at other schools. Dr. D.'s intention then becomes to speak with the program director and raise the timeline concern as well as the potential misrepresentation of the students' status on graduating. Dr. D. decides that, regardless of the program director's reaction, she will present the case as fairly and reasonably as possible. She will express concern about the expectation the students may have given the public status reports.

Dr. D. decides not to speak with other faculty or students regarding her concern because they have no decision-making authority on how the program is presented. Dr. D. wants to express her interest in continuing to teach, but even though her statements might disadvantage her she has decided that she cannot by omission participate in misrepresentation to students.

If Dr. D.'s concerns are ignored, she must decide the route she might take in reporting ethical violations if informal resolution does not work. She has several options, including contacting a higher level of administration at the school, the APA Ethics Committee, or the state licensing board, among others. Dr. D. could also contact the APA accreditation office with any questions about the accreditation process. Dr. D. is anxious about proceeding in this matter but is also relieved that she has decided to take action and has determined the means by which she will try to rectify this dilemma.

Standard 7.02, Descriptions of Education and Training Programs

Psychologists responsible for education and training programs take reasonable steps to ensure that there is a current and accurate description of the program content (including participation in required course- or program-related counseling, psychotherapy, experiential groups, consulting projects, or community service), training goals and objectives, stipends and benefits, and requirements that must be met for satisfactory completion of the program. This information must be made readily available to all interested parties.

This standard guides training psychologists to identify and describe the elements of the training program that are required or expected to be met by students and that contribute to student decision making regarding the selection of a training program. Training programs usually have criteria that are prescribed by accreditation, certification, or licensing bodies and therefore have expectations across programs that students must fulfill. In addition to these, however, programs may develop various emphases in research and practice. Programs with a greater focus on clinical practice may require more psychotherapy training, clinical field experiences, possible experiential courses, and more application than research-focused programs, which may expect participation on a research team, in grant writing, and more courses in research design and methodology.

The conditions of participation in the training program are valuable for students to know in advance of commitment to a program and may include, for example: (a) stipend or assistantship possibilities and what they entail, (b) length of time expected in the program, (c) matriculation costs, (d) accreditation status, and (e) type of supervision. Program faculty should make known the expectations for students to participate in experiences that could be influence their decision of whether to apply to the program. For example, the requirements to participate in one's own therapy, participate in group therapy with classmates, matriculate the program within a certain time frame, and disclose personal information to the faculty can influence students' decisions about the focus and desirability of the program.

Conditions of a program can certainly change beyond the control of the program faculty. The university may withdraw assistantships, practicum sites may close, and faculty who led popular research teams may leave. Program faculty can be expected to make public only those developments that can reasonably be anticipated or become known. This standard is meant to ensure that students are able to make reasoned decisions about training based on the most accurate and relevant information available.

Standard 7.02, Case 1

Case Illustration. Mr. J. has been matriculating in his accredited doctoral program for several years and is planning his final coursework and programmatic activities and requirements in order to finish. He has been encountering several situations that may challenge his progress in the program.

Mr. J. is taking an advanced course in treatment interventions, and the professor is conducting the class through activities and exercises in which students are required to participate. Some of the activities involve clustering into small groups and relating the principles being learned to how students perceive each other and their relative interpersonal characteristics. Other exercises involve variations on students' experiences of each other in relation to self, others, and professional development. The syllabus states that students are required to participate in in-class exercises but says nothing about experiential groups in which students would be required to self-disclose and share perceptions of each other. When Mr. J. speaks to the professor about his discomfort with these activities, the professor retorts that these exercises are not what he considers experiential and that he is not requiring that the students disclose the types of personal information addressed in Standard 7.04, which the professor realizes would be an ethical violation. Mr. J. is required to take this course. Other professors teach this course in other semesters; however, the drop–add period has already passed, and he would have to ask for special circumstances, and a reason would have to be provided in order to withdraw. He would not be able to pick up another course and therefore would be short a course, which could jeopardize his assistantship. The professor is steadfast in his position and appears to Mr. J. to be exasperated with him.

Ethical Dilemma. Standard 7.02 requires any participation in experiential groups to be made readily available to any interested parties. Mr. J. knows that this course is required, but the course description does not make clear that these types of activities could be required. He does not know whether the other faculty who teach this course also require these activities because the syllabi are very similar to each other and use similar wording to describe the course. His professor believes that "in-class exercises" is an accurate description of the activity. Mr. J. thinks that these activities are a violation of Standard 7.02, but the professor does not. Other students are also uncomfortable with the activities, but they all have decided to say nothing because they do not want to challenge the professor. Mr. J. feels exploited because he is expected to make observations about peers with whom he has collegial relationships, and he thinks that the professor who facilitates the class experiences seems to enjoy directing these activities as a director of a play. Mr. J. realizes that Standard 7.04 does not directly apply because the professor is not asking him to disclose specific personal information.

Mr. J. has already approached the professor and feels he has been rebuffed. He knows that he has the right to ask for special circumstances to withdraw or to present the problem to the training director; however, he knows that the training director and the professor have been colleagues for years and he is unsure how his complaint would be received. Mr. J. realizes for the first time that words and phrases such as *experiential, in-class exercises,* and *interactive activities* can have very different meanings and are not typically specified in syllabi. He does not want to appear to be a troublemaker. He feels very alone in his decision and conflicted about his course of action.

Mr. J. also thinks that these activities fail to respect Principle E: Respect for People's Rights and Dignity in regard to the public treatment of his fellow students, and Principle A: Beneficence and Nonmaleficence in that the professor may not be safeguarding the welfare and rights of the students and that his actions may lead to misuse of his influence.

Decision-Making Factors. Informed consent is a foundational concept in Standard 7.02 that is meant to give students information on which to base decisions. Without this standard, students could unknowingly make choices based on a lack of information or based on misinformation that result in potentially disadvantageous consequences. Mr. J. realizes that Standard 7.02 is meant to protect both programs and students by informing students what is expected of them by the program and by informing programs that require-ments and expectations must be known to prospective students.

The term *experiential* has referred to a variety of practices across time, and Mr. J. is caught between differing interpretations. He realizes that role plays, practicing techniques and interventions, and engaging in hypothetical situations for the purpose of demonstrating skills and competencies are a vital part of learning. The activity in question, however, does not seem to Mr. J. to have learning objectives and is not a route to further understanding of con-cepts or principles taught in the class. It also seems to Mr. J. that the exercises potentially exploit the power differential between the professor who is facil-itating this exercise and the students who are expected to make comments about others that they would not otherwise make. Furthermore, the professor is hearing the observations that could affect both the his evaluation of the students and students' perceptions of each other.

In thinking about what to do in this situation, Mr. J. factors in several questions:

- Can I stay in this class and participate in a way that does not require me to be incongruent with my professional values and my interpretation of the Ethics Code?
- What are the possible effects on my relationship with my peers if this group plays out as the professor has planned?
- Are there faculty members, such as my advisor, to whom I can go for support and assistance?
- How will my course trajectory be affected if I drop this class, and what will be the impact of this on my attitude about the program?
- Is there a mentoring program available to me through which I can get assistance unrelated to the program?
- How will I be affected in terms of my attitude about my depart-ment, program, other students, and myself if I do intervene and if I do not?

Decision Options. Mr. J. realizes that there could be several ways to influence the professor's practice in class. He thinks about discussing the problem with his fellow students to determine whether others are willing to participate in talking with the professor again about their discomfort and the implications for their relationships with each other if they continue this exer-cise. If others are not willing to participate, Mr. J. may think about approach-ing the professor again himself. He realizes the professor may react badly, but he weighs the potential consequences of participation versus pursuit of the problem with the professor.

Mr. J. considers others in the department to whom he can go and thinks about the likely course of events if he talks with his advisor, training director, or others. He also realizes he may be able to seek consultation from professional organizations, such as the local ethics committee. He knows that the power differential within the training context is a factor that presents itself in various decision-making situations for students. The level and quality of support and assistance available to students in their departments, and the systems in place to protect students and faculty from exploitation, are factors in decision making that must be considered on an individual basis. If Mr. J. does have support among other faculty, or if procedural systems are in place to help deal with this situation, he may feel more confident about questioning the professor. If these conditions do not exist, then Mr. J. must base his decision on the relative consequences to himself, his peers, and the effect on him in the continuance of his training and professional development.

Standard 7.02, Case 2

Case Illustration. Mr. F. is a second-year student matriculating in a psychology doctoral program. His program has developed relationships across the university with other programs and has advocated with the administration for the importance of financial assistance for doctoral students in the program. As a result, all students in the program have typically been assigned assistantships within either the department, in teaching and research assistantships, or across the campus, in academic enhancement, admissions, athletics, student affairs, or academic departments that use assistantships for academic advisement. The program includes in the application materials the fact that full-time students are able to acquire assistantships through the program, and the training director sees this information as a strong recruitment factor. The admissions material for the program describes the expectations of the program that students matriculate full time. The program does not have the resources or the curriculum model for a part-time program. The student handbook defines full-time matriculation as enrollment for 12 credit hours in the fall and spring semesters each and states that to hold an assistantship students must be matriculating full time.

Mr. F. had an assistantship the 1st year of his program and received good evaluations from his supervisors. He knows that he had been favorably evaluated and that he received a desirable assistantship in his 2nd year partly because of his performance during his 1st year. Mr. F. wants to pursue a part-time job in the emergency room of the local hospital to enhance his experiences in public sector and primary care settings. He thinks this will be very beneficial in preparation for his application for an internship. Mr. F. knows that he cannot work all of his commitments into his schedule, so he decides to sign up for 6 hours (two courses) instead of 12 hours (four courses). This would save him considerable time because one of the courses he defers is known to have a heavy reading load.

Mr. F. is shocked when the training director tells him that he cannot continue in the assistantship because he does not have full-time status in the program. Mr. F. is very angry and feels mistreated because he had performed well in the assistantships he had held. He reminds the training director that the promise of an assistantship had been cited in the application materials, the admissions materials, and in the student handbook. He decides that he will file a complaint based on unfair treatment and a failure of the program to follow through on program commitments. The training director is surprised and concerned when she receives the complaint and notes that a copy had been sent to the provost and to the APA Accreditation Office.

Ethical Dilemma. The training director assembles all of the materials that were given to students at all phases of the program. These include application materials, Web site information, admissions forms, and the student handbook. In addition, the training director knows that she met with all of the students regularly and gave considerable information verbally, but she knows that what counted was what was included in standard written and electronic materials.

The application materials and the information on the Web site state very clearly that the program was full time and that assistantships were available for all students. These materials, however, did not explain the requirement that students must be full time in order to have an assistantship. Only the student handbook given to students after they entered the program specifically defined full time as carrying 12 hours per semester.

The training director is now uncertain whether her program had met the requirement of Standard 7.02. She believes that when the materials were developed the application information was accurate, and she thinks that what is there still is accurate. She does not know whether the materials were complete enough. Mr. J. is claiming that even though the requirement to be full time was in the initial material, the program has not advised and mentored students in an ongoing way that would keep students apprised of the requirements.

The program faculty who put the materials together advise the training director that they think it is sufficient to refer in the admission materials to assistantships being available for students with full-time status, without mention of the number of hours required to be full time, and that further details of number of hours required for full-time status as well as other particulars of the faculty expectations would best be introduced when students begin matriculation. The training director is stymied about what to do.

Decision-Making Factors. Standard 7.02 presents conditions of participation as ethical expectations within education and training. Conditions of participation require disclosure and transparency from training programs regarding requirements for students and give faculty a protective context through which faculty and programs enforce expectations. Informed consent is bidirectional and therefore provides protection not only for students but also for programs. Autonomy and responsibility are applicable factors if the student accepts his or her offer of admission to the program.

In this case, the training director may consider the materials the program provided and evaluate whether the materials met the expectation of Standard 7.02. There is a reasonableness in the expectations created by Standard 7.02 in that the student bears some responsibility for becoming familiar with the program materials and taking some initiative to clarify ambiguity in his or her own progress through the program. The director may also evaluate the engagement of the student and whether the student has met the expectations cited in the materials. The training director and the faculty realize that they need to think through the dissemination of information; how official information is conveyed; and, most important, for purposes of professional development of students, how they identify faculty responsibility and teach student responsibility.

In addition, the training director thinks about the effect this event might have on the other students in the program. The other students are compliant with the matriculation requirement, and they have been assigned assistantships. What are the obligations of the training director to maintain consistency and congruity in application of policies involving students? Any difference in application of the policies to Mr. F. could appear to be favoritism or differential treatment of a single student.

The training director may think about several factors that can influence her decision:

- Is the application material specific and clear that the program is a full-time one?
- Does the material imply that assistantships are automatically given to all students, or are qualifiers clear about the assistantship?
- Does the training director or other faculty meet with students periodically to update them on policies, decisions, and activities in the program related to their successful matriculation?
- Is the student handbook treated as a contract in that students must agree to abide by the handbook policies, procedures, and requirements, or is the handbook treated as less than a contract?
- What are the responsibilities of the students in becoming informed and prepared for participation in the program?
- How can the faculty and the students collaborate in maximizing informed consent and transparency for both?
- How might the director and the faculty respond to the actions taken by the student in informing others outside the department of the grievance?

Decision Options. In keeping with the intent of transparency and full disclosure, the training director decides to meet with the individuals involved in the situation. She meets with the faculty to receive their input and feedback and to process their perspectives on the circumstances. The training director and Mr. F.'s advisor also meet with Mr. F. and discuss the expectations they had for the program in regard to full disclosure of requirements as well as their expectations of the students to understand the information and to be aware of the policies of the department as they pertain to students.

The training director realizes that Mr. F. had not connected the assistantship and the full-time requirement together and gives him the opportunity to pick up classes in order to become a full-time student and keep the assistantship. She determines that the policy, however, cannot be modified for Mr. F. because there is a reasonable expectation that he should have understood these requirements and, furthermore, she thinks it is important that requirements be equally applied to all students.

The training director notifies the provost and the APA accreditation office of the resolution of the problem without providing all of the details of the case. Failure to notify might be viewed as tacit agreement that an unethical action had occurred, and the training director thinks the program has provided enough information that this is not the case.

The faculty does realize, as a result of this experience, that they want to adopt a policy regarding both program and student responsibility that would be detailed in written documentation and that would be discussed and explained in group and individual advisory meetings.

Standard 7.03, Accuracy in Teaching

Psychologists who teach or train students must be mindful of the importance of transparency and accountability in the presentation of materials, expectations of performance, and means of evaluation. Psychologists who teach also should be mindful of the commitment to the scientific bases of knowledge in determining content and curricular experiences required of students.

Standard 7.03(a)
Psychologists take reasonable steps to ensure that course syllabi are accurate regarding the subject matter to be covered, bases for evaluating progress, and the nature of course experiences. This standard does not preclude an instructor from modifying course content or requirements when the instructor considers it pedagogically necessary or desirable, so long as students are made aware of these modifications in a manner that enables them to fulfill course requirements. (See also Standard 5.01, Avoidance of False or Deceptive Statements.)

Just as the student handbook of the program, department, or university represents the students' contract with the program, so too does the course syllabus typically function as the instructor's contract with the students for the course. The syllabus contains the explanation of requirements for the student and describes the knowledge and experiences that students will gain as provided by or through the instructor. This standard is meant to promote a fair and equitable agreement between faculty and students on the expectations of both for performance in the course. In developing a syllabus, faculty might ask the following questions:

- When one reads the syllabus, are the instructor's expectations of students clear?
- Are the experiential or applied experiences clear and understandable in terms of requirements versus elective experiences, the conditions of the experiences, and the expectations for disclosure?
- Is the content in the syllabus congruent with the title of the course and the description offered by the instructor at the beginning of the course?
- Are the means for evaluation accurate and reasonably clear?
- Are all of the factors involved in evaluation cited in the syllabus?
- Are required out-of-class experiences explained?
- Are the activities necessary to complete the course outlined in the syllabus?
- Are modifications to the requirements made in such a way that students can comply with expectations?

These are questions that instructors may review when composing a syllabus and course material toward the goal of transparency among faculty, program, and student expectations.

Standard 7.03(b)

When engaged in teaching or training, psychologists present psychological information accurately. (See also Standard 2.03, Maintaining Competence.)

A valued tradition in academe is the freedom of opinion and expression. The graduate school experience inherently promotes independent thinking, academic debate, and engagement in discourse without fear of consequences. Psychologists balance freedom of academic expression with accuracy and inclusion of material germane to the course. Psychology as a discipline lends itself to investigation, critical thinking, and pursuit of knowledge. This pursuit allows a wide breadth of scientific inquiry and hypothesis building. Academic psychologists should engage in the freedom of ideas while maintaining their commitment to accuracy and the scientific method.

Standard 7.04, Student Disclosure of Personal Information

Psychologists do not require students or supervisees to disclose personal information in course- or program-related activities, either orally or in writing, regarding sexual history, history of abuse and neglect, psychological treatment, and relationships with parents, peers, and spouses or significant others except if (1) the program or training facility has clearly identified this requirement in its admissions and program materials or (2) the information is necessary to evaluate or obtain assistance for students whose personal problems could reasonably be judged to be preventing them from performing their training- or professionally related activities in a competent manner or posing a threat to the students or others.

Respect for professional boundaries is well described in several sections of the Ethics Code (e.g., Section 2, Competence; Section 3, Human Relations; and Section 10, Therapy). Boundary concerns cluster around two factors: (a) loss of objectivity by psychologists and (b) potential exploitation of individuals with whom psychologists work. This standard assists psychologists in defining potential boundary issues, in particular in the context of training, and illuminates the means by which objectivity and exploitation can become threats in the training environment. Principle D: Justice and Principle E: Respect for People's Rights and Dignity are applicable to this standard in that they promote and protect student privacy and engagement in just treatment.

The potential for loss of objectivity becomes a threat to professional faculty–student relations when students' personal disclosures reveal information that may affect the faculty's perception of students. Students may recount experiences in their histories that, in the frame of reference of the faculty members, indicate weakness, poor judgment, relational problems, or other perceived shortcomings that could affect faculty's and supervisors' views of students' current capabilities. Often psychologists do not realize they have lost objectivity until a series of events occurs in which their interactions seem to be based on information, affect, or beliefs not known or understood by others. Without effective cognitive compartmentalization, individuals can blend information and interpretations that subsequently affect judgment and decisions regarding others. This standard protects students from inadvertent loss of objectivity by individuals who have decision-making and judgment power over their training experience.

When one individual is significantly more disclosing than the other, a dynamic may develop in which the disclosing individual feels more vulnerable on the basis of being more known than the other. Differential disclosure is a common factor across psychotherapeutic methods and may be viewed as an element of therapeutic treatment. Intentional disclosure and encouragement of disclosure are also elements of forensic interviewing, organizational interviewing, and clinical intake interviewing. We identify these examples simply to note that disclosure is understood as a significant factor in psychological transactions and that a resulting vulnerability of the disclosing person is a likely possibility. In the training context, students are vulnerable to training psychologists' judgment and decision making because of the impact of those decisions on their lives. When students are encouraged to be disclosing of personal information or experiences that are not typically known through contemporary interactions, their level of vulnerability is significantly increased.

The exceptions for which personal information may be requested are noteworthy. These exceptions balance autonomy and privacy with the need to ensure competency and safety. Programs that value disclosure as a variable in their teaching model should include full descriptions of these expectations in their training materials. This information must be made available to students in the decision-making stage of application, not after the student has accepted his or her admission offer to the program. Programs typically differentiate *student handbooks*, which are given to entering students, from *admissions materials*, which are provided to potential students before they make a decision. Requirements, including disclosures that could be factors in program choice, should be explained in the initial materials.

When personal problems or questions of safety are encountered in training settings, psychologists may request information that could contribute to decisions about students' welfare and training capability. The condition of having personal problems is not the central focus of this exception; more important is the effect of problems on students' ability to competently proceed in the training program. Psychologists should be alert to the fact that clinical experiences in training include students offering psychological services to the public through psychotherapy, assessment, consultation, and other activities that prepare them for professional performance. Supervisors should be aware that a student's state of well-being is a factor in the quality and competence of services he or she provides to others. When students cannot proceed in training because of personal factors, or when the individuals served by students receive compromised services, psychologists may request information needed to make effective and useful decisions about the course of training.

Standard 7.04, Case 1

Case Illustration. The clinical training director of a psychology doctoral program is apprised by faculty that two very problematic situations have occurred, both of which need her immediate attention. In Situation 1, a doctoral student, Ms. A., is receiving individual supervision from Dr. D. Ms. A. is carrying a full caseload that includes some complex cases that involve diagnoses of borderline personality disorder, depression, and eating disorders and that include clients with histories of childhood sexual and physical abuse and other traumas. Ms. A. believes she is capable of working with these clients because she has had prior supervisory experience with these kinds of cases and because she is diligent in her focus on each client, her preparation for sessions, and her knowledge of how to develop appropriate treatment plans. Dr. D.'s conceptualization of supervision is one in which the clinicians/therapists bring their own personal history into their active frames of reference in session. Dr. D.'s thinking is that empathic capacity hinges on the therapist's ability to relate his or her own feelings from past experience to the client. Because of this perspective, Dr. D. begins asking Ms. A. questions in supervision regarding her own personal history. When discussing a case in which the client had experienced childhood sexual abuse, Dr. D. asks Ms. A if she has had any similar experiences with which she could relate to the client. Dr. D. continues to inquire about Ms. A.'s personal experience with each disclosure by the clients about their traumatic experiences, which include suicide, eating disorders, and relationships with parents. When Ms. A. shows some reluctance to discuss her personal history, Dr. D. asks if she is in therapy and wonders aloud whether this might be the reason she is reluctant to discuss her history. Ms. A. speaks to her advisor about her concern. Her advisor asks Dr. D. about the incident, and Dr. D. reiterates that Ms. A. is resistant to supervision and that Dr. D. was only doing what was right. The advisor decides to speak with the clinical training director.

Situation 2 involves Dr. M., who also conducts individual supervision with some of the doctoral students in the practicum course. Dr. M. makes it a practice to focus on clinical skills and competencies of the students and does not make inquiries into the students' personal lives. Dr. M. understands and appreciates that students can have reactions to clients that tap into the students' own experiences, values, or attitudes. Dr. M. teaches the students to be aware of their own reactions that could interfere with their effectiveness in conducting psychotherapy and tells them that they can decide how to present those dynamics in supervision. Dr. M. is careful and specific in teaching students the difference between focusing on their own experiences and understanding their personal reactions to clients that could influence their objectivity. Given this perspective, Dr. M. is particularly concerned about how to handle an alarming development concerning one of her supervisees, Ms. R. Ms. R. has appeared depressed, lethargic, and less communicative in supervision. She has missed several supervisory sessions without explanation. Other students have reported unpredictable outbursts among the classmates, claims that others were conspiring against her, and sensitivity resulting in crying and arguments with classmates. Ms. R. also has missed several client appointments.

When approached by classmates, she retorts that she does not know what they were talking about and asks them to leave her alone. Dr. M. learns from another faculty member that Ms. R. has been missing other classes also. Dr. M. decides to meet with the clinical training director to discuss the concerns.

Ethical Dilemma. The ethical dilemmas in Situation 1 and Situation 2 involve the interpretation of Standard 7.04 regarding student disclosure and the application of the exceptions. Psychologists—in this case, faculty and supervisors—must decide about the appropriateness and application of required student disclosure. The standard prohibits these inquiries unless one of two exceptions can be met: (a) the requirement is clearly identified in the program's admission materials or (b) the information is needed to assist a student whose personal problems might be preventing him or her from performing training-related activities in a professional manner or who is deemed a threat to others. If not, even though the information might be helpful, interesting, or pertinent, students have a right to privacy in regard to their personal experiences and their past, as well as in contemporary personal experiences, such as whether they are in therapy at the time of matriculation. Faculty who might think that such information would be useful and might find a rationale for asking must remember that this standard gives guidance by offering two exceptions, one of which must be met in order to proceed with personal inquiry.

Decision-Making Factors. The clinical training director, the faculty, and the students who are involved in Situation 1 and Situation 2 are all aware that the program had not identified this requirement in its admissions materials. This decision was deliberate and not an oversight. The program had decided that student privacy was an important value in their program. Situations 1 and 2, therefore, must look for exception in the allowance and appropriateness of the requirement of disclosure in regard to the second instance: "The information is necessary to evaluate or obtain assistance for students whose personal problems could reasonably be judged to be preventing them from performing their training or professionally related activities in a competent manner or posing a threat to the students or others."

Considering Situation 1 in light of the above-mentioned second exception, Dr. D. has not indicated concern for Ms. A.'s personal status or of her ability to work with her clients. Dr. D.'s rationale is based on theoretical orientation and therapeutic style. Dr. D. trained during a time period and in a program in which student disclosure was acceptable and in some cases expected. Dr. D. thinks that this practice is an effective training approach and that this is a way in which students can develop greater insight, introspection, and awareness.

Regardless of the intentions of Dr. D., the clinical training director knows that Standard 7.04 is meant to protect the psychologist and the student from the potential of exploitation or loss of objectivity. Knowledge about students' past experiences or present personal or therapy content could inadvertently affect the faculty members' evaluation of students in their matriculation. Moreover, disclosures may result in the students' feeling vulnerable while in evaluative circumstances.

Situation 2 appears to be applicable to the second exception mentioned in Standard 7.04. Dr. M. does not inquire about Ms. R.'s personal information; however, Ms. R.'s behavior has raised reasonable concern regarding her mental health status. The two criteria for inquiry of personal information include (a) the existence of problems that could prevent students from performing training- or professionally related activities or (b) actions that may pose a threat to other students or others. Dr. M. and the training director take steps to verify the reports they have received and then assess the risk implied by those actions. Both conclude that Ms. R. is at psychological risk given her actions and the statements she has made. Given her outbursts and accusations of conspiracy, they consider her to be a risk to other students. Harm to others cannot be assessed without further information; however, Ms. R.'s psychological status does indicate an impediment to her ability to perform professionally related activities. No decision or judgment would be made until further assessment and evaluation of Ms. R.'s health status, but there is enough evidence for concern and for the appropriateness of further personal inquiry. Standard 7.04(2) allows psychologists to obtain assistance for students whose health status is in question and gives latitude in helping students find sources of professional help. This standard also gives psychologists who have responsibility for students in training the ability to act in a protective manner for the welfare of students under their auspices as well as for the clients of the students.

Decision Options. The clinical training director realizes that Dr. D.'s actions do not fall within Standard 7.04(2) and finds Dr. D.'s retort that the supervisee is resistant to not be a relevant perspective. The director considers the fact that supervisors can misinterpret inquiries about personal information as helpfulness, promotion of self-awareness in relation to conducting psychotherapy, or educative. These perceptions of standards of training do not now meet the ethical expectations of psychologists. Faculty and supervisors must be mindful of the evolving ethical values of respect for the autonomy and privacy of individuals with whom they work. Although this standard does not specifically prohibit asking for personal information, but only prohibits "requiring" it, the power differential between faculty and students may result in students feeling coerced. Furthermore, psychologists cannot know how they will react to information about students, that is, whether the knowledge could affect their evaluation as well as their interpersonal assessment. The blurring of information, feedback, and observations of a professional nature with personal information about students' past experiences and current personal life can interject personal observations into professional evaluation apart from the intention of the psychologists.

In Situation 2, Dr. M. and the training director agree, after verification of the reports and information regarding Ms. R.'s behavior, that they must intervene and determine what action will be most helpful to her. She may not be receptive to the concerns being expressed and may not want to accept feedback or involvement by the faculty. After an initial assessment by Dr. M. and the training director, they will decide how to proceed with any action regarding her status in the program, disclosure to family or others relevant to her welfare, and recommendations for professional assistance. The clinical training director and Dr. M. think that they have engaged in the proper assessment of Ms. R.'s actions and believe that they are following the spirit of Standard 7.04(2) in becoming involved with inquiries about her personal information.

Standard 7.05, Mandatory Individual or Group Therapy

Expectations for psychologists to avoid exploitation and loss of objectivity are conveyed consistently through the ethical standards that pertain to relationships between psychologists and those with whom they work. Standard 7.04 defines the context in which personal information may be asked, and Standard 7.05 defines the context of a particular type of personal information: individual or group therapy. The vulnerability that students may feel from disclosure and the faculty authority associated with evaluation gave rise to Standard 7.05.

Standard 7.05(a)

When individual or group therapy is a program or course requirement, psychologists responsible for that program allow students in undergraduate and graduate programs the option of selecting such therapy from practitioners unaffiliated with the program. (See also Standard 7.02, Descriptions of Education and Training Programs.)

Autonomy and privacy are balanced with health and quality of training in allowing students choices for therapy that are unaffiliated with the training program. Group therapy in training is likely to be composed of student peers, and therefore the vulnerability in disclosure can affect student–student relationships as well as faculty–student relationships. Multiple role conflicts can arise when students shift roles from peers and colleagues to therapeutic roles within a group even though there would likely not be an evaluative component in these relationships. Furthermore, the student and training psychologist roles can assume multiple and conflicting aspects. Depending on the training environment and the focus of the program, training psychologists who do not directly evaluate students may still have an indirect influence on the students' progress. For example, programs that encourage multiple working relationships between faculty and students, such as mentoring roles, research teams, joint grant writing, community service collaborations, and other shared activities, result in faculty and students working together without a direct evaluative component. Programs in which an apprentice model, for example, is encouraged may result in students working closely with a select few faculty and never having direct connection with the majority of the training faculty. This standard does not prescribe the conditions of therapy but instead creates choices for students that are compatible with the training environment and student goals.

Postdoctoral training programs may well include required experiences of a therapeutic nature. The pursuit of intrapersonal growth, self-awareness, or the importance of experiencing the client/patient phenomenon can be a central focus in postdoctoral training. Standard 7.05 is not meant to be applicable to postdoctoral training. The postdoctoral programs in which therapy is an integral part are selected by individuals because those individuals are seeking these experiences. Furthermore, if postdoctoral trainees are unsatisfied with the program expectations, they can more easily change a postdoctoral site than a doctoral training program.

Standard 7.05(b)

Faculty who are or are likely to be responsible for evaluating students' academic performance do not themselves provide that therapy. (See also Standard 3.05, Multiple Relationships.)

The caution described in other standards (e.g., Standard 3.05, Multiple Relationships) applies here to faculty who may be in therapeutic and evaluative roles with the same individual. These two roles are inherently incompatible for five reasons: (a) the therapeutic progress can be impeded by the reluctance of the client/student to disclose personal information to a faculty member; (b) the therapist/faculty member may lose objectivity when learning personal information about the client/student; (c) the potential for exploitation increases because the therapist/faculty member has both academic and therapeutic influence over the client/student; (d) if the client/student does not progress successfully in the program, questions may arise about the role of the therapist/faculty member; and (e) other students may question the status of the client/student in relationship to them and their academic performance and the role of the therapist/faculty member in their training experience.

This standard speaks to faculty "who are likely to be responsible for evaluation" in a broader definition than direct faculty–student relationships such as instructor and advisor, which are examples of direct faculty influence over students. Faculty who are involved in the administrative activities of a program can be members of curriculum committees, assistantship committees, and other policy groups that make decisions that affect students' progress. As a result, some faculty members can exercise considerable influence over students who may never be enrolled in their courses. Training psychologists determine the nature of their anticipated roles with individual students and use their judgment in proceeding with therapeutic engagement with students. Decision-making questions psychologists may ask include the following:

- What are the possible courses the psychologist may teach, and what is the likelihood that these students may enroll in the class?
- Is the psychologist teaching elective courses only, or could required courses taught by the psychologist be needed in order for the students to graduate?
- Does the psychologist have the authority to refuse admission to a class on the basis of the prior therapeutic relationship with the students requesting enrollment?
- Has the psychologist informed the students that being in individual or group therapy with the psychologist will limit their professional engagement with the psychologist in regard to evaluative experiences?
- Does the psychologist participate in any policy- or decision-making committees that could affect the matriculation of the students in the therapy experience?

Standard 7.06, Assessing Student and Supervisee Performance

Standard 7.06 is anchored in the concept of informed consent. Psychologists who are in evaluative roles in regard to students convey the information students need to know in order for them to understand and respond to expectations. Timeliness, specificity, and established criteria must be known to all affected persons and are critical to a fair and just evaluative process.

Standard 7.06(a)
In academic and supervisory relationships, psychologists establish a timely and specific process for providing feedback to students and supervisees. Information regarding the process is provided to the student at the beginning of supervision.

The authority to evaluate is at the crux of the power differential between faculty and students. For this reason, evaluation must be conducted in a thoughtful, fair-minded, and objective manner. Training in psychology requires more than accurate information acquisition and retention. The many facets of training, including didactic coursework, clinical performance in psychotherapy and assessment, multicultural competencies, research skills, and consultation and organizational skills, call on evaluating psychologists to apply varying methods of assessment. Psychologists may adopt a record-keeping frame of reference in identifying and then documenting, through syllabi or other means, their expectations for levels of performance. Graduate training in psychology includes many performance expectations that are not measured through course syllabi, such as professional interpersonal competencies, ability to collaborate on research teams, interviewing skills, and dissertations. Evaluating psychologists who implement a documented means by which students can be apprised of these expectations will avoid student uncertainty and confusion.

Evaluation is the outcome measure for student performance at intervals during the training program; it may include course examinations, research projects, and paper submissions as well as culminating experiences such as special projects, comprehensive examinations, and dissertations. Assessment of student performance not only includes a final evaluation of a training experience but also is meant to assist students during the learning process in taking corrective action, focusing on areas of needed improvement, and receiving feedback information in the formative stage of learning. Feedback on performance during the process of learning provides students with information to help them redirect their efforts toward the expected level of competency. Training activities in psychology are diverse and lend themselves to many different means of evaluation. Performance in didactic courses may well be measured by paper-and-pencil tests, whereas clinical performance may be measured by observation of particular skill sets or successful demonstration of therapeutic factors (e.g., therapeutic relationship, therapeutic stance, application of theoretical model).

The evaluation process adopted for student performance in courses, supervision, and other psychological activities within the program should be conveyed and described to students at the beginning of the learning experience. This timely procedure enables students to prepare to meet performance expectations through time management, allocation of resources, and other preliminary activities that may promote successful accomplishment of requirements. This standard does not suggest the means by which training psychologists may evaluate students but instead deems that students be apprised of their performance in an ongoing manner and not be taken by surprise by a negative terminal grade.

Standard 7.06(b)

Psychologists evaluate students and supervisees on the basis of their actual performance on relevant and established program requirements.

Psychologists in training settings are privy to many facets of student performance and conduct because of the multiple training roles in which they work with students, such as when a student is an enrollee in class, advisee, research team member, graduate assistant, clinical supervisee, or involved in other appropriate academic training. Psychologists can become aware of students' personal characteristics, capabilities, interpersonal and learning styles, and style of interaction with faculty and other students. Psychologists who have thoroughly and specifically defined criteria for performance will be better able to evaluate students whose extraneous characteristics could interfere with objectivity. When means of evaluation are not clearly identified, psychologists could be subject to loss of objectivity in evaluation either in unjustifiably positive or negative assessments.

Standard 7.06, Case 1

Case Illustration. Dr. S. is the instructor of record for the doctoral practicum course in the fall semester. He has taught this course several times and enjoys it very much. The department does not have an in-house training clinic, and therefore all of the practicum sites are in the community and the surrounding area. Dr. S. holds the group practicum meeting for 2 hours every week. The individual supervision as well as the clinical experience take place at the practicum site in the community. Dr. S. realizes the importance of a syllabus; he always composes a syllabus for the course and discusses the requirements during the first class meeting of the semester.

In the syllabus, Dr. S. includes the five requirements of (a) attendance in the group supervision class as well as the individual supervision session; (b) participation in class and in individual supervision; (c) accurate and thorough record keeping, including case management and progress notes; (d) documentation of practicum-related activities, both direct and indirect hours; and (e) performance on a midterm and final examination in which clinical scenarios were offered for assessment, diagnosis, and treatment planning.

Mr. C. is enrolled in the practicum course and, by Dr. S.'s observation, performs very well in class. He frequently makes observations about other students' cases that are accurate and informative. He comments on assessments of the clients and possible diagnoses, and he always has positive and helpful observations regarding treatment planning. As the semester progresses, Mr. C performs quite well on the midterm, and at the end of the semester he submits an exceptionally good paper and does well on the final exam.

During the last week of the semester, Dr. S. receives a phone call from Mr. C.'s site supervisor. The supervisor regrets to say that she has grave concerns about Mr. C.'s clinical abilities. Mr. C. is able to talk about his clients articulately in supervision, but when the supervisor watches his videotaped sessions she observes his inability to form a therapeutic relationship, his didactic nature, his tendency to lecture and give informational advice, his insensitivity to multicultural competencies, and other in-session activities that were detrimental to clinical progress. The site supervisor reports that when she talked with Mr. C. about these concerns he was polite but not open to hearing negative feedback, and he did not respond to corrective recommendations. Mr. C.'s clients often do not return after the first couple of therapy sessions, and the site supervisors decide that they will not be able to offer him a placement the next semester. The site supervisor declares that she will not be able to pass Mr. C.

Dr. S. is stunned by this conversation because, by his evaluation, Mr. C. would have received a grade of A. Dr. S. decides that when considering the combined performance evaluations, Mr. C. will receive a C in the class. Mr. C. is very surprised and upset when he receives his grade. He meets with Dr. S. and points out that he had met all requirements on the syllabus and intends to appeal his grade.

Ethical Dilemma. Dr. S. begins to realize that he had overlooked a critical component of the evaluative process for practicum. Because Mr. C. is so capable of articulating clinical concepts in the didactic format, Dr. S. had not considered that he would not be successful in clinical performance. Dr. S. also begins to realize that he had not thoroughly represented the evaluative aspects of the course in the syllabus. Dr. S. realizes that he is struggling with both Standard 7.06(a) and 7.06(b). He still thinks that he met the requirement to provide a timely and specific process for providing feedback for the didactic portion of the class, and he thinks that his evaluation of Mr. C.'s performance in didactic activities was accurately outlined in the syllabus and conducted in an acceptable manner. Dr. S. realizes, however, that he had not consulted with the site supervisor in the timely and specific way that would have given him this information earlier, and therefore he was not able to give the student timely and specific feedback during the semester but instead just at the end of the semester (Standard 7.06a). Dr. S. also had not specifically cited performance in the clinical arena, students' attitudes learning, interpersonal competence, openness to supervision, or growth toward clinical competency as integral components of the evaluation for the grade (Standard 7.06b).

Decision-Making Factors. Dr. S. faces several factors in his decision about how to proceed. He had developed his syllabus as he had for many other semesters, but heretofore he had not faced the incongruity of didactic and clinical performance that was now revealing the inadequacy of his syllabus. His evaluation criteria were focused on recitation of information and case conceptualization that took place in the group didactic format. He had evaluated students on paper-and-pencil tests and a term paper. Also, he realizes that he has based evaluation on summative performance in class and on paper and, except for the paper-and-pencil midterm examination, had not implemented any formative evaluation or feedback. On these counts, he has not met the expectations of Standard 7.06(a) in being timely and specific in regard to the clinical requirements at the practicum site.

In addition, Dr. S. had not cited in his syllabus, or at the beginning of class, that clinical performance as assessed by the site supervisor was an integral component of the overall evaluation for the course. Dr. S. had assumed that because this was a practicum class, all of these measures would be taken into account in the grading. He sadly realizes that he has not been in ongoing contact with the site supervisor regarding Mr. C.'s performance. He did not have an understanding with either the site supervisor to accept responsibility of informing Dr. S. if there were clinical training problems on site or with Dr. S to initiate contact with the site supervisor regarding Mr. C. to receive the feedback from the site supervisor. As a result, Dr. S. realizes that he has not met the expectations of Standard 7.06(b) in evaluating this student on established course requirements.

Dr. S. has mixed thoughts about the role of the student in this situation. He would have had more empathy for Mr. C. had the site supervisor not been direct and candid to Mr. C. about his performance or had the supervisor waited until the end of the semester to give Mr. C. the negative feedback. It seems that the site supervisor conducted her role appropriately in giving direct feedback and in a formative manner, except for the fact that she did not convey the negative evaluation to Dr. S., the instructor of record. Mr. C., then, knew of his clinical performance problems but was not open to the feedback from the site supervisor and did not discuss the problems with Dr. S.

Decision Options. Dr. S. decides to make several changes in his doctoral practicum course. He revises his syllabus to reflect clinical performance, interpersonal competency, and effectiveness as a trainee in the practice of psychology. Dr. S. also deliberates on the vehicles by which he could make these evaluations other than through written papers, recitation of information, and other paper-and-pencil measurements. He realizes that videotaping, direct observation, simulation, standard client modules, and similar methods would be more appropriate for clinical evaluation. Dr. S. now values the importance of making the expectations for performance and the method for evaluation clear not only through the initial distribution of the syllabus but also through ongoing discussion and explanation in the group practicum class.

The site supervisors for the program had not been integrally involved in the ongoing evaluation of students at their sites. Dr. S. determines to meet regularly with them to establish a working relationship and to confirm the contractual agreement between the program and the sites in knowing which entity was responsible for each part of the course. Dr. S. decides also to collaborate with site supervisors on the method for evaluation and to establish an early warning system for students who may be having difficulties either in clinical, interpersonal, or other site-related problems.

In disappointment, Dr. S. realizes that he had not given sufficient attention in group supervision to the developmental level of his students in terms of their openness to learning, fears or uncertainties about performance, ability to hear feedback, and their perspective on actually practicing what they are training to do. He decides to restructure the group practicum class and to build in time to attend to these concerns. He also begins including in his group supervision class a more focused and infused awareness of multicultural competencies and the subsequent clinical expectations of those competencies. Dr. S. has learned the importance of formative as well as summative evaluation and the value of being alert to training difficulties before final evaluation occurs. He decides to establish a means by which he can collaborate with site supervisors on formative evaluation that would help the supervisors as well as the trainees. In consideration of the grade assignment, Dr. S. decides to delay assigning grades, as well as deciding whether students should repeat the first semester, until the second semester of the practicum had been completed. This case highlights the value of program mechanisms that will bring the faculty together to discuss progress of students. Such mechanisms can be particularly helpful when adjunct faculty play a significant part in training.

Standard 7.07, Sexual Relationships With Students and Supervisees

Psychologists do not engage in sexual relationships with students or supervisees who are in their department, agency, or training center or over whom psychologists have or are likely to have evaluative authority. (See also Standard 3.05, Multiple Relationships.)

Because of the expanding scope of psychological training across academic departments, community agencies, hospitals, organizations, and forensic settings, training psychologists increasingly have responsibilities and authority across multiple sites and through differing roles, such as department liaison to a community agency, adjunct faculty of a teaching hospital, and consultant to an organization. As a result, psychologists have broader influence across settings and roles than in direct faculty–student evaluative roles only. For this reason, Standard 7.07 calls on psychologists to be aware of the many means by which they can affect the academic lives of students both in current circumstances and in anticipation of potential evaluative authority. This standard also calls attention to the status of *supervisor* as distinct from *faculty*. Psychology trainees often receive supervision from psychologists in the community and at professional training sites that may or may not have official affiliation with the academic department. The role of supervisor reflects the same relational elements as that of faculty and student. Supervisors hold an evaluative role over students in the same manner as do faculty.

The power differential in faculty–student relationships corresponds to that in therapeutic relationships with current and former clients/patients (see Standard 10.05, Sexual Intimacies With Current Therapy Clients/Patients, and Standard 10.08, Sexual Intimacies With Former Therapy Clients/ Patients). Students and clients/patients have expectations of trust (Principle B: Fidelity and Responsibility and Principle A: Beneficence and Nonmaleficence) from training psychologists and from treating psychologists, respectively. The ability of students and clients/patients to extricate themselves from harmful dual relationships is diminished because of the work investment in the training program for students and the emotional investment in treatment for clients/ patients. Further consequences could occur when other students in the program are aware of dual-role relationships and are affected either through their relationship with the student or the psychologist.

Standard 7.07, Case 1

Case Illustration. Ms. E., a doctoral-level psychology student, is very excited about being invited by her program advisor to participate in a multisite research project as her advisor's research assistant. She knows this position will allow her to pursue her research interests, that she will be working with several faculty members from her own program, and that she will meet psychologists from other sites and will be able to learn so much from them and from the experience. She will be working on a team in collaboration with other students and psychologists and will be in pursuit of important research questions. After Ms. E. has been working on the team for a few months, she begins to notice that the psychologist who is principal investigator (PI) and project director has begun seeking her out for discussions, asking for her opinion on research procedures, and spending more time with her than with the rest of the team. At first, she is honored, because she thinks the PI must think she is doing a very good job, that she has strong research potential, or that she is particularly dedicated to the project and therefore can be depended on to follow through. After a few weeks, however, she begins to feel uncomfortable because the PI would ask work-related questions initially and then begin to be self-disclosing and to ask Ms. E. questions about her private life. Just as Ms. E. is going to speak with the PI about their interactions, the PI asks to meet with her. He tells her that she is the most interesting, attractive, bright, and fun person he has ever met, and he expresses a strong desire for them to begin seeing each other outside of work. He says that he thinks they "may just click."

Ms. E. is reeling from this statement and is quite dismayed and uncertain how to handle this situation. She tells the PI that she is not interested in pursuing a personal relationship with him. The PI begins to explain to her that their having a personal relationship would not be a professional or ethical problem because they are not in the same academic department; the PI is not her supervisor or advisor, and he has no authority over her matriculation in the program. The PI asks Ms. E. to think about the proposal and to remember that they could have a very special relationship together.

Ethical Dilemma. Ms. E. is very mindful of the ethical prohibition of specific sexual relationships within the profession, and she is particularly aware of the proscription of relationships involving students. She knows that earlier APA Ethics Codes had cited direct authority or evaluative capability over students as the criteria for prohibited sexual relationships. She also knows that the current code has been revised from the 1992 Ethics Code[2] to include relationships between psychologists and students or supervisees who work in the same department, agency, or training center. The intent of this revision is to recognize the influence that professional psychologists may have in their work settings regardless of official positions of authority or reporting lines. Ms. E. feels certain that the roles she and the PI hold would be applicable to Standard 7.07, and she understands how the problems anticipated by Standard 7.07 could play out in her situation.

Ms. E. is very certain that she does not want to become embroiled in such a potential relationship and ethical conflict, but she is uncertain how to proceed. She realizes that the PI could be embarrassed, angry, or spiteful if he is turned down. Ms. E. does not want to jeopardize her advisor's position of significance on the project, her own research assistantship, or her relationships with others on the project. Even though the PI is correct in that he has no direct authority over her, Ms. E. can see that there are many ways in which this development could negatively affect her. She knows that she will not accept the PI's offer, but she is anxious about how to proceed.

Decision-Making Factors. This standard, as well as others that explicate relationships that reflect an inherent power imbalance, brings to light many other problematic aspects of these situations than only the sexual relationship, although the sexual component is a singularly ethical problem. In this situation, the PI is not Ms. E.'s direct supervisor, but he does have authority over the entire research project and, as such, he could conceivably affect any aspect of the research project. Ms. E.'s advisor is a tenured full professor; however, the roles, status, and assignments made on the project could be influenced by the PI. Only the advisor can dismiss Ms. E. from the project, yet the allocation of funds for research assistantships, the number of assistants retained across time, and the allocation of funds and assistants to other psychologists could also be affected by the PI's decisions. Some of the research assistants have assignments at the major site, working side by side with the psychologists. Other assignments include field work, surveying the commu-

---

[2]American Psychological Association. (1992). Ethical principles of psychologists and code of conduct. *American Psychologist, 47,* 1597–1611.

nity, and doing analyses on weekends. These are viewed as less desirable by the students. The PI does not make these assignments, but he could be involved in methodological decisions if he so desires.

The effects of such an ethical breach can reach beyond the unethical action itself. In this case, other research assistants have already become aware that Ms. E. has been spending more time in the presence of the PI than they. They have begun to wonder what this means and whether Ms. E. is receiving special consideration, talking about the other research assistants to the PI, or receiving information about the project that they do not have. They also wonder how her relationship with the PI might affect them and why the PI is not giving them equal access.

The students have concerns based on the power imbalance and the limited control they have in the academic research and professional environment. Other faculty and researchers working on the research team could have different concerns, regardless of their autonomous positions on the team. The appearance of a special relationship between a student and the PI could raise questions among team members regarding the student's access to information, the influence of the student on the PI's decision making, and the relationship of the team and the other research assistants to the student. Such a relationship within a work team in which roles, tasks, and functions are established and known by all can affect the productivity, trust, and motivation of any member. These repercussions of such a situation can surreptitiously pervade a project, department, program, or agency.

Decision Options. Ms. E. might decide to consult with her advisor or another trusted faculty member. The academic climate, trust of identified others, and anticipation of consequences may guide her in determining whether to seek consultation. Ms. E. already knows that she will not consider the PI's offer, and so the purpose of a consultation would be to decide how to respond to the PI. Ms. E. also wonders whether the attention she received has already been noticed and whether this means she should do anything to counteract any negative perceptions other team members might have. Any gossip or grapevine activity on this situation could only be damaging. For this reason, because Ms. E. is not confused on the ethical standard in question, and is not interested in a relationship with the PI, she might decide either not to consult someone or to talk with someone unrelated to her academic community. She also needs to think through the effect of trying to exert damage control on perceptions already being held. She understands the broader spirit and meaning of Standard 7.07 and can express this concept to the PI. She is certainly taking a reasonable and circumspect ethical stance, even if it is contrary to that of the PI. She might also expect that once her contact with the PI changes the team members will notice, and their concerns will diminish without her direct involvement.

CONCLUSION

In summary, Section 7 of the APA Ethics Code identifies and describes the primary components of ethical practices in academic and training setting in which psychologists work with students and supervisees: Informed consent clarifies both the program and faculty's responsibility and commitment to the students and the students commitment to the program; the conditions of evaluation define boundaries of academic practice that could either in perception or actuality compromise students personally, academically, or professionally; and relational boundaries specifically identify prohibited sexual relationships with students and supervisees. These standards of education and training guide psychologists in making decisions that guard against loss of objectivity or engagement in exploitation and provides students with a road map for expectations of self and others through informed consent.

The following questions facilitate decision making in each of the three components just described. These questions are neither exhaustive nor comprehensive, but they do suggest a means of comparison between ethical and questionable program status in the context of education and training standards:

- Will successful matriculation result in students meeting expected professional requirements if that is what the program has indicated is the result of successful graduation?
- Does the admissions material represent the current requirements of the program?
- Does the admissions material accurately identify program expectations of the students?
- Are required activities and elective activities delineated from each other?
- Would an individual be able to read the admissions material and have a very accurate assessment of the training experience?
- Have recent graduates of the program identified perceived incongruent or misrepresented aspects of the program?
- Would a potential student have an accurate assessment of costs, resources, practicum sites, supervision, pedagogical focus of the program, assistantship possibilities, and other factors that affect the quality of the training experience?
- When faculty perceive a need for personal information, has the purpose been to assess the status of the student in the program, assist the student, determine whether the faculty need to make an intervention based on competency concerns, or protect the interests of clients and others in service with the student? If not, how would the information be used, and to what purpose?

- When program faculty conduct required therapeutic experiences for students, how do the faculty determine that no evaluative transaction will occur with those particular students? How does a faculty member document this position?
- How do the faculty identify the method of evaluation for students? Do the faculty have descriptions of the means for evaluating different requirements than didactic classes, such as the expectation to develop interpersonal skills, clinical skills, and professional collaboration skills?
- Do the faculty members and supervisors have a means to document their perception of their roles with students and what these relationships mean for professional conduct?

8

RESEARCH AND PUBLICATION

The fundamental value conveyed through each standard in this section is the protection of individuals who could be exploited or harmed and the protection of the integrity of the scientific enterprise during the pursuit of scientific advancement through research and the dissemination of knowledge through publication. The individuals who are affected by these standards are research participants and creators of original professional works. The design of Section 8 provides a framework for professional conduct through which the 2002 American Psychological Association's (APA's) "Ethical Principles of Psychologists and Code of Conduct" (hereinafter the *APA Ethics Code* or the *Ethics Code;* see http://www.apa.org/ethics/code2002.html)[1] promotes both the protection of these individuals and a context of honesty, integrity, and fairness in the pursuit of science and the dissemination of psychological information. Aspects of each of the Ethics Code's General Principles have significant application to psychologists' perspective in conducting research. General Principle A: Beneficence and Nonmaleficence alerts research psychologists to the importance of safeguarding the welfare of others, including human research

---

[1]American Psychological Association. (2002). Ethical principles of psychologists and code of conduct. *American Psychologist, 57,* 1060–1073.

participants and animal subjects. The commitment to promote the welfare of others applies not only to research participants with whom psychologists work directly but also to those who may be affected by the professional actions of psychologists in conducting research. The Ethics Code (in Standard 2.04, Bases for Scientific and Professional Judgments) directs psychologists to base professional work on scientific and professional knowledge. General Principle B: Fidelity and Responsibility, moreover, underscores not only the importance and the responsibility of conducting research that benefits society but also psychologists' obligation to conduct research and to be active participants in the development of research that benefits society and communities. General Principle C: Integrity values psychologists' accurate and truthful representation of data through research, publication, and treatment of emerging knowledge in scholarly pursuits. When conducting research in which hypotheses require deception, or when misrepresentation inadvertently occurs in disseminating information through scholarly publication, psychologists are mindful of the fact that, first, they must explain the deception and correct the misrepresentation as soon as possible and, second, identify and resolve any possibility of mistrust or harm that has resulted from their professional actions. General Principle D: Justice guides psychologists in thinking about fairness and justice in research areas of investigation and about different groups' access to the benefits of psychological research. Psychologists should ask themselves who is benefiting from the research and who is not benefiting. They also are aware of the use of their research resources and whether their resources are primarily benefiting some groups over others. These factors inform psychologists when making decisions about their research pursuits. The development of research ethics over recent years is reflected in General Principle E: Respect for People's Rights and Dignity and is central to psychologists' thinking about how they treat people who are research participants. The foundational role of informed consent in research grows out of General Principle E and provides direction for the implementation of these values in conducting research and in participant decision making.

The framework of protection for research participants and creators of original works is developed primarily through two concepts: (a) informed consent and (b) identification of authorship and accurate reporting of original works. Informed consent, exceptions to informed consent, and qualifications of informed consent can form the underpinnings of psychologists' thinking and decision making regarding research design and implementation.

INFORMED CONSENT

Standards that underscore the value of the accurate reporting of research results and of accurately identifying published original works serve as parallel concepts between research and publication. The credibility of the scientific

contributions of psychology rests with the veracity and reliability of information developed and reported by psychologists. The culminating process of reporting scientific findings, theoretical concepts, and new ideas that advance knowledge is the vehicle through which the public accesses the contributions of the profession. Psychologists are mindful of the ethical importance of their scientific representations to the public.

The APA Ethics Code standards that define the treatment of original work give psychologists parameters within which to think about collaboration and appropriate use of others' works, protect the scientific enterprise, and provide open access to review. Psychologists should be mindful that their responsibility to participate in and advance research is framed within a mandate to conduct research ethically and to ensure that scientific endeavors are made in an ethical manner that will contribute to the profession's knowledge base. These ethical standards balance the importance of independent scientific pursuit with respectful acknowledgment of the original work of others. Scientists must be able to work in professional environments of consultation and mutually respectful inquiry and to build on the advancements contributed by others. The publication standards serve to promote a professional environment in which the work of research psychologists is nurtured and respected.

Standard 8.01, Institutional Approval

When institutional approval is required, psychologists provide accurate information about their research proposals and obtain approval prior to conducting the research. They conduct the research in accordance with the approved research protocol.

The requirement for research proposal approval by designated review committees of sponsoring universities, federal agencies, or other parent entities of research initiatives has developed over the years within the scientific community. The term *institutional sponsor* has traditionally meant the host institution at which or through which the research will be done. The principle here is that psychologists would not go into settings to conduct research without acquiring that setting's approval and then following the agreed-on protocol. An institutional review board (IRB) is often, but not always, the vehicle by which institutions oversee research. It is also the case that the funding or sponsoring institution that employs the researchers may also require institutional research review of their employees/researchers. It is not atypical that researchers would need to acquire approval from both institutional entities.

The potential for abuse, misrepresentation, and risk to participants has resulted in development and adherence to standards, uniformity in procedure, and the researchers' responsibility for consequences. Standards 8.01 and 8.02 both address disclosures of information that represent core elements of the

proposed research initiative. Standard 8.01 focuses on informed consent from the institution to do the research, and Standard 8.02 addresses getting informed consent from the participants to ensure that they understand both expectations and possible consequences of involvement in research initiatives. Standard 8.01 addresses provision of information regarding procedures and protocol that will serve as the blueprint for implementation of the research design. Psychologists who are developing IRB requests for approval might describe the characteristics of the research that will most likely affect the safety or risk to participants and that define the expectations of the participants, the researchers, and the institutions.

Psychologists should be aware of the required procedures specifically cited in the standard that note the importance of accurate information; the acquisition of prior approval, not post hoc approval; and following through in the same manner that was proposed in the request. In other words, after researchers describe the proposed study they have an obligation to adhere to the conditions that were approved. Modifications may be necessary in implementing and conducting research; however, these proposed changes should be made before deviating from the approved proposal.

Standard 8.01, Case 1

Case Illustration. Dr. D. is a professor at a nearby university. In recent years, he has developed an interest in research involving victims of disaster and people who have experienced trauma. His research has focused on the immediate aftermath of disasters and the coping reactions of the affected individuals. Dr. D. has also broadened this research line to include the experience of people displaced by disasters. He went to New Orleans during the aftermath of Hurricane Katrina and conducted research there for 2 months. Dr. D. has just learned that an earthquake has hit a region in southeast Asia and that hundreds of people have been affected. The news of the earthquake has just reached the national news. Dr. D. has begun to think about the value of collecting data in another country and comparing the experiences recorded from the Katrina victims with those of persons in this Asian region.

Dr. D. has collected data for his research projects for years, and he has always gone through his university's IRB. The IRB has made several changes recently, and Dr. D. is aware that approval for research is now taking at least 3 weeks to process. Dr. D. has not faced this problem before because his data have been collected in the United States and he has been able to expedite the approval through earlier procedures that are no longer in place. Dr. D.'s participants have been individuals living within the United States. He begins to ask himself why he would need to have IRB approval because the participants would not legally be under the auspices of the United States. He thinks that if he travels to the site of the earthquake he can get tacit approval from

the on-site authorities, either the local government officials or the Red Cross. He realizes that if he waits long enough to go through the IRB that he will lose valuable exposure time to the individuals displaced by the earthquake and that time is of the essence.

Ethical Dilemma. Several ethical standards should inform Dr. D.s' decision. Standard 8.01 instructs psychologists to gain institutional approval before conducting research and states that research must be conducted in accord with approved research protocols. This may be complicated in an international context, and Dr. D. does not know yet what institutions may be involved and whether institutional approval will be needed. He also realizes that he is unclear regarding what requirements his own university may have for approval in such circumstances. He thinks possibly that because he is not asking for financial support for the travel to collect data, he is not responsible to the university. Dr. D. is also approaching an ethical violation of Standard 2.01(a), which decrees that psychologists must conduct research with populations and in areas only within their boundaries of competence and states that it is essential that psychologists understand the factors associated with competence in providing services to individuals of a different age, gender, gender identity, race, ethnicity, culture, national origin, religion, sexual orientation, disability, language, or socioeconomic status. Inadequate attention to any one of these factors can forseeably result in Dr. D. inflicting harm on the victims of this disaster. Dr. D.'s prior disaster research has not included international sites or participants. As a result, he could be in violation of competency standards on several factors. Applicable in this dilemma are three general principles. General Principle A: Beneficence and Nonmaleficence directs psychologists to strive to benefit those with whom they work and to do no harm and that, furthermore, psychologists must attempt to safeguard the welfare and rights of the individuals with whom they interact. General Principle B: Fidelity and Responsibility reminds psychologists of their responsibility to the communities in which they are working and states that they must clarify their roles and obligations and consult and cooperate with other professionals and institutions to the extent needed to serve the best interests of those with whom they work. General Principle E: Respect for People's Rights and Dignity cautions psychologists to be aware that special safeguards may be necessary to protect the rights and welfare of persons or communities whose vulnerabilities may impair their decision making. Psychologists should be aware of and respect cultural, individual, and role differences, including those based on age, gender, gender identity, race, ethnicity, culture, national origin, religion, sexual orientation, disability, language, and socioeconomic status, and they must consider these factors when working with members of such groups.

Decision-Making Factors. Dr. D. is torn between his motivation to advance his research through this window of opportunity and uncertainty about his professional obligations. He has ethical obligations to sort out, but he also thinks about the cultural, ethnic, and political implications of the actions he is considering. In consideration of Standard 8.01, Dr. D. realizes that his professional role is inextricably related to his university post. Because he will present himself to the individuals in charge of the disaster site as a psychologist from his university, he is bound by the policies of the university's IRB. If Dr. D. intends to return to the university, analyze his data, and include this data set with other data he will continue to collect, then his work is still being supported by the university. If he has a grant or other source of funding for this prospective research project, he would be bound by the research protocol of that grantor. If he wants to consider himself unencumbered by restrictions of institutional policies, he will nonetheless eventually be asked by the editors of journals to which he submits his work about the procedures he followed in collecting his data.

Reflecting on the cultural, ethnic, and political implications of his decision gives Dr. D. much to consider. The APA Ethics Code General Principles cited earlier call on psychologists to respect the dignity and worth of all people and to recognize the right of individuals to privacy, confidentiality, and self-determination, and the pertinent ethical standards require Dr. D. to achieve a level of understanding and of professional competence in working with diverse individuals. Given the region in which the earthquake occurred, Dr. D. would need to be competent, at least, in working with individuals of diverse ethnicity, race, national origin, religion, and language. In thinking about the fundamental elements of his research procedures Dr. D. will become aware that obtaining appropriate informed consent (Standard 8.02) is essential before he includes participants' data in his research. Dr. D. then should also begin to think about the use of interpreters (Standard 2.05). Both informed consent and use of interpreters would be essential aspects of his research process.

If he decides to pursue this research project, Dr. D. would be putting himself in the context of international disaster relief, which carries with it an expectation of competency in and familiarity with international disaster work practices. For this reason, he might wish to familiarize himself with practice guidelines and standards for international disaster and emergency services. These factors include awareness of the impact on individuals within their communities when asking them to participate in research and engaging with investigators. Without understanding the political and social structures of governments, communities, and internal systems, psychologists may risk causing unintended harm by violating laws, customs, and cultural practices. The potential for perceived exploitation may be significant when psychologists enlist individuals for research participation who do not share their cultural context.

Decision Options. Dr. D. begins to realize that although initially this opportunity could be most valuable to his ongoing research commitment, ethical and professional participation in this research activity would require a steep learning curve in his attempts to accomplish the necessary levels and kinds of competencies, skills, and broad cultural awareness. Dr. D. also realizes, given his ambitious research agenda in this arena, that even though he would not engage in international pursuits now he has much work to do in preparing himself to pursue his research. These pursuits would include multicultural education, engagement in multicultural and other diversity experiences, and extensive study and experience in response practices to international disasters. Dr. D. also realizes that he does not want to begin circumventing his university's policies and procedures, with which he has worked throughout his research career.

Standard 8.02, Informed Consent to Research

Informed consent is one of the foundational concepts on which the Ethics Code is built. Informed consent in direct application of psychological science or practice is addressed through several specific standards in addition to Standard 8.02, including Standard 3.10, Informed Consent; Standard 9.03, Informed Consent in Assessments; Standard 10.01, Informed Consent to Therapy. Participants in research, just like students and supervisees, depend on the psychologists/researchers to provide accurate and complete information in an understandable way with which the participants can make a decision of whether to participate. The risk of misinterpretation, loss of objectivity, investigator bias, and other aspects of research procedures that could influence participants' decisions is minimized when informed consent is thorough, accurate, and understandable. When the research activity is experimental, the expectations of informed consent for established procedures as well as additional criteria must be met to ensure protection and full disclosure to participants.

Standard 8.02(a)

When obtaining informed consent as required in Standard 3.10, Informed Consent, psychologists inform participants about (1) the purpose of the research, expected duration, and procedures; (2) their right to decline to participate and to withdraw from the research once participation has begun; (3) the foreseeable consequences of declining or withdrawing; (4) reasonably foreseeable factors that may be expected to influence their willingness to participate such as potential risks, discomfort, or adverse effects; (5) any prospective research benefits; (6) limits of confidentiality; (7) incentives for participation; and (8) whom to contact for questions about the research and research participants' rights. They provide opportunity for the prospective participants to ask questions and receive answers. (See also Standards 8.03, Informed Consent for Recording Voices and Images in Research; 8.05, Dispensing With Informed Consent for Research; and 8.07, Deception in Research).

Informed consent is an organizing value that is conveyed throughout the Ethics Code, most explicitly in Section 3, Human Relations; Section 8, Research and Publication; Section 9, Assessment; and Section 10, Therapy, as well as through General Principle B: Fidelity and Responsibility, General Principle C: Integrity, General Principle D: Justice, and General Principle E: Respect for People's Rights and Dignity. Standard 8.02 builds on the primary informed-consent standard, 3.01, as do the other informed-consent standards referenced in this paragraph. Informed consent represents psychologists' commitment to ensure that individuals affected by professional psychological activities have a full understanding of the actual and potential impact of those activities. Informed consent is the means through which psychologists accomplish transparency in intent, effect, and the consequences of participants' involvement with psychological activities. Choice, as much as possible, is given to individuals in participation of those activities. Adherence to participants' right to know and to choose contributes significantly to all aspects of psychological training, research, and practice.

The essential elements of informed consent are discussed and documented for all research in Standard 8.02(a). Standard 8.02(b) addresses studies of experimental therapies.

Psychologists conducting research involving human participants must consider the following eight basic factors in attaining informed consent as required by Standard 8.02(a):

1. *Purpose*. An explanation of purpose includes logistical conditions of participation and conceptual aspects of the study. These conditions may include information regarding length of time of commitment, frequency of participation, intensity of any treatment or intervention factors, type of experience in the relevant topic or subject, and an overview of the expectations of the participants and the researchers. Conceptual aspects may include information on the eventual use of the findings and how the outcome may contribute to the advancement of science and knowledge. Psychologists are not expected to provide information, however, that may compromise the research. When deception or distortion is necessary, other ethical expectations would apply, including subsequent debriefing. Furthermore, researchers may provide participants an overview of procedures that will be followed and that describe the participants' role in accomplishing

these (see also Standard 8.05, Dispensing With Informed Consent for Research; Standard 8.07, Deception in Research; and Standard 8.08, Debriefing).

The important factor for psychologists in explaining the purpose of the research is to ensure that individuals understand the experiences they are going to have and the information they need to make a decision of whether to participate in the proposed study. Psychologists will want to be alert in the informed-consent procedure to explanations for children, individuals with cognitive impairments, and individuals with language-specific needs, recognizing the relevance of Standard 3.10(b) in such cases. A meaningful explanation of informed consent is most important with all participants, in particular with populations that involve inherent power differentials because of physical or cognitive limitations for participants or because of interpretive needs.

2. *Right to decline.* Psychologists must be committed to conveying the true optional nature of involvement in research to the potential and actual participants. They should be particularly aware of those individuals who are vulnerable to the influence of a power differential, such as students, assistants, and others in continued relationships with the investigators as well as individuals with diminished capacity, such as children, older people, or people with cognitive impairments. In addition, individuals who may seem to be impervious to undue influence may have personal inclinations to being accommodating or helpful and therefore may have a vulnerability to influence based on their personal values or characteristics. Presentation of the right to decline or withdraw can be a difficult discussion for the investigators who do, indeed, want participation yet are committed to the objective and unbiased explanation of the right to decline.

3. *The foreseeable consequences of declining or withdrawing participation.* Psychologists who explain the consequences of non-participation may be aware of a two-pronged purpose to their descriptions. First, they will want to discuss both the likely and reasonable consequences of participation as well as the fears and concerns on the part of the participants, including those not likely or realistic but that may nonetheless inform participants' decisions. For example, undergraduates may fear declining participation in a research experiment out of concern that their grades would be affected. On the one hand, psychologists/researchers should address these concerns and reassure potential

participants that such fears are groundless when that is the case. On the other hand, forfeiting the information that would be gained in the experiment is an actual consequence. Psychologists may ask prospective participants what they anticipate the consequences to be and how they perceive the decision of not to participate. Any concern about punishment or penalty must be discussed and alleviated. Psychologists should recognize that individuals who have an impairment or those who are subject to a power differential may not be willing to express a concern about punishment, and in these cases psychologists will want to introduce and clarify the subject themselves. In regard to the second purpose of explaining the consequences of nonparticipation, psychologists will also want to thoroughly describe the continuation or discontinuation of other benefits or conditions of the research participation. The status of any treatment benefits, continued services, remuneration, supplies, equipment, referral access, consultation, and other tangible benefits to participants should be very specifically defined following the termination of participation.

4. *Reasonably foreseeable factors that may be expected to influence people's willingness to participate, such as potential risks or adverse effects.* Psychologists will want to think comprehensively about risk and effects in full disclosure of the range of experiences involved and in commitment to the transparency of intent, effect, and possible consequences that is the foundation of informed consent. Risk and adverse effects can materialize in ways not expected by the investigators. Researchers are certainly not expected to anticipate all possible outcomes, but they can be informed by thinking expansively about several potential variables:

- Will the effects manifest through sensory, physical, affective, behavioral, or cognitive modalities, and what will be the likely form that each will take?
- Could the nature of the effects differentially affect individuals; that is, could the treatment experiences possibly be traumatic for some and benign for others?
- Could individuals' values, morals, or lifestyle practices be challenged, compromised, or otherwise be injected into the experience unwittingly?
- Is the status of personal identification and/or anonymity clear to the participants, and are there exceptions to the expected procedure?

- Have the investigators considered the language, level of language, and interpretive needs of the participants?
- Has the process of debriefing been determined for all potential participants, including those who withdraw?

5. *Any prospective research benefits*. *Benefits* should be distinguished from *incentives* offered for participation. Benefits are often realized as part of the treatment application or the results of the treatment, such as educative information, strategies for behavior change, cognitive shifts, and self-improvement (e.g., weight gain/loss, improved physical condition). Researchers should make every effort to be realistic and accurate in suggesting benefits and to avoid misleading the participants into expectations that cannot be met.

6. *Limits of confidentiality*. Confidentiality limits in training and practice often are transacted by the supervisors and practitioners who may serve as gatekeepers of information; that is, disclosure of confidential information often involves the psychologists who participated in generating the information. Research data can evolve from the point of original collection to archival status and should be accessible by individuals other than only the original investigators. Research psychologists should explain to participants the potential for access by others and the implications of such access, any legal or ethical limits given the nature of the information, any multiple uses of the data that would suggest additional access, and implications regarding the electronic transmission of data.

7. *Incentives for participation*. Incentives can enable individuals to participate who otherwise would not be able to overcome impediments to participation such as costs and inconveniences of transportation, meals, logistical costs of being available when and where necessary, and loss of time and income. Psychologists are specific and thorough in describing the incentives, the condition of receiving incentives, and the circumstances under which incentives will cease.

8. *Whom to contact for questions about the research and research participants' rights*. The researchers responsible for the informed consent should provide the names and contact information of the individuals who can answer questions and provide information regarding participants' experiences. Phone numbers, e-mail addresses, and office addresses are means by which participants may have access.

Standard 8.02(b)

Psychologists conducting intervention research involving the use of experimental treatments clarify to participants at the outset of the research (1) the experimental nature of the treatment; (2) the services that will or will not be available to the control groups(s) if appropriate; (3) the means by which assignment to treatment and control groups will be made; (4) available treatment alternatives if an individual does not wish to participate in the research or wishes to withdraw once a study has begun; and (5) compensation for or monetary costs of participating including, if appropriate, whether reimbursement from the participant or a third-party payor will be sought. (See also Standard 8.02a, Informed Consent to Research.)

Informed consent in experimental treatment involves a heightened obligation to fully disclose the possible impact of the treatment on participants. Experimental treatment introduces variables that may cause effects for participants that are unknown to researchers. Psychologists may consider the following five aspects of experimental research as they provide information to participants:

1. *The experimental nature of the treatment.* Psychologists explain the difference between treatments of known effectiveness and experimental interventions to participants and must not leave the meaning or effect of experimental treatments up to the interpretation of participants. It is understandable that psychologists do not know the actual effect of experimental treatments, yet to the extent possible they should explain the experience that the participants can anticipate during treatment and explain the impact and consequences of the experience.

2. *The services that will or will not be available to the control group.* When the outcome of studies would be affected by fully informing participants of their classification, participants should be apprised of their role within the control group and the options for the control group participants after the study is complete. Often, however, participants' behavior or cognitions may be affected by the knowledge of their classification in the study. The standards of informed consent are not meant to interfere with research design that necessitates withholding the classification of participants. The researchers should describe any options for treatment either within the activities of the study or as a referral function.

3. *The means by which assignment to treatment and control groups will be made.* Research design and the means of categorizing participants may or may not be explained during the treatment procedure, depending on the methodology of the study. The intent of

this standard is to ensure two things: that participants understand (a) that they may or may not be receiving the anticipated treatment and (b) how the assignments to treatment and control groups will be made. The options for subsequent follow-up should be explained clearly and understandably at a feasible time. Benefits and risks of participation must be clearly explained in language understandable to the participants.

4. *Available treatment alternatives if an individual does not want to participate in the research or wishes to withdraw once a study has begun.* Psychologists should be alert to the possibility that potential participants may think the only alternative for treatment is to participate in the proposed research study. This perception may result in individuals feeling indirectly coerced into participation if the research study is seen as the only available treatment. Investigators, therefore, will want to ensure that potential participants understand treatment alternatives and accompanying conditions.

5. *Compensation for or monetary costs of participating.* Participants should understand any monetary effect on their participation, whether it be compensation paid to them or costs for the treatment, including billing a third party, self-payment, or reimbursement. This practice ensures that participants understand the relationship between monetary aspects of the agreement and the actual participation in the research. Any special conditions that would alter the monetary agreement must also be explained fully to the participants so that there is no appearance of deception or exploitation in the agreement for participation between psychologists and participants.

Standard 8.02(a), Case 1

Case Illustration. Dr. B. is a psychologist who is the director of the IRB for a large urban teaching hospital. She also practices in the hospital and teaches psychology and medical interns. One of Dr. B.'s review teams asks her to render an opinion on a research request that is giving them concern. She is surprised to realize that the proposal comes from one of her psychology faculty colleagues, Dr. M., who has several large grant-funded research projects underway. Dr. M. supervises trainees who provide health services to the hospital's low-income residents from a five-county area, and she conducts research in which many of the patients participate. Dr. M. has been given a grant to research particular psychosocial behavioral treatments with patients who have been diagnosed with HIV/AIDS. The individuals are already being seen for medical treatment as well as for psychotherapy, both individually and in groups. Dr. M's grant would implement a psychosocial treatment model that is intended to positively affect behavioral patterns and subsequent health risk levels.

In her proposal to the IRB, Dr. M. includes in the informed consent the purpose of the research and procedures, prospective benefits, limits of confidentiality, incentives, and a contact person. She does not include the right to decline or withdraw; foreseeable consequences of declining or withdrawing; or potential risks, discomfort, or adverse effects. Dr. B. meets with Dr. M. and asks about these omissions. Dr. M. responds that these participants are already patients and that some of them have been receiving medical services there for years. They are very used to involvement in research projects. Their only source of medical and psychological services is the clinic, and she knows that none of the patients has declined to participate in the years she has been there. She also sees no need to upset the patients by talking about hypothetical negative consequences.

Ethical Dilemma. Dr. B. begins to consider how she would approach Dr. M. about the ethical aspects of informed consent in question. She is mindful of Standard 8.02, which educates psychologists regarding the essential elements of informed consent for all research studies (Standard 8.02a) and for studies that include experimental treatments (Standard 8.02b). This standard explicitly lists the required components of informed consent. The three components of the standards in question serve important functions in participants' decision making. The right to decline to participate and the right to withdraw once participation has begun are both essential aspects of making an independent choice (Standard 8.02a[3]). Understanding the possible results of one's decision also is necessary information in making an informed and independent decision (Standard 8.02a[4]). Any factors that could manifest in the participation that could influence a person's original decision to participate is also an important aspect of the participants' independent decision.

Dr. B. is also aware that General Principle D: Justice recognizes the importance of fairness and justice in exercising access to processes, procedures, and services and that psychologists must be cautious about potential biases that could lead to unjust practices. Similarly, General Principle E: Respect for People's Rights and Dignity identifies the importance of respect for the dignity, worth, and self-determination of all individuals and psychologists' obligation to safeguard individuals whose vulnerabilities may impair their autonomous decision making. Furthermore, psychologists must guard against biases or prejudices that are based on, in relevance to this case, ethnicity, culture, race, disability, and socioeconomic status. Dr. M. may have made assumptions about the compliance of the patient population that was based in part on their socioeconomic status. Dr. M. may assume that, given the limited choices these patients have for health services, they will welcome any services she might offer, in particular for no fee. She may have imagined that the patients' need for health assistance was great enough that any considered choice to decline the research participation would not happen, and therefore she overlooked the procedures related to independent decision making. Dr. M.'s decisions reflect at least the appearance of a disregard for the related ethical standards and principles.

Decision-Making Factors. In thinking about the right to decline or withdraw from participation (Standard 8.02a[2]), Dr. B. understands that most of the prospective participants are patients at the hospital and have received medical and psychological services there for some time. These individuals rely on the hospital and the clinic for all of their health care. They are predominantly low-income individuals and from a financial point of view do not have, or see themselves as having, options or the ability to make choices. They could easily relate their current and ongoing health care to their cooperation in requests for research participation. Even though Dr. M.'s practice would not be to negatively affect the individuals who did not participate, the perception that their health service could be at risk is very possible. Dr. M. has made an assumption that this population would certainly want any treatments that they could get, thinking that they could not afford to seek these or other treatments elsewhere, and therefore she has neglected an explanation of the foreseeable consequences of declining (Standard 8.02a[3]). Dr. B.'s perspective, however, is that the population might fear that declining participation would entail missing out on a treatment that would help them and that they would not have another chance to receive such treatment. She knows that many of the patients do not have a sense of choice and independent decision making and that they feared bucking the system. Last, in regard to informing the potential participants of factors such as adverse effects or potential risks (Standard 8.02a[4]), the treatment involved in this study would require participants to make behavioral changes, including nutritional, exercise, and relational changes. These treatments would include practices that could affect the participants' relationships with others, such as making choices for one's support system; education in empowerment; and decision-making, communication, and parenting skills. Dr. B. realizes that if the participants implement some of these behavioral changes their family, support network, and friendship relationships could be affected. Dr. B. thinks that Dr. M. probably sees these changes as positive and does not consider the relational shifts that could have negative consequences for the participants. Dr. B. also thinks that Dr. M. has overlooked the foundational perspective that General Principle D: Justice and General Principle E: Respect for People's Rights and Welfare give to this situation, but she thinks it most important to encourage Dr. B. to incorporate these principles in her general thinking about her ongoing research.

Decision Options. Dr. B. decides to meet with Dr. M. and explain the aspects of informed consent and the overall perspective on research decisions that the APA Ethics Code general principles bring. Dr. B. recognizes that the omission of these factors in informed consent is just one example of how important perspective-taking is in decisions that affect others with whom psychologists work. She is reminded of the importance of cultural competence and psychologists' understanding of the populations with which they work. Dr. B. anticipates that Dr. M. will either be defensive, or feel bad, or both. This could well be a difficult conversation; however, Dr. B. is committed to an ethical resolution of the situation because she feels strongly about the importance of these aspects of research, and she sees Dr. M. as a strong researcher who had much to contribute.

Standard 8.03, Informed Consent for Recording Voices and Images in Research

Psychologists obtain informed consent from research participants prior to recording their voices or images for data collection unless (1) the research consists solely of naturalistic observations in public places, and it is not anticipated that the recording will be used in a manner that could cause personal identification or harm, or (2) the research design includes deception, and consent for the use of the recording is obtained during debriefing. (See also Standard 8.07, Deception in Research.)

Electronic transmission of information has become complex and commonplace. Psychologists should be mindful of the fact that the audio- or videotaping of individuals who can be recognized must be conducted only with the permission of the individuals. Just as masked records may not need consent for use, audio- or video-taping that does not identify individuals is also considered permissible. The guiding concept for psychologists in this situation is the importance of Principle E: Respect for People's Rights and Dignity and, of special note, the privacy and confidentiality of the individuals with whom psychologists work. There are some harms that may arise from disclosure of personal identities; however, in some circumstances—in particular, in the research of individuals who belong to a classification or subgroup—the context of the research may be used to advance political, social, or economic goals or for use by third parties. When these uses or interests are known, the researchers must inform the participants.

Standard 8.03, Case 1

Videotaping introduces a variable into informed consent in that the images of the participants are recorded and often render the participants identifiable. In the following sections, we present two cases as illustrations of Standard 8.03. In the first case, informed consent was obtained, but essential factors of the use and purpose were not included. In the second case, the researcher erroneously thought that the data collection was applicable to Standard 8.05, Dispensing With Informed Consent for Research.

Case Illustration. Dr. C. is a research psychologist who has studied human behavior in crisis and disaster settings for several years. Dr. C. has found many challenges in conducting research in this area but has decided that there also are many opportunities because disaster and emergency activities are becoming an ever-more-recognized field for investigation, and he would like to be on the ground floor. Dr. C. lives in a community located about 1 hour inland from a coastline that has frequently been battered by severe weather systems. One year earlier, a very strong hurricane had come through on that very coastline and caused much destruction. It was the worst weather event in the country in several years. Dr. C. realizes the opportunity to further his research by collecting data at the site, and so, on learning of the disaster, he immediately travels to the site and sets up a research team in the heart of the confusion and destruction. Dr. C. had filed appropriate documentation with his university, which he always has handy in case of immediate need for action. Dr. C. begins his data collection the day after the hurricane had hit. His purpose is to interview individuals who had experienced the destruction of the hurricane to determine their reactions, means of coping, processing of the event, and other emotional and decision-making factors. Dr. C. obtains consent from the participants by asking them to sign a form giving him permission to use their interviews in his research reporting and presentation of findings at a later date. Dr. C. then proceeds to interview many individuals on the scene; he videotapes the interaction and their responses.

Six months later, Dr. C. and his team complete their analysis of the interview data. As the research project evolved, Dr. C. had decided to include a hypothesis about those participants who were seeking help from aid workers and those who were present during the immediate service delivery process but who did not actively seek aid. They received aid and assistance only when Red Cross or other workers approached them. Dr. C. hypothesizes that the individuals who sought assistance had other positive attributes, such as resilience and effective coping and problem-solving characteristics. He classifies those who received but did not seek aid as passive and having poor problem-solving skills and coping skills. When Dr. C. submits his study for publication, the participants remain anonymous. He also, however, begins giving presentations on his findings and using the videotaped interviews in his discussions. The individuals who were interviewed by Dr. C. and his team are clearly identifiable, but Dr. C. thinks this was not a professional or ethical problem because the participants had signed consent forms for the interviews.

Ethical Dilemma. Dr. C. does, in fact, have signed consent forms for the interviews to be used, including the videotaped version of the questions. Dr. C. is aware of Standard 8.03. He believes that he has met the spirit and letter of Standard 8.03 through his informed consent because the research consisted solely of naturalistic observations in public places and that because personal identification was possible, he had attained the approving signatures of the participants. There was no deception involved in his study, and therefore he believes that he did not need to attain additional consent during the debriefing. Dr. C. has failed to realize that even though he had acquired participants' consent for use of the images and recorded voices during the interviews, he had not informed the participants that one of his hypothesis for investigation was a categorization of the participants as passive or active and that positive or negative characteristics would be attributed to the participants in accordance with their behavior during the time of the interviews. He had accounted for the factor of personal identification but not for the possibility that an assignment of negative attributes could be harmful to the participants. *Harm* as expressed in Standard 8.03 means not only physical harm or harm to safety but also psychological or emotional harm.

Decision-Making Factors. During one of his first workshops in using the recorded voices and images in this manner, a workshop participant approaches Dr. C. and suggests that his use of the identifiable individuals during a time of great distress for them, coupled with the negative categorization, constitutes an ethical breach. Dr. C. is taken aback by this observation. His first tendency is to deny the observation and defend his carefulness in acquiring the consent signatures. As Dr. C. continues to think about the opinion, he realizes that there are many factors to consider. Dr. C. had invested much of his grant funding in this project. He had taken about 1 month to be at the site and to gather these data. As a result, he has a host of peer reviewed articles, manuscripts in process, and a book underway primarily based on the variations of research questions that emanated from these video- and audiotaped interviews. Furthermore, his department and the research institute at his college are banking on this line of investigation for continued grant acquisition and to significantly increase the stature of the college at the university for the purpose of funding allocations and rankings of the top research departments in the country.

On the other hand, Dr. C. begins to realize that in his enthusiasm for the development of the research questions he had not thought from the frame of reference of the participants regarding his labeling and characterization of the individuals. Dr. C. does not want to throw away 2 years of work on this research project and yet fears that he might, in fact, be in violation of the Standard 8.03 if he continues. Dr. C. is particularly distressed to realize that the written transcripts of the interviews do not convey the important factors in the study in the way that the videotapes capture the essence of the hypotheses and findings.

Decision Options. Dr. C. has several choices regarding how he can decide the course of the research project. He could, of course, discontinue use of the data for this component of his investigation, but that would be a significant and pervasive loss. Dr. C. thinks about using only the audio portion of the interviews but realizes the possibly, albeit remote, that the voices could be recognizable. If he disguises the voices, then the effect of the interview is significantly diminished. Dr. C. has developed written documentation of the interviews in a very thorough and qualitatively rigorous method. The fact remains, however, that without audio and video together the classification of participants is not effective, because the movements of the participants during the entire period of observation are instrumental in the interpretation of their level of assistance seeking. Dr. C. realizes the complexity of ethical application of informed consent, in this case, in particular with video imaging as integral data elements. He begins reformulating the way he thinks about informed consent. Dr. C. has been conscientious about obtaining individual informed consent for research and for the use of videotaped images. Dr. C., however, had not thought about the identification of the participants linked to the findings as being potentially harmful.

Standard 8.03, Case 2

Case Illustration. Dr. V. is a social psychologist who studies parent–child interactions along several dimensions, including gender. More recently, she has conducted qualitative studies that may include ethnographic design, various interview methods, and naturalistic observation. Dr. V. is interested in the following research question: In the process of parent–child play interactions, do fathers and mothers interact with sons differently than they do with daughters in regard to the type of play activity, activity rigor (e.g., playing ball vs. board games), differential attention when both son and daughter are present (e.g., throwing the ball to boys more often that girls), encouragement of gender role play (e.g., girls playing with dolls and boys playing with toy vehicles), and other observational variables? Dr. V. decides to do a naturalistic observation in a local park that is a popular place to take children because of the play equipment and layout of the park. Dr. V. positions herself in a location where she can see many parents and children interacting together. Dr. V. decides that videotaping the activity would be the most accurate way to both record and code the interactions later. She is well aware of the ethical expectations for recording voices and images (Standard 8.03) but is confident that her observations meet the criteria of naturalistic observations defined in Standard 8.05. As a result, she does not seek informed consent from the observed participants. Their interactions are public behaviors, and therefore she thinks confidentiality is not a factor to be considered.

When Dr. V. completes her video file for this project, she begins coding the behaviors and interactions between parents and children. She does, in fact, find distinct differences on many factors, in particular, type of activity and gender role activity. Dr. V. writes an article based on these data, which is accepted for publication in a prestigious social psychology journal. Dr. V. decides that the article has been so successful that she will include discussions of this study in her social psychology course and in presentations that she often makes at professional association meetings. She thinks the presentation will be more effective if she includes some of the videotaped scenes. When Dr. V. shows the videotapes, she talks about the differential treatment in play of fathers and mothers with their sons versus daughters. The implication is that both fathers and mothers show differential attention to daughters and sons. Dr. V. does not think it important that in about half of the frames the parents and children are identifiable. At the end of one of her presentations, a colleague expresses concern to Dr. V. regarding the implication of distress to the parents if they knew the videotapes are being shown.

Ethical Dilemma. Dr. V.'s research question and methodology began in a reasonable and ethical way of thinking through the question and determining the most effective way to gather data that would answer the question. Dr. V. was also initially in good standing in thinking that her observations would not need informed consent by the observed participants because she was engaged in naturalistic observations. When Dr. V. decides to match the video images with research findings that made interpretations of quality or type of parent–child interaction, however, she began to drift into a status in which observers could feel judged or criticized and that value-laden results and conclusions could be perceived to cause distress or harm (Standard 8.05). When distress or harm becomes a possibility, then the research activity in which psychologists are engaged would no longer be categorized as exempt from informed consent. Standard 8.02 reminds psychologists to obtain informed consent for research and, in application to this case, to inform participants about both the purpose of the research and reasonably foreseeable factors that may be expected to influence their willingness to participate. Dr. V's decision to use the videotape in the described manner shifts her research study from being applicable to Standard 8.05 to Standard 8.03.

Decision-Making Factors. Dr. V. does not initially think that she is engaging in ethically questionable activity because she had written the highly touted article with no feedback from her peers on her methodology. She has done many naturalistic observations while investigating parent–child research questions for several years now without concern from peers or others, and she has shown videotapes of observed participants many times without concern. Dr. V. does, however, want to think through the comments made by her colleague a person whom she respects and whose judgment she trusts. Dr. V. begins to think about how this presentation and treatment of the data might be different from her other many presentations. Dr. V. thinks about the fact that her article, even though it used the same data, gave anonymity to the participants because she simply coded the behaviors and because no identifying information was included. Without commentary, the videotaped observations still met the criterion of naturalistic observation without distress or harm because the scenes observable and could have been viewed by any other person who was in the park that day, and the participants would have no expectation of privacy.

Dr. V. has spent recent years studying gender-based parent–child play and other variables that distinguish treatment of male and female children by male and female parents. She thinks of these exhibited patterns by parents as factual, not her opinion. She also thinks of these patterns as reflecting a sociological context, cultural and ethnic origins, the influence of age of the children, family customs, and other variables that shape behavioral choices. She does not think of her results and the description of her findings as being value laden.

As Dr. V. thinks about the way in which she has described and coded the behaviors recounted in the presentation and the categorization of the findings from an observer's point of view or from one of the parent's perspective, she realizes that she can understand how a parent could think that he or she was negatively evaluated regarding treatment of his or her children.

Decision Options. Dr. V. considers the fact that she can omit the videotape from her presentation of the study. This option, however, might make the presentation less interesting. She thinks she can blur the features of the individuals in the videotape and remove any identifiable objects so that she can continue to use the video. Dr. V. is in a quandary, however, regarding the fact that she has already shown the tape in which individuals are identifiable. She does not know the identity of the observed participants and therefore cannot contact them. She considers that if she did know their identities, she would contact them, explain what had happened, and inform them of her corrective actions.

Very important to Dr. V. is the lesson that she has developed a certain research perspective on her work that had affected her judgment in how third parties and the public might view research results and interpret findings, in particular when participants are identifiable.

Standard 8.04, Client/Patient, Student, and Subordinate Research Participants

When research participants are affiliated with the program, research team, faculty, researchers, or in any way have a continuing relationship with the research entity, then specific criteria must be upheld to avoid negative consequences, or even the perception of negative consequences, that could affect the decision of those participants to begin and continue in the research. Standard 8.04 identifies means by which participants can be given choices in an equitable and protected manner.

Standard 8.04(a)
When psychologists conduct research with clients/patients, students, or subordinates as participants, psychologists take steps to protect the prospective participants from adverse consequences of declining or withdrawing from participation.

The Ethics Code is committed to the welfare and equitable treatment of the individuals with whom psychologists work. These individuals are often in positions of lesser influence in their respective roles within the psychological context and may be chosen from a closed hierarchical system, such as a graduate program, specific work environment, correctional system, or undergraduate participant pool. The individuals may be clients/patients, students, employees, or research participants. Sections 3 (Human Relations), 7(Education and Training), 10 (Therapy), and the standards addressed in this Section (Research and Publication) lend particular specificity to these classifications and to the importance of psychologists' conduct in these contexts. Clients/patients, students, and subordinates are particularly vulnerable because they will continue to be in professional interactions with the psychologist investigators after the research study has ended. Psychologists are mindful that participation by their students, employees, or clients/patients in research projects constitutes a dual relationship between the researchers–psychologists and the participants and that this circumstance requires particular sensitivity and awareness of ethical implications.

Psychologists accept the responsibility for ensuring that these individuals do not suffer negative consequences, and they think through implications of nonparticipation that may occur incidentally, such as missing out on extra course credit, not receiving the treatment variable, and not being oriented to the educative component offered to research participants. Psychologists will want to ensure that these individuals understand the difference between consequences of nonparticipation and adverse actions directed at them.

Standard 8.04(b)
When research participation is a course requirement or an opportunity for extra credit, the prospective participant is given the choice of equitable alternative activities.

Psychologists may reasonably offer involvement in research both for the knowledge advancement of students and to expand the research possibilities for students and researchers. If a selection of activities from which to choose is not offered, the perception of coercion or exploitation is possible.

In developing alternative activities for comparable credit, psychologists may consider the learning benefits to the student; the range or variety of experiences offered; involvement with other faculty or researchers; time, duration, frequency, and logistical factors; possible effect on the participants of involvement; and approximately the same burden of providing alternative educational experiences.

INFORMED-CONSENT REQUIREMENTS FOR EXCEPTIONAL CIRCUMSTANCES

Standard 8.05, Dispensing With Informed Consent for Research

Psychologists may dispense with informed consent only (1) where research would not reasonably be assumed to create distress or harm and involves (a) the study of normal educational practices, curricula, or classroom management methods conducted in educational settings; (b) only anonymous questionnaires, naturalistic observations, or archival research for which disclosure of responses would not place participants at risk of criminal or civil liability or damage their financial standing, employability, or reputation, and confidentiality is protected; or (c) the study of factors related to job or organization effectiveness conducted in organizational settings for which there is no risk to participants' employability, and confidentiality is protected or (2) where otherwise permitted by law or federal or institutional regulations.

The intent of informed consent is to protect individuals from harm, exploitation, distress and adverse consequences of psychological activities that can occur when they are not fully apprised of the experience they will have as a research participant. When data collection does not jeopardize these protections, the Ethics Code allows psychologists to use their professional judgment in determining the appropriate consent status of their proposed research. The concept of *minimal risk* is helpful to psychologists in deciding the likely consent status of a research study. Minimal risk is considered a level not greater than risk ordinarily experienced in daily living or that which is experienced in standard testing.

There are three identified contexts for data collection in which dispensing of consent is often acceptable. Psychologists will also note that confidentiality is maintained and secured in all cases when consent is not sought.

1. *The study of normal educational practices, curricula, or classroom management methods conducted in educational settings.* Psychologists who conduct research within learning environments are aware that information is typically collected for the purpose of

record keeping, comparative progress data across students and for individual students, organizational reporting, and measures of quality and effectiveness of educational experiences. The dispensing-of-consent exception may be applied to use of information that is routinely gathered by the school or institutional entity. Psychologists who are deciding whether consent is needed for their research interests may ask themselves the following three questions: (a) Does the method or type of information collected need to be altered for the research? (b) Does additional information need to be acquired specifically for the research? (c) Does information need to be selectively manipulated or altered to serve the research purpose? If the answer to these and similar questions is yes, then the researcher will want to re-evaluate the necessity of consent.

2. *Only anonymous questionnaires, naturalistic, observations, or archival research for which disclosure of responses would not place participants at risk of criminal or civil liability or damage their financial standing, employability, or reputation, and confidentiality is protected.* Anonymity requires that individuals' identities cannot be known or traced even by the researchers. Naturalistic observations are equivalent to public behavior in which individuals might, or should, know that they could be observed. Archival data include information for which consent has already been given at an earlier time or in which the data have been formatted to mask the participants' identities. All three of these conditions are characterized by the criterion that individual identities are not known or recorded for observable purposes.

   This standard is intended to protect participants not only from consequences of the research conditions but also from incidental exposure that could have repercussions simply from identification, such as criminal or civil liability or effects on one's financial standing, employability, or reputation. Participants' confidentiality must still be protected when any possibility of identification exists.

3. *The study of factors related to job or organization effectiveness conducted in organizational settings for which there is no risk to participants' employability, and confidentiality is protected.* Institutions and organizations typically collect information regarding the operations of the entity for many reasons, including general productivity, effectiveness, quality of operations, and other facts that can improve the wellbeing of the organization. Psychologists who consider dispensing with consent under this standard might ask themselves

the following questions: Is the information descriptive of the organization's characteristics or those of the individuals from whom the information is collected? Will this information enable the researchers to answer questions about the functioning of the organization or about individuals in the organization? Will the results of the study be informative about the organization or about the individuals who work in the organization? If the answer to these and similar questions is that the information rendered is disclosing of the participants rather than descriptive of the organization then the researchers will want to reconsider the dispensation of consent.

Permission by law or regulation is a standard that is applied in several contexts within the Ethics Code. This statement allows psychologists to work within the framework of the state or federal system in which the Ethics Code is being applied.

Standard 8.05, Case 1

Case Illustration. Dr. N. is a licensed psychologist who practices in a moderate-sized community on the outskirts of the city where she is a member of a research group that consults with organizational and psychoeducational institutions in pursuing grants and in funding needs of the respective groups. She has always enjoyed working with school-age children and adolescents and so has found a happy medium in working with the research group but also doing her own private consultation with the school system in the community. Dr. N. has done quite a bit of professional work for the school system, including testing, evaluation, professional development for teachers, surveys of parents, and conducting workshops. She is well known and respected for her competence and ability in working within the system. Students and teachers alike are used to Dr. N. being in their classrooms and meetings and conducting administrative activities. All of Dr. N.'s activities are conducted within the school's authority to gather data, and so she has never had to pursue informed consent from parents or to explain the purpose of her operations to teachers, except informally should they individually have questions.

Dr. N. and her research team have received a grant to investigate the occurrence of mood disorders, in particular, anxiety and depression among school-age children. Dr. N. has conducted many interviews with children in the community school system and with teachers on their attitudes, perceptions, and experiences regarding bullying, relationships, communication, teamwork, and other subjects that focus on personal factors. She has also conducted several studies in which she has gathered data on personal factors, all within the realm of normal educational practices.

Dr. N. and her team interview children and teachers in several of the schools in conducting the investigation for the grant. Dr. N. uses personality instruments for children and adolescents that are intended to measure personality disturbances. After Dr. N. completes the data collection and her initial findings are made known, word gets out that more children in certain schools are depressed and anxious than those in other schools. Parents, teachers, and administrators alike are angry to learn of this information coming out. Administrators of schools in which the children are reputed to be more depressed and anxious are crying foul. The teachers feel manipulated and are under assault from parents who want to know why their children are depressed and anxious in school. Parents take issue with the fact that instruments that could reveal serious problems were administered without their permission.

Ethical Dilemma. Dr. N. is completely taken aback initially, because to her conducting this study does not seem any different from many other activities and services in which she has engaged in the schools. She knows most of these parents and teachers and has had many prior conversations with them about testing outcomes, surveys, interviews, and other professional services offered within the school. The data in her study were completely anonymous, and one could not determine which students were in which groups and which schools measured high or low on indexes of depression and anxiety, and she had not imagined that the information would cause distress or harm.

Dr. N. begins to realize that the reactions she is receiving all center ultimately on informed consent. She has always thought of her professional conduct as being well within ethical bounds, and she wants to be an ethically practicing psychologist. She consults with colleagues about her situation and begins to realize that even though she thought she did not need additional informed consent from her standard procedures, she may well have violated Standard 8.05. Dr. N. reviews Standard 8.05 and thinks that her research meets the following two requirements: (a) it would not reasonably be assumed to create distress or harm and (b) involves the study of normal educational practices, curricula, or classroom management methods conducted in educational settings. Dr. N. also becomes aware that she had compromised her adherence to General Principle A: Beneficence and Nonmaleficence, particularly in the passage that directs psychologists to do no harm and to safeguard the welfare and rights of the individuals with whom they interact. Furthermore, Dr. N. is reminded of General Principle B: Fidelity and Responsibility, which states that psychologists should establish relationships of trust with the people with whom they work.

In fact, Dr. N. has overlooked the fact that personality testing is typically not a standard psychoeducational evaluation given as part of an educational process. Furthermore, she had not pursued publication or public distribution of the information in her other activities within the schools. She thought that because the children and adolescents were anonymous no distress or harm could come to them individually. However, determining mood disorders in children attending specific schools did identify at least the possible groups and children who were represented in the study.

Decision-Making Factors. Dr. N. takes small solace in the fact that she knows she had not intentionally or knowingly acted unethically. She realizes that the people with whom she works seem to have lost confidence and trust in her. They feel manipulated by her use and development of school information to which she had easy access because of her long-standing presence in the school system. Some parents feel betrayed that she had not talked with them directly about the purpose of her study. The children who understand what had happened are worried that Dr. N. has found something wrong with them. The research team is counting on this study and its outcomes because these are important findings that will more than fulfill the grant sponsors' expectations. Dr. N. begins to reflect on what she has done in an attempt to sort everything out. In retrospect, she realizes that she did violate Standard 8.05 by inappropriately dispensing with informed consent in her study. Heretofore, Dr. N. had not understood or realized several aspects of Standard 8.05 that are applicable in her circumstance: She had not thought that distress or harm would be caused, all individual participants were anonymous, and she had thought of the testing as constituting "normal educational practices."

Dr. N. reflects on an aspect of Standard 8.05 that she now thinks about differently than before she conducted her study: that is that even though participants may be treated anonymously in a research project, when the findings are known the participants, and sometimes others, know that the information in the findings is, in fact, descriptive of them. When the location, size of the group, distinguishing characteristics, and other specific information can associate individuals with their roles as participants, then harm can be caused even though the individuals are not identified.

Decision Options. Dr. N. decides that her first obligation is to meet with each of the groups that have been affected by her actions. She determines that she will hear the reactions of the groups and respond as best she can to their feedback, complaints, and questions. She decides that she cannot go forward with the use of the data and will retract the data from any current analysis by the research team, and she will communicate this commitment to the individuals and groups with whom she meets. She also will need to explain her decision to her research team. Dr. N. will continue work with the community in a deliberate way to redress the harm that has been done and to regain the trust of those with whom she worked. Dr. N. was impacted by her experience of losing sight of ethical decision making when conducting research in her own practice and consulting settings.

Standard 8.06, Offering Inducements for Research Participation

The importance of making a reasoned judgment regarding inducements to participate in research is that the nature or amount of inducement could become the factor participants weigh more heavily than their genuine willingness to participate without the inducement. An inducement that is, in fact, the primary reason for participation becomes either coercive or taps a need of the participant that cannot reasonably be gained otherwise (e.g., money, consultation, merchandise, treatment). The effect of these conditions is that the participants do in fact feel forced because they have limited access to the inducement otherwise, or participants may misrepresent themselves in order to be included.

Standard 8.06(a)
Psychologists make reasonable efforts to avoid offering excessive or inappropriate financial or other inducements for research participation when such inducements are likely to coerce participation.

The threats in meeting this standard are excessiveness of an inducement or inappropriateness of an inducement. An acceptable reason for inducements is that the individuals would not otherwise be able to participate because of cost, time lost, transportation, or other factors that are realistic impediments to participation. In these cases, the inducement serves as a counterbalance to the impediments. Excessiveness may take the form of an amount of money that would be an inducement in and of itself or merchandise that has value beyond what the person would receive through fair monetary reimbursement. Researchers have difficult decisions to make in matching a compensatory amount of money across individuals of different means. Ten dollars may be significant for one person yet insignificant for another. Psychologists may think about the inducement as compensation for impediments or unintended costs to the participants in time, money, or activities forgone.

Standard 8.06(b)
When offering professional services as an inducement for research participation, psychologists clarify the nature of the services, as well as the risks, obligations, and limitations. (See also Standard 6.05, Barter With Clients/ Patients.)

A useful frame of reference for psychologists who are considering services offered is one in which they are engaged in private practice, public sector practice, or in a training facility. Informed consent in the full sense of disclosure about all relevant information regarding the services is expected. Those factors that would typically be described and explained in offering services, such as duration and frequency of services, costs, time commitment, reasonable expectations of both participants and researchers, risks, and the nature of the service, also apply in this research context. Psychologists may refer to Standard 3.10, Informed Consent, and Standard 10.01, Informed Consent to Therapy, in structuring and defining the services to be offered.

Standard 8.07, Deception in Research

Standards 8.07(a) and 8.07(b) offer psychologists parameters in assisting decisions regarding the use of deception. Several specific factors should be considered in qualifying the deception as necessary to the integrity of the study. Once a psychologist has determined that deception is appropriate, Standard 8.07(c) gives direction on how to proceed with disclosure of deception to the participants.

Some research designs incorporate omission rather than deception. These include occurrences of restraint from explaining and defining characteristics of treatment groups or reasons that participants are assigned to control versus treatment groups. Omissions are typically made to prevent bias, fulfillment of expected behavior, anticipation of outcome effect, or in attempts to accommodate the hypotheses. Omissions are not made in attempts to control or contrive resulting participant behavior but rather to avoid contrived participation.

Standard 8.07(a)

Psychologists do not conduct a study involving deception unless they have determined that the use of deceptive techniques is justified by the study's significant prospective scientific, educational, or applied value and that effective nondeceptive alternative procedures are not feasible.

Psychologists are obligated to determine that the value of the anticipated study outweighs the risk of harm to or distress of the participants. This criterion calls on psychologists to make very measured decisions about the import of the research and the possible value that could result from the findings. Professional judgment is used to ensure that the value being assigned to the potential outcome of the study is not frivolous or inconsequential. Psychologists may want to consult colleagues in making this decision.

Psychologists are committed to determining that the integrity of the study would be compromised if deception were not used. Deception is not meant to be a viable alternative in equal consideration with other methodologies but rather a means by which significant studies and meritorious hypotheses may be pursued that otherwise would go uninvestigated.

Standard 8.07(b)

Psychologists do not deceive prospective participants about research that is reasonably expected to cause physical pain or severe emotional distress.

The allowance for deception described in Standard 8.07(a) rests on the value and justification of the proposed study. That qualification does not apply when physical pain or emotional distress are reasonably expected outcomes; that is, when researchers anticipate that these conditions may affect the participants, deception is not allowed. Psychologists have an obligation to safeguard the welfare of participants and therefore do not have the option of deception when the welfare of participants may be in question.

Standard 8.07(c)

Psychologists explain any deception that is an integral feature of the design and conduct of an experiment to participants as early as is feasible, preferably at the conclusion of their participation, but no later than at the conclusion of the data collection, and permit participants to withdraw their data. (See also Standard 8.08, Debriefing.)

Psychologists are mindful that full explanations must be offered to participants regarding the deceptive conditions as soon as is feasible. Often, a study may have an extended data collection phase, or the researchers may have reason to think that participants may convey aspects of the deception to other participants. In these circumstances, researchers may delay the explanations until the data collection is complete. Psychologists carefully attend to the reactions of the participants and any effects of the deception on participants, including anticipated or unanticipated effects. The researchers themselves decide the proper response to concerns (e.g., counseling, extended debriefings, consultation, referral). Psychologists are particularly aware of the vulnerabilities of certain populations in reaction to deception, including children and individuals with cognitive, physical, or other functional limitations, and should make attempts to explain the deception in terms understandable to the participants.

Standard 8.08, Debriefing

Psychologists' responsibility for research participants reaches beyond the selection, treatment or intervention, and participation of individuals to responsibility for the effects of the research after participation has concluded. Psychologists must include in the informed consent any anticipated consequences of participation. In addition, psychologists respect and attend to information requests, conditions of information dissemination, possible effects on participants, and other pertinent needs of participants.

Standard 8.08(a)

Psychologists provide a prompt opportunity for participants to obtain appropriate information about the nature, results, and conclusions of the research, and they take reasonable steps to correct any misconceptions that participants may have of which the psychologists are aware.

Providing information to participants that describes the study in which the participants took part is an opportunity for individuals who have interest in the nature of the study, the implications, and the potential use of the results to be apprised of the research. The vehicle by which participants may be informed may vary in accordance with the population, location, length of time after which the study information becomes available, and communication means of the researchers. Information from an institutional, organizational, hospital, or any singular facility may be made available through postings, inter-facility mail, group meetings, or individual mailings. It is typical at the end of research participation for the investigators to ask individuals to indicate their interest in being informed of the results. Psychologists are not expected to go to extensive lengths or costs to accommodate the dissemination but instead to use reasonable communication means.

Information provided for debriefing is quite different in purpose and function from information provided following deception. Psychologists have an obligation to inform participants of variables subject to deception that may have affected them that were not disclosed or included in informed consent. Debriefing has an information-only purpose; it is a demonstration of accommodation and courtesy to the participants.

When debriefing participants, psychologists may be aware of common misconceptions or false impressions that were existent during the data collection or afterward. They should make an effort to dispel any known misconceptions so that participants have an accurate explanation of the research nature and purpose. Psychologists, however, are not expected to be alert for uncommon or little-known perceptions regarding the research.

Standard 8.08(b)

If scientific or humane values justify delaying or withholding this information, psychologists take reasonable measures to reduce the risk of harm.

In particular when they are working with special populations or groups with specific limitations, psychologists use professional judgment in the timing, format, or extent of the debriefing offered. When individuals may not understand the information or misconstrue in an anticipated manner, psychologists may alter or withhold the debriefing. If, however, psychologists have reason to think that participants may be at risk of harm based on misperception or misunderstanding of the study, they should clarify and correct those misperceptions. In working with children or individuals with cognitive limitations, psychologists may consider providing debriefing to parents, custodians, or others who are caring for the individuals.

Standard 8.08(c)
When psychologists become aware that research procedures have harmed a participant, they take reasonable steps to minimize the harm.

Even though researchers screen candidates for participation, it is possible that participants may be harmed by various personal or psychological circumstances that predate the research experience. Participants may experience a variety of reactions, including posttraumatic stress disorder, a phobic reaction, depression, or other mood alterations. Psychologists remain alert to the need to respond effectively with consultation, referral, or other means of minimizing the harm to the participants.

Psychologists are mindful that participants may be inadvertently harmed by the experience of the research treatment or by the information received in explanation of deception or in debriefing. Professional judgment is important in discerning and implementing the most useful course of action to minimize the effect.

Standard 8.09, Humane Care and Use of Animals in Research

Psychologists who conduct research with animals accept a designated responsibility for all aspects of their care. Standards 8.09(a) through 8.09(c) define psychologists' role in the administrative and treatment components of working with animals, including legal, regulatory, and supervisory responsibilities. Standards 8.09(d) through 8.09(g) describe standard of care regarding pain and discomfort that the animals may experience.

Standard 8.09(a)
Psychologists acquire, care for, use, and dispose of animals in compliance with current federal, state, and local laws and regulations, and with professional standards.

Psychologists who involve animals in their research are responsible for the comprehensive oversight, monitoring, and supervision of the animals' care. The guidance for the standard of care, treatment, and disposition of animals is provided through several sources. Psychologists should be in compliance with the regulations of the entities to which they are directly responsible. These typically include the funding agency, the university or institute through which the research is being conducted, the APA Ethics Code, and any current APA guidelines developed specifically for the care and use of animals. Several federal agencies, including the National Institutes of Health and the Department of Health and Human Services, disseminate regulations, policies, and procedures regarding research with animals. Psychologists should be informed of the standard of care established by these entities and incorporate these standards in their research.

Standard 8.09(b)

Psychologists trained in research methods and experienced in the care of laboratory animals supervise all procedures involving animals and are responsible for ensuring appropriate consideration of their comfort, health, and humane treatment.

This standard offers two specific criteria in identifying competence for psychologists who work with research animals. First, they must have specific research training and education regarding the involvement of animals and acquire experience in working with the particular species of animals involved in their research. Psychologists would expect to have different knowledge sets depending on the species with which they are working and will want to develop competence both in research procedures and in familiarity with the specific species.

Second, psychologists are responsible for the supervision of other individuals involved with the animal research. Psychologists accept responsibility for supervision of all individuals, including research assistants and other people working on the actual research project, including those who are responsible for the care and maintenance of the animals. The conditions (e.g., housing, temperature, environmental variables) in which the animals live apart from their research involvement are considered an integral part of the care and maintenance of the animals.

Standard 8.09(c)

Psychologists ensure that all individuals under their supervision who are using animals have received instruction in research methods, and in the care, maintenance, and handling of the species being used, to the extent appropriate to their role. (See also Standard 2.05, Delegation of Work to Others.)

Psychologists use their professional judgment in evaluating the training and supervisory needs of their assistants and balance these factors in accordance with the level of expertise needed in the care of animals. Those assisting in the research should have appropriate training in all aspects of animal contact in which they are involved, including research procedures and methods. The level of training required of assistants may be a factor for psychologists in deciding the level of supervision needed.

Standard 8.09(d)
Psychologists make reasonable efforts to minimize the discomfort, infection, illness, and pain of animal subjects.

Several aspects of animal care are applicable in this standard. The housing, care, and maintenance of animals include: (a) conditions in which they live; (b) quality of food and consistency of food and water, temperature control, and other environmental variables; (c) sanitary and clean conditions; (d) adequate physical care, such as medical needs; and (e) minimal or no physical pain to the extent possible.

Standard 8.09(e)
Psychologists use a procedure subjecting animals to pain, stress, or privation only when an alternative procedure is unavailable and the goal is justified by its prospective scientific, educational, or applied value.

Two conditions must be met in subjecting animals to adverse conditions: (a) The probable benefit to scientific advancement, benefit to humans, or benefit to other animals must supersede the aversive treatment administered to animals; and (b) no adverse interventions may be used if there are alternative methods available that would cause less pain or distress to the animals. This standard is intended to underscore the importance of respect and care for animals, in particular in physical and psychological conditions of pain and distress.

Standard 8.09(f)
Psychologists perform surgical procedures under appropriate anesthesia and follow techniques to avoid infection and minimize pain during and after surgery.

Psychologists must accept responsibility for the preparation of animals for surgery, the surgical procedure, and the postoperative care. Psychologists ensure that the individuals performing surgery and surgical care are trained and qualified. Proper medical procedures and medications should be administered to maximize the comfort of animals, including anesthesia, other medications as appropriate, and sterile surgical conditions. Postsurgical care is expected and must be included in the ongoing care of animals.

Standard 8.09(g)
When it is appropriate that an animal's life be terminated, psychologists proceed rapidly, with an effort to minimize pain and in accordance with accepted procedures.

Psychologists use their professional judgment in determining the disposition of animals that are no longer involved in research. If animals are able to be given over to the care of others, or if they may be released, psychologists should decide their disposition on the basis of the reasonable possibilities for the animal's life. If the animal's life must be terminated, psychologists will want to be aware of relevant professional guidelines for conducting appropriate procedures.

ACCURATE REPORTING OF ORIGINAL WORKS

Standard 8.10, Reporting Research Results

The pursuit of psychological knowledge through scientific inquiry must be credible, trustworthy, and able to withstand scrutiny. If psychologists' investigative endeavors are not scientifically sound, professional psychology could not advance as a profession or science in practice, training, or research. As a result, the accuracy of the reporting of scientific data is critical to the welfare of the profession.

Standard 8.10(a)
Psychologists do not fabricate data. (See also Standard 5.01a, Avoidance of False or Deceptive Statements.)

Prohibition against false statements regarding research is cited in Standard 5.01, Avoidance of False or Deceptive Statements, which addresses public statements made by psychologists regarding their credentials and work. Standard 8.10(a) prohibits false or deceptive activity in the collection, analysis, and presentation of data as scientific findings. Fraudulent conduct in scientific endeavors violates two important values of psychologists: honesty and integrity, which are fundamental values of the profession. Principle C: Integrity pledges accuracy, honesty, and truthfulness in science, teaching, and practice. The advancement of scientific research and knowledge builds on existing findings, so researchers must be able to verify the accuracy of existing data and to be confident that research findings are in fact valid.

Standard 8.10(b)
If psychologists discover significant errors in their published data, they take reasonable steps to correct such errors in a correction, retraction, erratum, or other appropriate publication means.

Errors in the presentation of scientific results can occur either through mistakes in the analytic process of the data or mistakes in the printing and publication process. Psychologists will want to correct either or both of these errors in a timely way and in the manner most appropriate. Researchers should identify and explain the corrections to the individuals who are most likely to have the access and authority to correct the errors in the publication at the earliest reasonable time.

Standard 8.11, Plagiarism

Psychologists do not present portions of another's work or data as their own, even if the other work or data source is cited occasionally.

Plagiarism in scientific writings may take the form of presenting material expressed or written by another individual as one's own. Psychologists are aware that plagiarism in scientific writings may take several forms. The ethical violations applicable to plagiarism include both written and oral content, the paraphrasing of material in addition to quoted citations, and acknowledging others in a generic way but not crediting specific passages originated by another individual. Psychologists must acknowledge and credit ideas, concepts, models, and copyrighted material of other individuals. Often in the literature review and preparation for scientific writing, writers may be uncertain about the origin of material. A psychologist may ask him- or herself whether any other individual has expressed concepts or ideas on which the psychologist is drawing in advancing a hypothesis or concept. If the answer is yes, then the psychologist must credit the source by supplying a pertinent citation.

IDENTIFICATION OF AUTHORSHIP OF ORIGINAL WORKS

Standard 8.12, Publication Credit

Authorship of scientific findings is often a shared status in that research is increasingly collaborative. Furthermore, the training context for generation of scientific findings is often a mentoring or advisement relationship between faculty researchers and student research assistants or advisees engaged in the development of a dissertation. Standard 8.12 gives direction to psychologists in authorship decisions and provides a standard by which students, early-career faculty, and others who may have a vulnerable status in a collaborative may know their rights and by which psychologists may know their responsibilities.

Standard 8.12(a)

Psychologists take responsibility and credit, including authorship credit, only for work they have actually performed or to which they have substantially contributed. (See also Standard 8.12b, Publication Credit.)

The product of a publication can involve many people, complex writing processes, and multiple efforts that result in the final article. Psychologists attempt to discern the accurate and fair allocation of responsibility and credit for scientific products, including those that are multifaceted. Psychologists may consider the following five aspects of this complex process in making authorship decisions:

1. The many roles taken by psychologists in the scientific process, including investigator, adviser, supervisor, teacher, administrator, and trainer. All of these roles are applicable to research collaboration and are fairly considered so in allocating authorship credit.
2. Research projects are often structured across multiple sites with multiple investigators. The research teams confer as soon and often as necessary to ensure accurate and fair responsibility and acknowledgement.
3. Intellectual contributions made in the publication process, including development of the hypotheses, data collection, analysis, interpretation, or other significant contributions, are fairly considered.
4. Stages of production of the publication are original works of one of the participants and are acknowledged as such. Individuals who contributed to an aspect of the article will read and edit their own original works.
5. Accurate publication acknowledgement also applies to materials other than scientific writings. Newsletters, flyers, newspaper articles, and other writings intended for the public or audiences other than the scientific community fairly and accurately identify the authors of the content. Psychologists do not accept authorship for materials written by anonymous or unknown authors. If the author is not known, then psychologists acknowledge that the material was provided by other sources.

Standard 8.12(b)

Principal authorship and other publication credits accurately reflect the relative scientific or professional contributions of the individuals involved, regardless of their relative status. Mere possession of an institutional position, such as department chair, does not justify authorship credit. Minor contributions to the research or to the writing for publications are acknowledged appropriately, such as in footnotes or in an introductory statement.

This section helps psychologists identify factors to be considered in ranking the order of authors and in deciding between authorship and acknowledgment elsewhere in the manuscript.

The first author is the person who made a distinguishably greater intellectual contribution to the article than others. The additional ordering of the remaining authors is also determined by the criteria of relative intellectual contribution, which could be defined as amount of time and effort in actual writing, being the originator of the conceptual and organizational structure, interpreting the results from the data, or other significant contributions.

Also, involvement in the research project that does not qualify as intellectual contribution is acknowledged elsewhere in the manuscript than in the authorship. Examples of contributions that are not applicable to authorship include providing the laboratory setting or office space, financial support, allocation of research assistants to the project, computer programming, scheduling participants, or editing of the manuscript. Psychologists may consider these and other criteria before making decisions regarding the relative type and degree of acknowledgment for all who are involved with a research project.

If individuals commit to a defined amount and type of contribution and then do not fulfill their obligation, the originally decided authorship may change in accordance with the actual rather than planned amount and quality of contribution by authors. These qualifiers could take the form of lesser quality of writing than expected; failure to produce the material promised; and/or failure to participate in the agreed-on format, style, or content of the manuscript.

When psychologists of differing rank, status, and power differential collaborate on a publication, the senior psychologists are aware of the potential exploitation of co-authors who are dependent on the senior writers for other professional involvement in their careers, such as promotion and tenure voting, assignments within the department, and overall impact that senior faculty can make on junior faculty or students of lesser status.

Standard 8.12(c)

Except under exceptional circumstances, a student is listed as principal author on any multiple-authored article that is substantially based on the student's doctoral dissertation. Faculty advisors discuss publication credit with students as early as feasible and throughout the research and publication process as appropriate. (See also Standard 8.12b, Publication Credit.)

This standard protects the doctoral students who are primarily responsible for the intellectual contribution to their dissertations and is cited as a separate standard because of the difficulty students may have in obtaining equal participation in authorship discussions. Exceptions to the principal-authorship standard for student dissertations may apply; however, psychologists will want to ensure that these exceptions are notable, clearly demonstrated, and agreed on before principal authorship is changed on a student dissertation. There may be exceptions to the principal-authorship standard, for example, if the dissertation came out of a larger, ongoing or longitudinal project through which the student did not participate in a primary way, or if the data were retrieved from an archival source or existing database collected, maintained, and developed by others. Psychologists discuss and decide in advance of the research onset the authorship and the ranking of authorship with students and others involved with student collaboration. Psychologists ensure that periodic discussions and agreements are conducted when authorship or other significant aspects of the publication are modified. All other faculty and student collaborations other than dissertation meet the criteria of Standard 8.12(b) for authorship status and ranking of authors.

Standard 8.12(c), Case 1

Case Illustration. Dr. P. is one of many psychologists involved in a multi-site research project that is supported by a multimillion-dollar federal grant. Dr. P. is able to support financially several of her students on the grant through assistantships. One of the incentives for the students, in addition to assistant-ships and their general pursuit of research experience, is that this project had approved the use of some of the data for dissertation topics. The psychologists at the multiple sites had agreed that they would identify certain components of the data that could be used for student research, but they had not discussed authorship of any such endeavors. Many studies with subsequent publications would come out of the research project over the years based on the compre-hensiveness of the study. The psychologists had discussed, early on, the devel-opment of primary, collateral, and secondary studies in terms of importance and contribution to the primary research questions. Furthermore, the psychol-ogists had decided on the method of determining authorship among the psy-chologists on all publications.

Mr. B. is one of Dr. P.'s students and has an assistantship on the project. He is very excited about use of the archival data from the project because his research interests are very close to the research questions of the project, and the particular data in which he is interested are exactly what he needs to complete his dissertation data. Mr. B. proceeds to analyze the data and write the final draft of his dissertation. After his committee accepts the dissertation, he begins to write an article for publication based on his dissertation. When Dr. P. tells the team that her student hopes to publish his dissertation and that he will be listed as the first author, they take issue with this. They claim that they had all decided about shared authorship among themselves, and if her student publishes under his name as first author, they will have to count this as one of Dr. P.'s publica-tions from the grant. They consider all studies as collateral studies emanating from their data-collecting and funding authority. Students who use existing data that have been made available only because of the psychologists' grant acquisition and their extensive development of the research project have not earned first authorship, they maintain. When Dr. P. cites Standard 8.12(c) to them, they retort that their position comes within the standard's "exceptional circumstances" clause.

Ethical Dilemma. Dr. P. reconsiders Standard 8.12(c), because she has always thought of the student's first authorship on the dissertation publication as standard professional procedure. The exceptional circumstances are not, in Dr. P.'s opinion, meant to be applied in the manner in which her colleagues are thinking; that is, the source of funding, assistantship status, and data collection itself were not primary factors in authorship. Dr. P. also considers the fact that this standard states that psychologists take authorship credit only for work they have performed and to which they have substantially contributed. She also considers that the standard cites the importance of relative contributions in deciding authorship regardless of the authors' status and specifically states that holding a specific position does not merit authorship. Dr. P. realizes that Standard 8.12(c) also calls on faculty advisors to discuss publication credit as early as feasible and to continue to do so throughout the publication process. In this case, Dr. P. and Mr. B. had not failed to establish the authorship; in fact, she and he did discuss the authorship early on, and she concurred that he would be first author. Dr. P. finds herself at odds with her colleagues, not with Mr. B.

Decision-Making Factors. Dr. P. considers the position of her colleagues and the implication their response holds for her. She realizes that when authorship was discussed that student research was mentioned but that student authorship on any faculty/student collaborations was not specifically mentioned. Because most of the psychologists do not have student assistants but instead are paying individuals to be on the project at their data collection site, they viewed student authorship as giving Dr. P. more access to publication than they had. At this point, she could ask for their reconsideration, and she would consider doing so, but she also realizes that resentment toward her might ensue given their already-stated position. Dr. P. has to admit to herself that continuing to be a member of the project was important to her because she hopes to be promoted to associate professor and eventually to full professor, and her entire research focus is wrapped up in this longitudinal series of studies. Dr. P. wants to do the right thing by Mr. B. and herself, but she does not want to jeopardize her position on the team. She could reassert her request, but she realizes now that the research team does not intend for students ever to be first author on any study coming out of their project and that their consideration of allowing this to count for her publication is a concession they are giving her.

Dr. P. also feels an obligation to Mr. B. to follow through on her commitment, not only because she and he had made the agreement earlier but also because she thinks this is the ethically correct thing to do. She does not interpret "exceptional circumstances" as her colleagues do and, in fact, thinks that the other areas of Standard 8.12 underscore the importance of authorship being consistent with the actual contributions of individuals on the project. Even though Dr. P.'s professional affiliation with the research group might be in jeopardy, she is committed to conducting herself ethically and professionally in regard to Mr. B. and does not want him to have such a questionable experience at this point in his early professional development.

Decision Options. Dr. P. feels strongly about keeping her professional commitment to her student. She considers whether and how much of the conflict regarding his publication that she would reveal. She does not want Mr. B. to have a negative perception of collaborative research, yet there are lessons to be learned, and this could, in fact, benefit Mr. B. in his future collaborations. Dr. P. also realizes that authorship is one of the professional topics that can be hard to discuss, which she surmises is the reason that early and ongoing discussion is stated in the APA Ethics Code. The additional factor in her decision to support Mr. B. is the pervasive and unavoidable power differential between faculty and students. Authorship is a difficult subject for peers and even more so in faculty–student relationships.

Ironically, Dr. P. finds herself in a power differential among her colleagues because she is a junior person on the team, untenured, and this is her first grant. Dr. P. could consider making another request for Mr. B.'s publication not to count as her allocated publication, and she can decide that option on the basis of her relationship with her colleagues, their attitude toward publication, and the consequences as she perceives them. She may decide to accept Mr. B.'s publication as her allocated publication for that period and to learn from this experience of the importance of specificity and full discussion of options.

Standard 8.13, Duplicate Publication of Data

Psychologists do not publish, as original data, data that have been previously published. This does not preclude republishing data when they are accompanied by proper acknowledgment.

The issue addressed by this standard is sometimes referred to as *self-plagiarism*. Psychologists must use their professional judgment in discerning the proper delineation of research findings into singular versus multiple publications. The publication of the same data across more than one article gives the readers the impression of multiple new findings or, at least, multiple verifications of findings, which in these cases is misrepresentative. This practice also misrepresents scholarly contributions as evidenced within one's curriculum vitae and implies a greater amount of original research than may be the case. Furthermore, authors who include already-published material in additional publications risk copyright violation of the original material even if the author originally wrote the results or findings being cited. Psychologists can be alert to these potential violations by typically citing the specific original work and alerting the editors of the publication to which the manuscript is being submitted of the following three factors: (a) when research was previously presented in the proceedings of a meeting or as a report at a professional meeting; (b) whether the complexity of the research project results in the need for separate and multiple publications; and (c) whether the project is multiphase, longitudinal, or multisite.

Standard 8.14, Sharing Research Data for Verification

The availability of data from which research findings and interpreted results originate is valuable to the integrity of scientific investigation. A fundamental principle of scientific research is that the scientific community must have confidence in the validity and integrity of information on which knowledge is based. Standard 8.14(a) is applicable to researchers who have originated the data being requested and are the authors of any published works based on the data. Standard 8.14(b) is applicable to individuals who are requesting the use of the data from the originating researchers for the purpose of verification.

Standard 8.14(a)
After research results are published, psychologists do not withhold the data on which their conclusions are based from other competent professionals who seek to verify the substantive claims through reanalysis and who intend to use such data only for that purpose, provided that the confidentiality of the participants can be protected and unless legal rights concerning proprietary data preclude their release. This does not preclude psychologists from requiring that such individuals or groups be responsible for costs associated with the provision of such information.

Psychologists are committed to maintaining raw data from research publications in order for other researchers to be able to verify the analysis process, accuracy of the findings, and outcome, or to evaluate the integrity of the research. Researchers are obligated not to share their research findings for other general reasons, or with those individuals are not competent to properly use the data, but instead for the purpose of scientific rigor and accuracy. Depending on the form of the data being requested, the costs may be substantial. Researchers are not expected to bear the costs and, in fact, can expect the requesting researcher to pay the expenses of transferring the data.

There are two exceptions to this standard. If the confidentiality of the participants could be compromised or leave the control of the authorizing researcher, and/or if the manuscript is currently owned by a publishing house, university, institute, or other research entity, then the originating researcher is not obligated to share data. It is not the originating researcher's responsibility to seek permission for release from another party in order to accommodate the requestor.

Standard 8.14(b)

Psychologists who request data from other psychologists to verify the substantive claims through reanalysis may use shared data only for the declared purpose. Requesting psychologists obtain prior written agreement for all other uses of the data.

This standard prevents individuals from using another researcher's existing database to ask new questions; analyze data for related or indirect purposes; and to, in essence, use another researcher's data as a new data set for additional research. If the requesting researcher does wish to use the data for reasons other than verification, he or she must make this inquiry in advance of the data request and must obtain a written agreement from the originating researcher so that the originating researcher is fully informed of the nature of the intended use before releasing the data.

Standard 8.14 , Case 1

Case Illustration. Dr. A. has expertise in psychological aspects of physical conditions and a particular interest in children with asthma and the psychological and academic implications of these children's conditions. Dr. A. sees an article in a psychology publication about the vulnerability of children with chronic disease and observable conditions to bullying. He is most interested in the school and peer experiences of children and how they cope in the school environment. He writes to the author of the publication, Dr. M., and expresses his interest in the findings. He asks Dr. M. for the data on which the article is based so that he can take a first-hand look at the variables and reanalyze the data and follow through the process for himself. Dr. M. sends Dr. A. the data on the basis of which the article was published. As Dr. D. peruses the data, he sees that the demographic information actually includes coding for asthma. Here is a huge compendium of information on asthma that took considerable time and access to accumulate.

Dr. A. begins to think about the fact that Dr. M. is not at all interested in asthma and has never published on asthma as a variable. He had clearly listed several chronic and apparent conditions that could be noticed by other children and that therefore could be factors in the selection of these children as targets for bullying. Dr. M. had asked for endorsement of those conditions for the purpose of categorizing chronic conditions, not to pursue asthma as a variable. Dr. A. believes that if he uses these data for asthma research he will not be impinging on Dr. M.'s research domain. In fact, these data would advance his study of asthma considerably, because of the methodology, the sample size, and the demographics known about the participants. He feels certain that Dr. M. would have said yes had the question been asked, but at this point Dr. A. is concerned that this additional request will seem like a bait-and-switch tactic.

Ethical Dilemma. Standard 8.14 reminds psychologists that without prior written agreement they cannot use data obtained for verification for any purpose other than verification of the findings or claims made by the originating researcher. The Ethics Code explicitly calls for prior written agreement, not requests that may occur after the data are shared. Standard 8.14(a) requires researchers to share their data for verification purposes and therefore this part of that standard is a correlate to the requirement to share data and further determines that psychologists who receive data for such purposes must treat the data as originally stated and requested. Dr. A.'s logic will lead him into problematic behavior if he pursues this line of thinking. He is presupposing that Dr. M. would not pursue the same research questions or hypotheses as Dr. A., and he considers this probability a rationale for other use of the data. He further tells himself how helpful research with these data would be for children with asthma. Even if Dr. M. never uses the data to pursue these hypotheses, that fact begs the question. Dr. A. should also be reminded that the informed consent for treatment with minors would have specifically described how the data would be used. Further, Dr. M.'s application to his IRB would have also included intended use, access, and other specific aspects of the study that were already conducted. Dr. A. realizes that he can propose the additional use of the data, but he does not seem to realize that it is critical that he do so. Although this may have felt awkward, it would have been much better to describe the process by which he became interested in the additional use of the data and to ask whether Dr. M. will consider allowing Dr. A. to use the data.

Decision-Making Factors. Dr. A.'s thoughts about use of the data for purposes other than verification have inherent ethical problems. He should be aware that asthma is a disability classification under the Americans with Disabilities Act. Dr. A. is aware that Standard 2.01(b) requires that an understanding of factors associated, in this case, with disabilities is essential when conducting research with this population. Dr. A. would be conducting research within his area of competence, yet one could raise a question regarding his respect for the rights of the minor participants and their custodians. Psychologists must safeguard and protect the rights and welfare of persons who might have vulnerabilities based, in this case, on disabilities (General Principle E: Respect for People's Rights and Dignity). Dr. A.'s rationale does not diminish the clarity of the violation and does not provide a reasonable explanation for his potential actions. Dr. A. must decide whether to ask Dr. M. for permission to conduct his proposed study given that Dr. A. has not yet asked permission to use the data in the manner he wishes and given that this may well be noted by Dr. M.

In this case, however, Dr. M. may not be able to give Dr. A. permission given several factors implicit in this study. The informed consent involved treatment of minors, as well as the permission the parents gave, was for the specific purpose, conditions, consequences, benefits, and other factors required in Standard 8.02(a). The option of asking the parents for extended use of the data might yield permission from some or all of the parents; however, Dr. A. must consider the possibility of perceived undue influence on the participants, a sense of exploitation, and a possible violation of the limits of confidentiality. Even though the identities of the participants are not known to Dr. A., solicitation for further research purposes by different investigators was not stated in the original informed consent and may give the custodians the idea that their information is being shared beyond their agreed-on use.

Decision Options. Dr. A. realizes that if he proceeds as he would like, he will be in clear violation of Standard 8.14(b). Given the factors involved in the informed consent and the extent and type of informed consent that Dr. M. has acquired, there may not be the possibility of further use of the data. Dr. A. will need to decide whether he is willing to approach Dr. M. given the circumstances of failure to ask in advance and in writing for extended use of the data. If Dr. A. does not raise this question with Dr. M., then no use of the data within ethical parameters is possible other than to reanalyze the data as Dr. M. had done, for verification purposes only. If Dr. A. decides to ask Dr. M., and if Dr. M. agrees, then there are substantive actions that must be taken before any use of the data could occur. These involve review of the conditions of informed consent and action taken to rectify any incongruence with the original consent and the proposed use of data. Dr. A. should be mindful that the participant population comprises minors with a chronic condition and that special care should be taken to avoid exploitation and undue influence and to be alert to the potential vulnerabilities of the participants with whom he is working. Dr. A. should also resubmit his request through both Dr. M.'s IRB and his own IRB to obtain consent. Dr. A. did not intend to use or misuse data in his original request to review and is somewhat surprised about how the possibilities these data could bring to him influenced his thinking for a period of time.

Standard 8.15, Reviewers

Psychologists who review material submitted for presentation, publication, grant, or research proposal review respect the confidentiality of and the proprietary rights in such information of those who submitted it.

Psychologists who review professional and scientific works have a specific responsibility—and honor—in that they have access to new ideas, concepts, and scientific findings. This responsibility requires psychologists to commit to confidential treatment of the content and to respect the ownership of the material by the authors. These proprietary materials include grants, articles, papers, and presentations developed for delivery at professional meetings. Psychologists are aware that neither oral nor written use nor reference to reviewed material is acceptable.

CONCLUSION

In this chapter we have defined the rights and responsibilities of psychologists and the individuals with whom they work, specifically in conducting research and the subsequent publication of research. Psychologists often engage in professional activities with individuals over whom they may exercise influence. Research and publication are two professional activities in which psychologists' influence over students, research participants, assistants, and supervisees is significant. This chapter has identified standards that direct psychologists to be mindful of their professional roles and the impact they may have on others. Psychologists have a responsibility to the people with whom they work to engage them justly and respectfully. Students, research participants, supervisees, and others who work with psychologists are encouraged to be aware of their rights and the expectations the profession has for their welfare and equitable treatment.

9

ASSESSMENT

The scope of professional psychology is expanding in complex and challenging ways. Central among the domains that are evolving within the profession is assessment. Psychologists receive instruction in general assessment in their doctoral training experience, but unless they incorporate assessment into their professional work they may have no further training in or application of it. The foundation of testing and evaluation has grown from general psychological evaluation to many areas of assessment that are specific in purpose, instruments used, and questions addressed. Five of these areas of specialty are (a) a range of forensic assessments, including evaluations for custody, parental fitness, fitness for duty, competence to stand trial, and correctional placement and treatment; (b) educational testing, including learning and behavioral problems, attention-deficit/hyperactivity difficulties, giftedness, and special placement; (c) neuropsychological testing, including specialty evaluation for gerontologically related problems; (d) diagnostic evaluations (e.g., posttraumatic stress disorder) and treatment, and (e) industrial and organizational assessment, including employment selection, organizational efficiency, and executive placement. This enumeration is not comprehensive but identifies the range and multiplicity of purpose and use of evaluation.

Several of the general principles of the American Psychological Association's (APA's) "Ethical Principles of Psychologists and Code of Conduct"(hereinafter the *APA Ethics Code* or the *Ethics Code*; see http://www.apa.org/ethics/code2002.html)[1] resonate closely with the professional activity of assessment. General Principle A: Beneficence and Nonmaleficence is most important in assessment in that psychologists must strive to benefit others and do no harm. Assessment as much as any psychological service can affect individuals' lives in very significant ways. To avoid harm, psychologists must ensure that their degree of knowledge and judgment is competent. General Principle D: Justice reminds psychologists that equal quality and fairness in treatment of others in assessment is critical because of the consequences to individuals when bias, incompetence, and/or limited expertise results in unjust practices. Last, General Principle E: Respect for People's Rights and Dignity is important because often the individuals being evaluated may have vulnerabilities that impair their decision making and limit their ability for informed consent. Furthermore, General Principle E underscores the importance of fairness and respect for cultural, individual, and role differences among diverse groups.

Ethical violations in assessment often arise from the slippery slope phenomenon rather than from deceptive intent; that is, assessment has become specialized and complex in such a manner that well-meaning psychologists may underestimate the training and knowledge base needed for an evaluation, which may result in them engaging in assessments that are beyond their competence levels. A deceptive aspect in failure to discern a specific assessment need is that some of the same instruments psychologists use in general assessment may also be part of a custody or neuropsychological assessment, and psychologists may mistakenly think that because they have training in the general or clinical use of the instruments they are competent to conduct assessments using those instruments in other arenas as well.

A second slippery slope phenomenon is the case in which psychologists who are not thinking of themselves as expert witnesses or evaluators do, however, offer an opinion, thinking that they are simply voicing their perspective. When psychologists even unwittingly enter the forensic, neuropsychological, or any other specialized area of assessment any opinion is regarded as an officially rendered one. Once again, psychologists can, with no ill intent, make ethically unsound judgments in the assessment arena if they are not familiar with the APA Ethics Code and other legal and professional documents relevant to their assessment activities.

---

[1]American Psychological Association. (2002). Ethical principles of psychologists and code of conduct. *American Psychologist, 57,* 1060–1073.

Section 9 of the Ethics Code assists psychologists in understanding the ethical aspects of preparation for assessment, professional interaction with clients/patients, understanding assessment procedures, and the use and treatment of data. The standards that comprise the assessment section provide psychologists guidance at each of these stages of engagement with assessment.

Standard 9.01, Bases for Assessment

A guiding standard of the Competence Section is Standard 2.04. This standard reflects the importance of psychologists basing their work on established scientific knowledge and professional judgment. Standard 9.01 addresses the application of this competence to assessment. Accurate and sound scientific documentation for findings is the core concept of Standard 9.01, including sufficient substantiation of findings, required individual examination sufficient to support statements, and bases of conclusions and recommendations required when a review does not include examination. Psychological evaluations often result in findings and recommendations that affect the course of individuals' lives. Standard 9.01 and other standards in this section are intended to ensure that assessments are grounded in scientific knowledge and judgment to most accurately and fairly support the function of assessment.

Standard 9.01(a)
Psychologists base the opinions contained in their recommendations, reports, and diagnostic or evaluative statements, including forensic testimony, on information and techniques sufficient to substantiate their findings. (See also Standard 2.04, Bases for Scientific and Professional Judgments.)

Reliance on substantive information and techniques is a critical factor in ensuring the credibility, soundness, and accuracy of psychologists' opinions. Psychologists, therefore, carefully evaluate the merits of the information they themselves have acquired and, to an equal degree, evaluate information provided by others that may be used in forming their opinions.

Five of the reasons for the difficulties that often arise in meeting this standard are (a) going beyond the scientific and professional information available, (b) overstating the findings, (c) misconstruing the information, (d) mistaking hearsay information for verifiable information, and (e) drawing on information that is not applicable to the case.

Several pitfalls affect psychologists as they choose factors from which to formulate their opinions. Psychologists may have strong beliefs about a case either regarding the individuals involved, the nature of the case, personal values, or other persuasive factors that influence their thinking, resulting in a predisposition of opinion. Psychologists also may develop an approach to evaluation that involves either techniques, instruments, interview formats, or other procedures with which they have expertise and therefore have confidence in conventionally applying this same approach. When the purpose of the evaluation requires different reference materials, psychologists may not recognize the importance of using other, perhaps less familiar, procedures. They may find themselves misled by information that is sound, convincing, valid, and accurate but that does not apply to the case at hand well enough to answer questions or be informative. The Ethics Code encourages psychologists to think carefully about the particular instruments they choose in a given case. There is an ethical aspect to psychologists being able to answer why they have chosen a particular test to answer a particular question in a case. Psychologists give tests not for the sake of giving tests but because they think that a particular instrument helps answer the assessment questions. They may find that when they render opinions, in particular in forensic settings, others may entice or pressure them to go beyond what the data support. Depending on the context, psychologists may not realize the extent to which they have gone beyond what the data support until after the proceeding. Psychologists may face many challenges in determining the usefulness and substantive nature of information on which they rely. There are several questions psychologists may ask themselves in developing source information:

- What are the assessment questions to be answered?
- Are the reference materials both able to yield answers to the questions and appropriate to use in answering the questions?
- Why does one choose a particular instrument to answer a particular question?
- Are these the most useful and appropriate materials to use in formulating opinions?
- Was the information garnered by the psychologist or by other individuals? If it was gathered by others, what steps can be taken to ensure the accuracy and applicability of the information?
- What steps can psychologists take to ensure that information received by others is not biased or inaccurate?

Standard 9.01(b)

Except as noted in 9.01c, psychologists provide opinions of the psychological characteristics of individuals only after they have conducted an examination of the individuals adequate to support their statements or conclusions. When, despite reasonable efforts, such an examination is not practical, psychologists document the efforts they made and the result of those efforts, clarify the probable impact of their limited information on the reliability and validity of their opinions, and appropriately limit the

nature and extent of their conclusions or recommendations. (See also Standards 2.01, Boundaries of Competence, and 9.06, Interpreting Assessment Results.)

Psychologists are aware that opinions of theirs rendered through reports and evaluations are used to make decisions that can significantly affect individuals' lives. Conducting a personal examination is central to making professional judgments and is often a dynamic rather than static process. If psychologists are going to make statements or draw conclusions, they will want to conduct an examination adequate to support their findings and recommendations. If they cannot accomplish the needed examination, then they must document the efforts they have made, clarify the probable effect on the outcome of their evaluation, and express the probable limitations.

Prior reports, interviews, previous evaluations, and other sources of information are useful in developing opinions and may certainly be included in reports and recommendations; however, when evaluated psychological characteristics of individuals are factors in decisions that affect those individuals, psychologists are conscientious about conducting the relevant examinations. Psychologists use their judgment in deciding the components of the examination and ensure that the information that is necessary for rendering an opinion on the specific questions asked can be addressed through that examination. Psychologists are also careful not to develop a standard examination for different evaluative purposes but should attempt to construct an examination that will most effectively assist in the decisions to be made.

Psychologists make reasonable efforts to conduct an examination. An examination may not be feasible for various reasons, including the following: the individual is not in the geographical area any longer; the individual refuses the examination; an intervening occurrence, such as illness, prevents contact; or legal representation of the individual prevents the communication. When such a circumstance occurs, psychologists should follow ethical procedures to incorporate the limitation into their opinions and recommendations.

This standard is intended to provide guidance to psychologists when they are proceeding in the context of limited data (e.g., absence of a clinical interview) or are unable to apply appropriate techniques (e.g., selected instruments). The following four steps may be useful in determining how psychologists may reasonably provide a report yet recognize limitations in the recommendations:

1. *Document efforts*. Psychologists provide evidence that they themselves have not been obstacles to conducting the examination by citing their actions and interactions in the process. They may document variables such as the varied and ample times offered

during which to conduct the examination, geographical and logistical access for the meeting, examples of written and verbal attempts to schedule a meeting, any financial implications for the examinee, and enlistment of court assistance.

2. *Document the results of the efforts.* Reporting the resulting status of data access, after efforts to conduct an examination have ceased, assists both psychologists and the recipients of their opinions. Relative importance of unavailable data and that which are accessible can be helpful to psychologists in formulating their opinions of the impact of missing information.

3. *Clarify the impact on reliability and validity of opinions.* Once the limiting conditions have been defined, psychologists describe how the limitation qualifies their opinions and how the impact of the omission affects the parameters of the report. When a parent is not interviewed, and this fact is stated, it is important that further explanation of how that omission affects psychologists' judgment be described. A psychologist might state, for example, "The mother was not interviewed and, as a result, the validity of my observations regarding the behavior of the children is limited because I do not have access to her perspective on the well-being of the children."

4. *Limit the nature and extent of conclusions or recommendations.* Even when psychologists fully describe the limits of their opinions and conclusions they should make a particular effort not to draw conclusions that go beyond the scope of the available information. In a child custody case in which one parent is not examined, psychologists may still include information regarding that parent that is reliable and valid, such as frequency of visitation or activities in which the parent has engaged the child. Psychologists, however, must not make a custody recommendation or observations about the qualities of a parent who has not been examined. This is one example of types of recommendations that are not made given the absence of data. Psychologists will want to explain the ways in which their opinions and reports are limited and to carefully qualify conclusions and recommendations.

Standard 9.01(c)

When psychologists conduct a record review or provide consultation or supervision and an individual examination is not warranted or necessary for the opinion, psychologists explain this and the sources of information on which they based their conclusions and recommendations.

A common professional activity for psychologists is to review existing records, files, or documents in order to make a specific decision or additional determination. Psychologists should be familiar with record review parameters and discern for themselves the applicability of an examination. Some of the typical record review variables they might consider include quality control review of decisions already made by other professionals, review for reconsideration of an action (e.g., workers' compensation appeal), or administrative review (e.g., management review of insurance claims). Psychologists may consider the appropriateness of an examination along three parameters: (a) if the case involves making an initial decision, (b) if there is evidence that significant changes with the individual have occurred since the last examination, and (c) if the record presented for review has not included direct access information. Psychologists should specify the bases for their opinions to make clear that their work is a record review.

Standard 9.01(a), Case 1

The challenges of Standard 9.01(a) often manifest through the use of insufficient or inappropriate techniques and going beyond the information available. In the following vignettes, two psychologists act in ways that question their compliance with this standard.

Case Illustration. Dr. W. receives a referral from a colleague who is a school counselor in a local middle school. The referral is for a 9-year-old African American boy named Billy, who, as reported by the counselor, is having behavioral problems in the classroom, as evidenced by out-of-seat behavior, challenging classmates, and general acting-out behavior. Dr. W. assumes that the counselor is referring Billy because Dr. W. is known for her psychotherapy with adolescents and for her ability to assess and treat behavioral problems. Dr. W. has found, in her 15 years of experience, that a battery consisting of a brief personality screener, a behavioral checklist given to parents and teachers, and an extensive interview with parents yields the information she will need for her assessment. In fact, she prides herself on being able to distill this information into very targeted observations, diagnoses, and recommendations. She has been recognized many times for her astuteness and mastery in the use of this approach.

After completing all aspects of her evaluation, Dr. W. determines that Billy has conduct disorder. She reports to the parents and to the school her assessment and her recommendations for remediation, including special placement in the school and behavioral interventions. Unbeknownst to Dr. W., Billy's reading teacher has noticed some atypical characteristics in Billy's oral reading and in his written responses in reading comprehension exercises. She refers Billy to the school psychometrist, who identifies a significant reading disorder with dyslexia.

Ethical Dilemma. When Dr. W. learns of this information, she initially assumes that this diagnosis is an additional finding to her evaluation and recommendations. She begins, however, to be uneasy about whether the findings are coincidental. She consults a colleague who is a learning specialist and explains the circumstance. Dr. W. learns that children often turn to behavioral coping choices when they are confronted with a potentially embarrassing in-class performance situation. Often, children will divert the teacher and classmates when they are asked to read out loud, go to the blackboard, or do any other performance activity in which they know they will underperform in the presence of other children. Negative behaviors are chosen more frequently than positive ones because the other children may laugh and enjoy the student's antics, and thus the event becomes positive for the child rather than negative. Dr. W. feels as though the rug has been pulled out from underneath her. She realizes that she had fallen into a pattern of evaluation that could result in the misdiagnosis of children based on the inability of her battery to identify many possible educational problems. She also realizes that she had inadvertently not followed the intent of Standard 9.01(a) in that she was not able to assess Billy accurately with her battery. She does know how to use the instruments that would have detected the reading disorder, but she is not as familiar or skilled in these instruments as she is with others, and she had thought that her expertise in her particular battery could suffice for a broader array of diagnosis than was true.

Decision-Making Factors. Dr. W. knows that she needs to intervene in the remediation and treatment of Billy and that she must rethink her approach to assessment and diagnosis. This is a very difficult realization for Dr. W., because it brings into question her competence and skills. After seeking and receiving consultation, Dr. W. learns that assessment instruments, trends in the education and learning community, and ways in which learning problems are perceived have changed significantly during the past several years. Dr. W. has been very conscientious in acquiring continuing education in behavioral problems, she had not been aware of the parallel developments in other areas, such as learning, that can have considerable impact on children's behavior. Dr. W. also faces the likelihood that she had not developed skills in multicultural and diversity competencies. This deficit may have contributed to her acceptance of the counselor's assessment, at face value, without making her own initial assessment of the presenting concern. Dr. W. has already delivered her feedback and recommendations to the parents and to the school and, in fact, Billy has already been reassigned to the special education classroom for behavioral disorders.

Decision Options. Dr. W. meets with Billy's parents immediately and tells them about the evolving aspects of the referral and the very significant implications of her treatment recommendation. She describes to them how the diagnosis was made and the errors in her approach that led her to the diagnosis and recommendation. She does consider that she cannot, at this point, render any opinion at all about Billy's eventual behavioral characteristics that would be present after remediation and accommodations for his reading disorder. She does know that the reading disorder must be targeted and remediated before any other consideration of diagnoses related to behavior. Dr. W. further decides to commit herself to coursework and consultation in learning disorders and diversity competence in order to feel confident again in her assessment practice.

Standard 9.01(a), Case 2

Case Illustration. Dr. B. is an organizational psychologist who has a consultation practice in which he conducts evaluations for several companies in recommendations of candidates for executive management positions. Dr. B. has agreed to evaluate candidates for the chief operating officer position in a large financial corporation. Over the 15 years in which Dr. B. has been specializing in this practice area, he has developed a battery of tests and interview formats and a high level of expertise in personnel evaluation and selection. Dr. B. has great confidence in his battery and in his ability, through interviews and interpretation of test results, to present the best profile of candidates' strengths and weaknesses. Dr. B. has assembled tests that measure aptitude, knowledge and skills, and interpersonal style, and he administers a personality screening instrument based on a normal population. Dr. B.'s standard format is to interview the candidates first and then, for internal candidates, he interviews the coworkers and supervisors of those individuals. After interviewing Ms. C., a candidate for the chief operating officer position, Dr. B. notes that she has an interpersonal and explanatory style that was demonstrative and affective. She was emphasizing particular points in the interview when he noticed this characteristic, but he did not find it distracting or questionable. He perceives Ms. C. to be very competent and knowledgeable about the corporation and the areas for which she would be responsible in this new position. The test information came in, and on the personality screening instrument Ms. C. is characterized as being very interpersonal, situationally aware of her environment, and being opinionated. She is also identified as valuing advocacy and egalitarianism and respectful of the opinions of subordinates. After surveying Ms. C.'s coworkers, Dr. B. finds that she is viewed by a few as being too assertive, being led by her feelings in decision making, and too sensitive and critical regarding reactions of others in team interactions. One supervisor recounts an argument he had had with Ms. C. in which, he said, "she became borderline on me."

When Dr. B. writes his reports on each candidate and presents his opinions to the search committee, he recounts the comments he has received from these coworkers and repeated the accusation of "becoming borderline" in his report. The committee struck Ms. C. immediately from consideration for the position. Two months later, through other sources, Dr. B. is told that the three people who had made these complaints had been identified by the new management team as being harassing and discriminatory toward women in the office. These three employees had been dismissed from the company. Dr. B. has a sinking feeling that he had miscalculated the work environment in the corporation and, worse, had done a great injustice to Ms. C. He also contemplates the ethical implications of his decisions.

Ethical Dilemma. Dr. B. appears to have become comfortable in using his standard battery, and it could be that had he been guided by his battery only and his own interview with Ms. C., he would have rendered different opinions than he did. Dr. B. has violated Standard 9.01(a) in that his report went beyond the information that would be needed to substantiate his finding; that is, Dr. B. did not rely on prior psychological reports, his own evaluation, the evaluation of other competent professionals, or the findings of any personality tests that could identify borderline personality characteristics. Dr. B. had also taken a questionable stance in regard to Standard 9.06 in that his interpretations of his survey data suggest a personality disorder diagnosis for which he was not assessing the candidate. Dr. B. has also disregarded General Principle A: Beneficence and Nonmaleficence in his failure to do no harm or to safeguard the welfare and rights of others. Further, he has failed to meet the standard of General Principle E: Respect for People's Rights and Dignity, which calls for psychologists to respect the dignity of others and to eliminate biases or stereotypes based on gender.

Decision-Making Factors. Dr. B. is faced with a reconsideration of his approach to consultation, evaluation, and recommendations. He also is living with the knowledge that his report had eliminated Ms. C. from consideration for the job in a very prejudicial way. Dr. B. thinks that if he approaches the president of the company and recounts all that has happened and all that he now knows, it could likely result in his not receiving any more consultation jobs from the corporation. He has had a good relationship with this corporation; it has been one of his larger clients. He realizes that one of his choices will pit his financial welfare and reputation against his ethical and professional stance. The chief operating officer position has been filled, but there is the matter of the company management having a biased view of Ms. C. by virtue of Dr. B's report, a view that might preclude her from consideration for future job openings.

Dr. B. also decides that he is uninformed about contemporary practices, changes, and ethical behavior in the workplace, including from a consultation point of view. He also realizes that what used to be state-of-the-art knowledge about assessment and evaluation is outdated.

Decision Options. Dr. B.'s consultation with the corporation has ended, but he wants to make every attempt to repair the damage he has done in the selection process. He meets with the president of the corporation, tells the president all that had happened, and takes responsibility for giving a flawed report. The president notes that another person had been chosen for the job and is already in place. The president does, however, acknowledge that Ms. C. had been a good employee and that the board had been somewhat surprised at the report. Dr. B. emphasizes that he is asking that his report be purged from company files and for these statements to be removed from Ms. C.'s record. Dr. B. asserts that he has apprised the company of the invalidity of his report and that even though the corporation now owns the report, if they use the report for any decision making, promotion, or salary consideration, they would then knowingly be using inaccurate information.

Dr. B. further decides to commit himself to continuing education and consultation to get up to speed on his perspective in his field. He also realizes that he is not competent in skills and awareness related to diversity factors and that he has missed the gender bias in this scenario. He still does not understand how he missed the accurate reading of the gender implication of the situation, and this factor also was persuasive in his commitment to become more knowledgeable and aware.

Standard 9.01(b), Case 1

Case Illustration. Dr. D. is a family psychologist whose practice primarily includes couples and families. Dr. D. conducted couples therapy 4 years ago with Mr. J. and Ms. K. They had two very young children, ages 1 and 3, who were not involved in the therapy. During the course of the year in which Dr. D. saw the couple, several very serious and painful problems were discussed in sessions. Mr. J. had struggled with a drinking problem that Ms. K. reported had caused harm and chaos to the family. During this time, Mr. J. diverted money to pay for the alcohol and often was not able to pay the necessary bills to keep the family going. Utilities would be shut off, and letters would be received about delinquent mortgage payments. The couple would have very intense and demonstrative arguments in session, and very painful things were said by both. Mr. J. was typically defensive and denying of the impact his drinking had on the family.

Shortly after marital therapy terminated with Dr. D., Mr. J. began to get control of his dependency and slowly worked his way back to approaching a healthier life. He had not had a drink in the last 3 of the 4 years since Dr. D. had seen the couple. He was gainfully employed in a responsible job that he liked. Within the past year, however, Ms. K. and Mr. J. had divorced. Mr. J. is now living during part of the year in another state, where he is taking care of his aging parents. He lives part of the year in the same town as Ms. K. and the children. Ms. K. does not want to share custody with Mr. J.; as a result, the court has requested that Dr. D. conduct a custody evaluation. Mr. J. and Ms. K. agrees that Dr. D. would be acceptable. They both consent to the release of Dr. D.'s records from the prior therapy. Mr. J., in fact, thinks that his progress over the last several years will bode well for him in the evaluation and assumes that Dr. D. will contact him so that he can update Dr. D. and report his progress. Dr. D. conducts the evaluation during a time when Mr. J. is out of state and cannot return for another month. Dr. D. does include in the report that a recent interview with Mr. J. has not been conducted. He knows that, ethically, an examination of an individual is expected when statements or conclusions are made and opinions about psychological characteristics are rendered. In lieu of being able to evaluate Mr. J., Dr. D. bases his report and custody recommendation on the couple's earlier therapy. Dr. D. does not know that Mr. J. has made considerable progress in his recovery since being in therapy. In the report, therefore, Dr. D. recounts Mr. J.'s drinking problems, argumentativeness, and failure to be financially responsible for his family. In consideration of the custody report, the court awards Ms. K. sole custody of the children.

Ethical Dilemma. In an alternative attempt to meet the expectation of Standard 9.01(b), Dr. D. has violated the intent of Standard 9.01(b). Rendering opinions of the characteristics of individuals without examination or evaluation leads to bias and inaccurate portrayals. This standard applies to those circumstances in which decisions are being made that significantly affect an individual. In this case, Dr. D. realizes the importance of having a reference for evaluation of Mr. J. but drew on outdated information (Standard 9.08), in the process creating a distorted representation of Mr. J. Even though Dr. D. noted in his report that a contemporary interview or examination was not conducted, he did not cite the probable impact of this limitation on the validity of his opinion, nor did he qualify the nature or extent of his recommendations. Standard 10.02(b) is also called into question here in that Dr. D. was called on to perform a role that potentially conflicts with an earlier role. He is obligated to clarify or decline the current role.

Decision-Making Factors. When the custody decision is determined and the report becomes public, Dr. D. is made aware of the inaccuracy of his characterization of Mr. J. It is, in fact, the case that Dr. D. had not meant to be unfair or prejudicial to Mr. J., but because of his reliance on outdated information he had done just that. Dr. D. must now rethink his opinion in light of this new information about Mr. J. as well as reconsider his decision. His evaluative statements about Mr. J. were based on information that Dr. D. knew to be true at the time of his last association with Mr. J., but he had failed to consider the possibility of significant behavioral changes. Dr. D. has to admit to himself that he likely made this assumption because he considers these characteristics to be enduring and, therefore, he did not consider change. He realizes that he then, and perhaps at other times, has allowed stereotyping to affect his decision making. Dr. D. also has to accept the fact that his experience with Mr. J. occurred in the context of marital counseling and that he should not have substituted his assessment of Mr. J's participation in counseling for an objective parental fitness evaluation. Dr. D. had generalized his impressions of Mr. J. to pervasively affect his thinking about Mr. J. and his personal and parental attributes.

In seeking to rectify his mistaken statements, Dr. D. considers several relevant factors. What had been the impact on his prior therapeutic relationship with Mr. J. and Ms. K? Should he attend in some way to damage he may have caused to his separate relationships with Mr. J. and with Ms. K.? He had not known the couple's children, and he does not know whether the children were aware of Mr. J.'s drinking problem because they were very young at the time. He considered that his outdated information inadvertently introduced prior behaviors of Mr. J. that his children may not have known. Dr. D. also is embarrassed in a professional sense as he thinks about approaching the court and telling the judge that the custody decision had been made on the basis of inaccurate information.

Decision Options. Dr. D. would want to contact the court, meet with the judge for the case, and explain the inaccuracies of his report. He acknowledges that he both used outdated information and did not qualify his report to reflect that a contemporary interview and examination had not been conducted and that this fact should be recognized as informing the limitations of the report.

Dr. D. would want to contact Mr. J. and Ms. K. to process their reactions to his report and to explain his thinking and his errors. Dr. D. does not know in advance how to engage and what to expect, but he knows that he wants to ease the therapeutic damage that might have been done and to be responsive to their reactions.

Dr. D. reflects on the mistakes he has made in ethical terms and realizes that he misconstrued and overlooked several important standards. He was admittedly flattered when the judge specifically asked him to do the custody evaluation. He had worked in this judge's court quite often. The judge had said that he knew Dr. D. could keep his objectivity and that knowing the individuals could be helpful in doing the evaluation. Dr. D. now realizes that he should have given this evaluative role a great deal more thought before accepting it. Dr. D. had not connected Standard 9.08 with outdated information; he had thought of this standard as describing outdated tests, not information that is no longer accurate. Last, Dr. D. confronts the fact that he had substituted the outdated clinical information so that he would not have to write the report without making a custody evaluation. He would have been reluctant to make a recommendation without interviewing both parents, and the route he took was expedient, because he had not had to wait for Mr. J. to return to town. Dr. D. decides to pursue continuing education focused on forensic evaluation and custody in order to enhance his competency in forensic practice. Dr. D. realizes that an option would have been to refer the family for an objective custody evaluation in which he could have provided input.

Standard 9.02, Use of Assessments

Standard 9.01 asserts the importance of scientific documentation in substantiation of findings that render opinions and offer recommendations. Standard 9.02 correspondingly asserts the importance of choosing techniques, instruments, and methods appropriate for the populations and setting, the assurance of validity and reliability, and meeting the language needs of the individuals being served. This standard specifically conveys to psychologists the importance not only of using sound documentation but also of realizing that if the techniques, instruments, and methods of gathering data are not sound, then the data cannot substantiate findings.

Standard 9.02(a)
Psychologists administer, adapt, score, interpret, or use assessment techniques, interviews, tests, or instruments in a manner and for purposes that are appropriate in light of the research on or evidence of the usefulness and proper application of the techniques.

Determination of "appropriate" use can be complex because some of the same instruments, for example, can be used in custody evaluation, employment selection, therapeutic treatment, and disability evaluation. The data gained by using these instruments would be used very differently to answer the different questions asked for each of these evaluations and the instruments would make differential contributions to the overall examination battery depending on the type, manner, and purpose of the assessment. Psychologists may think about several aspects of assessment selection as they develop a battery of instruments, techniques, and methods of evaluation.

Psychologists who specialize in a particular area of assessment may become quite familiar with particular tests and methods, but they should be alert to the importance of selecting methods that serve the individual case. Even though psychologists may even think they have greater expertise with certain instruments than others and can glean more from those instruments than from others, they are committed to using the most appropriate instruments. The costs of new materials can be significant, and the tendency to continue with known instruments can occur. Psychologists become familiar with the conventional uses of methods and instruments as well as their limitations. The test manual can be reviewed for proper application of the material and to assist psychologists in not overstating the purpose and use of instruments. Without adherence to the defined supplication of the instrument within the test manual, psychologists could inadvertently use instruments to assess qualities beyond what the instrument can measure and beyond the purpose for which the instrument was developed.

Standard 9.02(b)

Psychologists use assessment instruments whose validity and reliability have been established for use with members of the population tested. When such validity or reliability has not been established, psychologists describe the strengths and limitations of test results and interpretation.

Psychologists are committed to the fair and equitable treatment of clients/patients, research participants, students, and others with whom they engage in psychological activities. Psychologists also are aware that they have significant influence on the lives of people for whom they render opinions that affect placement, treatment, jobs, and other life-impacting decisions. For these and other reasons, the use of appropriate measures in testing is a crucial factor. The validity and reliability of instruments should be assured before use; however, and just as important, the application of instruments to specific populations should also be determined through knowledge of norming procedures and other psychometric characteristics in the development of the tests. Examples of factors that can be particularly vulnerable to misapplication of tests are age, gender, race, ethnicity, culture, national origin, disability, language, socioeconomic status, and some diagnostic classifications.

Psychologists may face circumstances in which an evaluation for decision making is necessary to promote and protect the welfare of individuals yet there are no instruments available that are a good fit for the population. Psychologists may be called on to determine the instruments that will access the information needed for a decision that will not disadvantage or inaccurately represent the individuals. In these cases, the strengths of the instruments and reasons for using the instruments are thoroughly explained. The limitations and the particular cautions for interpretation also are well described. Psychologists make reasonable attempts to assemble instruments, materials, and techniques that are applicable to the individuals for whom decisions are being made.

Instruments are periodically revised and often are renormed. Psychologists are cautioned not to use obsolete tests (see Standard 9.08, Obsolete Tests and Outdated Test Results). When, however, psychologists are seeking instruments that best fit their population for the purpose needed, they should use their professional judgment in determining the appropriateness and best fit for the population and for the purpose. Some questions psychologists might ask themselves include the following:

- Which version of an instrument fits my examinees in terms of norms, standardization, and applicability?
- Do the examinees have disabilities (e.g., hearing loss, cognitive loss, verbal limitations) that render the standard tests inappropriate for them? What are the best options?
- Has the content of a test been changed with the norms remaining the same, or have the norms changed, and what is the effect for my purposes?
- Given that a test's validity and reliability are appropriate for my purposes, can the different versions of the test answer different questions?
- Can I present a sound rationale for variance in my choice of instruments that will support the validity and applicability of my report and recommendations?

Standard 9.02(c)

Psychologists use assessment methods that are appropriate to an individual's language preference and competence, unless the use of an alternative language is relevant to the assessment issues.

When conducting assessments, psychologists must be alert to the importance of language, hearing or speech special needs, or any aspect of communication that could be an impediment to individuals' performance in evaluation. Language *preference* is differentiated from language *competence* in that individuals may be very capable in oral communication, but not written, or they may be able to read another language in print but not speak that language. Also, individuals may be concerned that they will be disadvantaged if they show a preference for a language other than English and therefore not be forthcoming about their level of English understanding.

Psychologists are aware of the importance of choosing appropriate instruments for testing individuals who have speech, auditory, or visual difficulties. Individuals may not be cognizant of a hearing or visual loss. Therefore, psychologists should be alert to signs of difficulty during the testing and may refer clients/patients for hearing or vision testing.

If a particular language is important for the reasons the individuals are being tested, then a measure of competence in that language is appropriate. Some reasons for testing inherently include facilitation in a certain language either because the environment for placement, employment, or receipt of services requires understanding of a particular language. Psychologists must both understand this alternative need and select appropriate assessment measures for the purpose.

Standard 9.02(c), Case 1

Case Illustration. Dr. R. is a child psychologist who practices primarily in the evaluation of children for psychoeducational purposes such as learning problems, attention deficits, and development concerns. She receives a referral from a friend and colleague who is an elementary school teacher. The teacher explains that a 7-year-old Latino boy who recently moved to the area with his family has joined her second-grade class. The boy's language of origin is Spanish, and he speaks very well in English. The teacher finds the boy to be withdrawn interpersonally and distracted during class studies. She has worked with him for these past 2 months but has been unable to discern whether he is emotionally affected by the move, is having difficulty with the class material, or both. The teacher asks Dr. R. to evaluate the boy.

Dr. R. willingly accepts and determines that she will first interview the parents and then likely conduct evaluations to assess the boy's intellectual, achievement, and emotional status. The mother, accompanied by his older sister, brings the boy for testing. The father is working and cannot attend. Dr. R. meets with the mother, who is uncertain why her son is having difficulty in school, but she accepts the advice and recommendation of the teacher that an assessment is needed.

After the clinical interviews, Dr. R. begins testing and finds that even though the boy speaks very good English he is not able to read or write with enough proficiency to follow her instructions on several of the subtests. He tries to cooperate and is clearly upset and anxious that he cannot do what she is asking. Dr. R. does not have the instruments that she wants to use available in Spanish. She could have acquired Spanish test materials, but because the boy reportedly spoke English very well she had not thought it was necessary. Dr. R. does not want to tell the mother to come back, because the family had traveled quite a distance, and the logistics for them had been challenging. Dr. R. decides that she will proceed as best she can with the evaluation and considers that it might be useful to observe how the boy copes with test performance in such difficult and challenged circumstances. She has occasionally tested children with attention-deficit/hyperactivity disorder when they were not taking their medication in order to see how they would function without it, and she thinks this could be a similar learning opportunity.

When the boy becomes so distraught and upset that he cannot continue, Dr. R. remembers that the mother and sister are in the waiting room and that she can call on them to assist. She thinks that bringing the mother in might create unpredictable dynamics, so she decides to ask the sister to translate for her. The sister agrees to assist and participates in the evaluation by interpreting for her younger brother. At the end of the testing, Dr. R. thinks that even though there were some bumpy moments, the assessment worked out very well in the end.

Ethical Dilemma. Dr. R. has been a child psychologist for 10 years and reputedly was held in high regard by her colleagues for her assessment and diagnostic skills with children. Dr. R., however, has headed down the slippery slope of overlapping her knowledge domain with areas in which she has not achieved competence. Standard 9.02(c) directs psychologists to use assessment methods that are appropriate for an examinee's language preference and competence. Dr. R. did not recognize the common occurrence of individuals having differential written and language skills. She inappropriately continued with instruments that were possibly beyond the client's reading and writing capabilities. She further practiced beyond her own level of competence in conducting an evaluation that rightfully required a cultural sensitivity and a command of language ability that she did not have (Standard 2.01b). Correspondingly, Dr. R. did not verify that the instruments she used had established validity and reliability with the boy's cultural and ethnic origin (Standard 9.02b). By enlisting the sister in the testing, Dr. R. delegated work to others (Standard 2.05) and thereby was required to ensure that steps are taken to avoid tasking individuals who have a multiple relationship with those being served; that only a person who can be expected to perform competently on the basis of his or her education, training, or experience are enlisted to assist; and that the person who is asked to help can perform his or her services competently. Dr. R. did not adhere to the expectations of Standard 2.05. General Principle A: Beneficence and Nonmaleficence applies in this assessment case in that psychologists strive to benefit those with whom they work, do not cause harm, and promote the welfare of others. Even if she did so unintentionally, Dr. R. allowed her client to be in a stressful circumstance in which he was not able to respond to instruction, and this may have caused the boy to feel incapable. General Principle E: Respect for People's Rights and Dignity is applicable in that neither the boy, the sister, nor the mother was treated respectfully and with a regard for their right to choice.

Decision-Making Factors. Dr. R. should have considered several decision-making factors in approaching the challenges of this case. She treated the language preference as secondary to her choice of assessment methods rather than making instrument choices in accordance with the client's language facility. She should have been prepared to accommodate the child's language of origin in making a determination of intellectual and emotional status. In addition, she should have determined in advance whether her instruments of preference were psychometrically sound when used with individuals of the client's ethnicity.

Dr. R. should have considered her range of competence not in assessment expertise but in her competence to work with individuals of the client's ethnic origin, cultural experience, and language and in her competence to work with the family in understanding the context in which the child was having difficulties.

By enlisting the sister to participate in interpreting test material, Dr. R. opened up the testing conditions and her responsibility to the delegation of work of others. Dr. R. had an obligation, if including interpreters in test administration, to ensure no multiple relationships, a level of competence, and follow-through in performing competently. Dr. R. considered the sister to represent less of a multiple relationship than the mother; however, this is a false distinction because the sister's presence could have affected the perceived neutrality of the testing environment for the client as readily as the mother could have.

Perhaps as problematic as the failure to discern the relevant ethical standards was Dr. R.'s disregard for the importance of General Principle A and General Principle E. Dr. R. should have been more cognizant of her obligation to safeguard the welfare and rights of the boy and his family in this evaluation environment, one with which they were unfamiliar and were depending on the judgment of the teacher and Dr. R. to protect their interests. She should also have been more thoughtful in treating the family needs more respectfully and in protecting this family from even greater mistreatment.

Decision Options. Dr. R. should realize that the assessment administered, as well as any opinions, diagnosis, and recommendations rendered, should be retracted and that a new assessment, conducted by a psychologist competent in diversity, should be commissioned. Furthermore, Dr. R. should realize that the emotional status of the client has been underestimated as a factor in his despondence, and these dynamics should be identified before any diagnosis of learning difficulty or attention deficit is assigned.

Standard 9.03, Informed Consent in Assessments

Informed consent for participation in psychological activities, including assessment, research, and therapy, is a fundamental principle of ethical conduct in psychology. Standards that address informed consent are included in four sections of the Ethics Code and are consistent in their representation of values and the principles of individual freedom of choice and respect for the rights and dignity and welfare of the individuals with whom psychologists work. Psychologists are committed to ensuring that individuals who agree to participate in assessment have a full understanding of the possible implications, consequences, and effect that the assessment findings may have on those individuals, because participants in testing and assessment may not be cognizant of the impact that the outcome data may have on decisions being made regarding themselves. Furthermore, without full informed consent participants may be forthcoming with disclosure that could be detrimental to them. Without early informed consent, disclosing participants may feel manipulated by the appearance of psychologists' withholding consequential information.

Standard 9.03(a)

Psychologists obtain informed consent for assessments, evaluations, or diagnostic services, as described in Standard 3.10, Informed Consent, except when (1) testing is mandated by law or governmental regulations: (2) informed consent is implied because testing is conducted as a routine educational, institutional, or organizational activity (e.g., when participants voluntarily agree to assessment when applying for a job); or (3) one purpose of the testing is to evaluate decisional capacity. Informed consent includes an explanation of the nature and purpose of the assessment, fees, involvement of third parties, and limits of confidentiality and sufficient opportunity for the client/patient to ask questions and receive answers.

This standard identifies for psychologists the circumstances under which informed consent may be waived and the primary elements of informed consent for assessment in all other circumstances. Psychologists are encouraged to think about informed consent in a way that most accurately reflects the purpose of their assessments, the expectations of participants, and the effect on participants of involvement in the assessment.

Psychologists may consider the following four foundational elements of the informed consent for assessment:

1. *Nature and purpose*. Psychologists make reasonable attempts to ensure that individuals who agree to participate in assessment understand the implications of participation and the potential impact the results may have on decisions that affect them. Psychologists may consider aspects of informed consent that are not required by standard but that may be helpful, including the reason for testing; information that the testing intends to yield; the consequences or impact of the information, directly or indirectly, on the individuals; and the duration and frequency of assessment sessions.
2. *Fees*. Individuals must be informed of the fees involved in the assessment and any additional fees to be paid by them. Although this is not required by the standard, psychologists may also inform

those with whom they work of the involvement of any third parties either in payment of the fee for their assessment or third parties who may be billing the psychologists for services. If possible, psychologists may further apprise individuals during the initial phase of assessment of any possible changes in fee or alterations that could prevail under different circumstances.

3. *Third-party involvement.* As soon as it is feasible, psychologists should explain to the participants the role of third parties (e.g., insurance companies, organization, companies, schools, hospitals) in terms of access to information from the assessment. The persons being tested are not always the clients/patients. Psychologists must be mindful that before the participants disclose confidential or personal information, they should understand who the client is, who has access to the information provided by the participant, who owns the information, and who has access to transferring the information or sharing the information with other entities (see also Standard 3.07, Third-Party Requests for Services, and Standard 3.11, Psychological Services Delivered To or Through Organizations).

4. *Limits of confidentiality.* Psychologists will want to explain both their own obligations of confidentiality and the limits of confidentiality. Explaining the limits of confidentiality in advance of disclosure gives the participants the choice of disclosure and conveys the psychologists' respect for the participant's right to choose and right to privacy. Disclosure to participants of the following three possible conditions are not required in this standard; however, psychologists should be aware of the relevant statutes and regulations of their legal jurisdictions: (a) mandatory reporting of potential child abuse, (b) limitations of confidentiality to minors, and (c) the potential waiver of confidentiality for risk to self or others.

Three exceptions to the requirement for informed consent concern the acquisition of information that, for different reasons, may not involve the collaboration or require the permission of the participants:

1. *Information mandated by law or governmental regulation.* This standard grants to psychologists the ability to work within different state, federal, and organizational systems under varied laws and rules and shields psychologists from any incongruence between ethical standards and variation in law and regulatory policies that exist across the country and between jurisdictions.

2. *Data gathered through routine educational, institutional, or organizational activities.* When information is gathered routinely within educational systems, organizations, hospitals, or governmental entities, psychologists may use information without acquiring additional informed consent. If psychologists use information in a manner that identifies the participants or that extends beyond the scope of the existing informed consent, then additional consent would become necessary.
3. *Evaluation of decisional capacity.* When individuals' ability to make decisions comes into question, psychologists may be called on to evaluate the individuals for educational, placement, treatment, or special services needs. In these cases, the informed consent required by this standard is not needed (see Standard 9.03b).

Standard 9.03(b)

Psychologists inform persons with questionable capacity to consent or for whom testing is mandated by law or governmental regulations about the nature and purpose of the proposed assessment services, using language that is reasonably understandable to the person being assessed.

Persons of questionable capacity include children and individuals with cognitive impairments, developmental delays, or forms of dementia. An explanation of the *nature* of the assessment should address what will happen during the testing, how the process will go, and what the individual's experience is likely to be. An explanation of the *purpose* of the assessment also should be offered, in understandable concepts for the individuals' level of functioning and capacity for understanding. *Purpose* may include the ways in which assessment is meant to help the person and may, depending on the context, include descriptions of how the assessment might help in terms of resources, treatments, or placements. Psychologists weigh these factors carefully within the context of the client/patient's status when presenting explanations to persons with limited cognitive capacity.

Psychologists conducting mandated testing are working in a forensic context and therefore must be mindful of several factors that pertain to these procedures. Explanations of the nature of testing should include the same elements as the explanations given to persons with limited cognitive capacity but in addition may include more specificity about the features of the testing process and the likely effect of the experience on the examinee. Furthermore, the examinees would be informed of how the information may be used, by whom, and informed about access to information by others. The purpose of the assessment as explained in a mandated context may be significantly different from that offered in a context in which the examinees have limited cognitive capacity. Mandated testing typically results in a placement, a functioning decision, or an action that changes or redirects individuals' lives. Psychologists may wish to clarify the potential use and effect of testing results in guarding against individuals feeling manipulated into disclosures or finding that they have contributed unwittingly to decisions they dispute. Ethical Principle E: Respect for People's Rights and Dignity encourages psychologists to offer as much transparency as feasible given the conditions of the psychological services.

Use of reasonably understandable language means considering such factors as the examinees' actual first language or the language of greatest fluency or ability, given the purpose of the assessment, and the level of language use in terms of complexity of words, complexity of concepts, use of examples, and clarification of any apparent confusion regarding meaning.

Standard 9.03(c)

Psychologists using the services of an interpreter obtain informed consent from the client/patient to use that interpreter, ensure that confidentiality of test results and test security are maintained, and include in their recommendations, reports, and diagnostic or evaluative statements, including forensic testimony, discussion of any limitations on the data obtained. (See also Standards 2.05, Delegation of Work to Others; 4.01, Maintaining Confidentiality; 9.01, Bases for Assessments; 9.06, Interpreting Assessment Results; and 9.07, Assessment by Unqualified Persons.)

Psychologists take reasonable steps to ensure that individuals are both capable of understanding them and are being tested in the language most familiar to them for the purposes of the assessment; that is, individuals may have fluency in a second language but not be able to read or write adequately in that language. Psychologists are committed to providing testing environments and conditions that equalize individuals' opportunities to perform. If individuals are not proficient in the needed aspects of a language, then interpreters are necessary. Psychologists discuss the reasons for use of an interpreter with the examinees. They are mindful that interpreters are extensions of psychologists in conducting the examination and, therefore, they should educate interpreters about the important ethical standards and practices that pertain, including confidentiality, accuracy, respectfulness of the examinee, and any specific training the interpreter may need to participate in the assessment competently.

If the involvement of an interpreter affects the testing procedure, the performance of the examinee, or the resulting data acquired through the testing, then psychologists must explain those conditions in their reports, recommendations, diagnosis, and any findings or opinions they express regarding the assessment.

Standard 9.03(b), Case 1

Case Illustration. Dr. G. has just finished her postdoctoral studies in neuropsychology at a psychiatric hospital and decides to take a part-time teaching job at the nearby university and to start a part-time private practice in neuropsychology and forensics. She joins a group of psychologists who are well known for their geropsychology and forensic specialty. Dr. G. receives several referrals from psychologists in the group to start her practice. Two of the referrals represent distinct categories of clients/patients for whom the nature and purpose of assessment services must be explained: (a) questionable capacity to consent and (b) mandatory testing.

One of the referrals is from a family whose 87-year-old father, Mr. E., has been living alone in his own house for the 7 years since his wife died. The three siblings explain to Dr. G. that their father is still doing well but that they are concerned that he is alone much of the time and think that he would benefit from the socialization and activities that he could enjoy at an assisted-living facility. They ask Dr. G. to perform a thorough evaluation of their father so that they can find the best placement with the services and activities that he used to enjoy when he could drive and get around by himself. Dr. G. accepts the case and assembles the instruments she thinks will give an accurate portrayal of Mr. E.'s mental status. She also recommends a physical examination so that the family will also be apprised of any physical medical accommodations Mr. E. might have. When Dr. G. meets with Mr. E., she explains that his family has requested an examination of him so that they can find the best and most suitable assisted living facility for him. She adds that they know he misses the activities that he used to do and want him to move to a place that will allow him more socialization and activity. She adds that there are advantages to being among other people and that other patients have enjoyed that environment once they made their move. Mr. E. agrees to the examination.

When Dr. G. completes the report and meets for feedback with Mr. E. and his children, she describes her findings, which are that Mr. E. still has many capabilities and should fare very well in assisted living. She adds that he could even consider independent living in a managed facility in which his meals are provided and other select services, such as apartment cleaning and general maintenance, can be purchased. She explains, however, that Mr. E. has some age-related memory loss and that he and his family would want to be attentive to any changes in his ability to recall and retrieve information.

Dr. G. is quite taken aback when the siblings ask to meet with her separately. Mr. E. had given consent for Dr. G. to talk with them about his health. The siblings now take a very different perspective from when they first asked for the evaluation. They now say that they do not think their father is making sound decisions and that they are worried about others exploiting him and taking advantage of him. Mr. E. has considerable assets, they report, and they fear that he could make foolish decisions if he were in an environment around other people. They ask that Dr. G. re-evaluate the memory loss and any other finding she might have that would support them being awarded power of attorney over their father's estate.

Ethical Dilemma. Dr. G. is stunned at the change in the attitude of Mr. E.'s family. She is well aware of her ethical obligations to Mr. E. as her client. He had, in fact, given her consent to talk freely with his children, so Dr. G. does not think she has violated Standard 3.10. She can imagine, however, that when an older person is presented as having reduced capacity it would be easy for a health professional to discuss the specifics of the client's status more fully and freely than if mental competence were not a question introduced into the context. Dr. G. is well aware that Standard 9.03(b) cites the importance of explaining the nature and purpose of testing to persons who may have questionable capacity. The nature of her stated and actual testing was still congruent; however, the family is now introducing a very different purpose from the one Dr. G. had offered Mr. E. She had accepted the request for evaluation from the family but had made clear to them that Mr. E. would be her client even though they had his consent to receive the report and recommendation (see Standard 3.07, Third-Party Requests for Services).

Furthermore, Dr. G. feels that the intent of General Principle A: Beneficence and Nonmaleficence and General Principle E: Respect for People's Rights and Dignity would be violated if she complies with this request.

Decision-Making Factors. It crosses Dr. G.'s mind that the family may not have been completely forthcoming with her given the contrast in their initial request and later request. Their second request raises the questions of exploitation of one's client through misrepresentation of purpose (Standard 3.08, Exploitative Relationships) and of going beyond the information rendered from the evaluation in order to substantiate her findings (Standard 9.01a, Bases for Assessments).

Dr. G. reflects on her observation that Mr. E. understands her instructions and directions and had only somewhat lower performance scores on memory-related subtests. She had explained to Mr. E. that the nature of the test was for mental status evaluation and that the purpose was to identify the best fit for him in an assisted living facility. Now, she realizes that the request being made would take her outside of the realm of purpose that she had given Mr. E. Consideration of this new purpose could bring her compliance with Standard 9.03(b) into question.

In compliance with General Principle A: Beneficence and Nonmaleficence, Dr. G. believes that if she considers the family's request she will be doing possible harm to Mr. E. and not safeguarding his welfare and rights. She considers also that this request could be viewed as a misuse of her influence. In keeping with General Principle E: Respect for People's Rights and Dignity, Dr. G. thinks that her respect for Mr. E.'s dignity, worth, and self-determination could be compromised if she complies with this request and that, given his age-based vulnerabilities, she has a special responsibility to safeguard his welfare.

Decision Options. Given all of the factors she has considered, Dr. G. decides that the request for either continued testing or reinterpretation of elements of her existing report is not reasonable. She feels resolute and confident in this determination. She reflects, however, on how to proceed in expressing to the family not only her decision but also her reaction to their request. She also wonders whether to tell Mr. E. of his family's request. She could straightforwardly decline the family request and say no more. She decides, however, that the emerging value of asset management could unfairly affect other decisions made by the family. She decides to talk diplomatically with the family about their concerns. Dr. G. realizes that telling Mr. E. of the family's request could cause an uproar in the family, or at least a sense of diminishment and hurt on the part of Mr. E. But she also is concerned that if he is not informed of their request, he could be misled and deceived. In reviewing the case, Dr. G. concludes that the family's motives have more to do with gaining access to Mr. E.'s assets than his well-being. After reaching this conclusion, she decides that her obligation to safeguard her clients and those who are more vulnerable compels her to inform Mr. E. of the exchanges she has had with his family.

Standard 9.03(b), Case 2

Case Illustration. Dr. G. performs evaluations for the court and the Department of Juvenile Justice (DJJ). The court had mandated an evaluation for a 14-year-old boy, Joe, who had been involved in gang activity. He had been implicated in incidents of boys breaking into cars, attempts to shoplift in electronics stores, and gang fighting. When Dr. G. meets with Joe for the intake and initial evaluation, she explains that because he is in detention, the evaluation was mandatory and he is expected to participate in the assessment. She tells him, as she has been told, that the reason for the evaluation is for the DJJ to determine the best services for him and to help him get his life back on track. As Dr. G. proceeds through the intake, she feels much compassion for the boy. He reports having been raised in a family in which he was physically and verbally abused. He had spent several years in foster care, moving from family to family, and has health problems that he feels were caused by the bullying he has endured. Joe becomes more and more disclosing to Dr. G.

and tells her of even more near-scrapes with the law than were known by the DJJ. Dr. G. realizes that even though her explanation for the testing was accurate, she had not anticipated that the boy might disclose additional illegal activity during the intake.

Ethical Dilemma. Dr. G. is unprepared for the disclosures Joe has made and the potential implications of her obligation to report these. She is aware of Standard 9.03(b) and the importance of explaining the nature and purpose of assessment in mandatory testing situations. She thinks that she had appropriately explained both nature of the testing and the purpose. She now realizes that because Joe's disclosures could increase his exposure to additional charges and therefore a greater or more punitive sentence, she may not have accurately portrayed the purpose of the testing. Certainly, appropriate services were a reason for testing, but the potential for continued detention was a factor in implementing the services. Dr. G. reflects, as she did with the case of Mr. E., on her obligation to protect Joe's rights and welfare, in particular because his status as a minor creates a vulnerability that impairs his autonomous decision making (General Principle E: Respect for People's Rights and Dignity).

Decision-Making Factors. Dr. G. realizes some similarities between her treatment of the Mr. E. case and this case in that the implications for testing could vary from the initial purpose and explanation of testing. Dr. G. thinks that Joe's disclosures may be factors in the court's deliberations, and the implication that services may be delivered in a detention context could be factors in what the boy decided to disclose in that confidentiality may be compromised. Dr. G. is aware that the compassion she feels for Joe may have come through in her interviewing style and that her empathic stance may inadvertently have created a climate in which he felt invited to disclose. Dr. G. begins to think about how she has conducted this case in terms of consent and how she can ethically proceed from here. She thinks about the potential for the purpose for testing to shift as information is gleaned, the fact that explaining the purpose may be an ongoing part of the assessment rather than a discussion at the outset, and the fact that either the examinee or third parties' actions can impact psychologists' intentions.

Decision Options. Dr. G. decides that she will make some changes in several aspects of her testing procedures. She will become much more aware of her interviewing and interpersonal style, because even though she had informed Joe of the limits of confidentiality in their discussions she may have unwittingly encouraged disclosure through her interviewing style. Dr. G. would want to think about the congruity of her verbal and nonverbal communication. She realizes that the requester of services may have additional expectations of the outcome of testing than would be told to Dr. G. and that she would begin anticipating multiple implications of her reports so that she could moderate them.

In this case, Dr. G. stopped during the interview and refocused Joe on the informed consent. She reminded him that the information he shared was not confidential and that decisions could be made on the basis of his disclosures. She intervened with Joe before he told her anything that she thought would be damaging. She will have to report what Joe had already said, but she does think that some of the disclosure regarding aggravating circumstances potentially explains some of his choices. She realizes that with clients such as Joe, who may be very responsive to a caring and empathic listener, it may be necessary to repeat a statement of limits of confidentiality several times over the course of an interview.

Standard 9.04, Release of Test Data

Standard 9.04 is structured specifically as two parts: (a) one in which clients/patients have agreed to release of test data and (b) one in which psychologists do not have consent from the clients/patients to release test data. Standard 9.04(a) is a more complex segment of the overarching standard and is broken into three distinct parts: (a) the definition of test data, (b) the direction of when and to whom to release test data, and (c) identification of the two discretionary exceptions to consented release.

Standard 9.04 introduces the definitions of test data and test material (more fully referenced in Standard 9.11). The 2002 Ethics Code adopts terminology and definitions regarding assessment findings differently than the 1992 Ethics Code[2] did. In Standards 9.04 and 9.11, the definitions of *test data* and *test material* are clearly differentiated; also, the conditions of release of data and security of test materials are delineated.

Standard 9.04(a)

The term *test data* refers to raw and scaled scores, client/patient responses to test questions or stimuli, and psychologists' notes and recordings concerning client/patient statements and behavior during an examination. Those portions of test materials that include client/patient responses are included in the definition of *test data*. Pursuant to a client/patient release, psychologists provide test data to the client/patient or other persons identified in the release. Psychologists may refrain from releasing test data to protect a client/patient or others from substantial harm or misuse or misrepresentation of the data or the test, recognizing that in many

---

[2]American Psychological Association. (1992). Ethical principles of psychologists and code of conduct. *American Psychologist, 47,* 1597–1611.

instances release of confidential information under these circumstances is regulated by law. (See also Standard 9.11, Maintaining Test Security.)

A substantial transformation has occurred in recent years regarding privacy, access to information, respect for the welfare of individuals, and individual rights. The conditions of information maintenance, transmission, and criteria for information release have significantly shifted from institutional- and expert-based authority to the valuing of the self-determination of individuals with the right to control their personal information and decisions that affect their lives. These changes are reflected in federal and state laws, in practice codes, and in policies of institutions. Use of psychological assessment information has increasingly become an integral factor in decision making in the forensic, primary care, educational, organizational, and clinical arenas. As a result, requests from attorneys, judges, physicians, and other professionals for assessment and for access to findings have significantly increased. This context frames the perspective for psychologists who must decide how and to whom to release client/patient information.

Information that contains responses, observations, and data obtained from an examinee comprises test data, including materials that were components of a test kit, protocol, battery, or other test materials used by psychologists in conducting the assessment. Once individualized information is entered onto a data sheet, the materials become test data because they contain information that is descriptive of the examinee. Psychologists' perception of information as test material or test data can be a process of conversion. By virtue of adding information that is relevant to the examinee on a sheet of paper that is initially test material, psychologists convert that sheet of paper to test data.

When clients/patients or their legal representatives request release of test data to themselves or to others, psychologists must comply with the request unless they have reason to think the information may be substantially harmful, misused, or misrepresentative of the accurate context of the assessment. This standard does not require psychologists to confirm or give evidence for their concern in protecting the client/patient; however, they may be alert to the importance of explaining to the client their rationale and the potential negative outcome of data release and to the prudence of documenting their rationale. Clients/patients would typically not think comprehensively about the course and direction of their information after release; neither would they think about the repercussions of others having access to their information. There are several relevant aspects of this decision that psychologists might share with clients/patients:

- It is possible that sections of a report may not be able to be released selectively without releasing the entire report. If clients/patients are focusing on specific content for release, they should know that the rest of the content may have to be released as well.

- Clients/patients may think that their current behavior (e.g., addiction recovery, depression alleviation, reduction of phobic symptoms) will be seen positively, as it has been in their psychotherapy; however, an opposing position could present the same information in a negative light.
- Disclosing records for one intent may expose information in the records that is disadvantageous for other reasons (e.g., health, disability, or other types of insurance, financial status, employment status).
- If a decision is pending in court or in a medical setting, and there is an opposing stance or a dissenting opinion, the clients/patients' records are at risk for interpretation.
- When the examinees are not the clients in a case, psychologists explain this status as a function of informed consent. In regard to release of data, psychologists ensure that both the client entities (e.g., organizations, court orders, medical requests) and the examinees understand who has the authority to grant data release and to whom. Examinees must be apprised in advance of testing when the information they provide will not be available to them (see also Standard 3.11, Psychological Services Delivered To or Through Organizations).

Once psychologists have fully explained the possible course of information and completely disclosed the potential consequences and fulfilled their informed-consent commitment, the clients/patients may still want to release the information. Prevailing federal or state laws will likely affect psychologists' decisions of whether to release client/patient information; as a result, psychologists should ensure that they are familiar with the applicable rulings in their context.

Standard 9.04(b)

In the absence of a client/patient release, psychologists provide test data only as required by law or court order.

Standard 9.04(b) is the counterpart to 9.04(a) and addresses release of test data in the absence of client/patient consent. A similar parallel exists in Standard 4.05(a), which addresses disclosures of confidential information with the appropriate consent of the client/patient, and in Standard 4.05(b), which covers disclosure of confidential information without the consent of the client/patient. As in other standards that refer to requirements of law or court order, this standard removes psychologists from circumstances in which they might have a conflict between law and the APA Ethics Code. Psychologists must protect the confidentiality and privacy of the individuals with whom they work, unless they are required by law or court order to provide information. Psychologists should explain this policy to examinees in advance of assessment and ensure that all individuals involved understand the limitations as well as protections of the confidentiality status.

Standard 9.04(a), Case 1

Case Illustration. Dr. L. has had a 10-year practice specializing in forensic assessment, substance abuse, and psychotherapy. He receives a referral from his colleague for a client, Mr. M., who has been suffering from chronic depression, anxiety, substance abuse, and suicidal ideation. Dr. L. asks one of the partners in his practice to conduct an evaluation to determine Mr. M.'s primary therapeutic needs, general mental status, substance abuse effects, and suicidal risk. The evaluation does confirm clinical depression, generalized anxiety, a moderate level of suicide risk, and continued substance abuse. Dr. L. meets with Mr. M., who professes to be committed to treatment and to changing his life. After careful consideration, Dr. L. decides to accept Mr. M. as a client. During the next 2 years, they work very hard together in therapy, and toward the end of that time Mr. M.'s depression and anxiety are greatly reduced. He has had no suicidal ideation in a year, and he has not used any alcohol in a year.

One day, Mr. M. comes to his appointment, exuberant. He announces that he has tentatively been offered a new job in a good law firm in the southern part of the state. He needs to be interviewed by some additional management, attend an orientation session, and take some tests. The human resources department (HRD) representative has described these additional steps as formalities. If Mr. M. is offered the job, he will be moving in a couple of months. He has already made some initial contacts in the new community and wants Dr. L.'s recommendation in finding another psychologist there so that he can continue treatment. He is so happy with the progress he has made, and he attributes much of his change to Dr. L. and his therapeutic work with him. Dr. L. gives Mr. M. some references for a psychologist, and in 2 weeks, Mr. M. calls Dr. L. and tells him that he has made the contact with one of the psychologists. In order to provide continuity of care, the psychologist has requested the initial evaluation record and a summary of Dr. L.'s case notes. At the end of the conversation, Mr. M. incidentally mentions that when he went in for the last interview at the new firm, he was told that all new employees take some tests that help the company in placing new employees and making client assignments.

Mr. M. tells the HRD representative that he had already had a full battery of tests 2 years earlier, and she suggests that he have his evaluation sent to the HRD. He then asks Dr. L. to send a copy of his report and case notes not only to the referral psychologist but also to the HRD representative. When Dr. L. explains his concern about the company having access to Mr. M.'s case file, Mr. M. says that he is sure that when company officials learn of his struggle and successful recovery from depression, substance abuse, and suicidal thoughts, they will see his story as positive and see that he can be a very persevering, hard-working, and disciplined employee.

Ethical Dilemma. Dr. L. knows that the assessment in question might be helpful to the psychologist/psychotherapist in that background information, family history, case notes, history of medication, and diagnostic classifications could be informative in developing a treatment plan. The assessment, however, was not done for the same purposes for which the company's industrial and organizational psychologist would use the report (Ethical Standard 9.01, Bases for Assessments). Dr. L. considers the potential for evaluating Mr. M. against criteria measured in the industrial and organizational personnel testing and the risk for harm to Mr. M.'s position with the firm if the evaluation were misused or inaccurately used (Standard 3.04). Dr. L. would not have used this battery of tests in an evaluation for performance, placement, or personnel fitness, and therefore he is uneasy that another psychologist might act in just that manner (Standard 9.02). Dr. L.'s primary concern, however, is that Mr. M. has given his permission to release the evaluation, yet Dr. L. feels strongly that release of the assessment would most certainly be detrimental to Mr. M. Standard 9.04(a) cites two exceptions to the release of records with client/patient permission: (a) to protect a client from harm or (b) to prevent misuse or misinterpretation of the data. Dr. L. considers whether the context of Mr. M.'s situation would warrant Dr. L. withholding the evaluation even after Mr. M. has requested its release.

Decision-Making Factors. Dr. L. thinks about other cases in which he has considered not releasing test data even with the consent or the wishes of the adult client. He has encountered individuals in divorce or custody cases who wanted release of their evaluations thinking that they could select information from the report and withhold other information. Dr. L. has found that most individuals, when learning that select release is not likely or that once consent is given and that control of the content is significantly weakened, rethink their willingness to voluntarily release test data. On occasion, Dr. L. has seen couples who were divorcing who agreed to release data because one party thinks the other party would be cast in a negative light. Again, in such situations Dr. L. would clarified for them that information about both would be released and that the perspective taken by third parties cannot be accurately anticipated. In these and other test data release questions, Dr. L. has found that most people are much more circumspect about releasing their data when they understand the implications and possible consequences.

In addition to the ethical concerns about releasing the test data, Dr. L. has a very uneasy feeling about the law firm's use of the test data. Even though many reasonable qualities and characteristics that contribute to a successful position placement can be gleaned from the personnel evaluation, Dr. L. speculates that mental health, chronic conditions, temperament, Axis I or II diagnosis, insurance cost–benefit ratios, sick day use, and other benefits that result in a negative effect for the company would be decision-making factors regarding employment.

Dr. L. thinks that Mr. M. understands the potential for misuse or misinterpretation of his evaluation by the law firm, but at the same time, Mr. M. takes pride in his personal successes and believes that his achievements of the last 2 years would be seen as evidence of his commitment to recovery and to making a contribution even in the face of adversity. This is one of the only times that Dr. L., after a candid discussion with a client, finds that the client still disagrees with him regarding release of test data. Dr. L. considers that Mr. M. is proud of his progress and he perceives that Mr. M.'s satisfaction in gaining control of his drinking may play a part in his optimism over the way his accomplishment would be perceived.

Decision Options. This case is unusual for Dr. L. in that typically when he explains the possible pros and cons of releasing test data and explains how the information can be disseminated, clients become more circumspect about releasing data. In this case, Dr. L. has explained the possibilities, and Mr. M. still wishes to release the information. Dr. L. consults with the colleague who had conducted the original assessment, and the colleague agrees that any personnel decisions made from that assessment could represent inappropriate interpretations.

Dr. L. decides that although his not releasing the test data could significantly impact his therapeutic relationship with Mr. M., in good conscience he needs to do so. Dr. L. prepares to work with Mr. M. on termination and will endeavor to avoid a breach in their relationship. Dr. L. is aware that if he does release the information and it is used in a detrimental way by the law firm, his therapeutic relationship with Mr. M. could also suffer. Dr. L. does not have the same reservations regarding access to case notes and psychological evaluation by the new treating psychologist and, in fact, thinks sharing this information could be helpful to clients. Dr. L. considers the relevance of these two exceptions to Mr.'s case and decided that each might be applicable. Nonetheless, Dr. L. realizes that were Mr. M. to pursue obtaining the data he could almost certainly do so in asserting his legal right. For this reason,

Dr. L. decides to both have an in-person discussion with Mr. M. about the possible consequences and to write him a letter so that he will have a written documentation in consideration of Dr. L.'s reasoning.

Standard 9.05, Test Construction

Psychologists who develop tests and other assessment techniques use appropriate psychometric procedures and current scientific or professional knowledge for test design, standardization, validation, reduction or elimination of bias, and recommendations for use.

The psychometric soundness of test materials and procedures that psychologists use in evaluation is a fundamentally important aspect of assessment. Psychologists must realize their responsibility in making determinations that affect individuals' diagnosis and treatment for health purposes, educational placement, employment, medication, legal judgments, and other decisions that impact individuals' lives. They should be mindful of the aspects of psychometric procedures that must be considered in order to ensure that testing materials are appropriate and may ask themselves the following questions:

- Are the testing materials equally appropriate for all populations? If not, how will the test materials be accurately described so that proper use is ensured?
- Does the manual or descriptive materials define and explain the proper use of the test, language specifications, interpretation of scores, application across diversity and demographic variables, and norms and any standardization of administration?
- Are the validity and reliability tests psychometrically sound?
- What is the intended use of the test, and what are the limitations and qualifications?
- Are there scientific research findings or professional clinical data that support the purpose and construction of the test?

These questions are not comprehensive or definitive, but they are examples of the concepts that psychologists may consider in development and use of test materials.

Standard 9.06, Interpreting Assessment Results

When interpreting assessment results, including automated interpretations, psychologists take into account the purpose of the assessment as well as the various test factors, test-taking abilities, and other characteristics of the person being assessed, such as situational, personal, linguistic, and cultural differences, that might affect psychologists' judgments or reduce the accuracy of their interpretations. They indicate any significant limita-

tions of their interpretations. (See also Standards 2.01b and c, Boundaries of Competence, and 3.01, Unfair Discrimination.)

Psychologists are alert both to features of the test itself or the testing environment and characteristics of the examinee that might influence psychologists' judgment or affect the accuracy of their interpretation of the test results:

- *Purpose.* The psychometric description of instruments will define the purpose of tests, the administrative procedure, scoring, and interpretation. Psychologists make sure that the reason for evaluation of the client/patient and the questions posed are congruent with the purpose of the test and that the questions asked can be answered with the selected test. Psychologists should be mindful that tests are to be used with the expectation that they will yield information that is relevant for the purpose of the evaluation.
- *Test factors.* The testing environment and the factors related to the testing context can have an effect on the test procedure, results, and subsequent interpretation. Psychologists should be alert to any conditions in the environment (e.g., noise, lighting problems, temperature, space) or with testing materials (e.g., missing pieces, supplies, stopwatches) that could affect the accuracy of the interpretation.
- *Test-taking abilities.* Characteristics of the examinee during administration contribute to the behavioral observations made by the examiner. These factors may include coping strategies, distractibility, expressions of frustration, fatigue, persistence, motivation, and adaptation to new concepts. These and other variables should be appropriately factored into the psychological report because the examinee's characteristics are relevant to learning and performance. Psychologists continue to be alert, however, to any characteristics that may affect their perception unfairly or differentially and therefore may effect interpretation of information.
- *Examinee characteristics.* Language, cultural/ethnic origin, gender, age, and other demographics may be factors in testing performance. Psychologists should be aware of normative factors, standardization, language difficulties, speech or hearing difficulties, or any other variables that could affect the examinee's performance and the psychologist's subsequent interpretation.

This standard calls on psychologists to be mindful of any factors in the testing process that could affect their judgment, resulting in bias or inaccurate interpretations. A valued skill in assessment is the competence to select and conduct testing with instruments, materials, protocol, and procedures that are applied with equivalence to all examinees (or to explain the differences) and to then apply the results very individualistically, factoring in clinical interviews, the impact of the testing environment, examinee characteristics, background, interpersonal style, prior testing, records, and other information that culminates in the interpretation and recommendations.

Assessments may easily be affected by limitations either in the application of the instruments, factors related to the examinees, test environment, access to significant information, normative parameters, psychometric factors, and other variables. The challenge to and the commitment of psychologists are to be aware of limitations and to properly include them in the psychological report. They also include any aspect of interpretation in which accuracy or the judgment of the psychologist may be at risk.

Standard 9.07, Assessment by Unqualified Persons

Psychologists do not promote the use of psychological assessment techniques by unqualified persons, except when such use is conducted for training purposes with appropriate supervision. (See also Standard 2.05, Delegation of Work to Others.)

Psychologists may have authority over assessment activities in which they do not conduct all aspects of the evaluation themselves. In these circumstances, psychologists must accept the responsibility for ensuring the qualifications of others. These individuals are typically either employees who are not trained or licensed to conduct assessments independently or trainees. Psychologists who delegate work to others under their authority or who accept the role of supervisor for training purposes realize that they are still responsible for the work product. Standard 2.05 is applicable to this standard in that psychologists also are mindful of any multiple relationships others may have, of the competence of the individuals to whom they are delegating work, and to monitor that others do perform their work competently. The licensed psychologist is likely to be the person to sign any report and to render final opinions and recommendations. This action presents to clients/patients and to the public the impression that the psychologist is responsible for the assessment document. This responsibility underscores the importance of vigilance and oversight by psychologists when being accountable for the work of others.

Even though psychologists accept final responsibility for assessments, both employees and trainees must meet the appropriate level of competence and educational preparation for the tasks they are assigned. Employees and students may have exceptional competence and ability in psychological activities related to assessment that could be mistaken for training in evaluation. Employees should demonstrate specific skills and the requisite competence for the particular expectations of psychologists who are responsible for them. Students are by definition in training, yet they should have instruction and practice in assessment at the expected level of performance before conducting elements of an evaluation for decisional purposes. Psychologists should be reasonably careful in their decisions to assign levels of tasks to those whom they know have had the experience, education, and training to competently do the work.

Standard 9.07, Case 1

Case Illustration. A group of neuropsychologists have both a private practice and are on staff at the regional hospital. They need assistance with test administration and write-ups in their private practice. A psychometrist, Ms. S., who had worked 15 years doing testing for the county school system, applies for the job. Ms. S. has excellent recommendation letters and had an accomplished career before retiring. Her skill set for assessment is touted by those who know her, and she is recognized as most competent in her field. After conducting the interview, the psychologists are impressed; she talked confidently about her evaluation methods, and they like her interactive style. The psychology group is pleased and relieved to find such a capable person so readily available, and they hire her immediately. Two weeks into the job, one of the psychologists, Dr. P., begins noticing irregularities. Dr. P. had volunteered to give an orientation to Ms. S. and to work with her in becoming acclimated to the responsibilities of the job. Several psychologists in the group have begun to express concern to Dr. P. regarding Ms. S.'s practices. Some of her reports reflect a misinterpretation of the treatment plan; others fail to incorporate the important elements of the background and family history into the overarching summary and recommendation. Of great concern is her choice of instruments for some of the referral questions. Dr. P. meets with Ms. S. and approaches the concerns that have been voiced. Ms. S. is open to the feedback and to consideration of any problem, but she seems confused and uncertain about what Dr. P. is actually telling her. Dr. P. hopes that the discussion will correct the problems; however, 2 more weeks pass, and his colleagues are showing even greater concern on the same matters. Dr. P. meets again with Ms. S. and decides to review, along with her, two of the reports she has drafted. When they begin going through the first report, page by page, Dr. P. has a sinking feeling. He realizes that Ms. S. has been using a template for her choices of instruments, her format for the report, and her recommendations that are suitable for psychoeducational testing but not for neuropsychological testing. Even though she had indicated familiarity with some of the neuropsychological instruments, it becomes very clear in their review that she is not experienced in using these instruments and therefore the conceptualization from which neuropsychological testing must be considered is not within her methodology.

Ethical Dilemma. Dr. P. and the practice group have made a serious error. As they think back to Ms. S's initial interview, they realize that they were so pleased to have a strong candidate that they had not asked questions with the level of specificity necessary. Ms. S. was, as she had said, truly an expert in educational testing for learning disabilities, attention-deficit problems, phonological deficits, and other learning specific tests appropriate to educational settings. There was enough overlap in the interview discussion with memory scales and processing speed that the group had made a leap that she then would be familiar with more specific tests of memory, motor speed, and executive functioning as well as with other neuropsychological tests, most of which require specialized training. Dr. P. had always thought of Standard 9.07 in application to individuals who are not skilled and do not have an adequate knowledge base. In this case, however, Ms. S. is skilled and competent, and she has expertise, but she is unqualified for this particular type of testing. To make matters worse, Dr. P. realizes that a conceptual framework exists with testing domains and that Ms. S.'s thinking is conceptually more congruent with education purposes. This predicament also causes Dr. P. to think about Ms. S.'s ability to interpret assessment results (Standard 9.06). She is quite capable of learning, but for her to participate in testing with her current level of knowledge would call Standard 9.07 into question. The additional training necessary would take a considerable amount of time. Dr. P. sadly realizes that the practice has put Ms. S. in a very difficult situation. She had not deceived or misrepresented herself in any way. The evolving nature of assessment serves as a reminder for Dr. P. and the practice that competencies are a fluid and changing construct.

Decision-Making Factors. Dr. P and the group practice realize that with all good intentions, they had overlooked the emerging differences in areas of assessment given the specializations and practice domains that continue to develop and become individualized. Ms. S. is not unqualified to do psycho-educational testing and in fact has expertise in learning disabilities; attention-deficit difficulties; and other specific processing areas, such as achievement, cognitive evaluation, oral and written language, and visual–auditory learning. A reasonable degree of shared domain exists, in particular in memory and some executive functioning; however, for Ms. S. to competently do the preparatory work the group needs for neuropsychological testing she would need additional training and would need to be able to shift her perspective in conceptualization and interpretation. Dr. P. and the group know that they need to make decisions about the work already done by Ms. S. and to decide how they will go forward. The accurate assessment of Ms. S.'s competencies and skills will be a factor in deciding how to proceed.

Decision Options. Dr. P. and his group want to act professionally and ethically in their treatment of Ms. S., in their regard for their clients, and in the importance of accuracy in their testing recommendations. They realize that the testing that had been done would need to be reviewed and possibly revised. The group did not know of the problem at the time of assigning the evaluations, so Dr. P. thinks that if he and the group recall the evaluations and revise them, for no additional fee, the ethical aspect of the activity would be addressed.

Dr. P. and the group discuss offering Ms. S. either additional training or transition time to acquire another job. They decide they will invest in additional training and additional resources for Ms. S. to remain with the group and to learn the additional skills, if she is interested. Dr. P. resolves to meet with Ms. S. and to explain to her the circumstance in which they find themselves and to discuss the possibilities with her. He will further explain to her his professional and ethical concerns both for the clients and about the treatment of her and her professional participation. He thinks it important that he convey respect for Ms. S.'s skills and not portray the concern as being about her general competency. Standard 9.07 addresses the expectation for qualifications of those conducting testing, but also applicable, in this case, is General Principle E: Respect for People's Rights and Dignity.

Psychological assessment has evolved in recent years to include a much broader and specific range of purpose and method in testing. Custody evaluation, competency, workers' compensation, disability, psychoeducational, mental health status, diagnostic classification and treatment, forensic assessment, neuropsychological testing, and industrial and organizational management personnel appraisal are just a few of the assessment domains that represent the proliferation of psychological assessment services. Dr. P. is stunned as he thinks about the myriad purposes for evaluation that call for very different conceptualizations, instrument selection, interpretation, recommendations, and placements. He and his group realize that ethical behavior requires a significant level of attention and thinking through the purpose and nature of evaluation and matching the skills and competence of the individuals who can fulfill the expectations.

Standard 9.08, Obsolete Tests and Outdated Test Results

Standard 9.08(a) directs psychologists' attention to the potential for changes related to the examinee that may affect the validity of the test results, and Standard 9.08(b) alerts psychologists to the ramifications of choosing newer editions versus earlier editions of instruments. Both describe the decisions psychologists make in determining the best choice for when and how often to test an examinee and what instruments are the best choices to yield the data needed to answer the assessment questions. Furthermore, psychologists should note that the criteria for decisions under both standards are use for "the current purpose"; that is, a primary factor in decisions of instrument selection is first defining the current purpose. Subsequent decisions regarding instruments, clinical and collateral interviews, record review, and other elements of the evaluation will stem from the identified current purpose.

Standard 9.08(a)

Psychologists do not base their assessment or intervention decisions or recommendations on data or test results that are outdated for the current purpose.

Psychologists should determine the current purpose of an assessment on the basis of the need for case decisions (e.g., custody, educational placement, psychological treatment) or status determination (e.g., diagnostic classification, attention-deficit problems, cognitive impairment). Once the current purpose is determined psychologists decide to use existing data or to conduct additional assessment. Some of the concepts that psychologists may consider in making this decision include the following:

- Does the purpose call for a comparison of performance, skill, ability, or other variables either across time, in different settings, or in other comparative circumstances? If so, then psychologists may consider using both existing data and newly acquired data.
- Are the stability and reliability of performance, skill, or other variables in question? If so, then psychologists may consider use of both earlier and newly acquired data.
- Is current functioning a primary consideration for educational, job, or other placement purposes? If so, then currently acquired data may be preferred.
- Does the test manual cite psychometric limits or purpose of the test that would preclude use of earlier data?

Standard 9.08(b)

Psychologists do not base such decisions or recommendations on tests and measures that are obsolete and not useful for the current purpose.

Obsolescence is determined not by recency of test development but by the application of the test to the current purpose. Psychologists often must make decisions such as choosing between earlier and later versions of the same instrument or choosing to use an older instrument for which there has been no revision. Professional judgment should be used in determining the instruments that are most relevant and valid and that serve the purpose of the assessment. There are several factors that psychologists may take into consideration:

- Has the earlier version lost psychometric effectiveness or efficacy for use in any context?

- Which test demonstrates the most relevance and validity for the specific population being tested, and is there reason to think that a particular version of a test will most fairly and equitably meet the current purpose?
- Are the normative data appropriate for the population being tested?
- Are the stability and reliability of an older instrument's psychometric measures more valuable compared with newer instruments that have relatively sparse psychometric measures?
- Which instrument is based on the most appropriate theoretical underpinnings for the current purpose?
- Does the longitudinal nature or comparative needs of a research project render an earlier version of a test more applicable, and would a newer version introduce more extraneous variables, counterbalancing any benefits of using the newer instrument?

Expense, convenience, or additional training needs are not acceptable reasons to use obsolete versions or instruments that are not useful for the purpose. Psychologists should use the most advanced and psychometrically sound instruments available and not base decisions on these aforementioned factors.

Standard 9.09, Test Scoring and Interpretation Services

Standard 9.09(a) identifies ethical aspects of testing services for psychologists who offer services to other psychologists. Standards 9.09(b) and 9.09(c) provide guidance for psychologists who use test scoring and interpretation services. In both roles, psychologists accept the responsibility for the process and the product that they offer to other psychologists, institutional entities, or the public.

Standard 9.09(a)
Psychologists who offer assessment or scoring services to other professionals accurately describe the purpose, norms, validity, reliability, and applications of the procedures and any special qualifications applicable to their use.

Psychologists who provide testing services to other psychologists must equip them with psychometric, administrative and procedural, contextual, and application information that will fully prepare psychologists to properly use the services. These materials are provided as manuals, test materials, or other documents that describe the purpose and application for the service as well as the normative parameters, validity, and reliability measures. The service information should also include specific description of the application of the services and limitations of application, such as diversity (e.g., age, ethnicity, disabilities), language, reading level or other educational parameters, and generalizability.

Standard 9.09(b)

Psychologists select scoring and interpretation services (including automated services) on the basis of evidence of the validity of the program and procedures as well as on other appropriate considerations. (See also Standard 2.01b and c, Boundaries of Competence.)

Psychologists who use assessment services will likely have several from which to choose. Two important aspects of making this choice are (a) the soundness of the program itself in regard to psychometric properties and (b) the applicability to the specific current purpose and variables that describe the individual and define the assessment questions. A service may offer a scoring and interpretation package that has strong psychometric properties and is very marketable but does not fit the purpose or needs of the populations being assessed. A service may also offer a package that seems to be an excellent fit for the psychologists' purposes but does not demonstrate adequate validity and reliability. Psychologists should use their professional judgment in deciding on services that engender confidence that the data do in fact represent the fairest, most accurate, and useful profile of the information provided.

Standard 9.09(c)

Psychologists retain responsibility for the appropriate application, interpretation, and use of assessment instruments, whether they score and interpret such tests themselves or use automated or other services.

Psychologists who authorize or coordinate assessments accept responsibility for all aspects of evaluation, including interview and data collection, administration, scoring, interpretation, write-up, and the final report or recommendations. Even though psychologists may employ services that perform aspects of the evaluation, the authorizing psychologists retain the responsibility for all content of the report and the disposition of the results. Furthermore, psychologists who are providing these professional services in assessment have acquired the training necessary to conduct aspects of assessment themselves and be competent to cross-check automated and service-provided information to ensure accuracy.

Psychologists are mindful of several other aspects of scoring and interpretation service use as well:

- Services should announce changes in their software or service systems, such as updates, resolved and unresolved problems, revision information, and other modifications that enable psychologists to have current access to the program.

- Psychologists are alert to disparities in the provided data and their own clinical information and make reasonable attempts to correct any incongruencies.
- Copyright restrictions may be applicable in using commercial service products; psychologists will want to be aware of the copyright status of any material they use.
- Psychologists conceptually view an evaluation through a comprehensive perspective and therefore are committed to issuing opinions, reports, and recommendations that reflect the integration of individualized information such as clinical interviews, background information, presenting concerns, health status, prior testing, and other information that will render an accurate and valid interpretation.

Standard 9.10, Explaining Assessment Results

Regardless of whether the scoring and interpretation are done by psychologists, by employees or assistants, or by automated or other outside services, psychologists take reasonable steps to ensure that explanations of results are given to the individual or designated representative unless the nature of the relationship precludes provision of an explanation of results (such as in some organizational consulting, preemployment or security screenings, and forensic evaluations), and this fact has been clearly explained to the person being assessed in advance.

When psychologists form opinions of individuals that result in reports and recommendations that affect their lives, they should be committed to explaining the results of the assessment to those individuals. Some of the valuable factors that may be included in the explanation are the actual results, what they mean, how they will be used, what the effect will be for the individuals, and any short- or long-term consequences. The individuals also should be given an opportunity to ask questions and achieve clarity, if reasonably possible, about the effect of the evaluation on their lives. Psychologists themselves are not required to directly provide the explanation; the persons who had primary contact with the client/patient may have been trainees or employees. If the psychologists do not deliver the explanation themselves, they should ensure that the individual who does present the explanation is competent to do so.

When the examinee is not the client and is not the recipient of the explanation, psychologists must confirm and ensure, before conducting the assessment, that the examinee and other related parties are knowledgeable about who the client is and who will receive the results of the assessment. There are several reasons that the examinee may not be the client, in particular in organizational settings and forensic settings. Often, the examinee is not the client when employment, promotion, or program and institutional evaluations are conducted. Furthermore, in forensic settings the client is often the institution or court, for example, in fitness for duty, court-ordered testing for child custody or parental fitness, and evaluations of competency to stand trial. When distinguishing the examinee from the client is appropriate, psychologists should be mindful of the importance of explaining these roles and the resulting communication transactions before testing commences.

Standard 9.11, Maintaining Test Security

The term *test materials* refers to manuals, instruments, protocols, and test questions or stimuli and does not include *test data* as defined in Standard 9.04, Release of Test Data. Psychologists make reasonable efforts to maintain the integrity and security of test materials and other assessment techniques consistent with law and contractual obligations, and in a manner that permits adherence to this Ethics Code.

The integrity of psychological evaluation depends on the security, proper use of, and appropriate access to test materials. Psychologists and other professionals who have authorized access to test materials must accept the obligation to secure and protect materials that they acquire. Test construction and development of sound psychometric properties for a test is time and labor intensive; thus, testing corporations have proprietary policies and copyright privileges for many frequently used instruments. Standard 9.04 describes conditions of the release of test data, and psychologists become aware that *test material* may be converted to *test data* simply by the entrance of examinee information on the test material. Laws, regulations, and contractual obligations may limit psychologists' ability to maintain security.

When test data and test material are merged because of protocol format or the recording of data, psychologists should use professional judgment in decisions regarding proper shared use of client/patient information. Psychologists remain committed to the protection of test material, yet often the court, schools, and others involved in a placement, diagnostic, employment, or treatment decision regarding an examinee request aspects of the test data in addition to reports and recommendations that can reasonably be constructed separately from test material. When psychologists must make a determination on how to proceed when test security and request for information are in conflict, they may consider several factors. First, psychologists may request to send information only to others who are professionally competent to understand and respect test security. Second, if the request is a court order, psychologists may request a protective order, which eliminates exposure of the test material to a broader judicial audience and permits restrictive use in court. Last, prior to the inception of the testing, psychologists may attempt to record test data separately from test material.

Assessment is a domain of psychology in which the control of the evaluation product, supporting records, and collateral information is commonly needed and requested in order to successfully accomplish the purpose and outcome of evaluation. Psychologists who conduct assessments, whether educational, forensic, organizational, or clinical, should be mindful of the privilege and the responsibility they hold in conducting assessments within the context of respect and protection for test materials while meeting ethical commitments to their examinees and clients.

CONCLUSION

The ethical standards for assessment strive to be broad in application to the range of practice and to the emerging areas. The commentary in this chapter, along with the case illustrations, is intended to guide psychologists through the ethical implications of the stages of assessment and evaluation:

- Preparation for assessment includes identifying criteria for materials (Standard 9.02), guidance for assembly of materials (Standard 9.05), and criteria for determination of applicability of materials (Standard 9.08).
- Engagement with clients cites parameters for informed consent.
- Assessment procedures are asserted through description of conducting assessments (Standard 9.01), method for interpreting results (Standard 9.06), and procedure for explaining results (Standard 9.10).
- The use and treatment of data are identified in determining the circumstances of data release (Standard 9.04), differentiating between test data and test materials (Standard 9.11), outlining the importance of qualifications (Standard 9.07), and use of scoring and interpretation services.

Assessment is a dynamic core domain of psychology and contributes significantly to psychologists' professional identity. The established and the emerging areas of assessment include forensic assessments, educational testing, neuropsychological testing, diagnostic evaluations, and industrial and organizational and consulting assessment. Because these and other areas of assessment are rapidly growing, many conventional assessment practices of today were unknown 20 years ago, and in years to come, there will certainly be a need for assessment and evaluation in areas of psychology that have yet to emerge.

10

THERAPY

Section 10 of the 2002 American Psychological Association's (APA's) "Ethical Principles of Psychologists and Code of Conduct"(hereinafter the *APA Ethics Code* or the *Ethics Code;* see (http://www.apa.org/ethics/code 2002.html)[1] applies to therapy and therapeutic relationships. The general term *therapy* is used to apply to all dimensions of health intervention, such as psychotherapy, counseling, analysis, behavioral analysis, crisis intervention, career counseling, and other therapeutic interventions. All of the APA Ethics Code's general principles support the standards in this section. General Principle A: Beneficence and Nonmaleficence is relevant because it decrees that psychologists should actively work to benefit their therapy clients/patients and avoid harming them. General Principle B: Fidelity and Responsibility speaks to the importance of acting in ways that promote trust in the therapeutic relationship and of psychologists' accepting responsibility for their own behavior. Psychologists value honesty and truthfulness in their transactions and interactions with others and are responsible for keeping the best interests of their clients/patients primary, according to General Principle C: Integrity. General

---

[1]American Psychological Association. (2002). Ethical principles of psychologists and code of conduct. *American Psychologist, 57,* 1060–1073.

Principle D: Justice is relevant because it encourages psychologists to be mindful of their responsibility to promote and protect the right of all persons to fairness in access to psychological services and in access to benefits. General Principle E: Respect for People's Rights and Dignity is reflected in various provisions, especially those involving informed consent and the importance of respect for people's privacy, confidentiality, and self-determination. General Principle E also reflects the importance of respecting differences, including those based on age, gender, gender identity, race, ethnicity, culture, national origin, religion, sexual orientation, disability, language, and socioeconomic status.

Standard 10.01 describes the specific informed-consent provision involved in therapy with clients/patients. Standard 10.02 describes the requirement to inform clients/patients about the multiple-relationship issues that can surface when working with families or couples, and Standard 10.03 describes these requirements in regard to group therapy. Standard 10.04 addresses whether to offer or provide services to persons who are already receiving mental health services elsewhere. Standard 10.05 describes the clear prohibition of sexual intimacies with current therapy clients/patients, and Standard 10.06 likewise describes the clear prohibition of sexual intimacies with relatives or significant others of current therapy clients/patients. Standard 10.07 prohibits psychologists from providing therapy to former sexual partners, and Standard 10.08 addresses sexual intimacies with former therapy clients/patients. Standard 10.09 describes the expectations for interruption of therapy, and Standard 10.10 addresses termination of therapy.

The therapy section of the Ethics Code may be viewed as thematically clustered. Standard 10.01, Informed Consent to Therapy, is a foundational concept in the Ethics Code and has correlates within three other sections (i.e., Standard 3.10, Informed Consent; Standard 8.02, Informed Consent to Research; and Standard 9.03, Informed Consent in Assessments). Standards 10.02 (Therapy Involving Couples or Families), 10.03 (Group Therapy), and 10.04 (Providing Therapy to Those Served by Others) represent the format or category of the recipients of services. Standards 10.05 (Sexual Intimacies With Current Therapy Clients/Patients), 10.06 (Sexual Intimacies With Relatives or Significant Others of Current Therapy Clients/Patients), 10.07 (Therapy With Former Sexual Partners), and 10.08 (Sexual Intimacies With Former Therapy Clients/Patients) represent psychologists' behaviors regarding sexual intimacies. The final two standards—10.09 (Interruption of Therapy) and 10.10 (Terminating Therapy)—focus on the termination of therapy.

Standard 10.01, Informed Consent to Therapy

This standard has three components that address informed consent and are designed to guide psychologists in providing information that helps clients/patients (a) understand the structure of the relationship, (b) under-stand the nature of treatment and risks when recognized techniques and pro-cedures have not been established, and (c) know the name of the therapist's supervisor when the therapist is a trainee.

Standard 10.01(a)

When obtaining informed consent to therapy as required in Standard 3.10, Informed Consent, psychologists inform clients/patients as early as is feasible in the therapeutic relationship about the nature and anticipated course of therapy, fees, involvement of third parties, and limits of confiden-tiality and provide sufficient opportunity for the client/patient to ask ques-tions and receive answers. (See also Standards 4.02, Discussing the Limits of Confidentiality, and 6.04, Fees and Financial Arrangements.)

Informed consent is a foundational concept in the APA Ethics Code. It is first defined and discussed in Standard 3.10, Informed Consent. General Principle E: Respect for People's Rights and Dignity—specifically, the element of respect for the right of self-determination—is the heart of informed con-sent. Self-determination cannot adequately be honored unless informed con-sent is also valued. Informed consent is a process, not a moment in time, and it is foundational to the trust within the relationship between psychologists and clients/patients. Informed consent regarding treatment decisions and the implications of treatment stems from respect for the rights and dignity of the individuals with whom psychologists work. The concept of informed consent has evolved over time across ethics subject matter in psychology and other pro-fessions, including legal and biomedical ethics. The current perspective is the result of decades in which the professional therapist–client/patient relation-ship has been viewed in evolving ways. When it is clear that the client/patient is not capable of understanding informed consent, other ethical obligations are triggered. When older or medically compromised individuals are not able to provide consent, psychologists pursue other avenues (e.g., authorization from a guardian) and are aware of other legal elements, including knowledge of laws and statutes in one's own jurisdiction.

Standard 10.01 requires that several issues be discussed and that this dis-cussion occur at the beginning of therapy or as early as feasible. If a client is in crisis, obtaining informed consent in the first session may not be feasible, or it may be clinically contraindicated. In addition, the process of therapeutic informed consent may be ongoing as new information and issues arise.

The list of areas relating to informed consent must be discussed, and a sufficient opportunity to ask questions and receive answers is required. Many other topics may also be appropriate for discussion. Topics that psychologists should discuss with clients/patients include the nature and anticipated course of therapy (e.g., information about the therapeutic process, duration of sessions, goals of treatment, number of sessions), fees (e.g., expected cost of therapy, including the psychologist's fee, and/or client/patient deductibles and co-payments if insurance or organized health care or managed care system is to be used; types of reimbursement accepted; payment schedule; policies regarding missed appointments), involvement of third parties (previous therapists; primary care physicians; family members; legal guardians; health insurance companies; employers; organizations; or legal, military, or other authorities), and limits of confidentiality (confidentiality is provided except in cases involving mandated child or elder abuse reporting or duty to warn or protect; see Standard 4.02c, Discussing the Limits of Confidentiality). Psychologists are also encouraged to provide sufficient time and opportunity for client/patient questions and for therapist response and discussion about any aspect of therapy, and this process may continue throughout the therapeutic experience. More general information regarding this standard is referred to in Standards 3.10, Informed Consent; 4.02, Discussing the Limits of Confidentiality; and 6.04, Fees and Financial Arrangements.

As required by Standard 3.10(a), the information should be presented in language that is reasonably understandable to the client/patient. As required by Standard 3.10(d), consent may be written or oral, but in any case it must be documented by the psychologist.

Standard 10.01(b)

When obtaining informed consent for treatment for which generally recognized techniques and procedures have not been established, psychologists inform their clients/patients of the developing nature of the treatment, the potential risks involved, alternative treatments that may be available, and the voluntary nature of their participation. (See also Standards 2.01e, Boundaries of Competence, and 3.10, Informed Consent.)

This is a new standard in the APA Ethics Code that recognizes that there are potential risks and benefits to clients/patients of new therapeutic techniques, even if specific documented benefits and adverse effects are not known. Standard 10.01(b) also recognizes that innovation in the use of new, experimental, or innovative techniques in mental health services is critical to serve a diverse public. However, when providing such techniques psychologists respect the clients/patients by informing them of the experimental nature of the treatment, including the potential risks and benefits, and letting them know of other, more standardized treatments that may be available. The voluntary nature of the client/patients' participation must be determined, and their right to choose more traditional treatments should be clear. Standards 2.01(e), Boundaries of Competence, and 3.10, Informed Consent, are also relevant to this standard.

The 1992 Ethics Code[2] standard that addressed this issue, 1.04(c), conceptualized the issue primarily as one of competency:

> In those emerging areas in which generally recognized standards for preparatory training do not yet exist, psychologists nevertheless take reasonable steps to ensure the competence of their work and to protect patients, clients, students, research participants, and others from harm. (p. 1600)

Although this previous version of the APA Ethics Code addressed the importance of informed consent, it primarily focused on psychologists' responsibility to address problems in a competent manner and to protect clients/patients and others from harm. Those responsibilities are still implied, but the emphasis has shifted to the importance of informed consent.

Standard 10.01(c)

When the therapist is a trainee and the legal responsibility for the treatment provided resides with the supervisor, the client/patient, as part of the informed consent procedure, is informed that the therapist is in training and is being supervised and is given the name of the supervisor.

Clients/patients must be informed whenever the therapist is a trainee and the supervisor is legally responsible for that therapist's professional actions. Information that should be provided includes identification of the therapist as a trainee and his or her role as such as well as the fact that the trainee is being supervised and the identity of the supervisor.

This standard reflects the importance of General Principle E: Respect for People's Rights and Dignity because it states that clients have a right to self-determination, including information regarding the qualifications of their provider as well as the identity of the individuals who will have access to their disclosures. Although the standard does not require written disclosure of the trainee's status and supervisor's identity, it may be prudent to obtain acknowledgement in writing that the client/patient has received this information.

Standard 10.02, Therapy Involving Couples or Families

This standard underscores the importance of taking reasonable steps to clarify who the client is and the relationship the psychologist will have with each person involved when couples or families are the recipients of therapeutic services. The standard also provides guidance in addressing potential conflicting roles, should they arise. Doing so helps to avoid harm (General Principle A: Beneficence and Nonmaleficence), promotes trust (General Principle B: Fidelity and Responsibility), and conveys responsibility for keeping the best

---

[2]American Psychological Association. (1992). Ethical principles of psychologists and code of conduct. *American Psychologist, 47*, 1597–1611.

interest of clients as primary (General Principle C: Integrity). Clarification is also a way to promote fairness and to ensure that potential biases do not lead to unjust practices (General Principle D: Justice), and clarification conveys respect for the dignity and worth of each person (General Principle E: Respect for People's Rights and Dignity).

Standard 10.02(a)

When psychologists agree to provide services to several persons who have a relationship (such as spouses, significant others, or parents and children), they take reasonable steps to clarify at the outset (1) which of the individuals are clients/patients and (2) the relationships the psychologist will have with each person. This clarification includes the psychologist's role and the probable uses of the services provided or the information obtained. (See also Standard 4.02, Discussing the Limits of Confidentiality.)

This standard describes the informed-consent requirements when the clients/patients being treated have ongoing relationships with each other outside of the therapeutic context, such as formal family or marital therapy or collateral contacts, such as limited contacts with family members in support of the treatment of an individual. The standard requires that the psychologist take reasonable steps to clarify several issues and that the discussion occur early in the beginning of the joint meetings. The first area of clarification involves deciding which of the individuals are clients/patients, and the second involves clarification of the relationship that the psychologist will have with each person involved, including the role of confidentiality and privacy, especially when working with minors, and the role of secrets in family or couples therapy.

Standard 3.10(a), Informed Consent, has a corresponding purpose to Standard 3.07, Third-Party Requests for Services, in that both alert psychologists to the multiplicity of relationships involved in the therapeutic context; that is, psychologists are aware not only of the nature of their relationship to the identified client/patients but also of the fact that the clients/patients have relationships with each other. The complexity of the relationship matrix could complicate psychologists' therapeutic work. Standard 3.11(a)(3) and 3.11(a)(4) also identify the importance of knowing, within the multiplicity of relationships, who the clients/patients are, who the collaterals are, and what relationship the psychologists will have with each person and the organization.

The psychologist's approach to treatment, including whether he or she will conduct individual, conjoint sessions, or both, and how frequently sessions will occur, is also important to clarify. In addition, the psychologist may need to clarify in an ongoing manner the goals of treatment because each member of a family may have different treatment goals. For example, one member of a couple may have entered therapy to try to salvage a marriage, whereas the other partner may be in therapy as part of the process of dissolution of the marriage.

The role of privacy and confidentiality can be confusing in couples and family therapy, and although theoretical information should inform psychologists' decisions regarding keeping secrets versus not keeping secrets, this standard simply requires that therapists attempt to clarify the policy regarding family secrets at the beginning and throughout the process of therapy.

State law often determines confidentiality rules for minors. Most states allow for the parents/guardians of minors to have access to information generated from treatment. However, psychologists often negotiate agreements to withhold private information to allow minors a greater sense of privacy and thus encourage the therapeutic process. Psychologists are encouraged to be candid with parents and perhaps provide examples at the outset of therapy about what kind of sensitive information may be withheld, such as drug use or sexual activity. A limit of confidentiality is a situation in which the psychologist believes it necessary to break confidentiality if he or she determines the presence of danger to the patient/client's self or others. Judgment on the part of the psychologist is an important factor as to when high-risk behavior on the part of the minor reaches the threshold of dangerous. Standard 4.02, Discussing the Limits of Confidentiality, also is relevant here.

Standard 10.02(b)

If it becomes apparent that psychologists may be called on to perform potentially conflicting roles (such as family therapist and then witness for one party in divorce proceedings), psychologists take reasonable steps to clarify and modify, or withdraw from, roles appropriately. (See also Standard 3.05c, Multiple Relationships.)

One area in which an ethical dilemma can easily arise is when a psychologist is working with a couple or family who then becomes involved in litigation involving divorce, child custody, and child abuse allegations. The psychologist may then be asked by one or both parties to testify on their behalf, or he or she may be served with a court order to serve as a fact witness for the legal matter. This standard requires that the psychologist address potentially conflicting roles as soon as it becomes apparent that he or she may be called on to perform them. The emphasis in this standard is that the psychologist takes "reasonable" steps to clarify, modify, or withdraw from roles appropriately. *Clarifying* the potentially conflicting roles might consist of explaining what the roles are, in what ways they might conflict, and what effects such a conflict might have on the therapy. *Adjusting* roles might involve changing from being a couple's therapist to being the individual therapist for one member of the couple, if that is clinically indicated and not problematic for all involved. *Withdrawing* from an existing role may be an option, but this has to be balanced with the risk of the client/patient feeling abandoned by the psychologist. The psychologist might also simply decline to accept the new role.

As in all multiple relationships, a request to serve in a dual capacity risks impairing a psychologist's performance of one or both professional roles; specifically at risk are potential problems with objectivity and feelings of betrayal in the therapeutic relationship. (See Standard 3.05c, Multiple Relationships, for similar requirements to clarify role expectations and the risks involved in serving more than one role with a client/patient.)

Standard 10.02(a), Case 1

Case Illustration. Dr. C. provides professional services primarily to families and adolescents. He understands the difficulties in balancing ethical practices when working with minors, including confidentiality, mandatory reporting, and informed consent. Dr. C. has developed a fully explanatory informed-consent agreement for parents to sign and for minors to review. He makes the discussion of informed consent part of his intake interview and explains to families the conditions of the informed consent. Dr. C. provides for assent, including the request for privacy for the minor, despite the fact that the parents have legal rights to the session content in most cases. Dr. C.'s view is that confidentiality through informed consent and throughout the therapeutic process is vital to the success of therapy. As a result, he explains to families that confidentiality within the family therapy sessions is of utmost importance. He is careful to identify the limits of confidentiality, providing examples of relative harm to self or others and a proposal to negotiate mutual expectations among family members and him regarding privacy in those kinds of situations.

Dr. C. begins to see Family A for several presenting reasons, including stress from work of both parents. They have been receiving negative reports from their 8-year-old son's teacher about misbehavior and fighting at school. The parents are also quite concerned about their 15-year-old daughter because of her grades, her moodiness, and her isolation from friends and activities at school. After several weeks of family therapy, the parents privately report to Dr. C. that their daughter seems to be getting more despondent and uncommunicative. She talks easily with Dr. C. and seems to like him. They hope that Dr. C. will see her separately while continuing to see the family.

Dr. C. agrees to see the daughter, thinking that she might be more disclosing and interactive without her parents there. A few weeks have passed since Dr. C. has begun to see the daughter, and he thinks they are working well together; she has begun to be more disclosing of her feelings and problems. Suddenly, Dr. C. receives a call from the father saying that the parents have heard rumors that their daughter is involved in sexual activity within a group of her peers at school. They want Dr. C. to weave questions into her sessions that would lead her to discuss this subject. When he rejects this idea, they began to pressure her for this information and begin making veiled comments during family therapy. They do not want to discuss this matter in front of the son, so they suggest that he not come to all of the family sessions.

At this point, Dr. C. begins to feel as though the therapy is unraveling. The son begins to feel marginalized and wants to start seeing Dr. C. individually as his sister has. He also comments that his parents are not as worried about him as they are about his sister and that he can do something about that, too. The parents begin to pressure Dr. C. to reveal the content of his sessions with the daughter. When he reminds them of the informed-consent agreement, they retort that they had agreed to that before they knew about the rumor regarding their daughter's behavior. They claim that he cannot hold them to that now. The daughter had thought that she could trust Dr. C., but now, realizing the access to Dr. C. that her parents have, and knowing they can be formidable and intimidating, she begins to have doubts about Dr. C. and becomes suspicious of the entire therapy process.

Ethical Dilemma. Dr. C. is faced with thinking through the application of several ethical standards in this situation. Standard 10.01 describes the elements of informed consent. Those elements that Dr. C. should consider include informing clients/patients of the nature of therapy, involvement of third parties, and the limits of confidentiality. Standard 4.02 (Discussing the Limits of Confidentiality) also is applicable. Each of these issues was discussed when informed consent was agreed on and each family member was present. Dr. C., however, describes the parents' involvement and access to confidential information as very limited because they had agreed to not inquire about specific content. Standard 10.02(a) requires psychologists to clarify which individuals are clients, the psychologist's relationship with each person, the role of the psychologist, and use of information obtained. A parallel to Standard 10.02(a) exists in Standard 3.07 (Third-Party Requests for Services), which also applies in this situation because the parents are third parties who requested services for their daughter, and according to this standard psychologists must clarify their roles, identify the clients/patients, and explain the use of information obtained. Dr. C. begins to question whether the changing requests and actions by the parents and the changing reactions of the daughter and son have inadvertently shifted him into a questionable ethical situation.

Decision-Making Factors. Dr. C. realizes that the informed consent seems to adequately explain the elements of these standards. Now, however, the parents are making requests for which they have legal authorization but that violate the informed-consent agreement. Dr. C. could be in a difficult position in regard to two issues: (a) making differential use of information obtained than was originally agreed on and (b) facing a shifting relationship with each person. All of the family members are clients, but given the dynamics within the family Dr. C's professional role with the son and the daughter is beginning to deteriorate because the son is aware of the dynamics between the parents and daughter and perceives favoritism toward the daughter over him by both his parents and the psychologist. The daughter also is privy to the exchanges between the parents and Dr. C., and she thinks they are determined to eventually wear Dr. C. down into giving them session information.

The fact that Dr. C. is conducting family therapy with all four family members gives each member access within the family sessions that would not have been the case had they been individual clients and the family members been collaterals; that is, the parents' participation in family therapy gives them access in that setting to bringing in their expectation for information about the daughter's activities. Because the daughter and son are also participants in the family therapy, they are unavoidably in circumstances of deciding whether and how to react. The daughter may feel entrapped, the son may think he is simply an observer in his sister's therapy, and Dr. C. may feel co-opted.

Dr. C. is faced not only with decisions about how to proceed ethically regarding the standards that apply but also with reacting to the changing dynamics within the family and the ongoing communication among the family members, all of whom are clients. Dr. C. has no control over, or participation in, how these interactions affect therapy with each member or the family as a whole. The relationship of Dr. C. with each person (Standard 10.02a[2]), his role, and the use of information obtained all appear to be changing, and it is important that he clarify these elements of the standards.

Decision Options. Dr. C. has several possibilities and several obligations in the evolving situation. He may consider re-establishing the role of therapist with the family as a whole, including addressing the son's developing feelings of marginalization. With the entire family present, Dr. C. might discuss the role of the therapist concerning each person who is a client/patient and the limits and extent of confidentiality within family therapy and between family and individual therapy as it applies to this family. Dr. C. may also rethink his roles as family therapist and individual therapist for the daughter; it may be that he cannot effectively carry out both of these roles. Many uncertainties regarding confidentiality have developed in particular with regard to the two children. Moreover, the son may have perceptions of what is happening among Dr. C., the parents, and his sister, and he may feel that he is being left out.

Dr. C. must also be concerned about the parents' shifting agreement regarding extent of confidentiality and the implications for the use of information obtained. Dr. C. may meet individually with the parents and explain that a violation of the consent agreement as the daughter understands it could mean a significant setback in her therapeutic work; her relationship with

Dr. C.; and her relationship with the parents in terms of trust, access, and continued viability of family therapy. Dr. C.'s explanation to the parents of these potential consequences and their understanding of the implications will be highly significant to the outcome of the situation.

Standard 10.02(a), Case 2

Case Illustration. Dr. M. specializes in working with adolescents who are identified as having behavioral problems. These problems could range from acting out; being oppositional; having peer difficulties; and having academic, parental, and/or school-related problems. The parents of a 14-year-old adolescent boy named Sam bring their son to Dr. M. for therapy. They have heard about Dr. M. and know of his successful treatment of adolescents. They tell Dr. M. they are at their wits' end with Sam and that, given what they have heard about Dr. M., trust in his abilities to help their son. They report that Sam is very unresponsive to them, stays in his room or goes out most of the time, and has friends they have not met and about whom Sam seems rather secretive. They are concerned about his withdrawal from them and his secretiveness, but they think these behaviors might be part of a stage he is going through. Sam's parents travel quite a bit for their respective professional careers. Sam is an only child, and his parents consider him old enough to be at home by himself. When they both have to travel overnight, Sam's grandmother, who lives nearby, stays with Sam and is generally available.

Sam's parents readily sign the informed-consent document, which includes very restrictive access to session content. Dr. M. is very committed to the principle that, unless a client/patient's life or the life of another person is at risk, or child abuse/neglect is a concern, all information between therapist and client/patient is to be kept confidential. Dr. M. is certain that this condition of therapy and his adolescent client/patients' awareness of his conviction are reasons for the success of his practice.

Sam's therapy with Dr. M. progresses, and he begins to trust Dr. M. Early on, he admits to occasional marijuana use. Dr. M. does not think that the circumstances or the frequency merit reconsideration of the confidentiality clause. In fact, Sam's parents had alluded to their suspicion of this activity but had not asked Dr. M. to monitor or report any knowledge. Dr. M. thinks that this information could best be woven into the therapy while maintaining confidentiality. As time goes on, Dr. M. becomes very concerned because Sam begins reporting that his friends, who are several years older than he and of the age of majority, are buying drugs and selling them for extra money. Sam states that he is not involved in this activity but has seen his friends involved in these transactions. As a few weeks go by, Sam's description of his activities clearly points to his involvement in the buying and selling of a variety of drugs, including cocaine and methamphetamine.

Dr. M. begins to feel conflicted about his confidentiality stance given the potential consequences of Sam's participation in illegal activity and given the risk that arises in the context of buying and selling illegal drugs. Dr. M. asks to meet with Sam's parents with the intention of probing them for any awareness they may have and their perception of what is happening in Sam's life. Sam's parents ask to have a conference by phone because it would be difficult for them to have time to meet in person. Dr. M. agrees, not having any choice, and is not able to get beyond a superficial exchange with Sam's parents. They express how grateful they are that their son is being taken care of by Dr. M. and say they have felt great relief since the therapeutic relationship had gotten underway. They report that Sam is very happy seeing Dr. M. and say that he feels very trusting of Dr. M. The parents say they consider this to be a breakthrough and just want Dr. M. to know that they support him continuing to do whatever he has been doing.

Ethical Dilemma. Dr. M. begins to be concerned about the role and function of confidentiality in his agreement with Sam's parents and in his therapeutic relationship with Sam. Standard 4.02(a) calls on psychologists to discuss the relevant limits of confidentiality with clients/patients and, in the case of minors, with legal representatives. Standard 4.02(a) also discusses the foreseeable use of the information generated through psychological activities. In this case, Dr. M. might wonder whether the legal and safety risks of Sam's activities should outweigh the importance of maintaining confidentiality. Similar to Standard 4.02(a), Standard 10.02(a) states that psychologists must clarify at the outset their role in the therapeutic relationship and the probable use of the information obtained through services. Also in the balance, however, is the question of whether a waiver of confidentiality, albeit justified, would precipitate a rupture in the therapeutic relationship that would result in irrevocable damage.

Decision-Making Factors. Dr. M. is in a difficult and confounding spot. Typically, he is faced with parents who want to know more than he thinks is appropriate or ethical. In this case, the parents do not ask any questions, do not want to know anything, do not ask for a progress report, and generally leave Dr. M. in a solitary role regarding Sam's welfare. Dr. M. even has a sense that the parents have shifted some responsibility for Sam onto him, without that ever having been said or inferred. Dr. M. has been accustomed to presenting a protective view of session information and typically emphasizes the importance of information staying within the therapeutic relationship.

Dr. M. has conveyed the appropriate application of confidentiality to Sam and his parents about typical and often-occurring adolescent behaviors. The informed consent could have been construed to imply that only a knowledge of activities that pose a high risk to self or others could compromise confidentiality. In this case, buying and selling drugs carries potential consequences of legal action that could result in imprisonment as well as safety concerns. Dr. M. could now be worried not just about the role and status of confidentiality but also about the sense that the parents have left Sam somewhat in Dr. M.'s care and that his role is inadvertently and unintentionally expanding from the provision of psychological services to one of greater responsibility for the client/patient. Dr. M. has not agreed to this role, but he now wonders, if Sam were injured or arrested in a drug transaction, could Dr. M. be culpable?

Decision Options. Dr. M. has gotten caught in a slippery slope situation in which his agreement to confidentiality regarding controlled and arguably minor violations that have escalated during the course of therapy and become much more serious in nature. Dr. M. values and protects his confidentiality stance with adolescents, knowing that this is a factor in the trust level that adolescents value and expect from him. In this case, Dr. M. might hope to preserve the therapeutic relationship and confront the escalating concern about Sam's legal and safety risks. Dr. M. could rather easily define these risks as ethical reasons for waiving confidentiality, but he is just as concerned about the effect on Sam; how to approach Sam's parents, who seem disconnected from their son's situation; and how this would affect Dr. M.'s continued relationship with Sam.

Dr. M. may meet with Sam and directly express his concerns in terms of Sam's actions, the implications of buying and selling illegal drugs, the possible legal consequences, and the safety risks of which Sam may be unaware. Redirecting the therapeutic content to these topics and processing the meaning with Sam could contribute to the maintenance of the therapeutic relationship. Furthermore, Dr. M. and Sam may discuss the reason for Sam's involvement in drug dealing; any reinforcement Sam may be getting from this activity; and, most important, how Dr. M. may help Sam extricate himself from this situation. Dr. M. already knows that part of this activity was an attempt to get attention and to belong. Dr. M. suspects that Sam feels more a part of this group of peers than he does a part of his family. Dr. M. could focus Sam's therapy on this need.

After processing this material with Sam, Dr. M. would likely want to meet with Sam's parents and be very forthcoming about the imminent legal and safety concerns. Just as important, Dr. M. would need to stress the need for the parents' involvement with Sam through more time spent together, their willingness to understand Sam's needs for his family at this time and, possibly, family therapy.

Standard 10.02(b), Case 1

Case Illustration. Dr. S. is part of a group practice in which he sees families, couples, and children. Currently he is seeing a couple who has three children: twin 8-year-old girls and a 10-year-old boy. The couple has several presenting problems but seems committed to working through their problems for the sake of their marriage and the children. The wife had had an affair the year prior but had broken off the relationship and wanted to work on the marriage. The husband continued to have a problem with gambling, although neither of them called it an addiction. He realized that the problem was affecting their marriage, family, and financial stability because he would spend an inordinate amount of his salary each month on gambling. At first, he only bet on horse races but then expanded into sports betting. They had other differences, including in disciplinary styles with the children, their preferences for spending time with friends and family, and career goals. Dr. S. has worked with the couple for 6 months, but both he and they realize that the marriage is not improving. The couple decide to separate for a trial period but are concerned about the effect on the children. They want to discontinue their own couples therapy but hope that Dr. S. will see the children and help them through this change in their living arrangement and generally through the separation and subsequent family changes. Dr. S. agrees to see the children, who are upset about their father moving out and about what is happening between their parents.

As Dr. S. continues to see the children over several weeks, the children became more talkative about what they thought had happened when their father still lived at home and what is happening now. All three children report that their mom and dad had fought a lot and would hit each other but never hit the children. They would, however, according to the children, say bad things to each other during their fights. The children also tell Dr. S. about events that would happen at their dad's place and at home with their mom. They report that their father is nice to them at his new place, but he does not pay much attention to them, and sometimes he naps or runs errands and leaves them alone. They report that their mom is now stricter with them and shouts at them a lot. She always seems to be either upset with them or depressed and crying. She does not want them around when she feels bad, according to the children.

One day, Dr. S. receives a subpoena from the court clerk directing him to appear at the couple's divorce and custody hearing. Dr. S. is being asked to give testimony as a fact witness. Because Dr. S. had seen the couple first, he has access to detrimental as well as positive information about both individuals that he would not have if he had seen only the children in therapy. Moreover, because Dr. S. is seeing the children, he also has information that he would not have known had he seen only the parents. Dr. S. has considerable information from all five family members about both parents and now has to decide what information can ethically be shared and what the procedure should be for his participation in this process.

Ethical Dilemma. Dr. S. should think about several standards in deciding how to proceed. Standard 10.02(b) recognizes that psychologists may be called on to perform conflicting roles. In this case, Dr. S. was a therapist first for the couple and then for the children. He is now being asked to be a witness in the divorce and custody hearing and therefore provide information about the couple learned both from the couple's therapy and from the children's therapy. Dr. S. knows the information from both the couple and children had never meant to be used in any way other than for therapeutic purposes. Dr. S. also should be aware of Standard 4.02(a), which addresses both the limits of confidentiality and in the foreseeable use of the information generated. Standard 10.02(b) also cites the importance of taking reasonable steps to clarify and modify or withdraw from roles appropriately. Although the APA Ethics Code does not explicitly bar Dr. S. from rendering an opinion regarding custody, there are multiple potential ethical and legal pitfalls in doing so.

Decision-Making Factors. Dr. S. is indeed in the situation of being a therapist for the couple and subsequently for the children and now giving testimony that not only could be damaging to both parents but also would be a breach of confidentiality of all parties. Dr. S. suspects that each parent has given permission for release of information thinking that the damaging information would be about the other person. Dr. S. may pursue a further understanding of the status of confidentiality and the application of privilege in this case in light of the jurisdictional statutes that prevail. If both parents gave permission to use information, then Dr. S. would want to explain the potential ramifications of release of information for both of them. Also, even though the content of what the children told him could not be verified, Dr. S. feels certain that the parents do not know what the children have told him about their behavior since the separation.

If only one parent withdraws the waiver of confidentiality, then Dr. S. would need to think about challenging the subpoena on the grounds of privilege because the records of the couple's therapy could not be parceled out, and he would be concerned about an inappropriate breach. Moreover, if one parent withdraws the waiver, then the same dilemma might apply to the information learned from the children, although in some states one parent might be able to waive privilege for the children. Dr. S. takes the additional precaution of ensuring that the parents waived privilege in order for him to testify on behalf of the children.

Dr. S. also is concerned about the impact on the children of him disclosing what they have told him. Dr. S. had explained the meaning of confidentiality to them as appropriately for their ages as possible. The fact remains that the children could feel responsibility for their parents' separation and divorce, their role in the circumstance, and the consequences for them. Dr. S.'s therapy with the children is an important resource, and his testifying to what they have told him might irreparably harm their future therapy with him or another therapist.

Decision Options. Dr. S. should have specific conversations with each of the parents regarding the totality of the content that could be involved, the consequences to them and to the children of these disclosures, and the purpose of his testimony. These should be primary factors in each parent's decision about authorizing the testimony. Dr. S. may clarify to the attorneys and the court the role of the therapist in this case and the conflicts inherent in providing testimony that would involve confidentially disclosed information. He should specifically note the impact of any disclosure on his ability to act effectively as a therapist for the children. He has already terminated therapy with the couple, and he could withdraw from the therapist role with the children, but the conflict would remain in that the testimony would be focused on content already shared. Dr. S. could ask the judge to withdraw the request for testimony based on the conflict of roles. He would very likely want to talk with the children about what was happening and his intended and unintended role in the proceedings in a way that they could best understand.

Standard 10.03, Group Therapy
When psychologists provide services to several persons in a group setting, they describe at the outset the roles and responsibilities of all parties and the limits of confidentiality.

This is a new standard that recognizes the importance of informed consent in the provision of group therapy. Psychologists describe at the outset of treatment the unique roles and responsibilities of both the therapist and the clients/patients in the group therapy situation. Goals of group therapy, the relationship of the therapist to the group members, expectations of group members, and guidelines for effective treatment, as well as the limits of confidentiality, may be provided. Psychologists are professionally obligated to maintain the confidentiality of group clients/patients, except when required by law to reveal child or elder abuse, or threats of harm to self or others. However, although group members must be advised to maintain confidentiality about other group members, they are not held to professional codes of conduct, and all group members should be informed about these limitations of confidentiality.

Other specific issues to consider discussing for ethical and clinical reasons are these: the nature of the group; whether the group is time limited or ongoing (and, if ongoing, how clients/patients can decide to end group treatment, including for what reasons and what the preferred process is); whether the therapist agrees to see individual clients at the same time that they are group members, and vice versa, and, if so, how information gleaned in individual therapy is handled by the therapist in group therapy; as well as whether contacting group members outside of group is discouraged or encouraged and how those contacts should be handled. Although the standard does not require written informed-consent documents, it may be helpful for clinical reasons to have group members sign such a document, including agreement to all the group rules and guidelines, including confidentiality.

Standard 10.04, Providing Therapy to Those Served by Others

In deciding whether to offer or provide services to those already receiving mental health services elsewhere, psychologists carefully consider the treatment issues and the potential client's/patient's welfare. Psychologists discuss these issues with the client/patient or another legally authorized person on behalf of the client/patient in order to minimize the risk of confusion and conflict, consult with the other service providers when appropriate, and proceed with caution and sensitivity to the therapeutic issues.

This standard allows psychologists to provide services requested by the client as long as this is done with sensitivity. The 1981 Ethics Code[3] prohibited offering services to someone receiving similar services from another professional. However, the Federal Trade Commission influenced the allowing of provision of services as long as psychologists do not engage in uninvited, in-person solicitation of therapy clients or other persons who because of their particular circumstances are vulnerable to undue influence. Psychologists are responsible for attending to the impact of their actions and decisions and steps, including consideration of the treatment issues in promotion and protection of the client's welfare; discussion of these with the potential client is suggested. A client/patient may have legitimate reasons to discontinue therapy with one therapist and move to another but may, for example, be angry with a therapist, and encouraging the client/patient to address the issues with the other therapist may be a more appropriate response.

The scope of psychological practice has expanded in recent years in such a way that a client/patient could reasonably be receiving services from several health professionals. A family could be working with a family therapist, a child specialist in behavioral or developmental concerns, a psychologist performing a learning disability assessment for a child, and a psychologist serving as a consultant for corporate advancement of one of the parents. These multiple professional services may not be overlapping in nature but could still call on psychologists to explain and clarify the roles of each and to consult with the other professionals involved as appropriate.

---

[3]American Psychological Association. (1981). Ethical principles of psychologists. *American Psychologist*, *36*, 633–638.

Standard 10.04, Case 1

Case Illustration. Dr. J. has received two referral requests for services from clients of her colleagues, Psychologist A and Psychologist B. Both clients state that they want to continue their therapy with their respective psychologists but want to see Dr. J. for specific purposes. Dr. J. has a general practice as well as several specialty areas. She knows both colleagues well and decides to call them to inquire about the referrals. Psychologist A has been seeing Client A for several reasons, including performance anxiety regarding public speaking expectations of her job, parenting concerns regarding behavioral problems of her young daughter, and academic challenges related to going back to college. Psychologist A explains to Dr. J. that Client A will be continuing to work on treatment goals in ongoing therapy but that she is quite certain that Client A has an eating disorder. Psychologist A does not work with eating disorders and hopes that Dr. J. will work with the client because she has a specialty practice in eating disorders. Dr. J. talks with Client A, reporting that she has consulted with Psychologist A in order to ensure that she understands the status of Client A's treatment and the purpose for her involvement with Client A.

When Dr. J. calls Psychologist B, he explains that he has been seeing Client B for several months and that Client B has been working on current relationship problems and conflicts on the job that could impede his career objectives. He also states that Client B has some symptoms of social phobia, for which he has been treating him. Psychologist B goes on to explain that Client B, while talking about some early occurring events, had disclosed a difficult relationship with his father and experiences of neglect. Client B remarked that Psychologist B reminded him somewhat of his father. He is not comfortable talking with Psychologist B about these unpleasant memories but thinks they are important to pursue. Psychologist B explains that Client B does not want to terminate therapy with him because he is making progress on other goals, but he wonders about seeing another psychologist to work on the early childhood experiences and to continue seeing Psychologist B for his other treatment goals. Client B expresses the same request when he calls Dr. J.

Ethical Dilemma. Dr. J. is likely to be well aware of cases in which the same client sees more than one psychologist, because in her specialty work it is a relatively common occurrence. In these cases, Dr. J. would want to think through both cases to decide whether the request for additional services is reasonable and in the best interest of the client/patient. She would want to be mindful of elements of Standard 10.04, in particular the treatment factors, the client's welfare, and the importance of discussing these matters with the potential clients and, when appropriate, with the referring colleagues. She should weigh the appropriateness of seeing Client A specifically for eating disorders treatment and Client B for early childhood trauma. There may be cases in which it would not be appropriate for the psychologist to contact the original mental health professionals, but in these cases Dr. J. determines it is appropriate and does talk with the current therapists.

Dr. J. may also be aware of Standard 3.09, which encourages psychologists to cooperate with other professionals in the spirit and purpose of providing the best and most effective service to clients. Furthermore, Standard 5.06 reminds Dr. J. of the prohibition against in-person solicitation of clients who are vulnerable to undue influence. Dr. J. has not solicited these clients and therefore is primarily concerned with meeting the expectations of Standards 10.04 and 3.09.

Decision-Making Factors. Multidisciplinary professional services(e.g., nutritionist, speech therapist, audiologists) are commonly employed. As the scope of psychological practice expands, the need for and appropriateness of multiple psychological services provided by more than one psychologist may increase. The development of specialization in psychological services and identified areas of expertise provides a context in which psychologists may provide different services to shared clients. In the case of Client A, Dr. J. received a referral from Psychologist A because treatment of eating disorders was outside the scope of the latter's practice, yet the additional psychological treatment needs can still be provided by Psychologist A, and a therapeutic relationship has been built. It would be important for the client and the other treating psychologist to understand the parameters of each psychologist's area of practice with the client and to ensure that the client would understand the distinctive areas of treatment provided by Dr. J. as separate and different from Psychologist A.

Dr. J. is less certain about the request from Client B. When talking with Psychologist B about the referral, Dr. J. realizes that the client, not the psychologist, had suggested the referral. Psychologist B told Dr. J. that he wanted to work with the client as effectively as possible and thinks that because the client is requesting this separation of services he will cooperate for the sake of the client's welfare. In terms of the treatment needs, Dr. J. does not provide any different expertise than Psychologist B. On considering the dynamics described by Psychologist B, it might seem to Dr. J. that the client is experiencing transference with Psychologist B or has some residual feelings regarding his childhood that arose in the therapy context. Dr. J. may consider that if this were the case, a similar dynamic could arise with Dr. J. that would not only be detrimental for the client and the therapeutic progress but also a challenge to the therapeutic relationship. Dr. J. may want to meet with Client B to determine the client's expectations and the therapeutic relationship and to get Client B's perspective on the shared provision of services. Dr. J. may also be concerned about the overlap of process, goals, coordination of treatment plans, and the potential for early experiences to have further effect on other aspects of treatment.

Decision Options. If Dr. J. decides to consider Client A for specific treatment of eating disorders, he may want to meet with Psychologist A first to determine the range of treatment provided by each professional and any collaborative agreement for ongoing consultation and to be sensitive to the therapeutic issues. Some overlap in content and process could be expected, but Dr. J. would not want to risk providing counterindicated treatment or to be working at odds with Psychologist A. It also is notable for Dr. J. that Psychologist A sought the referral and encouraged the client to consider additional treatment, indicating that the two may share a collaborative and cooperative purpose. Dr. J. may also want to meet in person with Client A before accepting the case to assess the client's ability and willingness to agree on the specific and targeted role of Dr. J. in order to avoid a blending of or confusion between the roles of the two psychologists. Dr. J. would not want to risk triangulation or a manipulation between psychologists.

Dr. J. may understand Client B's case to be very different from Client A's in the potential to differentiate treatment plans and to collaborate without confounding the purpose and method of treatment. In the case of Client A, Dr. J.'s services would be clearly additive, whereas in the case of Client B Dr. J.'s entrance onto the treatment team would be an attempt to save the existing therapeutic relationship by removing the current relationship impasse. Dr. J. could discuss these observations with Psychologist B and then also with Client B to encourage them to continue working not only on the aspects of therapy that were going well but also on the therapeutic impasse. This could be a therapeutic opportunity for the client to resolve the conflicts.

Standard 10.05, Sexual Intimacies With Current Therapy Clients/Patients
Psychologists do not engage in sexual intimacies with current therapy clients/patients.

Sexual intimacies with current clients/patients have been explicitly prohibited since 1977. The prohibition had been indirectly implied by other standards before that time. The evidence is clear that sexual contact with clients/patients has a high potential for harm partly because the power differential and influence that psychologists have result in exploitation of the vulnerabilities of the client/patient. It also harms psychologists' public image, and the prevalence of sexual involvement of mental health providers with clients/patients has resulted in an increasing criminalization of this behavior in over half of the states in the United States. This standard's prohibition applies only to clients/patients receiving therapy services; prohibitions against sexual relationships involving nontherapy clients and others with whom psychologists work (e.g., supervisees, employees, students, research participants) are covered by other standards (see Standard 3.04, Avoiding Harm; Standard 3.05,

Multiple Relationships; Standard 3.08, Exploitative Relationships and Standard 7.07, Sexual Relationships With Students and Supervisees).

The term *sexual intimacies* has been previously defined as any sexual touching between therapist and client/patient; this includes the tone and climate of the therapeutic environment. The Ethics Code does not confine the interpretation of *sexual intimacies* to physical contact or verbal communication. Sexual intimacy may be a way of interacting with others that involves fostering or allowing an erotic quality between psychologists and clients/patients. Even in a circumstance in which the client/patient initiates the interest in sexual intimacies, psychologists must maintain the focus of the professional relationship for the benefit of the client/patient and must not allow erotic material to come into the relationship in such a way that the benefit to the client/patient is lost. Sexual intimacy represents a violation regardless of whether the client/patient or the therapist initiated the possibility.

A complicating issue is that although the standard does not prohibit nonsexual touching (some clients and therapists have cultural or other orientations that allow for nonsexual hugs, handshakes, or other forms of affectionate communications), psychologists are encouraged to be cautious about how easily touch can be misunderstood as a sexual overture by some clients/patients, in particular those with a history of incest or other similar violations.

It is also important to note that sex therapy does not include romantic or erotic interaction between the therapist and client/patient, although it may involve communication about explicit sexual information, instructions, or readings. Psychologists should still be cautious because clients/patients may perceive comments as erotic regardless of the psychologist's intent. The use of sexual surrogates is controversial, but if the psychologist endorses the use of surrogates, the surrogate must never be the psychologist.

Standard 10.06, Sexual Intimacies With Relatives or Significant Others of Current Therapy Clients/Patients

Psychologists do not engage in sexual intimacies with individuals they know to be close relatives, guardians, or significant others of current clients/patients. Psychologists do not terminate therapy to circumvent this standard.

This is a new standard that recognizes that problems can occur if psychologists become involved in romantic relationships with close relatives or friends of clients/patients. Sexual intimacies with individuals whom they know to be close relatives, guardians, or significant others of current clients/patients can impair psychologists' treatment objectivity, blur the therapist–client/patient roles and relationships, and risk exploitation of the client/patient to attain or maintain a sexual relationship with the individual involved. Close relatives can include a parent, brother, sister, divorcing or estranged spouse; significant others include boyfriends or girlfriends and/or cohabitants of clients/patients. It would not be legitimate to terminate the therapy relationship in order to begin a romantic relationship with the other person. The qualifier "they know to be" indicates that the standard recognizes the rare situation in which a psychologist may see someone romantically yet is not aware that the individual is a close relative, guardian, or significant other of a current client/patient. When psychologists become aware that such a multiple relationship (see Standard 3.05a, second paragraph) has occurred, they must take reasonable steps to resolve the conflict with due regard for the best interests of the affected person or persons (see Standard 3.05b).

Standard 10.07, Therapy With Former Sexual Partners

Psychologists do not accept as therapy clients/patients persons with whom they have engaged in sexual intimacies.

This standard clearly and simply prohibits psychologists from providing therapy to former sexual partners. The assumption is that the previous sexual relationship can compromise objectivity and thereby reduce psychologists' ability to exercise General Principle A: Beneficence and Nonmaleficence and to conduct an effective professional relationship. Role confusion for both parties can result from of the intimate and personal knowledge that each holds about the other. Risk of further sexual involvement is also problematic. Other standards may also be relevant here, such as Standard 3.04, Avoiding Harm, and Standard 3.08, Exploitative Relationships.

Standard 10.08, Sexual Intimacies With Former Therapy Clients/Patients

The 1992 APA Ethics Code explicitly addressed sexual involvement with former therapy clients for the first time. The APA Ethics Committee had established a policy statement in 1987 that addressed such behavior when there was an improper termination of therapy, but the 1992 revision made the provision an explicit rule. This standard is similar to Standard 4.07 of the 1992 Ethics Code, with only slight modifications. It has two parts: The first part simply states the prohibition against engagement in sexual intimacies with clients/patients for at least 2 years after termination, and the second part decrees that psychologists engage in sexual intimacies 2 years after termination only in unusual circumstances and addresses seven factors that psychologists must consider in demonstrating that there has been no exploitation.

The controversy as to whether the standard should be changed to an in-perpetuity rule—a rule stating that psychologist should never become sexually involved with a person who has been the psychologist's client/patient—continued during the last revision, but no consensus has emerged in the profession concerning this. A consideration in the decision against implementing the in-perpetuity rule is the relationship and natural tension between General Principle A: Beneficence and Nonmaleficence, specifically to strive to benefit those with whom psychologists work and to take care to do no harm, and General Principle E: Respect for People's Rights and Dignity, specifically the right to self-determination and respect for autonomy. There was also doubt whether an in-perpetuity rule could survive legal challenges in state courts. Nonetheless, there was a consensus that a prohibition should be continued "almost always" with former clients/patients because of the importance of doing no harm (General Principle A).

Standard 10.08(a)

Psychologists do not engage in sexual intimacies with former clients/ patients for at least two years after cessation or termination of therapy.

This standard applies only to therapy clients/patients and establishes an absolute prohibition of sex with former clients/patients for 2 years after cessation or termination of therapy. The rule means that such behavior is always wrong in less than 2 years, for the same reasons that sex with current clients/patients is problematic (see Standard 10.05, Sexual Intimacies With Current Therapy Clients/Patients). However, after 2 years, sexual intimacies with former clients/patients may still not be appropriate, given the factors addressed in Standard 10.08. The 2-year time period was chosen because research has shown that almost all such relationships began during the first 18 months after the cessation of therapy. Complaints about relationships that began 2 or more years after termination of therapy are rare.

Standard 10.08(b)

Psychologists do not engage in sexual intimacies with former clients/ patients even after a two-year interval except in the most unusual circumstances. Psychologists who engage in such activity after the two years following cessation or termination of therapy and of having no sexual contact with the former client/patient bear the burden of demonstrating that there has been no exploitation, in light of all relevant factors, including (1) the amount of time that has passed since therapy terminated; (2) the nature, duration, and intensity of the therapy; (3) the circumstances of termination; (4) the client's/patient's personal history; (5) the client's/patient's current mental status; (6) the likelihood of adverse impact on the client/ patient; and (7) any statements or actions made by the therapist during the course of therapy suggesting or inviting the possibility of a posttermination sexual or romantic relationship with the client/patient. (See also Standard 3.05, Multiple Relationships.)

This standard first acknowledges that sex with former clients/patients, even after 2 years, should almost never occur. In other words, Standard 10.08(b) should be interpreted as a rule that says that the psychologist should almost never get involved with former clients/patients and that doing so would occur in an acceptable manner only in the most unusual circumstances. The Ethics Code does convey that such sexual intimacies with former clients/patients would almost never occur. The standard places the burden on the psychologist who engages in sexual intimacies with former clients even after 2 years to demonstrate that there has been no exploitation, in light of all relevant factors listed. The standard provides a list of factors, which are not considered exhaustive. At least those seven considerations must be included in determination of exploitation, but other factors may be considered on a case-by-case basis.

The first factor, "the amount of time that has passed since therapy terminated," recognizes that shorter time periods after termination argue against involvement but in all cases must exceed 2 years. This allows for a condition in which a therapist and former client/patient may cross paths and decide to enter a different kind of relationship 2 years or more after termination of therapy. However, psychologists should keep in mind that clients/patients often consider their therapists as individuals to whom they can return to for future therapy services. In any case, other factors should be considered as well. Of course, sexual involvement would preclude the possibility of any further therapeutic relationship.

The second factor, "the nature, duration, and intensity of the therapy," implies that there is a difference between the intensity and depth of different therapies. For example, a client/patient in intensive psychoanalytic or psychodynamic therapy on the one hand and biofeedback for headaches on the other hand would have a different relationship with the therapist offering each treatment. In addition, there is a great deal of difference between a therapy of several years' duration as opposed to a one- to two-session therapy. In the former case, entering a sexual/romantic relationship even after 2 years would be considered more complicated and would present more risk of exploitation, as opposed to brief contacts for interventions that were not interpersonally in depth.

The third factor, "the circumstances of termination," recognizes that a termination that occurs because of problems in managing the therapeutic relationship—for example, substantial transference–countertransference issues—may permanently prevent a relationship from ever occurring without a very high likelihood of exploitation and harm. In fact, some therapies may result in unresolved transference over very long periods of time. Other signs of problems may include abrupt or explosive terminations. In addition, premature termination in order to hasten a romantic relationship would be a form of exploitation.

The fourth factor, "the client's/patient's personal history," recognizes that events in the client/patient's history, such as boundary violations like sexual or other abuse, may result in special, problematic involvement with a person with whom there is a power differential, such as a former therapist. A client/patient who has had little power because of his or her role in family or society may be at particular risk. This factor recognizes that such variables may increase the risk of exploitation and harm. This may occur in part because of the client/patient's tendency to re-enact past events in a current relationship, but the psychologist bears the responsibility of not exploiting this tendency.

The fifth factor, "the client's/patient's current mental status" at the time of entering the new sexual/romantic/intimate relationship, recognizes that an individual who is distraught and vulnerable is more susceptible to exploitation than a person whose mental status is stable. Emotional crises, life transitions and losses, mood disorders, or other conditions that may impair judgment would render the psychologist as having undue influence. Certain disorders, such as some personality disorders, involve factors that are chronic, and those relevant to mental status during the time of therapy would thus have a high likelihood of persisting over time.

The sixth factor, "the likelihood of adverse impact on the client/patient," requires consideration of the adverse effects of the involvement, including factors such as impaired ability to trust, identity confusion, and increased suicidal risk. Boundary violations can become recapitulated; if the new relationship does not go well (and many sexual/romantic/intimate relationships do not go well), the former client/patient may experience more severe damage and harm due to expectations engendered by the previous therapeutic relationship. The consideration is made with regard not only to the former client but also to other persons, such as family members; ex-spouses/partners; children; and other clients/patients in the psychologist's practice, including clients/patients referred by the former client/patient.

The seventh factor, "any statements or actions made by the therapist during the course of therapy suggesting or inviting the possibility of a post-termination sexual or romantic relationship with the client/patient," indicates that it is unacceptable for the psychologist to suggest at any time during the therapeutic relationships that a romantic or sexual relationship with the client/patient could occur after 2 years or at any time. In other words, the sexual/romantic/intimate relationship should never stem from the therapeutic relationship. Even nonverbal cues, such as initiating sexualized hugs and touching, are prohibited. Standard 3.05, Multiple Relationships, is also relevant in articulating concerns with multiple relationships, including promising a multiple relationship.

A significant portion of psychologists in the profession strongly believe in an *in-perpetuity rule*. As indicated earlier, consideration was given to the option of an absolute prohibition of sexual intimacies with former clients/patients for the last two revisions of the Ethics Code, but concerns about difficulty in defending such a prohibition constitutionally and socially resulted in maintaining the current prohibition, which is a very restrictive rule. After the termination of a therapeutic relationship, the weight of responsibility for beneficence and nonmaleficence is great. The standard is written in a form that leaves the psychologist bearing the burden of demonstrating that no exploitation occurred, regardless of the passage of time after termination.

Standard 10.08, Case 1

Case Illustration. Both Dr. A. and Dr. B. are experiencing difficult decisions in regard to sexual intimacies with former therapy clients. Psychologist A has a practice primarily in psychoeducational testing and evaluation. Her clientele tend to be children and adolescents, but she occasionally sees adults for various purposes of evaluation. She also conducts brief therapy or counseling when related to the findings of her evaluations. If a client/patient's therapeutic needs call for longer term or in-depth therapy, she refers him or her to one of her colleagues. Dr. A. moved 2 months ago into a different community and has attended several community gatherings. During one of these activities, a man who lives near her introduces himself as a person for whom she had conducted an evaluation 5 years earlier. She does not remember him at first. He recalls that he had moved 5 years ago to this community and had changed jobs. He had struggled in the earlier job and was worried about his new job at the time. He knew that several people in his family had had learning problems, and he was concerned about a learning disability. She had conducted the evaluation, found no learning problem, and met with him three times for brief therapy. She thought that he might be having an adjustment problem and recommended a colleague for services if he wanted to follow up. Dr. A. and this former client find themselves attracted to each other and want to consider beginning to date. Dr. A. recognizes that the person in question had definitely been a client to whom she had provided psychological services. She wonders whether contemplating a relationship would be a violation of Standard 10.08.

Dr. B. ran into a former client at a social event 2 months earlier whom she had not seen since termination of therapy 3 years ago. In this case, Dr. B. immediately remembers the client, because he had been in therapy with her for 4 years. He had been one of her most challenging cases and one of the most rewarding. The client had had several childhood traumas that were affecting his contemporary life in debilitating ways. Dr. B. had a broad theoretical perspective but had decided to treat this case with a quite intensive and themat-ically driven dynamic approach. This approach was effective with the client and was successful in helping him break out of some protracted patterns in his life. Dr. B. keeps running into the client while running, walking her dog, and at neighborhood events. He apparently lives several streets over. Dr. B is find-ing herself very attracted to the former client, and he to her. She is cognizant that the therapy had ended 3 years earlier, well past the 2-year time frame, and wonders whether she would be violating Standard 10.08 if they begin dating.

Ethical Dilemma. Both psychologists are facing similar circumstances in their reacquaintance with former clients. Both are concerned about the import of Standard 10.08 in light of the potential for a renewed relationship. Although not as primary as Standard 10.08, Standard 3.05, Multiple Rela-tionships, reminds and cautions psychologists about being in a professional role with an individual and promising to enter into another relationship in the future with the same person. This prohibition also takes the form of Stan-dard 10.08(b)(7) of inviting a posttherapy romantic relationship. Further-more, psychologists must be aware of relationships that could be exploitative or harmful to the person with whom they are in the professional relationship. In these cases, neither Dr. A. nor Dr. B. is currently in a professional relation-ship with the former clients, so Standard 10.08(a), which prohibits sexual intimacies within 2 years, is also not in question. Both psychologists must consider the implications for meeting the intent of Standard 10.08(b).

Decision-Making Factors. Dr. A. considers the terms of Standard 10.08(b) in the application of her professional service to the client and the potential effect on the client of this significant role shift in their relationship. The client had been seen 5 years earlier for five sessions of clinical intake, test adminis-tration, feedback, and follow-up with referral. The nature of the service did not include any thematic or dynamically based material but rather psycho-educational information, and personal history had not been sought, with the exception of what was asked on intake. The termination was predictable and expected in that it was time limited in purpose. The former client had become successful and was not in a vulnerable psychological state. Adverse impact could not be predicted.

In the case of Dr. B., the therapy had been extensive, both in duration and intensity, as reported by Dr. B. The therapy had ended appropriately, and the circumstances were acceptable and mutual; however, the client's history was one of conflict, betrayal, rejection, and neglect. The client had not expressed dependent feelings toward Dr. B., but for several years she had been his primary support and a key figure in his life. The potential for a negative impact on the client could be likely, and the conditions of therapy, coupled with its duration and intensity, would still be a major factor in the context of the contemporary relationship.

Decision Options. The two psychologists reflect on the identified factors cited in Standard 10.08 and are mindful of the evolving relationship between the obligation to do no harm and to safeguard the welfare and rights of those with whom they work (General Principle A: Beneficence and Nonmaleficence) and the right to self-determination and autonomy (General Principle E: Respect for People's Rights and Dignity). Both psychologists realize that the decision and the explanation for the decision are their responsibility, not the former clients'. Dr. A. determines that she would be able to demonstrate that there had been no exploitation in light of the factors listed in Standard 10.08(b). However, she is having feelings that are giving her pause because the treatment was more than simple assessment, the former client had feelings of gratitude for her work with him, there was no assurance that the relationship would work out, and angry feelings were always a possibility. Given that a professional relationship had once existed, Dr. B., after reviewing the relevant factors, comes to believe that the relationship could not be free of the characteristics of a psychotherapy relationship and therefore realizes that the conditions for a posttherapy relationship could not be met.

Psychologists cannot rely on the testimony of the former clients; instead, they should use their professional judgment in evaluating the conditions of 10.08(b), seek consultation, and make a reasoned decision on the basis of what they know to be the circumstances of the therapeutic variables, the nature of the therapeutic relationship, and their ability to meet the conditions of Standard 10.08(b).

Standard 10.09, Interruption of Therapy

When entering into employment or contractual relationships, psychologists make reasonable efforts to provide for orderly and appropriate resolution of responsibility for client/patient care in the event that the employment or contractual relationship ends, with paramount consideration given to the welfare of the client/patient. (See also Standard 3.12, Interruption of Psychological Services.)

The standard requires that psychologists make reasonable efforts to address several potential interruptions to therapy services in those situations when employment or managed care or other contracts may restrict services. Ideally, clients/patients and their therapists reach an agreement regarding the length of services based on the accomplishment of therapeutic goals. At times, a psychologist may choose a change in employment position, or his or her position or contract may be terminated. This standard requires that psychologists make reasonable efforts to ensure, at the time of the employment agreement or contract, that orderly and appropriate resolution of responsibility for the welfare of the clients/patients occurs, especially in regard for continuity of their care. Psychologists have the responsibility to read contracts carefully. The term *reasonable efforts* recognizes that in some situations policies, contracts, or administrative staff may be changed, resulting in a psychologist's inability to follow through on promises to protect clients/patients' welfare in a manner that is out of the psychologist's control.

Standard 10.10, Terminating Therapy

A previous portion of this standard in the 1992 Ethics Code (1992 Ethics Code Standard 4.09a) that addressed client/patient abandonment was dropped, in part because no definition of abandonment was provided or was able to be defined. Standard 10.10(c) of the 2002 Ethics Code addresses the ethical actions that psychologists should provide (e.g., pretermination counseling and referral to alternative providers). It was also previously noted that some clients may feel abandoned, no matter how much the termination is in the client's best interest and no matter what steps the psychologist had taken. General Principle A: Beneficence and Nonmaleficence is relevant to this standard in that psychologists are required to help clients and prevent harm around the termination period. The first part of this standard directs psychologists to terminate therapy when it is reasonably clear that the client/patient no longer needs the service, is not benefiting, or may be harmed by continued service. The second part allows psychologists to terminate when they feel threatened or endangered by the client/patient or another person with whom the client/patient has a relationship. The last part of this standard directs psychologists to provide pretermination counseling and suggest alternative providers as appropriate, except where precluded by the actions of clients/patients or third-party payors.

Standard 10.10(a)

Psychologists terminate therapy when it becomes reasonably clear that the client/patient no longer needs the service, is not likely to benefit, or is being harmed by continued service.

This standard identifies three conditions under which therapy must be terminated and implies that psychologists should regularly consider whether these conditions are present in therapy. Compliance with this rule might be made by reviewing progress and goals and, if treatment is continued, by documenting in progress notes the decision to continue treatment, perhaps with adjusted or continuing goals made with the client/patient.

The first two conditions under which therapy must be terminated, that the client/patient no longer needs the service or is not likely to benefit, suggest that clinical judgment is required. For example, a client may be working through a plateau in therapy, and it may be appropriate to continue services despite an immediate apparent lack of progress. On the other hand, endless therapy for a client who no longer needs the service is inappropriate. As with many ethical dilemmas, consultation with colleagues, as well as a discussion with the client/patient, may be helpful. On occasion, clients/patients may discuss issues over and over without behavior or other changes and may erroneously believe that as long as they continue in therapy they are doing something about their issues. Psychologists should continually assess the clinical picture of clients/patients regarding appropriateness of services. Clients/patients who have chronic or extenuating conditions (e.g., serious mental illness, pain management needs) may be advantaged by lifelong psychological care in preservation and maintenance of treatment benefits.

The third condition that addresses harm from continued therapy is a complex issue because often treatment stirs up the experience of increased emotional distress as part of the therapeutic process. This is not the kind of harm addressed by this standard. However, if a psychologist finds that a client/patient's mental health continues to deteriorate, consultation and/or referral to other services may be appropriate. The standard also suggests that psychologists may occasionally discover that a client's problems are beyond their level of competence and that other services may be more effective. In addition, if a client is being harmed by getting into destructive debt financially, or by the fostering of overdependence, termination or referral may also be appropriate. On occasion, a psychologist may find him- or herself unable to provide the conditions necessary for effective therapy because of negative countertransference and/or differences based on age, gender, gender identity, race, ethnicity, culture, national origin, religion, sexual orientation, disability, language, socioeconomic status, or other related issues. In such circumstances it may be best to refer the client/patient. Furthermore, psychologists will want to be aware that there may be cases in which the process of psychotherapy itself is not beneficial to an individual, unrelated to competency, quality of therapeutic relationship, or other factors.

Standard 10.10(b)

Psychologists may terminate therapy when threatened or otherwise endangered by the client/patient or another person with whom the client/patient has a relationship.

This is a new standard that allows psychologists to terminate therapy if threatened or endangered by a client/patient or someone related to or associated with the client/patient. Impending threats may involve personal injury to the psychologist, the psychologist's family or associates, or harm to the psychologist's property. The usual requirements for ethical termination, as in Standard 10.10(c), would not apply because psychologists have the right to protect themselves from harm. The limits of confidentiality (see Standard 4.05[b][3], Disclosures) include the valid purpose of protecting the psychologist or others from harm. As such, in addition to termination, psychologists may request a protective order or injunction against those clients/patients or others whom they suspect will threaten or harm them.

Some circumstances in which psychologists feel threatened may arise because the client/patient variables extend beyond psychologists' area of competence, leaving them uncertain how to proceed but feeling responsible for the client/patient's treatment. Psychologists are called on to be aware of their defined area of practice and consider whether a question of manageability of the case has been a factor in the emergence of a threat or endangerment concern. Given the many possible related factors in leading up to a necessary termination, psychologists should not lose sight of what is best for the client. Even in the most difficult circumstances, psychologists can, by phone, voicemail, or letter, encourage client/patients in the direction of appropriate other treatment.

Standard 10.10(c)

Except where precluded by the actions of clients/patients or third-party payors, prior to termination psychologists provide pretermination counseling and suggest alternative service providers as appropriate.

This standard addresses the appropriate steps to take toward the end of therapy. Psychologists are advised to provide pretermination counseling and suggest alternative service providers as appropriate. The standard also recognizes that there are numerous instances in which such steps are not feasible, such as when the client/patient abruptly leaves therapy, does not return, does not respond to calls or letters, or otherwise does not cooperate in this process.

In an ideal situation, therapy is terminated when both the psychologist and the client/patient agree to the appropriate time to end therapy services. Other appropriate reasons to end a therapeutic relationship may include when the decision is the psychologist's because he or she is relocating, retiring, becomes ill, or does not feel competent to provide continuing services, as when unexpected treatment needs arise, or a multiple relationship has arisen, or the client/patient repeatedly fails to pay for services. Other reasons include limits by the client/patient's insurance or organized system of health or managed care and the client/patient is unable or unwilling to pay for services directly.

Pretermination counseling prior to ending a therapeutic relationship may include providing clients/patients with advance notice or negotiating together the end date of services, review of gains made in treatment, and future challenges to be dealt with either outside of therapy or when the client returns to therapy. Providing referrals for alternative service providers may also be appropriate if the client/patient has ongoing needs.

Standard 10.10, Case 1

Case Illustration. Dr. K. has a booming psychology practice in a relatively rural area. Dr. K. is a generalist who does limited testing and some psychoeducational work, but mostly conducts psychotherapy with individuals, couples, and families. Dr. K. sees children occasionally and is continually vigilant about the fact that in the rural communities he could be asked to fulfill psychological service needs beyond his actual scope of practice. Dr. K. has two cases within the caseload that are particularly challenging and about which he is somewhat concerned. He is very experienced and has been in practice successfully for many years, but he has not experienced cases similar to these.

In Case A, the client had begun therapy wanting to assess his interpersonal abilities as applied to the work setting and to personal relationships. He was being passed over for promotions at work and had been having failed relationships in which the other person would end the relationship. Dr. K. is initially quite hopeful and positive about this client because the client is open to suggestions, seems to like the therapeutic process, and is interpersonally likeable. As several weeks go by, Dr. K. notes that the tenor of the sessions is becoming increasingly challenging, confrontational, and argumentative. The client seems to be changing before Dr. K.'s very eyes, and almost every session now is redirected toward anger management and impulse control. The client tells Dr. K. that a restraining order has been issued by the person who had broken off the most recent relationship and that the client is on probation at work for trying to start fights with other workers. The client begins implying that if Dr. K. had done a better job conducting therapy the client would not be in the current fix and that the client might have to make Dr. K. "pay." Dr. K. begins to feel unsafe when seeing the client and begins asking colleagues to stay in the office during the client's session time. Dr. K. has never been in this predicament before. He communicates to the client that an expression of anger and frustration is legitimate but that threats are not acceptable or appropriate.

In Case B, the client also presents with relationship problems, but of a very different nature from those of the client in Case A. This client has been very open to therapy and seems to just absorb what Dr. K. has to offer. She is very appreciative and complimentary and tells friends how gifted Dr. K. is. The client talks about how the therapeutic relationship has torn down walls and given a new direction to her life. Dr. K. is embarrassed on hearing these superlatives and sometimes thinks that the client is just being kind. Dr. K. thinks the therapy is going well, as does the client, until she begins having difficulties with parents and family. As Dr. K. tries to explore and engage with the client on this new development, she begins to accuse Dr. K. of being parental and not understanding. Over the next few weeks, Dr. K. never knows what to expect regarding whether the client will be volatile or adaptive. She begins showing up at the office when she is upset, regardless of when sessions are scheduled. Letters begin to come in for Dr. K. The client meets Dr. K. in the parking lot and insists on talking then and there. During this encounter, Dr. K. gently but clearly defines the boundaries about where the client can contact him. Dr. K. begins to make plans about how to deal with the client's inability to cope with her crisis. Dr. K. cannot believe it, but after years of practice, for the first time, he is facing two cases in which he is feeling threatened and endangered by clients.

Ethical Dilemma. Dr. K. begins thinking about Standard 10.10 and the conditions of terminating therapy. Neither of these clients wants to terminate, but Dr. K. does not feel safe and does not want to continue seeing them. He has begun to dread the clients' appointments and now is unsure when or where the client from Case B will appear. Standard 10.10(b) provides for the termination of therapy when psychologists feel threatened or endangered. Dr. K. thinks about this definition and believes that both of these cases meet those criteria. Before taking action, he decides to consult a respected colleague regarding these extraordinary circumstances.

Decision-Making Factors. Dr. K.'s colleague realizes that Dr. K. has determined that Standard 10.10(b) is applicable to both cases and that, unusual as the situation is, Dr. K. is on the verge of terminating therapy with both clients for similar reasons. The colleague, however, asks Dr. K. to talk through the circumstances of the clients' dynamics, the purpose and course of therapy, and the information that was available about the clients' experiences outside of therapy. This could be helpful in understanding how to think about the current decision to be made. As they talk, the colleague begins to think that Dr. K. has accurately identified a potentially threatening client in Case A. There is ample evidence that the client is repeating the threatening behaviors with Dr. K. that are being exhibited with others. The client is externalizing and blaming Dr. K. for his failures and seems to increasingly be taking an impulsive and angry stance. There is no evidence that any of the client's externalizations toward Dr. K. are grounded in any actual experience.

In Case B, however, Dr. K.'s colleague thinks it possible that Dr. K. has failed to diagnose the client accurately and that she has at least some characteristics of an individual with a personality disorder and/or chronic and entrenched posttraumatic stress disorder. Dr. K. may have failed to diagnose her accurately, develop an appropriate treatment plan, and engage interpersonally with her. If Dr. K. had had a more thorough understanding of the case and the therapeutic response needed, the client's reactions might have been more contained. The purpose of this analysis for Dr. K.'s colleague was to ferret out the actual dangerousness of the clients or the failure of Dr. K. to recognize a case that is outside his scope of practice. The colleague remarks that when one is not capable or competent to work with a clinical condition, the case could seem threatening when it is actually simply beyond the competence of the psychologist.

Ethical Options. Dr. K. feels some embarrassment for this misstep but also is grateful to learn this important differentiation. Dr. K. now believes that the client from Case A is truly dangerous and that he will likely decide to terminate. Dr. K. decides that the client in Case B is not actually dangerous but that he is not able to provide competent services to her and realizes that if the client were referred to another professional experienced in the needs of this client, the client could very likely work productively in therapy. Dr. K. would want to be mindful that Standard 10.10(c) delineates the expectation that psychologists provide pretermination counseling and suggest alternative professionals for continued service. Even though the experience Dr. K. is having with the client in Case A is very difficult and anxiety producing for Dr. K., this client also deserves a recommendation for other services. This action could be accomplished by phone, letter, or voicemail. Psychologists should not lose sight of the primary benefit of the client.

CONCLUSION

This chapter and section of the Ethics Code address standards specific to therapy relationships. Although all of the general principles are relevant to the standards involving therapy, most of the areas covered by Section 10 are largely based on General Principle A: Beneficence and Nonmaleficence; that is, psychologists should work to benefit their clients/patients and avoid harming them. In addition, General Principle E: Respect for People's Rights and Dignity is highly relevant in that psychologists respect the dignity and worth of all people and the rights of individuals to privacy, confidentiality, and self-determination. Balancing the tension that sometimes arises between these two general principles, such as with Standard 10.08, Sexual Intimacies With Former Therapy Clients/Patients, is an ongoing challenge.

INDEX

within boundaries of competence
(2.01), 48–49
maintenance, dissemination, and
disposal of confidential
records of professional and
scientific work as (6.02a),
192–193, 195–197
and personal problems and conflicts
that may interfere with (2.06b),
70–71
that prevent performance of
(2.06a), 70
Professional judgment, 12–13
bases for (2.04), 61
regarding potential ethical
violations, 34
Professionals
cooperation with (3.09), 105–106
providing therapy to those served by
(10.04), 355–358
use of other psychologists' work by,
13–17
Professional services. *See also* Psychological services
documentation to facilitate
provision of later services
(6.01[1]), 185
limitations to services based on fees
(6.04d), 203
maintenance, dissemination, and
disposal of confidential
records (6.02), 191–200
avoiding personal identifiers
(6.02b), 195
as a professional activity (6.02a),
192–193, 195–197
when withdrawing from positions
or practice (6.02c), 195,
198–200
offering inducements for research
participation during (8.06),
274–275
Professional work
documentation of (6.01)
to allow for replication of
research design and analysis
(6.02[2]), 186
to ensure accuracy of billing and
payments (6.02[4]), 187
to ensure compliance with law
(6.02[5]), 187–188

to facilitate provision of services
later (6.01[1]), 185
to meet institutional requirements
(6.01[3]), 186–187
maintenance, dissemination, and
disposal of confidential
records (6.02a), 192–193,
195–197
Psychological services. *See also* Professional services
delivered to or through organizations
(3.11), 113–121
informed consent for (3.11a),
113–114
when informed consent and
results of procedures are
not permitted (3.11b),
114–115
false or deceptive statements about
(5.01b), 167
informed consent for
in human relations context
(3.10), 106–108
services delivered to or through
organizations (3.11),
113–121
interruption of (3.12), 121–122
provided in emergencies (2.02),
58–60
reasonable effort to obtain necessary
competence for (2.01d),
50–51
third-party requests for (3.07),
99–103
Psychotherapy, defined, 165
Public accountability, 6–7
Publication credit (Standard 8.12),
282–287
accurate and fair allocation of
(8.23a), 282–283
accurate reflection of contributions
(8.12b), 283–284
for doctoral students (8.12c),
284–287
Public statements. *See also* Advertising
and Other Public Statements
(Section 5)
avoidance of false or deceptive statements (5.01), 165–168
about psychologists' degrees
(5.01c), 167–168

Public statements, *continued*
    about psychologists' qualifications
        or services (5.01b), 167
    knowingly false/deceptive public
        statements (5.01a),
        166–167
    by others (5.02), 168–172
        compensation of journalists or
            related professionals
            (5.02b), 169
        identifying paid advertisements
            (5.02c), 169
        responsibility for public statements
            (5.02a), 168–172

Qualifications, false or deceptive
    statements about (Standard
    5.01b), 167

Reasonableness, 8
Reasoned judgment in, 12–13
Recording of voices or images
    in research (8.03), 262–267
    during service provision (4.03), 138
Record Keeping and Fees (Section 6),
    183–214
    barter with clients/patients (6.05),
        207–213
    documentation of professional
        and scientific work and
        maintenance of records
        (6.01), 184–191
        for accuracy of billing and
            payments (6.02[4]), 187
        for compliance with law
            (6.02[5]), 187–188
        to facilitate provision of services
            later (6.01[1]), 185
        to meet institutional requirements
            (6.01[3]), 186–187
        for replication of research design
            and analysis (6.02[2]), 186
    fees and financial arrangements
        (6.04), 200–207
        consistent with law (6.04b), 202
        limitations to services based on
            (6.04d), 203
        misrepresentation of (6.04c),
            202–203
        pursuing collection of fees
            (6.04e), 203–204

reaching agreement on (6.04a),
    201–202, 204–207
maintenance, dissemination, and
    disposal of confidential
    records of professional and
    scientific work (6.02),
    191–200
    avoiding personal identifiers
        (6.02b), 195
    as a professional activity (6.02a),
        192–193, 195–197
    when withdrawing from positions
        or practice (6.02c), 195,
        198–200
referrals and fees (6.07), 213–214
withholding records for nonpayment
    (6.03), 200
Records. *See also* Documentation
    bases of assessment in review of
        (9.01c), 298–299
    withholding, for nonpayment (6.03),
        200
Referrals and fees (Standard 6.07),
    213–214
Relational boundaries. *See* Sexual
    intimacies
Relational competence, 46, 47
Relatives of clients/patients, sexual
    intimacies with (Standard 10.06),
    359–360
Release of test data (Standard 9.04),
    320–326
    in absence of client/patient release
        (9.04b), 322–323
    harmful consequences of (9.04a),
        320–326
Reliability of assessment instruments
    (Standard 9.02b), 307–308
Reporting
    of ethical violations (1.05), 38–39
    of original works, 281–282
        plagiarism (8.11), 282
        research results (8.10), 281
            correcting significant errors
                (8.10b), 281
            fabrication of data (8.10a), 281
Reports
    bases of assessment for opinions
        rendered through (9.01b),
        296–298, 303–306

ABOUT THE AUTHORS

Linda Campbell, PhD, is a professor at the University of Georgia and director of the Center for Counseling. She serves as the president of the Georgia State Board of Examiners of Psychologists, is a past chair of the American Psychological Association (APA) Ethics Committee and was a member of the 2002 Ethics Code Revision Task Force.

Dr. Campbell is a past president of the Georgia Psychological Association and of APA Divisions 29 (Psychotherapy) and Division 31 (State, Provincial and Territorial Psychological Associations). She is a Fellow of APA (Divisions of Psychotherapy and Counseling Psychology). She is a past chair of the APA Board of Educational Affairs, a member of the Council of Representatives for the Division of Psychotherapy, cochair of the Task Force for revision of the APA Model Curriculum for Psychopharmacology, and cochair of the Women Psychologists for Political Action.

Dr. Campbell has coauthored three books, published numerous professional articles and book chapters, and made many international and national presentations on the topics of ethics education, practicum training, competency-based evaluation, and psychopharmacology training.

She has received numerous awards, including

- Distinguished Psychologist of the Year Award, Division 29 (Psychotherapy);
- Distinguished Psychologist of the Year Award, Division 31 (State, Provincial, and Territorial Psychological Associations);
- Georgia State University Distinguished Alumni Association Achievement Award;
- APA Karl Heiser Award for advocacy in shaping the discipline of psychology; and
- APA State Leadership Award for Outstanding Psychologist.

Melba Vasquez, PhD, is a psychologist in full-time independent practice in Austin, Texas. She has provided extensive leadership service; she is a past president of the Texas Psychological Association and of American Psychological Association (APA) Divisions 35 (Society of Psychology of Women) and 17 (Society of Counseling Psychology). She is the first Latina elected to serve as a member-at-large on the APA Board of Directors (2007–2009). She is a Fellow of the APA and holds the Diplomate from the American Board of Professional Psychology (ABPP).

She is a cofounder of APA Division 45, Society for the Psychological Study of Ethnic Minority Issues and of the National Multicultural Conference and Summit (with Derald Wing Sue, Rosie Bingham, and Lisa Porche-Burke). She has published extensively in the areas of professional ethics, ethnic minority psychology, psychology of women, supervision and training and counseling and psychotherapy. She served on the task forces for the revisions of the last two versions of the APA Ethics Code. She is the coauthor, with Ken Pope, of *Ethics in Psychotherapy & Counseling: A Practical Guide* (2007, 3rd edition) and of *How to Survive and Thrive as a Therapist: Information, Ideas and Resources for Psychologists in Practice* (2005). She has received numerous awards, including

- Distinguished Psychologist of the Year Award, Division 42, Psychologists in Independent Practice, August 2008;
- Friend of the Asian American Psychological Association, August 2008;
- Alfred M. Wellner, PhD Senior Career Award for Outstanding Service to Psychology, National Register of Health Service Providers in Psychology, November 2007;
- Distinguished Professional Contributions to Independent or Institutional Practice in the Private Sector, American Psychological Association, August 2007;

- APA Karl F. Heiser Presidential Award for Advocacy, August 2007;
- APA Division 17 Presidential Citation for Outstanding Career Contribution to the Profession Via Excellence In Mentoring, August 2007; and
- Woman of the Year, 2006, APA Division 17 Section for the Advancement of Women James M. Jones Lifetime Achievement Award, American Psychological Association, 2004.

Stephen Behnke, PhD, received his legal training at Yale Law School and his doctorate in clinical psychology from the University of Michigan. In 1996, Dr. Behnke was made chief psychologist of the Day Hospital Unit at the Massachusetts Mental Health Center, a teaching hospital of Harvard Medical School. He held this position until 1998, when he was named a faculty fellow in Harvard University's Ethics and the Professions Program. Dr. Behnke then directed a program in research integrity in the Division of Medical Ethics at Harvard Medical School. In November 2000, Dr. Behnke assumed the position of director of ethics at the American Psychological Association. He holds an appointment in the Department of Psychiatry at Harvard Medical School.

Dr. Behnke's research interests focus on issues at the convergence of law, ethics, and psychology. He has written on multiple personality disorder and the insanity defense, on competence and informed consent to treatment and research, on forced treatment of the severely mentally ill, and on laws relevant to the work of mental health practitioners. He coleads an ethics discussion group at meetings of the American Psycho-analytic Association.

Robert Kinscherff, PhD, Esq., is a clinical and forensic psychologist and an attorney. He currently serves as director of clinical services at Easter Seals of New Hampshire. He has previously served as assistant commissioner for forensic mental health (Massachusetts Department of Mental Health), director of juvenile court clinic services (Massachusetts Administrative Office of the Juvenile Court), and director of training at the Law and Psychiatry Service of the Massachusetts General Hospital. He is senior associate for the National Center for Mental Health and Juvenile Justice. Dr. Kinscherff's professional practice and research areas include mental health law and ethics, and clinical and forensic practice with clinically complex adolescents and adults with sexually problematic, physically aggressive, persistently self-harming or other challenging conduct that risks justice system involvement and/or involuntary civil institutionalization.

Dr. Kinscherff is a member of American Psychological Association (APA) Divisions 12, 18, and 41. He is past two-term chair of the APA Ethics Committee. During his tenure as chair the most recent revision of the APA Ethics Code was completed and approved, and the adjudication procedures of the Ethics Committee were revised. He has served as APA chair of a Joint Task Force on Interdisciplinary Relations for the American Psychological Association and the American Bar Association. He is also a past chair of the Committee on Legal Issues and is currently a member of the Committee on Professional Practices and Standards, where he serves as liaison to the Task Force on Parenting Coordination. In 2006, Dr. Kinscherff received the Karl Heiser Award for Advocacy from Division 31.

He holds faculty appointments at Harvard Medical School and the Massachusetts School of Professional Psychology, where he is codirector of the Forensic Certification Program. At MSPP, he was the 2009 recipient of the Dr. Stephen D. Hayes Community Mental Health Award for dedication to underserved communities and community mental health. For over a decade, he also taught mental health law at the Boston University School of Law. He is on the Advisory Board of the Society for Terrorism Research and an associate editor for its journal, *Behavioral Sciences of Terrorism and Political Aggression.*